Asian English Language Classrooms

The teaching of English in the Asian context is always challenging and dynamic because both teachers and learners have diverse linguistic and cultural backgrounds. Equally important, where English is not widely used outside the classroom, English language classrooms are an authentic site of learner engagement. For these reasons, for all those concerned with contemporary English language teaching (ELT) in Asia, *Asian English Language Classrooms: Where Theory and Practice Meet*, provides an account of theoretical orientations and practices in the teaching of English to multilingual speakers whose primary language is not English. While covering the fundamental ELT areas (e.g., the teaching of language skills, educational literature, the use of technology in ELT, the role of pragmatics in ELT, social psychology of the language classroom, and language classroom management) with which every language teacher and teacher trainer must be concerned, this volume showcases how particular orientations shape ELT practices. We believe that practicing English teachers must have a heightened awareness of the theory behind their practice. At the same time, the theoretical stance must be firmly anchored in actual classrooms. Containing newly commissioned chapters written by well-regarded and emerging scholars, this book will appeal not only to beginning teachers or teachers in training but also to established teachers around Asia where English is used as a lingua franca. If you are a student teacher of English or an English teacher who would like to see what other progressive teachers like you are doing across Asia, this is the book you have been looking for.

Handoyo Puji Widodo, PhD is an Associate Professor at the English Language Center, Shantou University. He has published internationally in refereed journals and volumes.

Alistair Wood, PhD is a Senior Lecturer in English Language and Linguistics at Universiti Brunei Darussalam. He has spent more than 20 years teaching English for Specific Purposes (ESP) and applied linguistics in Asia, and published in such journals as Applied Linguistics and English for Specific Purposes.

Deepti Gupta, PhD is a Professor at Panjab University, India. Her PhD was in ELT. In addition to her 30-year teaching experience, Gupta has authored three books and articles in numerous national and international journals (e.g., *IATEFL Issues, Asian EFL Journal, Profile, ICFAI, Diviner,* and *ELT Journal*).

Routledge Research in Language Education

For a full list of titles in this series, please visit www.routledge.com

The Routledge Research in Language Education series provides a platform for established and emerging scholars to present their latest research and discuss key issues in language education. This series welcomes books on all areas of language teaching and learning, including but not limited to language education policy and politics, multilingualism, literacy, L1, L2 or foreign language acquisition, curriculum, classroom practice, pedagogy, teaching materials, and language teacher education and development. Books in the series are *not* limited to the discussion of the teaching and learning of English only.

Books in the series include:

Team Teaching and Team Learning in the Language Classroom
Collaboration for Innovation in ELT
Edited by Akira Tajino, Tim Stewart and David Dalsky

Teaching EFL Learners Shadowing for Listening
Developing Learners' Bottom-Up Skills
Yo Hamada

Teacher Agency and Policy Response in English Language Teaching
Edited by Patrick C. L. Ng and Esther F. Boucher-Yip

The Space and Practice of Reading
A Case Study of Reading and Social Class in Singapore
Chin Ee Loh

Asian English Language Classrooms
Where Theory and Practice Meet
Edited by Handoyo Puji Widodo, Alistair Wood and Deepti Gupta

Teaching and Learning Foreign Languages
A History of Language Education, Assessment and Policy in Britain
Nicola McLelland

Asian English Language Classrooms
Where Theory and Practice Meet

Edited by Handoyo Puji Widodo, Alistair Wood and Deepti Gupta

LONDON AND NEW YORK

First published 2017
by Routledge
2 Park Square, Milton Park, Abingdon, Oxon OX14 4RN

and by Routledge
711 Third Avenue, New York, NY 10017

Routledge is an imprint of the Taylor & Francis Group, an informa business

© 2017 selection and editorial matter, Handoyo Puji Widodo, Alistair Wood and Deepti Gupta; individual chapters, the contributors

The right of Handoyo Puji Widodo, Alistair Wood and Deepti Gupta to be identified as the authors of the editorial material, and of the authors for their individual chapters, has been asserted in accordance with sections 77 and 78 of the Copyright, Designs and Patents Act 1988.

All rights reserved. No part of this book may be reprinted or reproduced or utilised in any form or by any electronic, mechanical, or other means, now known or hereafter invented, including photocopying and recording, or in any information storage or retrieval system, without permission in writing from the publishers.

Trademark notice: Product or corporate names may be trademarks or registered trademarks, and are used only for identification and explanation without intent to infringe.

British Library Cataloguing-in-Publication Data
A catalogue record for this book is available from the British Library

Library of Congress Cataloging-in-Publication Data
A catalog record for this book has been requested

ISBN: 978-1-138-80086-1 (hbk)
ISBN: 978-1-315-75524-3 (ebk)

Typeset in Galliard
by Apex CoVantage, LLC

Printed and bound in Great Britain by
TJ International Ltd, Padstow, Cornwall

Contents

List of contributors vii
Acknowledgements xiii
Preface xiv

1 Introduction: re-contextualizing English language teaching in Asia today 1
HANDOYO PUJI WIDODO, ALISTAIR WOOD, AND DEEPTI GUPTA

2 Teaching listening in pre-tertiary and tertiary English education in Japan 14
TOMOKO KURITA

3 Developing speaking for intercultural communication: textbooks with critical and creative approaches 30
LIXIAN JIN AND MARTIN CORTAZZI

4 Teaching reading through multimodal texts 49
EVELINE CHAN AND ZUOCHENG ZHANG

5 Supplementing extensive reading for Japanese EFL learners 71
MEREDITH STEPHENS

6 Teaching writing to multilingual learners using the genre-based approach 83
JUSTINA ONG

7 Teaching communicative vocabulary 98
ANNA SIYANOVA-CHANTURIA AND PAUL NATION

8 What EFL teachers should know about online grammar tasks 113
REIMA AL-JARF

9	Teaching pronunciation to adult learners of English KAREN STEFFEN CHUNG	131
10	Fluency in language classrooms: extensive listening and reading ALISTAIR WOOD	150
11	Literature in an age of distraction ALAN MALEY	164
12	Expressing study abroad experiences in second language haiku writing: theoretical and practical implications for teaching haiku composition in Asian EFL classrooms ATSUSHI IIDA	180
13	Exploring ICT tools in English language learning: language, technology, and the globalized classroom PAOLO NINO VALDEZ, NESLIE CAROL C. TAN, AND LINDSEY NG-TAN	192
14	The use of photo story in the Indonesian English language classroom: working with multimodal tasks NUR ARIFAH DRAJATI, SRI REJEKI MURTININGSIH, WINDA HAPSARI, AND HASTI RAHMANINGTYAS	203
15	Social psychology of the language classroom HAMZEH MORADI AND DEEPTI GUPTA	216
16	The role of pragmatics in teaching English as an additional language ANDREW D. COHEN	233
17	Language classroom management ZEKIYE MÜGE TAVIL AND ARIF SARIÇOBAN	254
	Index	268

Contributors

Reima Al-Jarf taught ESL, ESP, and translation for 26 years. She has published over 220 books, ebooks, book chapters, encyclopedia, and journals articles in peer-reviewed international and national journals and conference proceedings. She has given 325 conference presentations and 50 workshops in 69 countries. She is a member of 22 international and national professional organizations. She reviews articles for numerous peer-reviewed international journals including some ISI journals. She has won three Excellence in Teaching Awards and the Best Faculty Website Award at King Saud University, College of Languages and Translation, Department and the two KSU women's campuses.

Eveline Chan is a senior lecturer in English and literacies education, University of New England, Australia. Eveline has worked in language education for over two decades, teaching English as an additional language (EAL) students in school and tertiary contexts, and in mainstream and Teachers of English to Speakers of Other Languages (TESOL) teacher education programs. Her research interests include language and literacy development (L1, L2/EAL), literacy pedagogy and assessment, classroom discourse analysis, multimodal representations of curriculum knowledge, image-language interaction in multimodal texts, and reading in hypertext environments.

Karen Steffen Chung (史嘉琳Shǐ Jiālín), originally from St. Paul, Minnesota, USA, has taught English and linguistics in the Department of Foreign Languages and Literatures of National Taiwan University since 1990; her current rank is associate professor. Her educational background includes a BA in East Asian languages from the University of Minnesota, 1976; an MA in East Asian studies from Princeton University, 1981; and a PhD in Linguistics from Leiden University, 2004. The title of her dissertation is "Mandarin Compound Verbs."

Andrew D. Cohen is an emeritus professor of second language studies from the University of Minnesota, living now in Oakland, CA. Cohen was a Peace Corps volunteer in rural community development with the Aymara Indians in Bolivia (1965–1968), taught four years at UCLA and 16 at Hebrew University of Jerusalem before spending 22 years at the University of Minnesota. He is co-editor of *Language Learning Strategies* (OUP, 2007), author of *Strategies in Learning and Using a Second Language* (Routledge, 2011), and co-author of *Teaching and Learning Pragmatics: Where Language and Culture Meet* (Routledge, 2014). His most recent book, *Learning Pragmatics from Native and Non-Native Language Teachers*, is forthcoming from Multilingual Matters. Aside from his books and his numerous chapters and articles on research methods, language assessment, bilingual education, language learner strategies, and pragmatics, Cohen has studied 12 languages, with Mandarin being the latest.

Martin Cortazzi is a visiting professor at the University of Nottingham, Ningbo, China. He has taught and trained teachers in Britain, China, Lebanon, Turkey, Iran, Malaysia, Norway, Cyprus, and elsewhere. He has published widely on aspects of applied linguistics, education, narrative, and metaphor analysis. For many years, Martin Cortazzi and Lixian Jin have been researching linguistic, cultural, and educational issues related to Chinese learners and edited *Researching Chinese Learners, Skills, Perceptions and Intercultural Adaptations* (2011, Palgrave Macmillan).

Nur Arifah Drajati earned a BA in English education from Sebelas Maret University (UNS Surakarta) in 1999. She had taught English at SMA Labschool Jakarta for 17 years. She currently teaches postgraduate students at UNS Surakarta. In 2008, she completed her MA at Jakarta State University, and in 2013, she completed her PhD in English education at the same university. She is also a member of the TEFLIN Board (The Association of Teachers of English as a Foreign Language in Indonesia, Teacher Development Division). Her research interests lie in technology in language learning, action research, and reading difficulty.

Deepti Gupta is a professor at Panjab University, India. Her PhD was in English language teaching (ELT). In addition to her 30-year teaching experience, Gupta has authored three books and articles in numerous national and international journals (e.g., *IATEFL Issues, Asian EFL Journal, Profile, ICFAI, Diviner*, and *ELT Journal*). She has conducted more than a hundred workshops and teacher training programs. She helps people become empowered through cognitive training. As a teacher, Gupta believes that counseling people towards a stronger life is part of her profile.

Winda Hapsari is an English teacher and teacher trainer at *Lembaga Bahasa dan Pendidikan Profesional LIA*, a language course institute based in Indonesia. She earned her master's degree in educational psychology from *Universitas Indonesia*. She has published her work in the area of ELT with TESOL Inc. and *TEFLIN Journal*. Her research interests include educational psychology, English language pedagogies, teacher professional development, and motivation.

Atsushi Iida is an associate professor in the University Education Center at Gunma University, Japan. He was awarded his PhD in English composition and TESOL at the Indiana University of Pennsylvania, Pennsylvania (PA), USA. His research interests include second language writing, literature in second language education, and writing for academic publication. He has published his work in various journals including *System, Scientific Study of Literature, English Teaching Forum, Asian EFL Journal,* and *Assessing Writing.*

Lixian Jin is Chair Professor in Applied Linguistics and Head of School of English at the University of Nottingham Ningbo, China. She has taught English and linguistics and led international research teams in Britain, Hong Kong, Turkey, Singapore, Malaysia, and China. Her publications and research interests are in these areas and bilingual clinical assessments, narrative, and metaphor analysis. She has also served as an editor or an executive editorial member on a number of international journals. Lixian Jin and Martin Cortazzi edited and contributed to *Researching Cultures of Learning: International Perspectives on Language Learning and Education* (2013) and *Researching Intercultural Learning: Investigations in Language and Education* (2013, Palgrave Macmillan).

Tomoko Kurita teaches English at the Jikei University School of Medicine, Jissen Women's University Junior College, and Tokyo Kasei University, Japan. She graduated from Teachers College Columbia University's MA TESOL program. She has taught English at elementary schools, junior and senior high schools, and universities in Japan. Some of her research interests include listening, project-based learning, and learner autonomy.

Alan Maley has been involved with ELT for over 50 years. He worked with the British Council in Yugoslavia, Ghana, Italy, France, China, and India (1962–1988) before taking over as director-general of the Bell Educational Trust, Cambridge (1988–1993). He then worked in university posts in Singapore (1993–1998), Thailand (1999–2004), Malaysia, and Vietnam (2004–2011). He is now a freelance consultant and writer. He has published over 50 books and numerous articles. He is a past president of IATEFL, and recipient of the ELTons Lifetime Achievement Award in 2012. He is a co-founder of the C Group (http://thecreativitygroup.weebly.com/).

Hamzeh Moradi holds a Ph. D in Linguistics from Panjab University of India. He works as a lecturer at the Department of English Language and Literature, at Shahid Chamran University of Ahvaz, Iran. He has several years of experience in teaching linguistics and English as a foreign/second language at various institutions. He has demonstrated commitment in research, mainly in the areas of linguistics, sociolinguistics, applied linguistics, bilingualism, second language acquisition, language and technology, and English language teaching. He has published several manuscripts in international peer-reviewed journals.

Sri Rejeki Murtiningsih, called Jackie, received her BA in English education from Universitas Negeri Yogyakarta. She earned her master's degree in education from Flinders University of South Australia. After receiving her PhD in education from the University of Oklahoma, Murtiningsih returned to Indonesia and started teaching in the English Education Department at Universitas Muhammadiyah Yogyakarta. Her research interests include teaching ESL/English as a Foreign Language (EFL) reading and writing, reflective practice, service learning, and curriculum development.

Paul Nation is an emeritus professor of applied linguistics in the School of Linguistics and Applied Language Studies at Victoria University of Wellington, New Zealand. His books on vocabulary include *Teaching and Learning Vocabulary* (1990) and *Researching and Analysing Vocabulary* (2011) (with Stuart Webb), both from Heinle Cengage Learning. His latest book on vocabulary is *Learning Vocabulary in Another Language* (second edition 2013) published by Cambridge University Press. Two books strongly directed towards teachers appeared in 2013 from Compass Media in Seoul: *What Should Every ESL Teacher Know?* (available free from www.compasspub.com/ESLTK) and *What Should Every EFL Teacher Know?* He is also a co-author of *Reading for Speed and Fluency. Books 1–4* (With C. Malarcher, 2007; Seoul: Compass Publishing).

Lindsey Ng-Tan is a lecturer in the Department of English and Applied Linguistics at De La Salle University-Manila (DLSU) where she teaches English communication, speech communication, and English research courses. She finished a masters in teaching English language (DLSU) and is currently pursuing Japanese language study (Philippine Institute of Japanese Language and Culture). She was also a speech consultant for four years in SpeechPower where she taught Speech for Beginners, Speech and Elocution for High School, English Conversation Fluency, Grammar, Pronunciation, and Reading Comprehension. Her research interests include computer-assisted language learning and second language acquisition.

Justina Ong is a lecturer at the Department of English Language and Literature, National University of Singapore. She was the runner-up of the 2011 Christopher Brumfit PhD thesis award. Her research interests include second language writing, applied linguistics, and second language acquisition.

Hasti Rahmaningtyas earned her bachelor degree in English language teaching from the State University of Malang. She obtained her MA in applied linguistics from the University of Adelaide in 2013. Her research interests are narrative study and technology in language learning. She is currently teaching at the English Department of Universitas Negeri Malang.

Arif Sarıçoban has been working as an associate professor of ELT at Hacettepe University for about 20 years. He is interested in ELT teacher education, testing, materials development, ELT methodology, teaching language skills, and educational linguistics. He has authored many textbooks and course books in ELT, and participated and presented many papers, both in national and international conferences and symposiums. He is acting as the chief editor of a prestigious online journal for language and linguistic studies, and also acting as a member of editorial boards and as a reviewer for many national and international journals.

Anna Siyanova-Chanturia is a senior lecturer in applied linguistics in the School of Linguistics and Applied Language Studies, Victoria University of Wellington, New Zealand. Anna works in the fields of second language acquisition, corpus linguistics, and psycholinguistics. Anna's primary research interests include cognitive and psychological aspects of second language acquisition, learner corpus research, bilingualism, usage-based theories, phraseology, and vocabulary. In particular, Anna's research investigates acquisition, processing, and use of multi-word expressions (e.g., idioms, collocations, binomials, lexical bundles, multi-word verbs) in a first and second language.

Meredith Stephens is on the faculty in the Department of Comparative Cultures at the Institute of Socio-Arts and Sciences at Tokushima University. She first studied Linguistics and Japanese at the University of Adelaide and then pursued a degree in applied linguistics at Macquarie University. Her current research focuses on English language pedagogy in Japan and cross-cultural experiences of English language speaking immigrants in Japan.

Neslie Carol C. Tan obtained her masters in English language education in De La Salle University with a thesis on critical thinking and literacy and an MA in cultural studies from the School of Oriental and Asian Studies, University of London. Her research interests also include educational technology focusing on computer-assisted language learning, and she has previously presented papers on this field in international conferences.

Zekiye Müge Tavil is a member of the teaching staff in the Department of English Language teaching at Gazi University. She received her PhD from the same university. She is particularly interested in teacher training and development and teaching language skills. She has presented papers at several conferences and has published in EFL journals.

Paolo Nino Valdez holds a PhD in linguistics from the Philippine Normal University, and his dissertation, which delves on culture and code switching, was a finalist for the Christopher Brumfit Outstanding Dissertation Award in 2008. He is currently associate professor and former graduate program coordinator of the Department of English and Applied Linguistics, and external affairs director of the College of Education, De La Salle University, Manila. His publications have appeared in the *Asia Pacific Education Researcher*, *Reflections in English Language Teaching*, and *Philippine*

Journal of Linguistics, as well as Blackwell's *The Encyclopedia of Applied Linguistics*. His research interests are in the areas of bilingual education, critical pedagogy, and contemporary sociolinguistics.

Handoyo Puji Widodo is an Associate Professor of English Language Center at Shantou University. Widodo has published extensively in refereed journals and edited volumes. He has been actively involved in a wide range of (teacher) professional development activities (e.g., joint research projects & peer mentoring programs) in Indonesia and overseas. His areas of specialization include language teaching methodology, language curriculum and materials development, systemic functional linguistics (SFL) in language education, and teacher professional development. His work has been grounded in socio-semiotic, socio-cognitive, sociocultural, and critical theories of language pedagogies.

Alistair Wood was until recently a senior lecturer in English language and linguistics at Universiti Brunei Darussalam. He spent more than 20 years teaching English for Specific Purposes (ESP) and applied linguistics in Asia. His main research interests are in ESP, scientific English, and Bruneian English, with publications in *Applied Linguistics and English for Specific Purposes*, among other journals. In addition, he was a member of a team running a large multi-year project by Brunei and the United States helping to upgrade the English language and English teaching skills of Association of Southeast Asian Nations English teachers and teacher trainers.

Zuocheng Zhang is a senior lecturer in TESOL Education at the University of New England, Australia. He teaches TESOL methodology, English as a world language, and teaching for cultural diversity. His research interests include business English; TESOL education; multimodality, genre studies, and language; and discourse and identity in professional contexts. He has published extensively in these areas.

Acknowledgements

We are grateful to the contributors to this volume for their professional commitment to this project, for sharing their creative thoughts with us, and for allowing us to hear their scholarly voices presented in this work. Our special gratitude also goes to Christina Low, editor of Routledge Education, Psychology and Linguistics, for encouraging us to proceed with this project, along with a debt of gratitude to Yuvaneswari Yogaraja and other editorial staff at Routledge who assisted with the project. We would also like to say thank you to two anonymous reviewers for their feedback on the initial proposal for the volume. We wish to extend our sincerest thanks and appreciation to Winnie Cheng at the Hong Kong Polytechnic University for her assistance at the volume proposal writing stage.

Preface

Despite an increasing number of Asian speakers of English, the English language is still often seen as a school subject or as a foreign language. However, we feel assured that Asia is a prospective market for English language teaching (ELT) enterprises because more and more institutions are concerned about designing and implementing ELT to help English learners become competent users of the language and to prepare these learners for English-speaking communities of practice in Asia and beyond. In line with this, more and more qualified English language teachers are needed to enhance the quality of ELT. Years of experience in ELT have witnessed the fact that Asian English language classrooms are always uniquely complex and diverse because each of the learning institutions has differing expectations and holds socio-cultural values that shape the teaching and learning of English. With this in mind, there is a need to equip language teachers with a solid understanding of principled ELT practices. These practices are grounded in theoretical orientations (e.g., multimodality, creative writing) and learners' and institutional needs.

For these reasons, we initiated this project by inviting contributors who have experience in ELT in Asia to make this volume possible. As teacher awareness of experimenting with different approaches and methods in ELT grows in Asia, where many language teachers are becoming unsatisfied with many current ways to teach, the volume could provide a focus for conversation. To us, one of the strengths of this volume is that it provides a wonderful opportunity for emerging scholars' voices to be heard. Another strength of the volume is that all the issues raised in this collective work are about what most of the Asian ELT teachers are concerned with in the area of ELT. Thus the tone of this volume reflects the power of English in Asia and the power of Asia in the globalized world, because in recent years, there have been an increasing number of Asian learners of English who would like to become members of the global community.

The volume consists of the introduction chapter and a further 16 chapters. In the introductory chapter, we contend that there is an urgent need for re-contextualizing today's ELT in Asia because of language classroom diversity and complexity. We maintain that classroom diversity and complexity are historically, socially, and psychologically situated. This re-contextualization aims to enhance the quantity and quality of ELT and to explore different teaching practices that make the teaching and learning of English meaningful and relevant to learners' needs and other stakeholders' expectations. Therefore, this book makes a significant contribution to the field by providing locally grounded information and ideas for designing and implementing ELT in Asian contexts.

The diversity and complexity of language classrooms challenge language teachers to experiment with different ways to teach and engage learners in differing texts and tasks. In the 16 chapters, each of the contributors voices a different perspective on the teaching of language skills, educational literature, or creative writing; the use of technology in ELT; the role of pragmatics in ELT; social psychology of the language classroom; and language classroom management. We hope that these voices can be an inspiration to Asian English language teachers who are always enthusiastic about new ways to teach English. We also hope that this volume will attract language teachers to continually make innovations in language classrooms in order to encourage learners to devote their time, energy, and effort to develop their English ability and finally participate in Asian and globalized communities of practice.

1 Introduction
Re-contextualizing English language teaching in Asia today

Handoyo Puji Widodo, Alistair Wood, and Deepti Gupta

As echoed in the special issue of the *Journal of Multilingual and Multilingual Development*, The Power of English and the Power of Asia: English as Lingua Franca and in Bilingual and Multilingual Education, Asia is a potential market for English language education inasmuch as English language teaching (ELT) industries have been burgeoning for a number of reasons. To begin with, "the number of [non-native Asian speakers] has already surpassed that of native speakers, if we count the number of people who use English as a second and foreign language" (Cheng, 2012, p. 327). At this point, it seems fair to say that regardless of the socio-political status of English, Asia has the largest number of English speakers in the world. This can be a motivation for Asian learners of English to become users of the language. Southeast Asian (e.g., Singapore) and East Asian countries (e.g., China, Japan, Korea, and Taiwan), the fastest growing regions, are key players in Asia's economic, cultural, and educational developments in today's world. In this respect, English plays various roles in Asia, such as an official or semi-official language, a lingua franca, a medium of instruction, and a school subject. For example, because each of the Asian nations uses different official languages, English enjoys the status of being both a lingua franca (when communicating with Asian fellows across the region) and the sole official working language used by organizations such as the Association of Southeast Asian Nations (ASEAN). This shows that English is increasingly becoming the language of Asia that enables Asians to communicate with one another. From time to time, Asian countries seek to make "determined and focused efforts to establish cadres of competent users of English in education, commerce and culture" (Kirkpatrick & Sussex, 2012, p. 3). This indicates that Asian countries would like their citizens to be part of the global community of practice. In recent times, these countries have been key players in language education because more and more Asians are competent users of the language who can be role models for English language learners (ELLs).

In many Asian contexts, socio-politically, English is still often seen as a 'foreign' language in formal school and university curricula. Because of the role of English as a lingua franca in Asia, English should be viewed as an additional language, or teachers should re-contextualize what the learning of English as a foreign and second language means to ELLs, because the learning of English is viewed as an instrumental vehicle or investment in building and maintaining social relationships and transnational collaboration, bridging transnational communication, mediating social and economic mobility, and facilitating international cultural and educational exchanges among others. What makes the teaching and learning of English in Asia unique is that most of the ELT programs are situated in multilingual and multicultural settings, which make such practices a site of struggle among ELLs. In this multilingual context, it is a common phenomenon that code-mixing and code switching commonly take place inside and outside the language classroom. These code-mixing and code-switching practices serve as "a natural and creative strategy and identity marker for multilingual users of English" (Kirkpatrick & Sussex, 2012, p. 2). Additionally, years of our teaching in Asia have witnessed the fact that designing and implementing ELT practices are always challenging, because many such practices are socially sited in geographic domains where English is not widely used in daily social encounters. What seems to be interesting in this context is that the teaching of English co-exists with that of other languages ranging from local languages to national or official languages. ELT in this regard aims to bridge a connection among Asian countries "[g]iven the diversity of official languages and sociolinguistic profiles among [Asian countries]" (Kam, 2002, p. 2). Even though each of the Asian countries "had its own special reasons for teaching English in the early days, the language is now spreading in the region for largely pragmatic reasons" (Kam, 2002, p. 2). The growing needs for teaching English are driven by a widespread use of the language in academic (e.g., overseas studies, international academic exchange programs), professional (e.g., overseas job placement), occupational (e.g., working as a nurse abroad), and survival (e.g., immigrant workers) settings.

In recent years, though, Western scholars have dominated much of the work on methodology in ELT. More and more work on ELT practices in the Asia region is beginning to be well represented or reported. There is a growing realization throughout the continent that English is an Asian language, yet pedagogical approaches and practice are still too often not rooted in the Asian context. To fill this need, this volume, *Asian English Language Classrooms: Where Theory and Practice Meet*, aims to explore different theoretical stances and practices of ELT in the region and to bring about a synthesis of what works best in contemporary English language pedagogy in Asia. By inviting scholars in the area of ELT who have teaching experience and know current ELT practices in the region, this book provides a fresh impetus for designing and implementing ELT, which is socioculturally grounded in Asian traditions where people hold different cultural values and social norms. Thus this volume provides a platform for both well-regarded and emerging scholars who voice their experience in ELT in Asian countries, such as Brunei Darussalam, China, India, Indonesia, Japan, Korea, Saudi Arabia, Singapore, Taiwan, the Philippines, and Turkey.

A need for re-contextualizing ELT in Asia today

Traditionally, classrooms are a place where teaching and learning takes place. They are also a site of engagement or social practice where "people, typically one teacher and a number of learners, come together for a pedagogical purpose" (Allwright, 1992, p. 267). Additionally, classrooms serve not only as a site of engagement where a teacher and students interact with one another but also as social events, which involve social roles (e.g., teachers as facilitators, students as teacher co-collaborators), social relationships (e.g., a teacher and students, students and their peers), and social interaction (e.g., a teacher and students, students and their peers, students and instructional text). These social roles, social relationships, and social interaction shape the diversity and complexity of classrooms. Thus

> the classroom is a rich resource for learning about learners' lived experiences, including their identities [who they are; what they are doing]. A number of classroom activities can be used that combine language learning with expanding [teacher] knowledge of the learners and their individual needs.
> (Murray & Christison, 2011, p. 63)

For this volume, the scope of English language classrooms extends beyond four-wall classrooms, but language classrooms are operationalized as a site of engagement/social practice, which takes place either in face-to-face or virtual environments. At present, language classrooms can occur in both face-to-face and virtual settings, commonly known as blended classrooms in which both teachers and students can interact with each other in face-to-face mode and virtually. This new paradigm changes the way both teachers and students see language classrooms as dynamic and fluid sites of engagement, which allow for a myriad of social practices promoting genuinely humanistic and process-oriented views of teaching and learning in general and of ELT in particular.

Methodology in ELT has been a topic of extensive discussion and research in recent years in the Asian region, as evidenced not only in the growing volume of journal articles and books dedicated to the topic but also in the prominence of the topic at international conferences, which are annually held, such as the Asian EFL Conference, Asia TEFL Conference (annually held in different Asian nations), CamTESOL Conference (Cambodia), JALT Conference (Japan), MELTA Conference (Malaysia), RELC International Conference (Singapore), TEFLIN Conference (Indonesia), TESOL Arabia Conference (United Arab Emirates), and Thai TESOL Conference (Thailand). We have witnessed the fact that the topic of methodology in ELT is always well-received. It is fair enough to say that a vast majority of the research and discussions concern methodology in ELT at all educational levels ranging from primary to higher education and from government-owned educational sectors to privately managed educational sectors as well as from formal education to informal education. Methodology in ELT in Asian contexts remains in demand because more and more language teachers and practitioners seek different ways to teach their learners based on their sociocultural contexts and needs. It is noticeable that a growing number of projects that touch on ELT practices are being conducted in Asian contexts.

To respond to this need, this volume provides insight into re-contextualizing today's ELT in Asian contexts. The idea of re-contextualization of today's ELT attempts to raise teacher awareness of how contexts exert influence on a choice of theoretical orientation and pedagogical practice (Widodo & Park, 2014). This choice making relies upon such factors as teachers, students, materials, needs, and institutionalized culture among others. The re-contextualization of ELT tries to respond to the reality that each language classroom is contextually unique because both a teacher and students engage in social practice informed by different goals, pedagogical values, and expectations (Tudor, 1996). This is a challenge for language teachers to play roles as agents of change. With this role in mind, language teachers need to understand the characteristics of the context in which they work. These characteristics can embrace the nature of learners, the features of classroom materials as learning resources, the features of institutions, and the broader world. Certainly, teachers need to know the nature of language and language learning as philosophical foundations of ELT as a whole.

Aims of the book

This volume contains a collection of newly commissioned chapters tailored for those who wish to explore different pedagogical principles and theoretical stances in actual Asian English language classrooms. It provides an up-to-date account of ELT praxis in Asia. It is designed particularly for students taking language master's level and teacher education courses. The practical focus on Asian language classrooms makes the volume particularly useful and relevant to those who engage in the profession of ELT in different Asian settings. For those with more ELT experience, this volume can also provide a way of surveying and updating the existing knowledge on ELT. Overall, the book aims to give a general introduction to fundamental areas of ELT for the beginning or more experienced teacher and thus covers those areas about which all English teachers need to know. Additionally, the volume raises an awareness of how English teachers contextually frame their pedagogical practices to cater to their students' local needs situated in a specific socio-institutional context. Specifically, the volume aims to

1 explore and unpack what English language pedagogies mean to English teachers and learners in the Asian context where English is mostly considered a subject language or a foreign language;
2 showcase how theory informs practice and how practice refines theory (Kumaravadivelu, 2006). In this regard, language teachers play the roles of agents of change and explorers of different pedagogical practices enmeshed in a particular theoretical stance in response to changing needs for meaningful English language pedagogies;

3 promote, among different stakeholders, discussion about, and exploration of theoretically informed English language pedagogies, which are deeply rooted in the notion that such a pedagogical enterprise is an art of exploration – that is to say, there is no best way to teach the English language in all pedagogical contexts because of diversity and complexity of language classrooms; and
4 produce exemplary and grounded work that promotes the idea that language teachers should experiment with their practical theory.

These goals serve as the foundation of exploring what best works in Asian English language classrooms.

Readership of the book

This volume can be a welcome addition to the previously published books on methodology in ELT. As the title of this volume indicates, the readership of the volume is varied. The book can be a core or required undergraduate text for such courses as Language Teaching Methodology and Language Curriculum and Materials Design and Development. We argue that the relationship between language teaching methodology and language curriculum and materials development is that both are informed by particular approaches (theories), methods, and principles. Language curriculum and materials are curricular artifacts, which shape language teaching methodology in action. Because this volume is a collection of papers written by Asian language scholars and scholars who have working experience in Asia and have in-depth knowledge of the ELT contexts in Asia, it can be selected as a required text for pre-service teachers in all ELT departments in Asia. The volume can also be a complementary resource book for such courses as Teaching Practicum and Microteaching at language teacher college and university levels. At the graduate level, it may also be a compulsory reference for second-year students and those who attend in-service courses, teacher certification training, and other in-service workshops, as it is designed to provide pre-service and in-service English teachers with a solid understanding of current language pedagogies in Asia.

The present text is definitely an invaluable guide text for teacher educators who would like to enrich their course syllabi and teaching contents, and provide students with a better understanding of what ELT means personally, professionally, and contextually. This means that teacher educators can help their student teachers acquire knowledge and develop competence in making methodological choices (e.g., approaches, methods, and designs) in teaching. For language researchers, the volume can be a reference for researchers who wish to investigate different macro- and micro-skill areas and features of ELT approaches, methods, and practices. They may test out or examine how they can modify or adapt the ELT practices discussed in the text to their own research context. Lastly, this edited work can serve as a guide for English teachers and practitioners who would like to broaden their horizons of current ELT practices and explore different approaches, methods, procedures, and techniques that may work for their own classrooms.

The foci of the volume

This volume contains 17 chapters (including this introductory chapter), which address different ELT issues. These issues embrace the teaching of language skills, the educational literature (creative writing), the use of technology in ELT, the role of pragmatics in ELT, the social psychology of the language classroom, and the management of the language classroom. The volume presents three genres of scholarly work: review, pedagogical, and original essays.

In Chapter 2, Tomoko Kurita provides an account of effective listening comprehension instruction in Japan's pre-tertiary and tertiary English education. This instruction is based on the two theoretical frameworks of listening comprehension: Anderson's (1995, 2009) model and top-down and bottom-up processes, highlighting the importance of teaching listening, focusing on the process. Despite the importance of process-based listening instruction, Kurita observed that listening is the last priority in classrooms in Japan (Blyth, 2010; Yanagawa, 2012), and the typical listening lesson seems ineffective, which is why Japanese people tend to have serious difficulties understanding what they hear in English even after learning English at school (Nihei, 2002). In addition, Japanese learners have often been exemplified as learners having difficulties in English listening, especially in word recognition, because of their first language (L1) phonological obstacles. The author suggests that listening pedagogy should focus on solving the students' problems in listening processes rather than correcting answers to listening comprehension questions.

Lixian Jin and Martin Cortazzi in Chapter 3 discuss intercultural communication based on the argument that this is crucial in contemporary contexts in which learners of English will need to interact with culturally diverse people both locally and internationally. They outline some aims and themes for intercultural skills in ELT linked with important aims of education: the need for learners to understand and reflect on cultural contexts in their own and other communities, and to develop critical and creative thinking. Jin and Cortazzi elaborate their practical application of this threefold model through their contribution to the development of textbooks in China. They contend that, as elsewhere in the Asian region, English classes in China are often large and an emphasis on oral skills is quite recent. There are constraints in teachers' training in this area, and most learners have little experience interacting with English speakers from outside China. The contribution of this chapter focuses on examples from two series of textbooks, which include specifically designed elements to develop intercultural understanding with creative and critical oral communication, particularly through authors' innovative 'Participation Activities,' which feature three stages of oral interaction to analyze and solve problems in intercultural situations.

In response to a need for increasingly multimodal reading materials in both print and digital formats, Chapter 4, written by Eveline Chan and Zuocheng Zhang, provides an overview of research and theory concerning contemporary multimodal texts and reading, explores some of the affordances of multimodal texts for developing ELT students' repertoires of reading, and outlines some of the challenges for innovating practice in Asian ELT contexts. Chan and Zhang argue that the conceptions of reading need to be broadened beyond processing meaning from the printed word to include meanings created in image, sound, and space, which interface with the written-linguistic mode. Images combined with words have the potential to convey powerful cultural messages, as exemplified in media texts and advertising campaigns. Digital texts combine sound effects and music with animated images to engage readers, and interactive elements bring an element of joint construction to reading and text composition. This historical shift in textual practices, coupled with the emergence of multiple World Englishes, necessitates a critique of ELT practices, particularly in settings where English is an additional language. It is no longer adequate to adopt the practices of inner-circle, English-speaking countries without first considering the local purposes for ELT and the global contexts for communication in English.

In Chapter 5, Meredith Stephens presents the incorporation of extensive listening and creative written responses into extensive reading in order to assist students to reap the benefits of the massive exposure to second or additional language, such as English, afforded by doing extensive reading and listening. Stephens also adds that the inclusion of creative written responses in these tasks is important in establishing a mental representation of spoken language in order to learn to read (Walter, 2008). Extensive listening is viewed as a means of attaining this skill. Furthermore, Wolf (2008) has explained the Vygotskian view that writing helps learners to refine and expand their thinking. Composing creative responses to the texts read in extensive reading is deemed a means of achieving this end.

In the area of second or foreign language writing, Justina Ong argues that learners face many challenges in writing. For example, at a text-based level, they face problems in grammar and vocabulary, also known as lexico-grammar, and in constructing syntactically appropriate sentences (Tang, 2012). Such problems could stem from their lack of understanding of the functional use of language and could be addressed through effective writing instruction. Driven by these concerns, Ong, in Chapter 6, discusses a genre-based approach to the teaching of writing to multilingual learners. Specifically, she focuses on one of the critical stages of Feez's (1998) teaching-learning cycle, 'modelling and deconstruction of text.' She demonstrates how teachers could deconstruct two advertising texts through highlighting the linguistic features (e.g., lexis, transitivity patterns, mood, modality, and attitudinal lexis) the writers use to build up the ideational and interpersonal meanings of the texts (see Christie & Derewianka, 2008; Halliday, 1994; Schleppegrell, 2004) and how the writers use language to achieve the social purpose of persuasion.

In Chapter 7, Anna Siyanova-Chanturia and Paul Nation focus on vocabulary and multi-word expressions (MWEs) in the context of communicative language teaching. Recent years have seen a growing interest in research looking at the acquisition and use of MWEs in a second and foreign language classroom. MWEs are phrases that exhibit a certain degree of fixedness and are recognized as being conventional by a native speaker. They can be of many different kinds, such as collocations (*strong tea*), multi-word verbs (*figure out*), idioms (*piece of cake*), and speech formulas (*What's up?*). MWEs are important because they constitute a large proportion of authentic spoken discourse and are considered an essential component of mature linguistic performance. The abundance of MWEs in speech puts them at the forefront of communicative vocabulary teaching and learning. In addition, classroom research suggests that using MWEs can be a quick way of developing fluency, particularly in the early stages of language learning. Thus this chapter addresses a number of questions pertinent to the vocabulary and MWEs needed for spoken use of the language. One of its goals is to show what kind of activities language teachers can use in order to aid communicative vocabulary learning in general and MWE acquisition in particular.

To cater to technologically oriented ELT in this digital age, Reima Al-Jarf, in Chapter 8, discusses online grammar tasks based on a local need situated at King Saud University (KSU), in Riyadh, Saudi Arabia. Al-Jarf observed that this university has a Blackboard account for each of the courses faculty members teach, but very few faculty members are actually using Blackboard in teaching, including those who teach English language courses at the university. The author noted that English as a Foreign Language (EFL) teachers at KSU find it difficult to select and perform online grammar tasks that are appropriate, beneficial, and helpful for EFL students. Therefore, this chapter addresses (1) the types of online tasks that can be integrated into blended grammar instruction for EFL/ESL (English as a Second Language) college students, (2) the performance of the online grammar tasks based on online grammar websites, (3) criteria for selecting online grammar tasks, (4) instructional stages with online tasks, and (5) how online grammar tasks are performed. Illustrative examples of websites that can be used to perform each type of task are also presented. The teacher's roles in performing the proposed tasks will be described as well. This chapter will be beneficial to EFL/ESL instructors who use an online course, a blog, a discussion forum, a mobile app, or any other form of technology as a supplement to in-class grammar instruction.

Karen Steffen Chung in Chapter 9 provides a practical account of how to teach English pronunciation to adult learners. She begins by providing a rationale for the teaching of pronunciation and suggestions about how to prepare teachers mentally for the course. Since pronunciation training often receives a low priority in ESL programs (Baker, 2013), teachers will need to have some convincing arguments ready to explain its importance to program administrators and colleagues, students, and even teachers themselves. Key aspects of brain function and general principles of language learning are also discussed. Chung also presents a list of practical hints for teachers and students, and a collection of highly effective strategies and methods for pronunciation improvement and overall language learning. A short list of resources and tools as well as a list of suggested pronunciation texts are provided in the remaining section of the chapter.

In Chapter 10, Alistair Wood discusses the integration of extensive reading and extensive listening. He argues that more recently, the concept of extensive practice has also been seen to include listening as well as reading. However, the idea of extensive listening has not been as widely accepted as extensive reading, and there is still debate as to the benefits of this approach. This chapter examines what both extensive reading and extensive listening bring to the language class and how they can be integrated effectively into more traditional approaches to these two skills. A comparison is made with the more traditional intensive approaches, particularly with regard to listening, and justification given as to why extensive listening should also have its place (Widodo & Rozak, 2016). It looks at them both in relation to the overarching criterion of fluency as an aim in language teaching and investigates how extensive reading and listening contribute to fluency. Recently, both of these approaches have been combined in one activity where students read and listen to texts simultaneously. Wood concludes by suggesting how teachers can make use of extensive reading and listening not only to motivate students but also to compliment the aims of intensive reading and listening and improve overall performance in these areas.

Alan Maley in Chapter 11 discusses the nature of the near-total and constant distraction in which we live, and other factors bearing on the way we use literature, including the rise of control culture, the role of English in the world, and the need for social and emotional intelligence. Three approaches are discussed: Literature as Study, as Resource, and as Appropriation, focusing on the last. Text selection can have a powerful influence on the relevance of literature, so options for enhancing the appeal of texts are presented. It then focuses on possible activities for implementing Literature as Appropriation. These include familiarization activities, extensive reading, creative writing, and manipulating texts. The conclusion reviews the challenges literature faces: the culture of speed and info-glut, the current utilitarian model of education, the need to validate local cultures through English, and the gap between English in the classroom and the plurality of Englishes outside it.

In Chapter 12, Atsushi Iida documented the way in which EFL students used *haiku* – a three-line Japanese poem – in a second language (L2) to focus and express their study abroad experiences. The qualitative analysis of poetry writing in English showed that each haiku on the study abroad experience written by four EFL students contained both the description of each event and the depiction of the writers' emotional states and that their voices were articulated as a result of their reflective and linguistic negotiations of personal experiences. More broadly, this study exemplifies the abilities of EFL students to express their personal experiences through expressive writing and demonstrates how haiku writing as a form of meaningful literacy practice can transform the L2 composition classroom.

Paolo Nino Valdez, Neslie Carol C. Tan, and Lindsey Ng-Tan in Chapter 13 flesh out the use of information communication technology (ICT). They point out that the rapid development of ICT in the age of globalization has pushed forward the boundaries of communication. Moreover, communication in globalized settings involves highly mobile, hybrid, and technology-competent individuals. In the educational context, therefore, teachers are faced with a new set of challenges as they come to the task of educating 'digital natives' possessing multiliteracies and shuttling between different linguistic, cultural, and multimodal worlds. Divided into two sections, this chapter initially describes the current thinking on ICT in the context of ELT and proceeds with the identification of thematic strands that influence practice in the field. Moreover, using the community of practice framework of Lave and Wenger (1991), the second section then elucidates preliminary findings of an English language classroom use of social networking in the development of media logs. As will be reported, students who participated in the project not only drew on rich cultural and linguistic resources in achieving their communicative purpose but also deployed their skills in the use of technology and social media. These skills, therefore, actualize the notions of mutual engagement, joint enterprise, and shared repertoire as they become part of a community of practice in a global classroom.

In another area of technology in ELT, a plethora of research on the use of multimedia such as Photo Story has been undertaken. However, little is known about how it is used in secondary-school settings of English as an additional language (EAL) classrooms, such as in Indonesia. With this in mind, in Chapter 14, Nur Arifah Drajati, Sri Rejeki Murtiningsih, Winda Hapsari, and Hasti Rahmaningtyas report an empirical study that examined to which extent the deployment of Photo Story mediated multimodal learning tasks in the EAL classroom. The study specifically looked at challenges and benefits of using Photo Story to develop students' writing and speaking competences. The study also investigated the roles of teachers and students in the entire learning process. A total of 35 students in grade 12 volunteered to participate in this study. In groups of four, they were assigned to perform a series of tasks. Drawing on students' postings, narratives, and interviews, this chapter reports on four major findings: (1) drafting and negotiating strategies for the creation of multimodal narrative texts, (2) framing the use of language in composing, (3) collaborating on text creation and improvement, and (4) positioning roles of teacher and students in the entire learning trajectory.

In Chapter 15, Hamzeh Moradi and Deepti Gupta address the social psychology of the language classroom to help teachers and language educators obtain a better understanding of socio-psychological forces related to language learning in the classroom, be cognizant of the implicit psychological features of the interaction between teachers and learners, manage the classroom and learning environment, and optimize classroom management. The authors maintain that social and psychological factors of language learning have been the focus of a significant amount of research during the past few decades. The importance of social psychology facets in the language learning process is one of the most pervasive themes in recent research on L2 acquisition. In fact, L2 acquisition is not only an innate aptitude and phenomenon but also a socio-psychological one. Thus it is important to consider the social and psychological conditions in which L2 learning occurs. This chapter reviews the most significant models related to the socio-psychological facets of language learning and clearly describes some of the indispensable concepts in the field such as self-efficacy, attitude, motivation, effort, literacy learning strategies, and self-awareness.

Andrew D. Cohen, in Chapter 16, provides an overview of the role of pragmatics in teaching English as an additional language by looking first at innovative approaches to research methods. Then the chapter looks at politeness and impoliteness, considering cross-cultural and ethnic differences, jocular insults, and swearwords. Next, examples of recent speech act research – focusing on complaints and requests – are considered. After that, Cohen looks at other areas of pragmatics: conversational overlap, back channeling, phatic communication, humor, sarcasm, and pragmatic function of discourse markers. The last portion of the chapter focuses on pedagogy. A number of issues relating to the teaching of L2 pragmatics are considered: teaching L2 learners a less-commonly taught speech act (criticism), teaching third language (L3; EFL) learners a commonly taught speech act (refusals), teaching pragmatics to learners for whom English is a lingua franca, materials development for L2 pragmatics, construction of pragmatics websites, and assessment of pragmatics. The chapter ends with a focus on the learner and on strategies for the learning and performing of pragmatics.

Fundamental to ELT is classroom management that supports a well-organized picture of learning. Classroom management enforces both learning in class and communication between teachers and learners. Effective classroom management has a noticeable impact on the language learners. The purpose of classroom management is to provide a constructive environment for both students and teachers; this is not possible with nonmotivated learners, so the teachers should be the managers in the classroom by involving all the students in the teaching and learning process. Effective classroom management helps learners not only spend more time on learning but also less time on destructive behaviors by appealing to the learners' interest. Apart from that, there are several strategies for scaffolding students to achieve fruitful outcomes, but the most crucial issue is to enhance teacher awareness of classroom management. Therefore, in the last chapter, Chapter 17, Zekiye Müge Tavil and Arif Sarıçoban discuss various strategies in relation to classroom management by underlining different solutions in accordance with recent approaches to classroom management.

Future directions: teacher innovation and creativity

Much work has discussed and documented different theoretical and conceptual orientations and methods in ELT in different geographic and institutional settings as well as different communities of practice. What is urgently needed in current ELT practice is teacher innovation and creativity. Innovation and creativity deal not only with translating theory into practice based on a particular context but also with experimenting with different theories in order to examine what works and what does not work in a particular ELT context. Grounded in the notion of innovation and creativity, language teachers are able to critically see the relevance and practicality of the adopted conceptual/theoretical stance. Innovation and creativity, of course, mean different things to every language teacher and arise from different perspectives. Because language classrooms are diverse in terms of pedagogical practices, there is a call for more exploration in teacher creativity and innovation in the adoption of theory-informed methodology, educational literature, the use of technology, and classroom management in

ELT across Asia, for example. As Muller, Herder, Adamson, and Brown point out, "Asia as a region is rich in ideas and theories based on local contexts, and these locally derived theories and solutions may prove more relevant to the Asian context than imported ideas" (2012, p. xii). With this in mind, it is high time for language teachers to explore their own practical theories in their own language classrooms.

In this introduction, we have outlined the rationale, aim, readership, and foci of the book, and the need for re-contextualizing today's ELT in Asia. We hope that this volume will motivate others to continue work on methodology in ELT in which the ideas of teacher innovation and creativity are addressed. We do expect that such work will generate proposals for other directions for the field of ELT and for the enhancement of our understandings of different perspectives on methodology in ELT. These efforts will need to be documented in different Asian ELT contexts. It is important to note that this volume does not impose dogmatic methodology on practicing teachers, but it gives fresh impetus for designing and implementing ELT practices, which are theory informed and contextually relevant to learners' and other stakeholders' needs.

References

Allwright, D. (1992). Making sense of classroom language learning (Unpublished PhD thesis). Department of Linguistics, Lancaster University.

Anderson, J. R. (1995). *Cognitive psychology and its implications* (4th edn.). New York: Freeman.

Anderson, J. R. (2009). *Cognitive psychology and its implications* (7th edn.). New York: Worth Publishers.

Baker, A. (2013, August 2012). Integrating fluent pronunciation use into content-based ESL instruction: Two case studies. In J. Levis & K. LeVelle (Eds.), *Proceedings of the 4th pronunciation in second language learning and teaching conference* (pp. 245–254). Ames, IA: Iowa State University.

Blyth, A. (2010). How teachers teach listening in Japan: Part 1. *Proceeding of PAC, The Pan-Asia Conference The 18th Annual KOTESOL International Conference, 2010,* 71–82.

Cheng, L. (2012). The power of English and the power of Asia: English as lingua franca and in bilingual and multilingual education. *Journal of Multilingual and Multicultural Development, 33,* 327–330.

Christie, F., & Derewianka, B. (2008). A functional approach to writing development. In F. Christie & B. Derewianka (Eds.), *School discourse: Learning to write across the years of schooling* (pp. 1–29). New York: Continuum.

Feez, S. (1998). *Text-based syllabus design.* Sydney: McQuarie University/AMES.

Halliday, M. A. K. (1994). *An introduction to functional grammar* (2nd edn.). London: Edward Arnold.

Kam, H. W. (2002). English language teaching in East Asia today: An overview. *Asia Pacific Journal of Education, 22*(2), 1–22.

Kirkpatrick, A., & Sussex, R. (Eds.). (2012). *English as an international language in Asia: Implications for language education.* New York: Springer.

Kumaravadivelu, B. (2006). *Understanding language teaching: From method to postmethod*. Mahwah, NJ: Lawrence Erlbaum Associates.
Lave, J., & Wenger, E. (1991). *Situated learning: Legitimate peripheral participation*. Cambridge: Cambridge University Press.
Muller, T., Herder, S., Adamson, J., & Brown, P. S. (Eds.). (2012). *Innovating EFL teaching in Asia*. New York: Palgrave Macmillan.
Murray, D. E., & Christison, M. A. (2011). *What English language teachers need to know Volume I: Understanding learning*. New York: Routledge.
Nihei, K. (2002). *How to teach listening*. ERIC. Retrieved from http://eric.ed.gov/?id=ED475743
Schleppegrell, M. J. (2004). Linguistic features of academic registers. In *The language of schooling: A functional linguistics perspective* (pp. 43–76). Mahwah, NJ: Lawrence Erlbaum.
Tang, R. (Ed.). (2012). *Academic writing in a second or foreign language: Issues and challenges facing ESL/EFL academic writers in higher education contexts*. London: Continuum.
Tudor, I. (1996). *Learner-centredness as language education*. Cambridge: Cambridge University Press.
Walter, C. (2008). Phonology in second language reading: Not an optional extra. *TESOL Quarterly, 42*, 455–468.
Widodo, H. P., & Park, G. (Eds.). (2014). *Moving TESOL beyond the comfort zone: Exploring criticality in TESOL*. New York: Nova Science Publishers.
Widodo, H. P., & Rozak, R. R. (2016). Engaging student teachers in collaborative and reflective online video-assisted extensive listening in an Indonesian initial teacher education (ITE) context. *Electronic Journal of Foreign Language Teaching, 13*, 229–244.
Wolf, M. (2008). *Proust and the squid: The story and science of the reading brain*. Thriplow, Cambridge: Icon Books.
Yanagawa, K. (2012). Do high school English teachers teach listening, and do students listen to spoken English? To explore washback effects of the introduction of the centre listening test in Japan. *Dialogue, 11*, 1–14.

2 Teaching listening in pre-tertiary and tertiary English education in Japan

Tomoko Kurita

Listening is an important skill for learners of English as a foreign language (EFL) as a means of comprehension and an input skill for acquisition (Rost, 2001a). It can be said that all language learners should be taught how to listen so that they can become independent learners because, as Rost (2001a) mentions, "a key difference between more successful and less successful acquirers relates in large part to their ability to use listening as a means of acquisition" (p. 94). Therefore, how to teach listening is a significant issue in any language-teaching context.

In Japan, teaching listening has recently been given more attention than in the past because listening has been increasingly incorporated into university entrance exams and international English exams such as the Test of English for International Communication (TOEIC) and Test of English as a Foreign Language (TOEFL) since it is recognized as a core skill of English proficiency. Under globalization, people in Japan, especially in the business community, have realized the importance of the communicative purpose of learning EFL. The Ministry of Education, Culture, Sports, Science and Technology (MEXT) has placed greater emphasis on the teaching of all the four skills as practical communication skills at school English education in Japan (MEXT, 2003, 2009).

However, Yoshida (2003) points out that there is a "serious discrepancy between the ideal language education policy objectives and the reality of English teaching" (p. 291). There is a gap between the need to teach listening in English education and the actual classroom practice in Japan. In spite of the importance, several studies (Blyth, 2010; Nihei, 2002; Yanagawa, 2012) reveal that teachers have hardly implemented listening pedagogy in Japanese school education. A lack of adequate listening instruction causes Japanese learners who were taught English for 6 or 10 years at schools have serious difficulties in listening comprehension (Nihei, 2002).

Students in Japan view listening skills as difficult because of issues such as speech rate, unknown vocabulary, and pronunciation (Noro, 2006). Furthermore, they recognize that those difficulties become causes of anxiety to them (Noro, 2006). It is not only because students in Japan are not taught how to learn listening effectively but also because English listening is challenging for the students whose first language (L1) is Japanese. In research on listening, Japanese learners of English have often been exemplified (Eastman, 1993; Erickson,

Akahane-Yamada, Tajima, & Matsumoto, 1999; Otake, Hatano, & Yoneyama, 1996; Rost, 2001b) as learners having difficulties in English listening, especially in word recognition because of their L1 phonological obstacles in the literature. It is because the Japanese sound system including the phonology system, phonotactic rules, and use of tone and use of stress are different from that of English. In teaching listening to Japanese learners, the L1 influences need to be taken into account. Thus an effective listening methodology for them is called for in pre-tertiary and tertiary education.

In this chapter, my goal is to explore effective approaches to listening comprehension for students in Japan as an EFL context. First, I discuss the current situation of English listening pedagogy in Japan. Second, I introduce two theoretical frameworks on the listening comprehension process: Anderson's (1995, 2009) model and the top-down and the bottom-up processes. Third, I highlight the importance of teaching listening, focusing on the process rather than the product. Fourth, I analyze the common difficulties that students in Japan often encounter in listening comprehension and discuss useful interventions in the classrooms. Fourth, I propose approaches for developing students' listening comprehension skills.

The current situation of English listening pedagogy in Japan

In Japan, teaching English listening has been paid more attention because MEXT and the business community have started to value the importance of communication on the international stage as related to globalization and developing communication abilities of Japanese people (MEXT, 2003, 2009). The most recent Course of Study places an emphasis on the need to develop students' practical English communication abilities such as accurately understanding and appropriately conveying information and ideas (MEXT, 2009). The language policy in Japan is based on the strong requests of the business community, which requires English as the international language of commerce (Yoshida, 2003, p. 291).

Listening skills have been increasingly included in university entrance exams and other English tests because of greater emphasis placed on the teaching of the four skills as practical communication skills (MEXT, 2003, 2009). In 2006, a listening component was introduced into the National Center Test for University Admission (Center Test) as one of the subpolicies of MEXT (Tahira, 2012). Furthermore, the number of TOEIC test takers has been rapidly increasing in Japan. The Institute for International Business Communication (2014) announced that about 2.4 million people in Japan took TOEIC compared to about 1.7 million people in 2009.

However, several researchers (Blyth, 2010; Nihei, 2002; Yanagawa, 2012) claim that teachers have hardly implemented listening pedagogy in Japanese education, even though the importance of teaching listening has increased since listening is recognized as an essential part of communication ability. Yanagawa's (2012) research, which explores the washback effects of the introduction of the listening test from Center Test, reveals that teachers do not put emphasis on teaching listening in their classrooms of third-year students in high schools. Although 98% of the teachers were interested in the listening component of the Center Test, 24% of the teachers answered that they spent more than 20% of the lesson time on listening instruction. Two percent of them spent none of their lesson time on listening. Additionally, the study found that students also spent little or no time in listening practice outside of school and that the students do not know how to acquire listening skills (Yanagawa, 2012).

Nihei (2002) also states that it is likely to be the biggest problem that although the importance of listening skills is widely acknowledged in Japan, the adequate instruction and materials to develop them have not been provided. He also points out the time limitation of listening as one of the reasons, and he estimates that the average time devoted to listening activities in every class is five minutes per day. In the interviews on how teachers taught listening in Japan, Blyth (2010) found that "most teachers said that listening often was last on the list of priorities, yet they claimed it to be higher on their own personal priority list" (p. 76). Some interviewees mentioned that there were some constraints in teaching listening: limited time, textbooks that did not include listening materials, and no permission to choose how to teach listening freely.

In pre-tertiary education, reading and writing have been emphasized since the 1960s when it was placing emphasis on grammar rules and language structures (Tahira, 2012). This traditional methodology seems to remain and to have become hidden constraints to teachers. In 2013, another test system called TEAP (Test of English for Academic Purposes) was introduced to assess high school students' English four-skills proficiency for academic purposes for university admission, expecting a long-term positive washback onto pre-tertiary English education (Taylor, 2014). The introduction aims to change the dominance of grammar-focused university entrance exams, which influence the EFL pedagogy in schools emphasizing a grammar-translation method.

Thus, regardless of the importance of teaching listening, listening is last on the list of priorities in classrooms with some constraints such as limited time and textbooks that did not cover listening materials, or a question-answer methodology. It is important to explore the methods of teaching listening comprehension that teachers are able to implement in the actual classrooms so that the students can learn how to learn listening and enhance their listening comprehension ability in pre-tertiary and tertiary education contexts.

Insight of listening process for comprehension

For improving listening skills as part of English communication ability, it is important for teachers and students to gain insight into the process of listening comprehension and to monitor how the students arrive at the right answer for the comprehension questions, or alternatively why comprehension breakdown happens.

It is critical to know these two theoretical frameworks of the listening comprehension process in order to implement a process approach to teaching listening. These frameworks assist teachers in analyzing students' breakdown in listening comprehension and identifying the problems that they need to address.

Anderson's model of language comprehension

Anderson (1995, 2009) breaks down the language comprehension process into three stages: perception, parsing, and utilization. In the first stage of perception, the listener is involved in the perceptual process that encodes the spoken message. Words are segmented from the speech stream and recognized by the listener. The second stage is the parsing stage, in which the words in the message are transformed into a mental representation of the combined meaning of the words. In this stage, the listener is involved in the identification of constituent structure or a basic phrase or unit in a sentence's surface structure. The third stage is the utilization stage, in which the listener uses the mental representation of the sentence's meaning. For instance, if the sentence is a question, the listener may answer; if it is an instruction, he or she may obey. The three stages are by necessity partly ordered in time; however, they also partly overlap. Listeners can make inferences from the first part of a sentence while they perceive a later part. It seems that it is the key to successful listening comprehension that the listener succeeds in processing information in each stage. For example, a process approach based on this model can be implemented to enhance a word recognition skill at the perception stage, to increase a mental representation skill at the parsing stage, and to gain better understanding of speakers' intention at the utilization stage.

Top-down and bottom-up processing framework

The second framework is the top-down and the bottom-up processing framework. It is generally agreed that top-down and bottom-up processes continuously interact to make sense of spoken input (Vandergrift, 2007). Top-down processing refers to the use of background knowledge in understanding the meaning of a message. Bottom-up processing, on the other hand, refers to using the incoming input as the basis for understanding the message. In listening comprehension, the combinations of top-down processing with bottom-up processing of information from the stimulus itself are used.

In other words, linguistic knowledge and world knowledge interact in parallel fashion as listeners create a mental representation of what they have heard (Hulstijin, 2003). For instance, it is possible to understand the meaning of a word before decoding its sound because we have many different types of knowledge, including knowledge of the world around us. We know what normally happens, and so we have expectations about what we will hear. Buck (2001) mentions, "While we are listening, we almost always have some hypothesis about what is likely to come next" (p. 3). Significantly, second language (L2) or EFL learners, who have limited processing ability with less linguistic knowledge, will depend on their ability to make use of all the available resources to interpret what they hear by top-down processes. The learners make use of context and other compensatory strategies to make sense of the aural form of a word (Vandergrift, 2006). Therefore, it is generally agreed that strategies to use compensatory mechanisms – contextual, visual, or paralinguistic information; world knowledge; cultural information; and common sense while listening – will determine the degree of listening success (Vandergrift, 2007). It seems that the key to successful listening is also that the learners can control both processes well to create a mental representation from what they have heard.

The findings in research on top-down and bottom-up processes have provided two approaches to listening instruction: an approach to raise metacognitive awareness about listening (favoring top-down processes) and an approach to develop lexical segmentation and word recognition skills (favoring bottom-up processes). According to Richards (2008), the top-down process approach includes exercises that develop the learners' ability to use key words to construct the schema of a discourse, infer the setting for a text, and infer the role of the participants and their goals. The bottom-up process approach includes exercises that develop bottom-up processing, which helps learners to recognize word and clause divisions, recognize key words, and recognize key transitions in a discourse.

The importance of focusing on the process

Because listening comprehension takes place within the mind of the listener, teachers tend to know how much students understand. Therefore, teachers give listening comprehension questions to students and focus on how many right answers they get – namely, product of listening. Field (1998), however, highlights the importance of teaching listening, focusing on process rather than product. Although the scores tell us something about how much the student can listen as a listening product, they tell us nothing about why they cannot listen as process. According to Field (1998), teachers focusing on the product judge the students' comprehension by the number of correct responses to questions or tasks. On the other hand, teachers focusing on the process follow up on incorrect responses in order to determine where understanding broke down and to resolve the problems.

Typical listening teaching methodology in Japan focuses on product, not process. According to Nihei (2002), in a typical listening lesson in Japanese school education, students either listen to the CD of a reading textbook or after listening to some materials answer some comprehension questions. In interview research on how to teach listening in Japan, Blyth (2010) found that five teachers out of seven claimed that the ultimate goal of listening in the classroom was to answer comprehension questions. Focusing on the product is just testing for the students, not teaching. The students in Japan do not practice listening skills and listening strategies for better comprehension (Nihei, 2002). If the students are just tested without learning how to improve listening skills, and correct answers are focused on too much, it is natural for the students to view listening as stressful. Jones (2008) points out that for many students in Japan, listening is often stressful and even potentially demotivating.

Noro (2006) reveals that Japanese college students have listening difficulties such as speech rate, unknown vocabulary, and pronunciation, and that those difficulties become a kind of stressor to them. Listening tasks without consideration for the students' difficulties in the listening comprehension process can discourage students from listening. Jones (2008) proposes that teachers should take into account why students may find the listening task difficult in teaching listening in order to help students increase their ability. It seems that the instruction focusing on the product has ignored addressing students' listening problems through examining the process and reduces their self-confidence because they will not have improved as listeners.

Moreover, teachers paying attention to the listening process can avoid confusion of approaches. Richards (2005) points out that it seems that current listening instruction in general seems to be mixed with both learning to listen and listening to learn. The same confusion could be found in Japanese classrooms. The confusion could happen if teachers do not know the difference between listening processes as comprehension and as acquisition. It is necessary for teachers to differentiate teaching listening comprehension from listening for acquisition because the two views of listening lead to different directions for classroom pedagogy (Richards, 2005). Teachers need to realize that instruction for learning to listen (that is, learning to understand spoken message) involves enhancing comprehension abilities in the language comprehension process. The learners use what they already know in order to comprehend. On the other hand, instruction for listening to learn (that is, learning the syntax and lexis of the language through listening) involves creating new meaning and form linking, and then repeating the meaning and form linking, which helps the learners to be ready for paying more attention to the syntax and lexis of the language through listening. The learners need to notice what they do not know for acquisition.

The confusion of the approaches could cause teachers to use inappropriate materials or activities and lead learners to listening difficulty and anxiety, which negatively affects listening performance. For example, if a teacher uses a spoken text for acquisition, including many unknown lexical items to learners as a text for comprehension task, the learners cannot achieve the listening comprehension task since there is a large impact of vocabulary knowledge on comprehension, and they will only feel that listening is too difficult. In general, unknown vocabulary is one of the sources of listening difficulties (Bloomfield et al., 2010; Buck, 2001; Noro, 2006). Using spoken text with low vocabulary coverage in teaching listening comprehension might discourage learners from listening, unless the purpose of listening is just inference. Thus the instruction focusing on the listening process enables teachers to choose appropriate approaches and activities.

Seeking insight into the difficulties students often encounter in listening comprehension may provide us with more effective listening instruction that focuses on the process so that students can also monitor their listening processes on their own.

Difficulties that students in Japan encounter

It is useful for teachers to analyze common difficulties that students encounter from a process-based perspective. In general, compared to reading, listening can prove to be more difficult for EFL and L2 learners (Jones, 2008). First, readers usually have the opportunity to refer back to a written text to clarify understanding, but listeners do not have the chance to refer back to a spoken text in most listening contexts (Jones, 2008). Second, while readers recognize spaces between words, listeners have to segment words (Osada, 2004). Stahr (2009) asserts,

> Spoken language is characterized by assimilation as well as unclear articulation, and lexical units are not necessarily as clearly marked as in written text; this lack of clarity of spoken language makes word segmentation an extremely difficult task for L2 listeners (p. 582).

Research on Japanese college students by Noro (2006) reveals that main sources of difficulties in listening comprehension are rate of speech, vocabulary, and pronunciation. Under real-time processing, they attribute their comprehension breakdown to the three sources of difficulties: speech rate, unknown vocabulary, and pronunciation. All the sources of difficulties make the bottom-up processing difficult. Next, I would like to discuss the three main sources of difficulties and suggest effective interventions by which teachers can facilitate students' listening comprehension.

Speech rate

The speech rate problem is mainly caused by a lack of automaticity. In order to understand speakers at normal speed, the listening process must be almost automatic. The average speech rate of a lecturer to non-native speakers is 140 words per minute, while that of conversations is 210 words per minute (Tauroza & Allison, 1990). It is true that the faster the speech is, the more difficult it is to understand, but slower speech rates do not necessarily help (Bloomfield et al., 2010). In general, listening to a foreign language is, even at higher levels of proficiency, a cognitively demanding activity because the capacity of working memory could affect the amount of information a learner can process.

In the case of students in Japan, however, just because speech appears fast, it might not mean that it is. Buck (2001) mentions L2 listeners often perceive that speech is too fast, but it is often due to a lack of automaticity, and if they learn to process the language automatically, speech seems to become slower. Students in Japan, who have had little listening experience, are likely to face a lack of automaticity. In successful listening, there is little time to think about meaning. The students need to develop the ability to process the language automatically.

The teacher should use effective intervention in the classroom by giving listeners additional processing time as a silent pause between constituent boundaries. Osada (2004) demonstrates, in a study on Japanese college students, evidence that less proficient listeners receive the auditory impression that listening passages with longer silent pauses are more comprehensible than those with no adjustment.

Unknown vocabulary

Unknown vocabulary also causes students' comprehension breakdown. This problem is the result of the overlap between the students' vocabulary knowledge and the vocabulary of the spoken text. If teachers choose an appropriate spoken text with adequate lexical coverage for the students, the students will have little difficulty.

The size of vocabulary knowledge that is needed for satisfactory comprehension of a spoken text is 98% (Nation, 2006; Stahr, 2009). Nation (2006) asserts, if we take 98% as the ideal coverage, a 6,000–7,000 word family vocabulary is needed for dealing with spoken text, while the first 1,000 plus proper nouns cover around 85% of spoken text. Spoken language makes slightly greater use of high-frequency words of the language than written language does. Infrequent vocabulary has a negative impact on listening comprehension (Bloomfield et al., 2010).

Authentic material may include much vocabulary unknown to students. It is, however, important for students to be exposed to authentic spoken English because "authentic language and real-world tasks enable students to see the relevance of classroom activity to their long term communicative goals" (Brown, 2001, p. 258). Therefore, if authentic material is used, the task should be an easy and achievable one such as "listening for gist," which refers to top-down listening where the learner tries to understand what is happening, even if the student cannot understand every phrase or sentence, or listening for main ideas. The effective intervention for students is to choose an easier spoken text ideally with 98% lexical coverage for the listening comprehension tasks or to provide pictorial support.

On the other hand, the students could perceive a familiar word as an unknown word if students remember the word with the wrong pronunciation or a different stress position. It is impossible to link the sound heard with the meaning of the word in their long-term memory. In such a case, they could perceive the word as an unknown word. Therefore, it is important to learn vocabulary with a proper sound image with correct phonemes and stress position.

Pronunciation

Pronunciation, which is viewed as a source of difficulty, is likely to cause problems with word segmentation or word recognition. For example, "soup or salad" can be misheard as "super salad." Students in Japan are not accustomed to the features of spoken English, which causes difficulties (Nihei, 2002). It is essential for them to know that spoken English is different from written English. In connected speech, phonological modification such as assimilation, elision, and intrusion, take place. In general, the lack of linguistic information in the bottom-up process may be made up by using non-linguistic information such as the listener's world knowledge in the top-down process. Therefore, if the listener had the contextual knowledge of the situation in the top-down process, s/he could hear "soup or salad." The effective intervention may be to provide topical knowledge or contextual information before listening, since they are used in the top-down process.

In general, Japanese listeners have a serious challenge in word recognition in spoken English. Rost (2001b) mentions that Japanese learners often have difficulty identifying key words in spoken English, which has a different stress system, while Danish learners of English have less difficulty because there are similarities of stress, tone, phonology, and phonotactic rules between English and Danish. The segmentation of continuous speech into words is an important part of listening ability and a prerequisite for word recognition. The Japanese language has a mora-based rhythm, which influences Japanese learners' segmentation procedure, even when they listen to English.

A psycholinguistic study (Murty, Otake, & Cutler, 2007) has revealed that "listeners rely on L1 language rhythm in segmenting speech; in different language, stress-, syllable-, or mora-based rhythm is exploited" (p, 77). Evidence shows that non-native listeners did not necessarily segment speech in the same way as native listeners (Murty et al., 2007). For example, Japanese learners of English tend to listen to English using their L1 mora-based rhythm (Otake et al., 1996). They often mishear because they try to represent a set consonant (C) and vowel (V) – namely, CV structure – as a mora, which is different from the CVC structure in English; for example, Japanese native listeners tend to hear the phrase "not at all" as "no ta tall."

Paying more attention to stress and rhythm seems to help Japanese students to segment words better. Native English listeners treat the stressed syllable as the beginning of a word by the Metrical Segmentation Strategy for English (Cutler & Norris, 1988). The linked and assimilated consonants and reduced vowels are produced by English stress timing. An effective method of intervention is repeated listening to the oral text and providing English subtitles or transcription.

The difficulties and the affective reaction

Facing the difficulties may cause the students' negative affective reaction. Noro (2006) clarifies the nature of listening anxiety by the qualitative analysis of the data obtained by both questionnaire and oral interviews with Japanese college students. Affective reactions in the face of the listening difficulties are irritation, lack of concentration, aversion, sense of resignation, and loss of self-confidence. He concludes, "The difficulties were some sort of 'stressor' to them" (Noro, 2006, p. 64).

Anxiety has a negative impact on listening comprehension, but it also could be a factor that allows listening to be stressful and potentially demotivating for many students (Jones, 2008). If students continue to experience unachievable listening tasks, this might be demotivating for the students. Chang (2008) found that listening supports such as repeated input reduced learners' anxiety on listening tests, and Chang and Read (2008) mention that the metacognitive approach is likely to be effective in reducing listening anxiety.

Thus, from the analysis of difficulties that students in Japan encounter, these feelings are caused by the lack of automaticity; insufficient vocabulary; which includes the problem of having wrong sound images; and the L1 phonological obstacles, which make speech perception such as word segmentation and word recognition difficult. Furthermore, those difficulties become some kind of stressors to listening anxiety, which cause lack of concentration, demotivation, and loss of self-confidence. The teacher should use the effective intervention methods to reduce their difficulties in listening activities as well as address their problems: for example, using spoken text with a silent pause between constituent boundaries, providing enough time to process the listeners without automaticity, or offering a choice of an easier spoken text with 98% lexical coverage for the listening activity.

Proposed approach as a solution

Based on comprehension process and common difficulties students in Japan encounter, how can we help the students improve their listening comprehension ability? The purpose of this section is to discuss a solution that can be implemented in pre-tertiary and tertiary English education in Japan.

Teaching listening strategies for developing the top-down process

I have clarified that the main three difficulties that students in Japan often encounter are perception problems in the bottom-up process. The normal process of listening comprehension uses not only the acoustic input in the bottom-up process but also the listener's knowledge, past experience, feelings, intentions, and intelligence to create the interpretation of the text in the top-down process (Buck, 2001). Therefore, students should be taught how to use the top-down process as well as avoid focusing on the bottom-up process too much. First, as a pre-listening activity, teachers should provide the students with background information to enhance the use of the top-down process. Second, teachers should provide students with listening activities focusing on a certain listening strategy – for example, listening for gist, listening for purpose, listening for main ideas, and listening for specific information.

Teaching metacognitive strategies for better managing the listening process

Recent research has revealed the importance of metacognitive strategies for L2 listening success. (Goh, 2008; Goh & Taib, 2006; Vandergrift, 2003, 2007). Richards (2008) defines metacognitive strategies as "conscious or unconscious mental activities that perform an executive function in the management of cognitive strategies" (p. 11) including assessing the situation, monitoring, self-evaluating, and self-testing. Teachers should encourage learners to use metacognitive strategies. If teachers have the students monitor what their own listening problems are and evaluate their listening performance even for a short time, the students learn how to use metacognitive strategies for listening. Anderson's (1995, 2009) model is useful for monitoring listening precisely. For example, Goh (2000) investigated listening difficulties in light of Anderson's model (1995). During perceptual processing, listeners reported the difficulties of not recognizing words, neglecting what follows, and not chunking the stream of speech. During the parsing phase, they reported the difficulties of quickly forgetting what is heard, an inability to form a mental presentation from words heard, and not understanding subsequent parts because of what was missed earlier. During the utilization phase, they reported understanding the words but not the message (Goh, 2000).

This provides teachers with the methodological implication that they can have the students do self-monitoring with a monitor sheet to see the process on the perception stage, the parsing stage, and the utilization stage (see Table 2.1).

Teachers who can take more time to implement listening activities should follow the sequence with "steps in guided metacognitive sequence in a listening lesson" (Goh & Taib, 2006). It consists of five steps (see Table 2.2): first, in pre-listening activity, in pairs, students predict the possible words and phrases that they might hear and write down the prediction in English or Japanese; second, in the first listen, as they are listening to the text, students circle those words or phrases they have predicted correctly, and they also write down new information they hear; third, in pair process-based discussion, students, in pairs, compare what they have understood so far and explain how they arrived at the understanding, and they identify the parts that caused confusion and disagreement and make a note of the parts of the text that will require special attention in the second listen; forth, in the second listen, students listen to the parts that have caused confusion or disagreement and write down new information they hear; fifth, in a whole-class, process-based discussion, the teacher leads a discussion to confirm comprehension before discussing with students the strategies that they used. It is a constructive approach that allows Japanese students to realize the efficacy of using metacognitive strategies.

Table 2.1 Monitor sheet

	Perception stage *Can you recognize words?*	Parsing stage *Can you visualize it when it's heard?*	Utilization stage *Can you understand the speaker's intention?*	Notes *Do you notice any other problems?*
Text 1				
Text 2				

Table 2.2 Steps in guided metacognitive sequence for students in Japan

1	Pre-listening	In pairs, students predict the possible words and phrases that they might hear and write down the prediction in English or Japanese.
2	First listening	As they are listening to the text, students circle those words or phrases they have predicted correctly, and they also write down new information they hear.
3	Pair process-based discussion	Students, in pairs, compare what they have understood so far and explain how they arrived at the understanding, and they identify the parts that caused confusion and disagreement and make a note of the parts of the text that will require special attention in the second listen.
4	Second listening	Students listen to the parts that have caused confusion or disagreement and write down new information they hear.
5	Whole-class, process-based discussion	The teacher leads a discussion to confirm comprehension before discussing with students the strategies that they used.

Teaching suprasegmental features for better word recognition

In the case of Japanese learners, the main problem of their listening difficulty seems to be word recognition, which seems to be caused by the failure of segmentation of English speech owing to the use of their L1 segmentation procedure.

Several researchers (Erickson et al., 1999; Hisaoka, 2004; Torikai et al., 2003) support teaching suprasegmental features such as rhythm, stress, and intonation as important linguistic cues to all Japanese learners. Torikai et al. (2003) argue that a great number of Japanese people, in spite of having a good knowledge of English vocabulary, fail to understand what native speakers say even at relatively slow speed. They recommend shadowing to learn the knowledge of the suprasegmental features (word stress, rhythm, and intonation) of spoken English. In a study by Yanagihara (1995), the results reveal that the shadowing method is more effective than the dictation method and that the use of the shadowing method or the dictation method is more effective than simply listening alone. Hisaoka (2004) also claims that the use of shadowing improves Japanese students' listening abilities, allowing them to articulate the suprasegmental features in connected speech such as rhythm, intonation, assimilation, elision, and linking. He explains that shadowing improves processing of fast speech because it enhances the phonological loop.

Besides shadowing, Cauldwell (2002) recommends observing and imitating the suprasegmental features of connected speech. Using a rubber band to focus on strong-weak, stress-timed rhythm in English is also helpful to students in understanding English stress. Thus teaching suprasegmental features should be integrated with speaking skills.

The three-part sequence of listening instruction and micro-exercises

Field (1998) proposed a three-part sequence consisting of pre-listening, while-listening, and post-listening and contains activities that link bottom-up and top-down listening. In EFL classrooms in Japan, the sequence is useful with some modifications to activities. First, in the pre-listening phase, providing topical knowledge is more helpful for the use of metacognitive strategies for students than the vocabulary review. Reviewing of key vocabulary forces students to focus on the bottom-up process too much, as a study by Chang (2008) revealed. Pre-listening should focus on the top-down process. The teachers can provide background information or stimulate their experience related to the topic integrated with speaking, reading, and writing activities.

In the while-listening phase, not only can comprehension exercises for the top-down process but also dictation or partially transcribing for the bottom-up process can be practiced. It depends on what the students need to monitor and improve. For example, transcription and dictation can tell more about the condition of learners' word recognition than their answers to comprehension questions. Listens should be repeated more than once so that the learner can identify the parts that caused confusion and breakdown, and the learner can pay special attention to those parts in the second listen. That may encourage learners to use metacognitive strategies. For low-level learners, the teacher should use spoken text with a lengthened pause between constituent boundaries for less demanding listening practice.

Finally, the post-listening phase should include more activities to diagnose listening problems. Teachers and learners can focus on sections that the learner could not follow or not understand. This may involve analysis of part of the text to enable students to recognize such features as linking, assimilation, and other features of spoken discourse that they were unable to process. For example, by reading the transcription of the spoken text, students will notice the gap between what they heard and the actual words used. The monitor sheet (Table 2.1) is also useful here.

Micro-exercises that focus on required skills in each stage in the Anderson (2009) model are effective; they are exercises aiming to enhance word recognition skills on the perception stage, creating metal representation skills on the parsing stage, and skills to understand the speaker's intention in the utilization phase. For example, one micro-exercise for the perception stage is a dictation exercise focusing on phonological modification. One parsing stage exercise is an exercise that involves the listener drawing what s/he heard, which includes a certain form of syntax. One utilization stage exercise is a turn-taking exercise, which makes the students think of the speaker's intention and reply. These micro-exercises can be integrated with speaking, reading, and writing. More importantly, the exercises need neither an extended amount of time nor any extra materials, so teachers can implement them easily in pre-tertiary and tertiary education contexts in Japan.

Conclusion

In pre-tertiary and tertiary education in Japan, listening instruction should be emphasized as well as teaching the other three skills. Teachers should pay more attention to process rather than product in listening pedagogy because the process approach can follow up on students' problems and help teachers to choose appropriate listening activities. In this chapter, effective listening comprehension instruction focusing on process has been explored, based on the two theoretical frameworks of listening comprehension – the Anderson (1995, 2009) model and the top-down and the bottom-up processes – and taking into account common difficulties students often encounter: first, teaching listening strategies to enhance the top-down process; second, teaching metacognitive strategies to cope with the difficulties; and third, teaching suprasegmental linguistic features such as stress, rhythm, and intonation, which are useful linguistic cues for better bottom-up processing. The lesson sequences including the top-down process approach and the bottom-up process approach, as well as the micro-exercises for improving the subskills for the perception, parsing, and utilization phase, are useful, and they can be integrated with speaking, reading, and writing. In spite of some constraints, teachers need to implement listening pedagogy focusing on process in Japan.

In order to develop better listening pedagogy, further research for listening pedagogy in Japan will be needed in the future. It will need to include empirical studies that prove the efficacy of process approaches through teacher perception, material development, learner motivation, teacher language awareness, curriculum pressure, and so on. Moreover, it seems that learning the stress-timed rhythm of English is necessary for students in Japan. Teaching suprasegmental features and linguistic phenomenon of connected speech is important to the students for developing the bottom-up process. Further research on the efficacy of explicit instruction of suprasegmental features and linguistic phenomenon in spoken language will be expected.

References

Anderson, J. R. (1995). *Cognitive psychology and its implications* (4th edn.). New York: Freeman.
Anderson, J. R. (2009). *Cognitive psychology and its implications* (7th edn.). New York: Worth Publishers.
Bloomfield, A., Wayland, S. C., Rhoades, E., Blodgett, A., Linck, J., & Ross, S. (2010). *What makes listening difficult? Factors affecting second language listening comprehension*. College Park: University of Maryland Center for Advanced Study of Language. Retrieved from www.dtic.mil/dtic /tr/fulltext/u2/a550176.pdf
Blyth, A. (2010). How teachers teach listening in Japan: Part 1. *Proceeding of PAC, The Pan-Asia Conference The 18th Annual KOTESOL International Conference 2010*, 71–82.

Brown, H. D. (2001). *Teaching by principles: An interactive approach to language Pedagogy*. White Plains, NY: Pearson Education.
Buck, G. (2001). *Assessing listening*. Cambridge: Cambridge University Press.
Cauldwell, R. (2002). *Phonology for listening: Relishing the messy*. Retrieved from www.speechinaction.pwp.blueyonder.co.uk/pdf%20files/Phonology%20for%20 Listening_Relishing%20the%20messy.pdf
Chang, A. C-S. (2008). Listening strategies of L2 learners with varied test tasks. *TESL Canada Journal*, 25(2), 1–26.
Chang, A. C-S., & Read, J. (2008). Reducing listening test anxiety through various forms of listening support. *TESL-EJ, 12*. Retrieved from www.tesl-ej.org/wordpress/issues/volume12/ej45/ej45al/
Cutler, A., & Norris, D. G. (1988). The role of strong syllables in segmentation for lexical access. *Journal of Experimental Psychology: Human Perception and Performance, 14*, 113–121.
Eastman, J. K. (1993). C-words and F-words: The importance of distinguishing content and function in teaching second language listening comprehension. *System, 21*, 495–502.
Erickson, D., Akahane-Yamada, R., Tajima, K., & Matsumoto, K. F. (1999). Syllable counting and mora units in speech perception. *ICPhS99*, San Francisco, 1479–1482.
Field, J. (1998). Skills and strategies: Towards a new methodology for listening. *ELT Journal, 52*, 477–493.
Goh, C. (2000). A cognitive perspective on language learners' listening comprehension problems. *System, 28*(1), 55–75.
Goh, C. (2008). Metacognitive instruction for second language listening development: Theory, practice and research implications. *RELC Journal, 39*, 188–213.
Goh, C., & Taib, Y. (2006). Metacognitive instruction in listening for young learners. *ELT Journal, 60*, 222–232.
Hisaoka, T. (2004). On the use of shadowing for improving listening ability: Theory and practice. *Gakusyuin Kotoka Kiyou, 2*, 13–30.
Hulstijin, J. H. (2003). Connectionist models of language processing and the training of listening skills with the aid of multimedia software. *Computer Assisted Language Learning, 16*, 413–425.
Institute for International Business Communication. (2014). *2013nenndo TOEIC Program sojukenshasu wa kako saiko no 258.5mannin ni* [In 2013, the TOEIC Program reached a record 25.85 million test takers].Retrieved from www.toeic.or.jp/press /2014/p011.html
Jones, D. (2008). Is there any room for listening? The necessity of teaching listening skills in ESL/EFL classrooms. *Kansai University Gaikokugo Forum, 7*, 15–22.
MEXT. (2003). *Eigo ga tsukaeru nihonjin noikusei no tameno koudoukeikaku* [Action plan to cultivate "Japanese with English abilities"]. Retrieved from www.mext.go.jp/b_menu/shingi/chukyo/chukyo3/015/siryo/04042301/011/002.htm
MEXT. (2009). *Koutougakkou gakushu shidou yoryo gaikokugo eigoban kariyaku* [Study of course guideline for foreign languages in senior high schools provisional version]. Retrieved from www.mext.go.jp/a_menu/shotou/new-cs/youryou/ei yaku/1298353.htm
Murty, L., Otake, T., & Cutler, A. (2007). Perceptual tests of rhythmic similarity: I. Mora rhythm. *Language and Speech, 50*, 77–99.

Nation, I. S. P. (2006). How large a vocabulary is needed for reading and listening? *The Canadian Modern Language Review, 63,* 59–82.
Nihei, K. (2002). *How to teach listening.* ERIC. Retrieved from http://eric.ed.gov/?id=ED475743
Noro, T. (2006). Developing a construct model of "listening stress": A qualitative study of the affective domain of the listening process. *Annual Review of English Language Education in Japan, 17,* 61–70.
Osada, N. (2004). The effects of lengthened silent pauses on listening comprehension of Japanese EFL learners with a special focus on auditory impression and free recall protocol. *JACET Bulletin, 39,* 105–121.
Otake, T., Hatano, G., & Yoneyama, K. (1996). Speech segmentation by Japanese listeners. In T. Otake & A. Cutler (Eds.), *Phonological structure and language processing: Cross-linguistic studies* (pp. 183–201). Berlin: Mouton.
Richards, J. C. (2005). Second thoughts on teaching listening. *RELC Journal, 36,* 85–92.
Richards, J. C. (2008). *Teaching listening and speaking: From theory to practice.* New York: Cambridge University Press.
Rost, M. (2001a). *Teaching and researching listening.* London: Longman.
Rost, M. (2001b). Listening. In R. Carter & D. Nunan (Eds.), *The Cambridge guide to teaching English to speakers of other languages* (pp. 7–13). Cambridge: Cambridge University Press.
Stahr, L. S. (2009). Vocabulary knowledge and advanced listening comprehension in English as a foreign language. *Studies in Second Language Acquisition, 31,* 577–607.
Tahira, M. (2012). Behind MEXT's new course of study guidelines. *The Language Teacher, 36*(3), 4–8.
Tauroza, S., & Allison, D. (1990). Speech rates in British English. *Applied Linguistics, 11,* 90–105.
Taylor, L. (2014). *A report on the review of test specifications for the reading and listening papers of the Test of English for Academic Purpose (TEAP) for Japanese University Entrants.* Retrieved from www.eiken.or.jp/teap/group/pdf/teap_rlspecreview_report.pdf
Torikai, K., Tami, K., Someya, Y., Tanaka, M., Tsuruta, C., & Nishimura, T. (2003). *Hajimete no shadowing.* [Shadowing for the first time]. Tokyo: Gakushukenkyusha.
Vandergrift, L. (2003). From prediction through reflection: Guiding students through the process of L2 listening. *The Canadian Modern Language Review, 59,* 425–440.
Vandergrift, L. (2006). Second language listening: Listening ability or language proficiency? *The Modern Language Journal, 90,* 6–18.
Vandergrift, L. (2007). Recent developments in second and foreign language listening comprehension research. *Language Teaching, 40,* 191–210.
Yanagawa, K. (2012). Do high school English teachers teach listening, and do students listen to spoken English? To explore washback effects of the introduction of the centre listening test in Japan. *Dialogue, 11,* 1–14.
Yanagihara, Y. (1995). A study of teaching methods for developing English listening Comprehension: The effects of shadowing and dictations. *Language Laboratory, 32,* 73–89.
Yoshida, K. (2003). Language education policy in Japan- the problem of espoused objectives versus practice. *The Modern Language Journal, 87,* 290–292.

3 Developing speaking for intercultural communication

Textbooks with critical and creative approaches

Lixian Jin and Martin Cortazzi

In this chapter, we present a brief rationale for developing intercultural communication as an aspect of enhancing learners' oral skills in English Language Teaching (ELT), and we outline some relevant aims and features of this topic. The key questions here are:

1. How can we develop textbooks for oral intercultural communication skills?
2. How can we integrate intercultural communication skills with approaches to develop students' thinking skills and their creative thinking?

We highlight our contribution to materials development: an approach that we have developed over a number of years, which links intercultural communication skills with the development of students' ability to analyse and reflect on contexts and situations of interaction, and to develop their own critical thinking and creativity. Together with developing students' professional skills for their future workplace communication, these can be seen as inter-related aspects of developing oral skills in English (see Figure 3.1).

As a specific application, we focus on the context of teaching oral skills in China. This is a significant case: China has many millions of learners of English. While Chinese ELT has developed enormously in recent years at all levels of education, the teaching of oral skills remains problematic in many places. Although many teachers and students are aware of the need to develop intercultural communication skills, there is little training for teachers and there are relatively few resources for this. Although increasing numbers of Chinese students and teachers travel internationally, this remains a very small proportion of the total numbers of learners and teachers: this is therefore an under-developed area of Chinese ELT. We show the application of the suggested approach through the use of published textbook materials and classroom activities for teaching English in universities in China, in particular through the use of 'Participation Activities'.

Contemporary communication, cultures, and ELT

Contemporary communication is specially characterized by the multiplicity of media, with the speed, complexity, and diversity of communication locally,

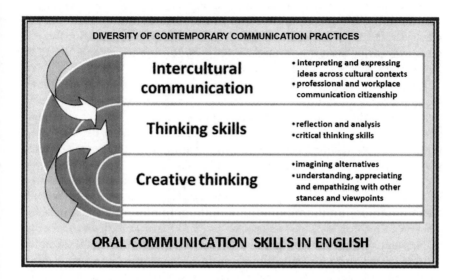

Figure 3.1 Three inter-related aspects of oral skills in English developed in this chapter.

nationally, and across national borders. Frequently, this means speakers of different languages and cultural backgrounds interact with each other in an increasing range of contexts: either face-to-face or less directly through electronic media. Thus, for more and more people, communicating in a second language with culturally diverse others is becoming a normal situation. It is quite likely to be a routine future situation for learners currently studying languages. Language education, therefore, needs to prepare students for these features of contemporary communication.

For the development of language learners' speaking skills, this is a crucial point. First, because it means that any individual or organization may sooner or later find a need to interact rapidly or at short notice with an unexpected range of culturally diverse participants. People with whom students may need to interact may include visitors or tourists, international students and teachers, or, for adult learners, clients, customers, and business and professional partners from around the world. Equally, as language users, students may travel or study abroad or interact directly, electronically, or vicariously through social and mass media with a widening range of other speakers. Second, language learners can be seen as current or future professionals and workers, citizens of societies whose cultural diversity in many places is multiplied through migration and population movements. An increasing number of places can be characterized by 'superdiversity.' This term underlines the complexity of urban populations in cities such as London, New York, or Melbourne where two to three hundred or more languages can be found, reflecting the enormous variety of cultures and ethnic groups among residents (Vertovec, 2007). Therefore, these intercultural communication contexts are not only international but also local: students need to learn to communicate with those from other cultural communities within their own locality. These points mean that intercultural communication skills have become a key part of the citizenship and professionalism, which is ultimately the context for which many learners develop competent speaking skills, not only in a first but also in a second or foreign language (Byram, 2008; Clyne, 1994; Guilherme, 2002; Scollon, Scollon, & Jones, 2012; Varner & Beamer, 2011) (see Figure 3.1).

The internationalization of ELT is a crucial part of this expansion of communication since in many education systems and business and professional organizations all around the globe English is the language of choice for communicating whenever a second language is required, so English needs to be taught and learned with intercultural contexts in mind. This development greatly extends any discussion about the role of culture in ELT: traditional concepts of a 'target culture' must now be pluralized to extend to a far greater range of 'target cultures' or 'source cultures' (those of the learners) for international students (Cortazzi & Jin, 1999). 'English' also needs to be pluralized to 'Englishes.' This problematizes ideas of 'native-speaker cultures' of English as the sole or main target since potentially any or every culture in the world is the cultural context of contemporary communication: interactants with whom students as future professionals may want to speak can represent this extraordinary diversity of backgrounds and contexts; many will be using English as a second or foreign language, quite possibly in expert but different ways, which reflect local or international Englishes (Kirkpatrick, 2007). Naturally, this range of contexts includes those where people use English as a first language, but they are by no means confined to first-language users who, globally, are vastly outnumbered by users of English as a second or other language. Since a pedagogic focus on one or two target cultures and contexts is plainly insufficient in this contemporary communication context, it is appropriate to develop intercultural skills in relation to a wide range of speakers from a wide range of cultural contexts.

Intercultural communication skills

The target for developing speaking skills must therefore include a dimension of developing intercultural communication skills. This will involve developing students' cultural awareness, knowledge, and understanding of diverse intercultural situations; development of positive attitudes; and engagement with and empathy for people from other cultures – some of these people will inevitably be unlike the learners themselves. Developing these skills will include developing students' ability to analyse and interpret unfamiliar situations in which intercultural communication is a key element. Cultural aspects of language learning should therefore include intercultural situations selected not only from different regions around the world but also locally so that in the ELT classroom, students can encounter diversity within their own country or context of learning.

Figure 3.2 shows some aims for developing intercultural communication skills in ELT (e.g., see Aldred, Byram, & Fleming 2003; Byram, 2008; Corbett, 2003, 2010; Jackson, 2014; Zhu, 2014). Several broad points should be salient: these skills are worth developing from an educational viewpoint as part of human

Intercultural communication aims for learners in ELT classes

Learners need to develop

- interest and open-mindedness about cultures and communication
- curiosity and confidence to explore intercultural situations and experiences
- understanding of and empathy for other cultural communities
- visions of themselves as 'intercultural'
- recognition of different dimensions of cultural beliefs and practices
- awareness communication styles, cultural ways of politeness and interaction
- explicit awareness of communication practices within their own cultural context
- ability to analyse situations and think critically about issues and problems
- mindful thinking and communication, sensitivity to stereotypes
- creativity in considering viewpoints and others' stances and experiences
- sensible risk taking in communication and action
- ability to accommodate to different audiences and different situations
- ability to negotiate language misunderstandings
- skills to manage intercultural conflict situations
- skills to make explicit and explain elements of different cultural practices
- ability to mediate and help others in situations of communication difficulties
- socio-cultural engagement, responsibility, and intercultural citizenship

Figure 3.2 Some aims for learners to develop intercultural communication skills.

development in a holistic approach to language education; the skills are worth developing in any language (a first, second, other or foreign language), and such aims can apply to all language skills, but the focus here is on developing oral skills.

These aims naturally take considerable time to realize in practice fully. Appropriate resources will be needed. Materials should include multimedia textbooks, which include video and audio recordings of speakers from different cultures, and literature in English from around the world to engage learners' imaginations. In practice, all materials need to be tailored to different levels and contexts for language learners. Students will need models of analysing intercultural situations and of talking about intercultural thinking and feeling. These models may be embodied in published materials or enacted by teachers.

Analysis, reflection, and themes

Teaching speaking for intercultural communication has a future orientation for students, to engage with contemporary communication situations and their concomitant complexity and diversity. However, developing these intercultural skills has an immediate present value for students too. It is important to help learners see this current relevance during teaching-learning processes. This is partly to help sustain student motivation and partly so that teachers give learners feedback on intercultural issues while they are learning intercultural skills. One rationale for including cultural issues in ELT is not only that students should understand target cultures but also to enable learners to analyse, understand, and reflect upon their own culture and identity. Similarly, teaching speaking for intercultural communication includes, by design, an element in which students analyse, understand, and reflect upon their own personal communication and upon ways in which people within their own cultural community express themselves (see Figure 3.2). This reflective element includes developing students' ability to be explicit and think critically about their own communication situations, including some in which they are personally involved and which include (inter) cultural elements.

To develop students' ability to analyse intercultural situations becomes crucial when the question of topics and situations is considered. These could productively involve one target context or target community. However, this misses the complexity and diversity of much contemporary communication. This means a global variety of topics and situations need to be included. Since not every culture or intercultural context can be represented within a syllabus or teaching scheme, representative sample situations are involved so that students develop sound knowledge of what aspects of contexts typically vary in intercultural communication and enhance their ability to analyse problematic situations.

The topics through which speaking skills are extended traditionally revolve around communicating about the family, food, travel, shopping, work and leisure interests, health and education, and daily life in one's own or a target country. At more advanced levels, topics often concern current problems and issues in society or cultural, geographical, and historical features of one or more target countries. Engagement in such topics can, of course, include intercultural dimensions. However, in our view, the list needs to be extended for a more sustained development of intercultural speaking skills, and over a long term, it should include the inter-related topics mentioned in Figure 3.3. One rationale for this is the complexity of contemporary communication patterns and the role of intercultural education for speaking skills related to future professional and workplace communication.

A slightly different rationale for topics in Figure 3.3 and the aims in Figure 3.2 is that the sustained teaching of oral intercultural communication skills really requires some specific training and teacher development. A problem here is that for many teachers, and even teacher trainers, intercultural communication has not yet been part of their training or professional development. One way to understand what might be involved in such professional development is to look at current textbooks about intercultural communication, which would be likely used in training programmes. There are now many introductions to this field (Chen & Starosta, 2007; Hurn & Tomalin, 2013; Jackson, 2014; Martin & Nakayama,

Aspects of intercultural communication for selective development of ELT topics

Develop students' awareness and increasing understanding of

- key features of contexts and how contextual variables affect communication
- World Englishes and international uses of English
- cultural ways of speaking, rhetorical and discourse practices in interaction
- non-verbal communication
- the pragmatics and interpretations of intercultural communication
- participants' diverse identities and how they relate to communication
- professional communication in intercultural situations, workplaces, and organizations
- issues in cultures of learning, international education, and study abroad
- tourism, travel, and hospitality
- well-being and health care
- personal relationships across cultures: friendships, love, marriage, and family life
- world views, religions, philosophies of living, and value systems

Figure 3.3 Some aspects and inter-related topics for developing intercultural communication in ELT.

2009; Piller, 2011; Spencer-Oatey & Franklin, 2009; Zhu, 2014) and collections of basic readings or papers (Christopher, 2012; Gudykunst, 2003; Holliday, Hyde, & Kullamn, 2010; Samovar et al., 2014) and handbooks (Jackson, 2012; Kotthoff & Spencer-Oatey, 2007; Zhu, 2011) and direct considerations for ELT (Corbett, 2003, 2010; Fennes & Hapgood, 1997; Fitzgerald, 2003; Hall, 2002).

These publications commonly feature the aims and topics we have outlined (Figures 3.2 and 3.3). Our approach, however, emphasizes the inclusion of critical and creative thinking, which we consider to be inextricably related strands of developing intercultural communication skills (see Figure 3.1) and which are less frequently considered in this literature.

Critical and creative thinking

In this approach, developing intercultural communication skills is intimately linked with critical and creative thinking. In many educational contexts, these skills are frequently discussed in their own right as central to the normal and effective development of human abilities (e.g., Boden, 1994; Gardner, 1993; Sternberg, 1988, 1999). They are widely recognized in study programmes and for English for Academic Purposes (Brink-Budgeon, 2010; Butterworth & Thwaite, 2013; Moon, 2008), but they are also considered in everyday English uses (Carter, 2004; Pope, 2005) and can be applied in many areas of learning (Cummins, 2012; DfEE, 1999; Tan, 2007). Critical thinking can relate to the analysis of intercultural contexts and communication situations, reflection on cultural themes in communication, and consideration of communication issues and problems for critical cultural awareness (Guilherme, 2002; Holliday, 2011; Spencer-Oatey & Franklin, 2009). Creative thinking can relate to recognizing others' cultural viewpoints, stances, and experiences, and to developing empathy for different perspectives while recognizing alternative explanations for misunderstandings and conflicting positions in communication. Critical and creative perspectives complement each other.

Developing oral skills in ELT in China

Teaching Chinese learners in China is a significant case for developing intercultural communication skills. They represent by far the largest national group of learners of English in the world. Because of China's role internationally, there are clear economic, social, and personal needs for Chinese professionals, tourists, and travellers to communicate with people from different cultures around the globe and, equally, for those outsiders visiting or working in China to communicate effectively with Chinese people, whether in English, Chinese, or another language. The concept of developing intercultural communication skills in relation to local cultural diversity and minority languages in China is now on the agenda of bilingual education but has so far not impinged greatly on ELT in China in terms of practical applications (Feng, 2007, 2011; Lo Bianco, Orton, & Gao, 2009).

However, as with many students in the Asian region, most Chinese learners are in a difficult position for learning intercultural skills. Opportunities to interact with those from outside China are limited. There are limited chances for most Chinese to interact with teachers or students from outside China. They may develop some intercultural skills through travel and study abroad. However, for those lucky enough to travel abroad, this is usually for short visits in which they may speak a lot of Chinese and little English. Thus visiting other cultural contexts and living abroad does not in itself guarantee the development of either oral skills or intercultural competence unless visits are arranged systematically with these aims in mind – even then students can over-estimate their own resulting intercultural development (Jackson, 2010; Dai & Chen, 2014). Research indicates that even though Chinese learners have a good background in learning English and attain acceptable scores on international tests, such as the International English Testing System and Test of English as a Foreign Language, as international students, many experience difficulties in communicating and learning in English, with associated intercultural problems of learning (Cortazzi & Jin, 2013a; Jin & Cortazzi, 2011, 2013).

Many Chinese universities, some schools, and private language institutes have a tradition of informal solutions to developing oral skills. This 'learning English with Chinese characteristics' includes the holding of English-speaking events for students through film and drama societies, book clubs with discussion circles, or English-speaking competitions (performances are sometimes shown on TV); the weekly informal gathering of students in an 'English Corner' of a park or square on campus for casual conversation; and in some places, Chinese versions of immersion English programmes to facilitate rapid language acquisition through massive exposure (Jin & Cortazzi, 2004).

In terms of ELT methodology, formal language teaching in China has moved beyond grammar-translation approaches to more active learner-centred approaches in which applications of knowledge of English to real-world contexts are emphasized. This includes learning to discuss and solve problems and develop collaborative skills in groups. Within this context, oral skills are considered far more important than was previously the case, and intercultural skills are more valued.

A major issue for many Chinese students abroad is that they have a limited willingness to speak in English. Many students are afraid to make mistakes and reluctant to take risks. Some who study abroad interact socially largely or exclusively with other Chinese students in Chinese and find it difficult to make friends with local people. This may partly be a result of a legacy of Chinese cultures of learning in which, in large classes, students are not encouraged to speak out, ask questions, raise issues in discussion, or proffer alternative viewpoints. Many Chinese students are seen by international teachers as 'passive' in class discussions: this is wrong labelling and perhaps a stereotype, since students in China listen mindfully and may be learning in different ways for cultural and social reasons in a different educational tradition (Cortazzi & Jin, 1996; Jin & Cortazzi, 1998). Most Chinese teachers of English manage the classroom interaction in their large classes rather effectively to promote learning in more formal ways (Cortazzi & Jin, 2001), but it has taken some years for English teachers to begin to feel comfortable with the classroom organization of pair and group work, which is typical of oral interactive approaches.

Further difficulties for developing students' oral skills relate to their teachers' professional skills. Most English teachers in China are Chinese: they have largely learned English in China, and few have had opportunities for an extended stay abroad. Very few Chinese teachers of English have had training in teaching intercultural communication skills. Most teachers in China teach large classes (primary and middle schools frequently have classes of over 40; university classes may have 60 or more students; even in oral language classes, numbers of well over 30 are commonplace). Teachers are aware of the importance of teaching oral skills, but only recently have listening and, to a lesser extent, speaking been included in tests at national levels in China. Traditional constraints in classroom practices include an emphasis on grammar and vocabulary taught in a teacher- or textbook-centred approach. This is changing with more teacher development in teaching oral skills and cultural aspects of ELT. A Chinese professional practice is that teachers learn skills and pedagogic techniques from observing each other in demonstration lessons, which may be video recorded. The recent generation of ELT textbook materials published in China has accompanying audio and video recordings, including recordings of situations with intercultural interactions, with tape scripts, and with intercultural notes provided.

Applications of this intercultural framework to ELT in China

Some applications to develop oral intercultural communication skills in second language situations in Western countries have been developed in Hong Kong universities and schools. These include prolonged student sojourns and academic exchanges with English-speaking institutions, short visits abroad, and ELT projects which develop direct oral interaction with local visitors and residents who speak English or with students abroad using the Internet. Some of these activities are within specific intercultural communication teaching modules. These are successful when supported by reflection and analysis through classroom discussion and journal activities supported by informed teachers (Jackson, 2010). Students can be prepared through ethnographic training to make the most of opportunities to understand the insider perspectives of others (Corbett, 2003; Roberts, Byram, Barro, Jordan, & Street, 2001). However, in most mainland Chinese ELT contexts, such possibilities are limited or impossible and therefore less direct oral experiences need to be provided through the use of multimedia resources and textbook materials, which include audio and video recordings of intercultural dialogues (scripted or authentic) and descriptions and narratives of intercultural interactions. These will form the basis of classroom interactions, perhaps supported by online resources.

In the following considerations and textbook examples, we refer to several series of materials for *College English* courses published in China jointly by Macmillan with Shanghai Foreign Language Education Press (SFLEP) (Smallwood, Li, Martin, & Green, 2002–5, 2004–5) and with the Foreign Language Teaching and Research Press (FLTRP) in Beijing (Greenall, Tomalin, & Friedland, 2008–9, 2009). These materials arguably lead developments in intercultural communication within ELT in China, and they have been linked with practical teacher development programmes over some years. We have been closely involved with these as series editor and cultural editor, materials writers, or authors of accompanying teacher's books, also as teacher trainers conducting related courses in key cities in China.

In this approach, it is not enough for learners to simply encounter a representative range of cultures through texts in order to raise their awareness and knowledge of other cultural communities. Rather, learners need to explore, investigate, and interpret intercultural interactions; identify the stances and interpretations taken by interlocutors and the values they draw on; and identify sources of misunderstandings and intercultural conflict. For this, learners need to be encouraged and guided to develop flexibility, mindfulness, and cultural adaptability, and eventually be prepared to mediate in situations of intercultural difficulty, misunderstanding, or conflict.

The FLTRP materials (Greenall et al., 2008–9, 2009) include audio and video recordings, both scripted and authentic, which with printed texts and dialogues give students access to a wide variety of cultural situations. Many of these scripts are models for Chinese and British participants are in interaction. Activities include many oral tasks for pair and group discussions and class presentations, often on cultural aspects of themes presented in the main texts, supported with 'Culture Notes.' These are further supported with focused activities related to a specific 'Reading across Culture' section on the theme of each unit, with discussion activities, which encourage students to express their own ideas and viewpoints on aspects of cultural life in different contexts. Some activities ask students to reflect on Chinese cultures and local situations. For example, on the theme of tourism, students are given the task to prepare in English their own recommendations of local places for international visitors and to describe significant sites taking into account the cultures of such visitors. Classroom presentations are made by groups and in the Teacher's Books, teachers are given communication criteria to evaluate these and give explicit feedback to learners. Later, after students have had the opportunity to internalize this process, teachers hand over this evaluation process to learners. Students draw up and apply their own criteria, including criteria of intercultural communication (e.g., that this should be appropriate, efficient, effective, and satisfying; Ting-Toomey, 1999; see Figure 3.6).

Oral expression is further developed through 'Developing Critical Thinking' – a section in each unit that encourages independent thinking about ideas presented in the main text or dialogues. The Teacher's Books give explicit guidance on different ways to manage the classroom organization of these activities. Many Chinese students are not accustomed to a lot of self-expression in English; some will feel a lack of confidence and the potential embarrassment of speaking out in class, and some will hesitate to verbalize their own ideas, so the Teacher's Books give full examples of answers and possible discussion points so that students can be supported. Some teachers use the Internet to make these available to their classes. These materials thus contain a lot of information and activities to raise awareness of cultural issues and to apply some intercultural communication skills – all the activities are, after all, conducted in English.

The SFLEP materials (Smallwood et al., 2002–5, 2004–5) also have this emphasis on oral interaction on cultural themes through active engagement in role plays, discussions, problem-solving, and interpreting ideas. The materials contain three kinds of additional innovations. One section has 'Intercultural Notes,' which specifically give intercultural information and guidance related to a unit theme. Examples of topics for these notes are gift giving in different cultures; perceived space between people, power, and language; World Englishes; intercultural marriages; languages and communication in Australia; exams across cultures; and questioning and learning in classrooms across cultures.

Another innovation is a section in each unit on 'Expanding Your Creativity.' This encourages oral expression in unexpected ways, which are quite different from both traditional and recent activities in Chinese ELT. This is a significant skill development in China (Cortazzi & Jin, 2013b). Each activity is by definition different from all others in the same textbook, but each asks students in pairs or groups to use English actively in new contexts in ways that go beyond accuracy and fluency. They emphasize interest, imagination, visualizing alternatives, engaging in problem solving, using judgement, or applying personal and social values (see examples in Figure 3.4). These creative activities lead to students' oral presentations in class, and students must give reasons or a rationale for their achievements here. These presentations can be evaluated by the teacher using criteria suggested in the Teacher's Book but are later evaluated by students themselves. The Teacher's Books have examples of guidance for students and of completed activities, but there is necessarily a creative range of outcomes for such activities.

Expanding creativity: activities for creative oral presentations of ideas

- put qualities for a successful personal relationship in rank order, from a given list (e.g., romance, honour, trust, family background, wealth, loyalty, accommodation)
- design a T-shirt with a message to express your thinking about a local environmental issue)
- decide what money means to people in your group (e.g., security, power, happiness, comfort, health and well-being, family status, property ownership)
- design a poster to advertise and recommend a newly issued book, song, or film
- interpret some intercultural data about good students and comment on its significance and interest for your group
- design an event for the Verbal Olympics: all events must emphasize people's verbal abilities (e.g., telling jokes or stories, presenting introductions, arguments and speeches . . . the longest/shortest/most moving/ most entertaining/ most expressive/ most informative. . .)
- make 'guidelines for the guides' – i.e., do's and don'ts for Chinese guides to interact with international visitors and tourists (e.g., explaining, sustaining interest, entertaining, organizing a group, timekeeping, visitors' cultural values)
- prioritize facilities for town planning in your locality (e.g., shopping, businesses, sports and leisure, entertainments, scenic landscaping, transport, tourist and visitor facilities, environmental aspects)
- write and perform a dialogue between a young person in love and their parents (who think their son/daughter is being unwise)

Figure 3.4 Examples of activities to develop creativity in oral skills in pairs and groups (based on Smallwood et al., 2002–5).

A third innovation is a 'Culture Corner' in each unit (authored by Jin).

This section systematically raises issues in intercultural communication which have been specifically observed to be problematic for Chinese learners of English in intercultural face-to-face interactions in China and internationally. These observations have been confirmed with key informants. The section shows how particular verbal events can be interpreted or misinterpreted by participants from different cultural communities – often this leads to wrong impressions, misunderstandings, or wrong evaluations of people, which can reinforce stereotypes (examples of topics are given in Figure 3.5). The section gives examples and information from different cultural viewpoints illustrated with cartoons and encourages students to observe and analyse interactions themselves by showing what features of context, cultural frameworks, interaction, and language to look out for.

'Culture Corners' are each followed by a 'Participation Activity.' This is an observed intercultural communication situation or critical incident, which has different cultural interpretations, which can lead to misperceptions, misunderstandings, misinterpretations, or conflict. Learners are presented with different choices for action or interpretation; they discuss and choose one which they feel is most appropriate, with reasons, and consider the consequences of other choices and who might make these other choices (see Cushner & Brislin, 1996). We call this a 'Participation Activity' to emphasize that students need to talk about and often re-enact or role-play such situations. There are no right or wrong answers, but through the Teacher's Book students are given further notes on the Culture Corner, key questions to help them consider the Participation Activity situations in more depth, and feedback comments for each choice. Thus, the main point of the activity is to consider and verbalize interactional choices, imagine, and discuss alternative cultural consequences and cross-cultural explanations of politeness, and to role-play similar scenarios – all in English.

Figure 3.6 shows three stages of Participation Activities. These can be related to the extracts from an example of '*Ask if you are not sure*' (Smallwood et al., 2004, 2005, 2006, Book 2: 49–50; Teacher's Book 2: 54–55). The Culture Corner elaborates with a cartoon illustration how second language users often

---

Culture Corner topics: raising awareness of politeness practices across cultures
- ways of listening
- expressing disagreement
- accepting invitations
- indicating preferences
- persuading others
- praising yourself
- ways of presenting arguments
- presenting balanced arguments
- asking questions in formal contexts
- asking when you are not sure
- using intonation to express meaning
- expressing feelings and emotions
- cultural views of classroom events
- culture shock and changes
- linguistic aspects of competitiveness
- topics for social chatting
- expressing humour
- politeness with emails

Figure 3.5 Developing intercultural communication with oral skills (based on Smallwood et al., 2004–5).

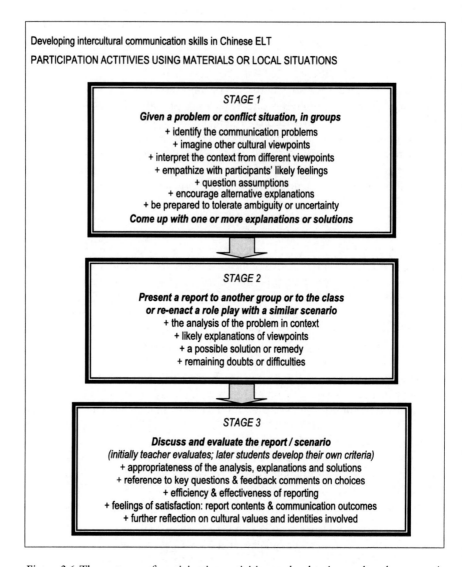

Figure 3.6 Three stages of participation activities to develop intercultural communication skills (based on Smallwood et al., 2002–5, 2004–2005).

do not understand what they are hearing: in some cultures, it is the listener's responsibility to understand, whereas in others, the onus is on the speaker to be clear; some people are embarrassed to ask or unsure how to ask for clarification; hesitating or waiting to ask may be interpreted as shyness or showing a lack of interest. Yet not asking may have serious consequences for misunderstanding (a humorous example of this is given):

Participation activity

You are attending a lively discussion about philosophy. Your Canadian professor is explaining the views of a contemporary British philosopher. The professor uses the word *Weltanschauung* during the discussion, and you don't know what it means. You try to work out the meaning from the context: 'Her *Weltanschauung* is interesting because it. . .' says the professor. 'This *Weltanschauung* is common among a group of people who. . .'

You think the word may have something to do with a newspaper; you know that *Die Welt* is the name of a German newspaper. It may be important for you to know this word; the professor has already used it twice. You would really like to know what *Weltanschauung* means.

With a partner, discuss the following courses of action open to you. Give reasons for your choice. You could

a) interrupt immediately, but politely, and ask for an explanation of *Weltanschauung*. Maybe everyone else wants to know, too;

b) wait until after the discussion has finished and look up the word by yourself; you don't want to look silly in front of the professor and the other students;

c) quietly ask your neighbour if he or she knows the meaning of the word; if your neighbour knows, you will obtain the answer without interrupting the class;

d) ask the professor for an explanation after the class has finished. This will avoid wasting class time if not everyone needs to know.

(*Weltanschauung* means 'world view' – a German expression often used by English speakers in discussions about philosophy, politics, and related areas.)

Notes in the Teacher's Book to help with stage 1 or later (Figure 3.6):

Students should consider

- how important it is to know such a term and whether this importance would only be known when you ask the teacher
- whether to interrupt the teacher and how to do this appropriately and politely
- whether talking to a neighbour will be considered an interruption to that student or to others nearby – and to the teacher
- whether asking the teacher might help the class
- whether asking the teacher after the class would interrupt the teacher then or delay the teacher in doing something else
- whether asking the teacher after the class is a good idea: it may help you but would it help other students?

Observation and research (Jin & Cortazzi, 1998, 2011) indicates that this situation does represent a real problem in intercultural communication for many Chinese people, and many Chinese students prefer choice (b) or (d), whereas Western European and North American students are far more likely to choose (a). In stage 1 (Figure 3.6), students are encouraged to envisage different cultural viewpoints and participants' feelings, while questioning their own assumptions. The Teacher's Book gives further considerations for each choice and its consequences, allowing the teacher to give guidance, comments, and elaborations on students' discussions and their reports (stages 2 and 3). Comments for choice (a) are especially helpful for Chinese learners:

> *If you do this, you should get an explanation immediately. However, you would need to think whether it is OK to interrupt the teacher in this way; in fact, most Canadian professors will not mind; they will probably see your question as a useful part of the class. You could use what you think you know as part of your question: 'I know that Die Welt is the name of a German newspaper but I am not sure what' 'Weltanschauung' means – is the term related to the newspaper?' (The answer is 'yes', indirectly, because 'Die Welt' means 'the world' and 'Anschauung' means 'view'.) Of course, although he teacher may welcome your question, it is possible that other students may not like your interruption, especially if your question is about something that they know and may think is basic knowledge. If it turns out that other students also wanted to ask, you will have helped them. You may also help the teacher because your question will help him or her to establish common ground which will be important for the rest of the explanation – perhaps the teacher presumed that some ground, such as this term, was common when in fact it is not. As the discussion is lively, your question is a way for you to join in . . .*

Together, the three stages (Figure 3.6) give students considerable practice for their oral skills, developing intercultural awareness with a critical-creative approach, which considers different views, experiences, and feelings.

Conclusions

In China, learners face considerable difficulties in their development of oral skills for intercultural communication. These are associated with the limited opportunities in their educational context, cultural traditions, and aspects of confidence and willingness to speak. Speaking skills are always developed in relation to particular topics: for intercultural communication, we have illustrated a range of these at different levels (Figures 3.3, 3.4, and 3.5) and through features in textbook materials.

Intercultural communication skills cannot be developed simply through language skills nor through knowledge of relevant cultures, nor by just knowing a few rules, politeness formulae, or examples of do's and don'ts. The materials we describe seek to develop overall awareness of likely differences, variables, and common ways of speaking in cultural styles of communicating within a framework of active student participation. The approach illustrated in Figures 3.1 and 3.2 highlights the fundamentals: the development of learners' ability to observe, analyse, and think flexibly. These underlying creative and critical strands of the cognitive and emotional engagement of this approach help to maintain student interest. They offset the inevitable fundamental difficulty of developing oral skills – their transience in real uses. Even with efforts to hold this transience, through uses of audio and video recordings, tape scripts, cultural notes, and intercultural guidance related to realistic scenarios, this difficulty remains for speaking skills.

Teacher comments on the materials we discuss, given in training sessions, indicate how they find this approach positive; they comment that it opens cultural and pedagogic horizons, not only for developing oral skills but also for a more holistic approach, which emphasizes pedagogic variety and creativity. This helps them to feel enabled to develop their own practices with their own ideas for local adaptations. While this approach and the examples are designed for ELT in China, we hope they provide principles, insights, and ideas for adaptation elsewhere. Within the current trends of communication and intercultural relations worldwide, this topic warrants all the effort and creativity we can put into its further development.

References

Aldred, G., Byram, M., & Fleming, M. (Eds.). (2003). *Intercultural experience and education.* Clevedon: Multilingual Matters.

Boden, M. A. (Ed.). (1994). *Dimensions of creativity.* London: MIT Press.

Brink-Budgen, R. V. D. (2010). *Critical thinking for students, learn the skills of analysing, evaluating and producing arguments* (4th edn.). Oxford: How To Books.

Butterworth, J., & Thwaites, G. (2013). *Thinking skills, critical thinking and problem solving* (2nd edn.). Cambridge: Cambridge University Press

Byram, M. (2008). *From foreign language education to education for intercultural citizenship.* Clevedon: Multilingual Matters.

Carter, R. (2004). *Language and creativity. The art of common talk.* London: Routledge.

Chen, G-M., & Starosta, W. J. (2007). *Foundations of intercultural communication.* Shanghai: Shanghai Foreign Language Education Press.

Christopher, E. (Ed.). (2012). *Communication across cultures.* Houndmills: Palgrave Macmillan.

Clyne, M. (1994). *Inter-cultural communication at work: Cultural values in discourse.* Cambridge: Cambridge University Press.

Corbett, N. (2003). *An intercultural approach to English language teaching.* Clevedon: Multilingual Matters.

Corbett, J. (2010). *Intercultural language activities.* Cambridge: Cambridge University Press.

Cortazzi, M., & Jin, L. (1996). Cultures of learning: Language classrooms in China. In H. Coleman (Ed.), *Society and the language classroom* (pp. 169–206). Cambridge: Cambridge University Press.

Cortazzi, M., & Jin, L. (1999). Cultural mirrors: Materials and methods in the ELT classroom. In E. Hinkel (Ed.), *Culture in second language teaching and learning* (pp. 196–220). Cambridge: Cambridge University Press.

Cortazzi, M., & Jin, L. (2001). Large classes in China: 'Good' teachers and interaction. In D. A. Watkins & J. B. Biggs (Eds.), *Teaching the Chinese learner: Psychological and pedagogical perspectives* (pp. 115–134). Hong Kong: ACER/CECR, The University of Hong Kong.

Cortazzi, M., & Jin, L. (Eds.). (2013a). *Researching cultures of learning: International perspectives on language learning and education.* Houndmills: Palgrave Macmillan.

Cortazzi, M., & Jin, L. (2013b). Creativity and criticality: Developing dialogues of learning and thinking through synergy with China. In T. Coverdale-Jones (Ed.), *Transnational higher education in the Asian context* (pp. 97–117). Houndmills: Palgrave Macmillan.

Cummins, D. D. (2012). *Good thinking: Seven powerful ideas that influence the way we think.* Cambridge: Cambridge University Press.

Cushner, K. W., & Brislin, R. W. (1996). *Intercultural interactions: A practical guide* (2nd edn.). Thousand Oaks, CA: Sage.

DfEE [Department for Education & Employment]. (1999). *All our future: Creativity, culture & education.* London: DFEE.

Dia, X., & Chen, G-M. (Eds.). (2014). *Intercultural communication competence: Conceptualization and its development in cultural contexts and interactions.* Newcastle upon Tyne: Cambridge Scholars Publishing.

Feng, A. (Ed.). (2007). *Bilingual education in China: Practices, policies and concepts.* Clevedon: Multilingual Matters.

Feng, A. (Ed.). (2011). *English language education across greater China.* Clevedon: Multilingual Matters.

Fennes, H., & Hapgood, K. (1997). *Intercultural learning in the classroom: Crossing borders.* London: Cassell.

Fitzgerald, H. (2003). *How different are we? Spoken discourse in intercultural communication.* Clevedon: Multilingual Matters.

Gardner, J. (1993). *The creators of the modern era.* New York: Basic Books.

Greenall, S., Newbold, D., & Friedland, D. (2009). *Real communication: An integrated course,* Books 1–4 (M. Cortazzi, L. Jin, & P. Leetch; Teacher's Books 1–4). Beijing: Foreign Language Teaching and Research Press.

Greenall, S., Tomalin, M., & Friedland, D. (2008–2009). *Real communication: Listening and speaking,* Books 1–4 (M. Cortazzi, L. Jin, & P. Leetch: Teacher's Books 1–4). Beijing: Foreign Language Teaching and Research Press.

Gudykunst, W. B. (Ed.). (2003). *Cross-cultural and intercultural communication.* Thousand Oaks, CA: Sage.

Guilherme, M. (2002). *Critical citizens for an intercultural world: Foreign language education as cultural politics.* Clevedon: Multilingual Matters.

Hall, J. K. (2002). *Teaching and researching language and culture.* London: Longman.

Holliday, A. (2011). *Intercultural Communication and Ideology.* Los Angeles: Sage.

Holliday, A., Hyde, M., & Kullamn, J. (2010). *Intercultural communication: An advanced resource book* (2nd edn.). London: Routledge.

Hurn, B., & Tomalin, B. (2013). *Cross-cultural communication: Theory and practice.* Houndmills: Palgrave Macmillan.

Jackson, J. (2010). *Intercultural journeys: From study to residence abroad.* Houndmills: Palgrave Macmillan.

Jackson, J. (Ed.). (2012). *The Routledge handbook of language and intercultural communication*. Abingdon: Routledge.
Jackson, J. (2014). *Introducing language and intercultural communication*. Abingdon: Routledge.
Jin, L., & Cortazzi, M. (1998). The culture the learner brings: A bridge or a barrier? In M. Byram & M. Fleming (Eds.), *Language learning in intercultural perspective* (pp. 98–118). Cambridge: Cambridge University Press.
Jin, L., & Cortazzi, M. (2004). English language teaching in China: A bridge to the future. In W. H. Ho & R. Wong (Eds.), *English language teaching in East Asia today* (pp. 119–134). Singapore: Eastern Universities Press.
Jin, L., & Cortazzi, M. (Eds.). (2011). *Researching Chinese learners: Skills, perceptions and intercultural adaptations*. Houndmills: Palgrave Macmillan.
Jin, L., & Cortazzi, M. (Eds.). (2013). *Researching intercultural learning: Investigations in language and education*. Houndmills: Palgrave Macmillan.
Kirkpatrick, A. (2007). *World Englishes: Implications for international communication and English language teaching*. Cambridge: Cambridge University Press.
Kotthoff, K., & Spencer-Oatey, H. (Eds.). (2007). *Handbook of intercultural communication*. Berlin: Mouton de Gruyter.
Lo Bianco, J., Orton, J., & Gao, Y. (Eds.). (2009). *China and English: Globalization and the dilemmas of identity*. Clevedon: Multilingual Matters.
Martin, J. N., & Nakayama, T. K. (2009). *Intercultural communication in contexts* (3rd edn.). Singapore: McGraw-Hill Education.
Moon, J. (2008). *Critical thinking: An exploration of the theory and practice*. Abingdon: Routledge.
Piller, I. (2011). *Intercultural communication: A critical introduction*. Edinburgh: Edinburgh University Press.
Pope, R. (2005). *Creativity: Theory, history, practice*. London: Routledge.
Roberts, C., Byram, M., Barro, A., Jordan, S., & Street, B. (2001). *Language learners as ethnographers*. Clevedon: Multilingual Matters.
Samovar, L. A., Porter, R. E., McDaniel, E. R., & Roy, C. S. (Eds.). (2014). *Intercultural communication: A reader* (14th edn.). Boston, MA: Cengage Learning.
Scollon, R., Scollon, S. W., & Jones, R. H. (2012). *Intercultural communication: A discourse approach* (3rd edn.). Chichester: Wiley-Blackwell.
Smallwood, I., Li, P. L., & Jin, L. (2004–2005). *Creative communication*, Books 1–4, and Teacher's Books (Series editor M. Cortazzi). Shanghai: Macmillan & Shanghai Foreign Languages Publishing House.
Smallwood, I., Li, P. L., Martin, S., & Green, C. (2002–2005). *Creative reading*, Books 1–4, (Series editor M. Cortazzi). Shanghai: Macmillan & Shanghai Foreign Languages Education Press.
Spencer-Oatey, H., & Franklin, P. (2009). *Intercultural interaction: A multidisciplinary approach to intercultural interaction*. Houndmills: Palgrave Macmillan.
Sternberg, R. J. (Ed.). (1988). *The nature of creativity*. Cambridge: Cambridge University Press.
Sternberg, R. J. (Ed.). (1999). *Handbook of creativity*. Cambridge: Cambridge University Press.
Tan, A-G. (Ed.). (2007). *Creativity: A handbook for teachers*. Hackensack, NJ: World Scientific.
Ting-Toomey, S. (1999). *Communicating across cultures*. New York: The Guilford Press.

Varner, I., & Beamer, L. (2011). *Intercultural communication in the global workplace* (5th edn.). New York: McGraw-Hill.
Vertovec, S. (2007). Superdiversity and its implications. *Ethnic and Racial Studies, 26*, 1024–1054.
Zhu, H. (Ed.). (2011). *The language and intercultural communication reader*. London: Routledge.
Zhu, H. (2014). *Exploring intercultural communication: Language in action*. London: Routledge.

4 Teaching reading through multimodal texts

Eveline Chan and Zuocheng Zhang

The teaching of reading in English language learning settings, and in the context of education more generally, is influenced by the purposes for reading and by the changing nature of texts brought about by the impact of digital technologies on reading practices. Digital technologies have transformed the way in which texts are produced, distributed, and consumed (Kress, 2005, 2010). Contemporary reading materials in both print and digital formats include a complex interplay of written text, images, and design elements. Such texts can be described as multimodal: they combine different sets of semiotic resources for making meaning, such as language, image, and spatial patterns, and communicate these meanings through multiple sensory modes and media (Jewitt, 2005, 2008; Kress, 2003; Lemke, 2006). For example, online news websites often include written articles accompanied by images, video, infographics, and interactive elements to engage and communicate information to readers; business reports may use graphics to summarise complex data or to highlight significant findings; and language learning materials frequently include images and audio to support the comprehension of written text to make meaning more accessible to learners. Images have the potential to convey powerful cultural messages, as they do in media texts and advertising campaigns. Digital texts readily combine sound effects and music with animated images to engage readers and often include interactive elements as well, bringing an element of joint construction to reading and viewing activities.

These changes in the nature of texts have substantial implications for teaching reading using authentic, contemporary texts in English language teaching (ELT). Proponents of multiliteracies pedagogy (e.g., Cope & Kalantzis, 2009; New London Group, 1996; Unsworth, 2001) have long held that (1) conceptions of reading need to be broadened beyond processing meaning from the printed word alone to include the integration of meaning across multiple semiotic modes, and (2) the teaching of reading needs to recognise the culturally and linguistically diverse contexts for communication in our increasingly globalised societies (New London Group, 2000, p. 9). There has also been a growing recognition of this shift in the ELT literature (e.g., Ajayi, 2012; Archer, 2000; Farías, Obilinovic, & Orrego, 2007; Lotherington & Jenson, 2011; Royce, 2007; Yi, 2014), with an emphasis on the need for teachers to be innovative in their teaching of English

(Baker, 2012; Tomlinson, 2005). Furthermore, practitioners are urged to recognise that it is no longer adequate to simply adopt the ELT materials and practices of inner-circle, English-speaking countries without considering both the local contexts and purposes for ELT and the global contexts for communication in English (Graddol, 2006; Kirkpatrick & Sussex, 2012; Muller, Herder, Adamson, & Brown, 2012).

Against this background, this chapter aims to (1) provide an overview of research and theory around contemporary multimodal texts and reading, (2) explore some affordances of multimodal texts for developing English language learners' repertoires of reading, and (3) outline some of the challenges for innovating practice in Asian ELT contexts.

Contemporary multimodal texts and reading

Changing nature of text

The dissemination of textual artifacts in the public domain is no longer constrained by the capacity of publishing houses and the printing press. Tools for digital text production make it easier to combine the semiotic resources of visual texts (static and dynamic images), audio texts (music, narration, sound effects), and kinaesthetic performance (drama, dance, other artistic performance) with those of spoken and written language. As a consequence, the consumption and production of multimodal texts has increased to a point where the printed word is no longer the primary mode for representing knowledge and communicating information (Bezemer & Kress, 2008; Jewitt, 2008).

This shift in textual practices can be seen in the design of resources for learning, and in particular, how knowledge is represented for pedagogical purposes. In a study of learning resources for secondary-school science, mathematics, and English from the 1930s, 1980s, and 2000–2005, Bezemer and Kress (2010) reported that images are increasingly displacing writing as the dominant mode of representation in textbooks, web-based resources, and teacher-produced materials. While many print-based ELT materials have typically incorporated images to support students' language learning, the influence of digital media on texts, images, and layout also can be seen in textbooks published over time (Ajayi, 2012). For example, in a study of 17 English as a Foreign Language textbooks for primary and secondary students in China published by People's Education Press between 2002 and 2006, Chen (2010a) reports the pervasive use of multimodal resources to engage readers dialogically. The study revealed how resources such as dialogue balloons, illustrations, labels accompanying images, and incomplete verbal texts mediate the "voices" of the editor, illustrated characters, and the reader by creating spaces for joint construction of meaning across visual and verbal modes.

The interaction of meanings across different semiotic resources in a multimodal text can be complex and multi-layered. Images, for instance, fulfill a range of different functions in textbooks and various learning materials. For example, an image may provide visual balance and cohesion in the design and layout of a page – it may be purely decorative or contribute predominantly to the *compositional* function of a text. Alternatively, multimodal resources may function primarily to complement verbal text in negotiating *interpersonal* meanings to engage readers, as in Chen's (2010a) study mentioned earlier. Furthermore, images may also play a significant role in representing *ideational* meanings in a text: a photograph can depict a setting relevant to target language use; pictures of various kinds are commonly used to support vocabulary development by providing redundancy in meaning; graphs and diagrams often present complex information in a more visually accessible format than written text; symbols in images can communicate powerful social and cultural messages (e.g., Zhang & Freebody, 2010). In other words, the semiotic work performed in contemporary texts in all three functional components – the representational (*ideational*), interactive (*interpersonal*), and compositional (*textual*) (Halliday, 2009, p. 314; Kress & van Leeuwen, 2006) – is distributed across a range of multimodal meaning-making resources. Thus meanings in a text are not confined to the words alone.

Changing concepts of reading

This changing nature of text has substantial implications for reading and the teaching of reading in ELT contexts. Reading extends beyond the processing of meaning from the printed word. Students are increasingly engaging with multimodal texts in print and on screen, through websites, social media, video games, advertisements, graphic novels, and textbooks. In order to make sense of such multimodal texts, students need some understanding of how language and other modes interact to make meaning. Kress (2000, p. 337) contended that it would be impossible to make sense of such texts, "even of their linguistic parts alone", without understanding how features such as images, words, colours, and sound contribute to the meaning of a text.

In the ELT research literature, there has been an increasing recognition that reading for authentic purposes requires more than an ability to decode linguistic meanings. For instance, Archer (2000), Lotherington and Jenson (2011), and Royce (2007) maintain that communicative competence in a target language must extend beyond a focus on linguistic meaning to recognise images as constructions of social and cultural meanings. English language students need skills to interpret images in order to understand how social, political, and ideological messages are constructed in text (Ajayi, 2012, p. 17), particularly with the expansion of online ELT resources and opportunities for direct intercultural communication via the Internet (Baker, 2012, p. 32).

To accommodate these broader purposes for reading, models of reading in ELT, and of literacy more broadly, have shifted over time from cognitive and behavioural approaches focused on skills and strategies (e.g., Goodman, 1988), to conceptualising reading as a sociocultural and situated process, and as a social practice, which varies across cultures, contexts, and social groups (Gee, 2008). An adequate model of reading then, needs to incorporate a broad repertoire of practices, which can account for the complex processes required to successfully make use of the meanings in print and multimodal texts in different institutional and social settings while being flexible enough to facilitate culturally relevant approaches to ELT.

As "a systematic way for interrogating . . . (reading as a sociocultural, situated) . . . practice", Freebody and Luke (2003, p. 57) identified four areas of reading competence: coding competence, semantic competence, pragmatic competence, and critical competence. These areas of competence, they argued, are a necessary repertoire of reading practices, or resources, associated with effectively engaging with print and visual texts (Freebody, 2007, p. 34; Freebody & Luke, 2003, p. 57; Luke & Freebody, 1990). Building on this "four resources" model (Freebody, 2007), multimodal communicative competence requires a reader to understand how grammatical, graphological, and phonological sound and visual conventions or patterns contribute to the meanings of a text (coding competence); to interpret its meanings (semantic competence); to know how to act on the different cultural and social functions that various texts perform (pragmatic competence); and to recognise the ideological messages in texts (critical competence). As shown in Figure 4.1, the four resources model can be effectively adapted to map multimodal reading practices (e.g., Bull & Anstey, 2010; Serafini, 2012; Tan & Guo, 2009).

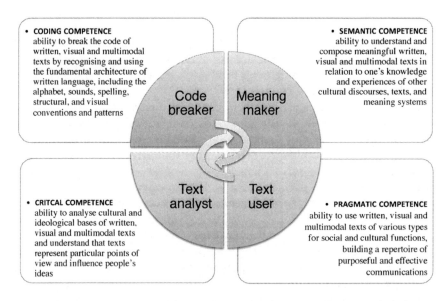

Figure 4.1 Multimodal reading competences derived from the "four roles model" of reading (Freebody, 2007, p. 34).

The four roles or areas of competence shown in Figure 4.1 are described in more detail in the following sections.

Code breaking (coding competence)

Reading multimodal texts involves not only decoding linguistic elements of written language or the printed word but also actively interacting with text to retrieve information from all modes of communication available during the meaning-making process.

In the decoding role, readers bring their knowledge about language to learn new vocabulary. They use their understandings about the relationships among sounds, letters, symbols, and word structures to identify unknown words. Grapho-phonic and lexico-grammatical cues are used to make sense of written text. Similarly, when visual material is included in the text, readers bring their knowledge of visual conventions and symbols to the decoding task.

Meaning-making (semantic competence)

Proficient readers are active readers who have clear goals in mind for reading and use reading strategies in their attempt to achieve comprehension. They participate in the construction of meaning from a text – they relate meanings in the text to their knowledge of the subject matter and experiences with other texts. They use their knowledge of vocabulary to construct meaning from the text and engage with both the literal and inferential meanings presented or implied in the text. When reading multimodal texts, they effectively integrate the complementary meanings represented in image, language, and other modes (Chan & Unsworth, 2011).

Text-user practices (pragmatic competence)

Competent readers not only read for meaning but also use their understanding to achieve various goals for communication. In this role, readers use a wide range of texts for authentic purposes – for example, in everyday activities, academic study, or work-related tasks. They understand the different social and cultural functions that texts perform in society and how they are structured differently to achieve their purposes (genre). They can be described as "writerly readers" (Cheng, 2008, p. 67; Hirvela, 2004) who have a working knowledge of the distinctive features of the text – for example, its tone, the degree of formality, and the sequence of components – and they can relate such features to the context based on their genre knowledge.

Text-analyst practices (critical competence)

Competent readers go beyond the text to analyse the underlying assumptions. The text analyst engages critical reading skills and uses knowledge of language and semiotic practices to identify how people, events, and ideas are portrayed in a text. They analyse the point of view of the author/composer and how the structure and features of a text, such as the choice of words or the juxtaposition of images, are used to achieve various purposes. In reading literary texts, the text-analyst role enables readers to exercise their "critical competence" in identifying how different characters, actions, events, and groups are represented. In factual texts, they can identify what facts are presented and omitted, and in what form "facts" are represented (e.g., statistically, graphically, in tables), and whose point of view is projected through these representations. In advertising and media texts, they recognise how print, sound, and image work together to construct an ideal product, a news story that sells, and the textual devices used to position and persuade the target audience.

Exploiting multimodal aspects of texts for developing repertoires of reading

Despite the diverse goals and settings for reading English in Asian classrooms, contemporary texts place new demands on English language teachers to shift their practices from skills-based to approaches that develop students' repertoires of practices for reading multimodal texts. Language, image, and other typographical features complement each other in communicating messages to the reader/viewer. The interaction of meaning-making resources in a multimodal text provides multiple cues for the reader/viewer to engage with text meaning. Salient features in images may indicate contrast, disproportion, or other key information in the text, or emotion as suggested by colour and framing. Explicit teaching about the features of language, image, design, and layout may be exploited to engage and enhance students' reading strategies.

The following sections provide some criteria for selecting texts, suggestions for addressing the four practices when teaching reading with multimodal texts, and assessment in multimodal reading.

Text selection

In many Asian ELT classrooms, textbooks are the predominant resource for teaching EL students. Therefore, teachers need to recognise the multimodal resources that are central to EL textbook design and students' learning. The following questions may be helpful in guiding teachers' selection and use of texts:

- What (cultural) representations are made in this text?
- Are they representative of students' diverse cultural experiences?
- Are they accurately portrayed?
- What biases are expressed?
- Are they relevant to students' interests, learning, and/or content requirements?
- Do they meet the requirements of state-mandated standards?
- What multimodal resources are available for meaning?

Code breaking – what does the text say?

When decoding the elements and structural composition of language and texts with pictures, graphic displays, and navigational devices such as on web pages, the following prompts may be useful:

- What type of text is this?
- What patterns and conventions can be seen in this text?
- What symbols or visual conventions appear in this text? (e.g., keys, legends, scales, units shown on axes of a graph, logos, icons)
- What does the student already know? (e.g., letters, words, punctuation, symbols, layout)
- What features of the text does the teacher need to teach explicitly?

An example of a code-breaking activity: reading texts with maps

Explicit teaching around identifying and decoding symbols, icons, visual conventions, and word labels on maps, such as Figure 4.2, can provide opportunities for building vocabulary and expanding students' visual literacy, depending on the level of the students and the lesson goals. The teacher can draw attention to the legend and the use of colour, guide students to identify icons and symbols, and

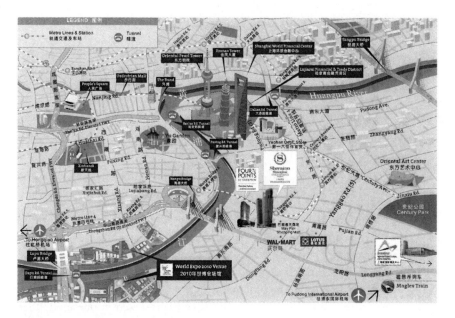

Figure 4.2 Tourist map of Shanghai.[1]
(Source: China Tour Advisors, Shanghai Maps)

Table 4.1 Example of code-breaking activity

Activity: Imagine you are visiting Shanghai for the first time. Use this map to find out how to get to the places you wish to visit. Ask your partner for directions. (This activity could be done as a class or in pairs.)	
How many metro lines are there?	• Where do they go? • (Identify visual symbols and colours, and what they represent)
I am staying at the Sheraton Shanghai. I want to visit Yu Garden.	• Which metro line do I take? • What is the nearest station to get on? To get off? • If I go by taxi, what bridge can I cross? • (Scan for visual symbols and decode word labels for place names)
Tomorrow, I want to go from the Bund to the Oriental Pearl Tower.	• Which is the nearest tunnel crossing? • (Identify visual symbols from legend; decode place name labels)

talk about what they represent. Students can then apply their decoding skills to task-based activities (Table 4.1).

Similar code-breaking activities can also be applied to texts with graphs, diagrams, and other kinds of images with labels.

Meaning-making – what does the text mean?

The ways in which images and other modes of meaning are interwoven to construct the content of a text need to be made explicit to English language learners. Questions to guide meaning-making activities include the following:

- What do the students already know about this topic?
- What are the possible meanings of this text?
- What facts or information can be found in this text?
- How are people, objects, events, and places represented?
- How do different modes in this text work together to create meaning?
    - What meanings are coded visually?
    - What meanings are coded verbally?
    - Are there meanings that are similar across modes?
    - Are there meanings in one mode that are additional or complementary to the meanings in the other mode?
    - Are there meanings that are alternately represented in one mode then the other (i.e., distributed across the modes)?
    - Are there meanings that are divergent in image and language (e.g., do they contradict each other?)?

Example of a meaning-making activity: reading explanatory texts with diagrams

Reading activities for meaning-making focus on gaining literal information from the text, making inferences or predictions, or summarising information, depending on the lesson goals and the level of the students.

Scientific explanations are commonly accompanied by diagrams, such as in Figure 4.3.

> The soil food web is the community of organisms living all or part of their lives in the soil. It describes a complex living system in the soil and how it interacts with the environment, plants, and animals.
>
> Food webs describe the transfer of energy between species in an ecosystem. While a food chain examines one, linear, energy pathway through an ecosystem, a food web is more complex and illustrates all of the potential pathways. Much of this transferred energy comes from the sun. Plants use the sun's energy to convert inorganic compounds into energy-rich, organic compounds, turning carbon dioxide and minerals into plant material by photosynthesis. Plants are called autotrophs because they make their own energy;
>
> they are also called producers because they produce energy available for other organisms to eat. Heterotrophs are consumers that cannot make their own food. In order to obtain energy they eat plants or other heterotrophs.
>
>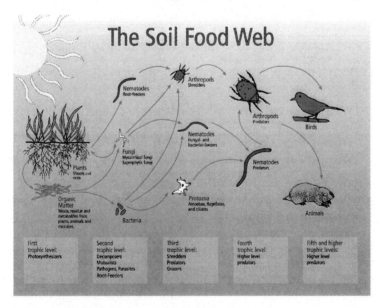
>
> *Figure 4.3* An example of a topological food web.[2]
> (Source: "Soil food web", U.S. Department of Agriculture. Wikimedia Commons)

The diagram shows the relationships among types of organisms in the soil, organic matter, plants, birds, and mammals. The words provide the technical vocabulary to classify the organisms into taxonomic groups. Along the bottom of the diagram, technical terms are also used to categorise different types of feeders according to their place in the food web. However, neither the words in the diagram nor those in the accompanying Wikipedia entry fully explain the relationships between the organisms represented in the diagram by arrows. In other words, meanings implicit in the diagram need to be inferred. Similarly, the intermodal relationships between visual and verbal meanings need to be recognised in order to understand the complex concepts, which are jointly constructed and distributed across modes in the multimodal text.

With such texts, successful meaning-making depends on understanding how the visual and written modes in the text work together to create meaning. Students' attention can be drawn to the affordances of each mode in representing different scientific concepts. When probing what meanings are made visually, students can be asked questions such as the following:

- Does the image symbolise, classify, or analyse?
- How are participants in the food web represented?
    - What images or symbols are used?
- What processes and relationships are depicted in the diagram?
    - What do the arrows mean?
    - What do the boxes along the bottom of the image mean?
- Are there meanings in language that are additional (or complementary) to those in the diagram?
    - What nouns and adjectives describe the organisms and concepts in the web?
    - What verbs and verb types are used?
    - What adverbs and phrases provide the circumstances of the processes or ideas?
- Why are some meanings made in different modes? How does this help your understanding of the text?

Text user – how do I use this text?

To develop pragmatic "text-user" competence, connections between texts and learners' cultural practices need to be made in ways that are significant for their learning. Some questions to draw attention to these connections are as follows:

- What is the purpose of this text?
- How is the text structured to achieve its purpose?

- What features make this text effective in achieving its purpose?
- How would this text be used in the community?
- What opportunities are there for students to use this text?

Example of text-using activity: reading research articles

When reading research articles, students may be guided by a range of questions to heighten their awareness of the genre:

- What kind of a research article is this? (e.g., is it a primary research article or a review of research?)
- What is the purpose of this kind of article?
- What sections do you expect to find in a research article? (e.g., abstract, introduction, methods, results, discussion, conclusion)
- What are the typical features of each section?

The results section of a research article presenting quantitative data may be exploited to this end. A visual display of results in tables or graphs is usually accompanied by a written commentary, which refers to the information in the table or graph. To begin the data commentary, the link between the visual and the verbal is usually signposted by expressions such as "as shown in the table/graph," which directs the reader to process the visual information in specific ways. It is usually the salient results such as trends, patterns, or features that are highlighted in the commentary for the reader. In some research reports, the commentary may go on to discuss these salient features to provide an interpretation or explanation of the findings.

Support materials such as a checklist of features may be provided to scaffold students' engagement with an exemplar text. Questions that focus attention on text features may be included as part of the scaffold:

- What lexical, syntactic, and organisational features have you noticed in the results section?
- How do these features make this section distinct from other parts of the research article?
- Why do you think the author chooses to organise the results in this way (e.g., the order of ascending or descending importance of information, the visual before the verbal, or vice versa)?
- What is the impact of this organisation on the reader?
- What devices are used to link the table/graph with the commentary?
- From your experience, which of these features are shared by other texts you have read in your discipline area?

Multimodal texts achieve their social purposes by exploiting the affordances of different modes of meaning valued by the discourse communities in which members recognise these genres as legitimate forms of social action. Teaching students explicit knowledge about genre and text equips them with the pragmatic competence to engage with text for effective communication.

Text analyst – what are the hidden meanings?

By probing how texts position readers differentially, various linguistic and visual devices deployed to influence interpretation and the reader may be identified as follows:

- Whose interests are served by this text?
- Whose voices or opinions are missing from this text?
- Does this text present a balanced point of view?
- What devices are used to influence the readers' thoughts or feelings?

Online media texts provide ready sources for text-analysing activities. Internet news websites can be used to compare different representations of news events. Multimodal advertisements can be used to identify the devices that are used to persuade consumers.

Example of text-analysing activity: identifying bias in multimodal news reports

The Asia News Network news story by Tan Hui Yee (2015, March 4), "Haze Rises to Unhealthy Levels in Chiang Mai", is accompanied by a photo (Figure 4.4), taken from a high angle, showing a city shrouded in smog (*The Straits Times* Asia report, Asia News Network www.straitstimes.com/asia/se-asia/haze-rises-to-unhealthy-levels-in-chiang-mai, March 4, 2015).

Both the language and the image convey the gravity of pollution in the city. The headline and lead, "Pollution Readings Far Exceed WHO Guidelines; Situation Could Worsen", make explicit that haze has reached a level that is detrimental to health. A comprehension question can be asked of students: *What do the text and image say about the haze in Chiang Mai?* Other more implicit meanings are distributed between the text and the image. Neither the text nor the image so far has touched upon the source of the pollution until one goes on to read the caption for the image.

The caption directly below the photo states:

> Haze is an annual problem in northern Thailand, as farmers practise open burning. During this period, many residents suffer breathing ailments and the Doi Suthep Mountain disappears from view.
>
> (*The Straits Times*, March 04, 2015)

Figure 4.4 Haze is an annual problem in Northern Thailand[3.]
(Source: Photo © The Nation/Asia News Network)

Farmers are singled out as the culprits in the dependent clause "as farmers practise open burning." The position of the clause in the first complex sentence gives it end weight and foregrounds the problem – haze and pollution. The next sentence highlights the effects of this problem – that is, "many residents suffer breathing ailments" and the mountain view is lost to the residents. Questions such as the following can be asked:

- What are the causes and effects of the pollution?
- Which residents suffer from it?
- Whose view is obscured by the haze?

This news report reflects the concerns of the city dwellers and presumably represents their interests. While it refers to the farmers' open burning as the source of the problem, the story does not explicitly state what they are burning and why. The "what" is answered in the second paragraph of the full news report: "It is an annual scourge in northern areas of the country from January to April as Thai farmers, as well as those in Laos, Myanmar and Cambodia, torch the land to clear scrub or agricultural waste." However, it does not explain why farmers burn their agricultural waste and what the government has done to intervene. Government action is mentioned in a much later paragraph of the news story: "The Thai government has had little success with its attempts to control open burning and encourage agricultural waste to be ploughed into the soil instead of being burnt". This information in itself does not explain the lack of success of the government intervention. There are no quotes from farmers to give them a voice in the issue, and other references to fires in the region are not linked explicitly to causal agents. The following questions to identify hidden meanings in the text can be asked:

- Whose interests are served by the news report?
- What evidence is there for this interpretation? In the image? In the language?
- How do text and image work together to construct this point of view?
- Whose view is not represented in this news report?

From the interplay of meanings in language and image, it can be argued that the news report, particularly the point of view represented in the image and its caption, is biased towards the urban community and the government, and thus sets up an opposition with the farming community.

Assessing reading of multimodal texts

Assessment practices in educational contexts dominated by formal, external examinations generally do not prioritise the multimodal aspects of reading in their test designs (Unsworth, 2014). Formal assessment lags classroom practice, where classroom teachers often take up the responsibility for formative assessment and assessment for learning.

Some considerations for assessing multimodal reading include the following:

- Do test stimulus materials represent an authentic range of the materials that students need to read and view in the English language curriculum?
- Are some of the test items multimodal?
- Do some test materials include features of online texts?
- Do test items represent a range of the types of reading tasks that students encounter in multimodal texts?
- What alternative forms of testing are best suited for assessing multimodal reading?

The suggestions in the aforementioned sections, while not exhaustive, point to some of the affordances of multimodal texts as rich resources for moving student readers from decoding text to engaging critically with meaning. Strategies such as inferring meaning from texts and integrating meanings across multiple sources of information are essential for effective reading of written, visual, and multimodal text types

(Chan & Unsworth, 2011). Some further benefits for teaching reading are afforded by teaching reading through multimodal texts:

1. Multimodal texts offer learners multiple points of entry into reading, allowing them alternative reading paths for interpreting texts from captions, images, colours, layouts, or words. Furthermore, differentiated reading paths are established along the lines of student backgrounds, interests, and needs (Ajayi, 2010).
2. Learners can access a wider range of semiotic possibilities for meaning-making by drawing on different modes. This can lead to increased student participation, collaboration, and negotiation of meanings (Ajayi, 2012).
3. A shift in the relations between textbook producers, teachers, and students enables more open, participatory relations in knowledge production (Bezemer & Kress, 2010).

Challenges for innovating practice in Asian English language classrooms

Transforming practice in settings where large classes, centrally controlled curricula, high-stakes assessment, and traditional methods of education are highly valued often presents a challenge for innovating pedagogy. For pedagogical innovation in ELT to be implemented in a sustainable way, specific local contexts for teaching and learning need to be taken into account. For instance, Littlewood (2007) mentions some constraints on the implementation of task-based language teaching in East Asia – namely, classroom management, avoidance of English, minimal demands on language competence, incompatibility with public assessment demands, and conflict with educational values and traditions. A similar concern with local and situational factors is echoed in Fang's (2012) discussion of the constraints of the new English curriculum mandated by the Chinese Ministry of Education. Fang (2012) identifies teachers' lack of knowledge about the curriculum and ELT approaches, form-oriented examinations as perceived by students and teachers, and student and teacher's faith in the effectiveness of communicative language teaching activities as barriers to innovation. The same mood is captured in Hu's (2005, p. 654) "ecological perspective on ELT," which calls for recognition of the complicated link between language instruction and the economic and sociocultural contexts specific to where learning and teaching take place. A closer examination of challenges to innovative practice in Asian ELT contexts, therefore, is warranted, and practical ways of overcoming them are necessary for effective English teaching in the classroom. Four dimensions of context, which contribute to these challenges are elaborated and discussed in the following sections: the ecology of English in Asian contexts, culture of learning in Asia, social and economic constraints, and ideology of text.

Ecology of English in Asia

English enjoys differential statuses in various Asian contexts. In India, for example, it has the status of an indigenized language, or New English, to contribute to the "triglossic" situation where varieties of English are used in different domains of Indian life (Gargesh, 2009, p. 92). In other contexts, such as China, Japan, and Thailand, for example, it is a foreign language and studied as a school subject. The ecological relationship (Haugen, 2006) between English and other languages, in particular the national languages, is important to consider for the teaching and learning of English. Social and individual attitudes towards English, material resources input by the government and society, and educational and employment opportunities mediated by English proficiency are all relevant.

Based on his survey of English teaching in 15 countries and territories (East Asia and Southeast Asia), Ho (2002) identifies several key features. There is much diversity of English teaching in the region. While English learning is made compulsory as an educational policy, it is not implemented effectively because of "under-funding, over-crowding of classrooms, shortage or even lack of textbooks, and ill-equipped teaching areas" (p. 14). The divide between the traditional rural areas and the urban areas results in different levels of student motivation for language learning and their achievements of proficiency. Language learning has a pragmatic goal – that is, to share the advantage of accessing communication, science, technology, and education opportunities through English. The tension between traditional forces and the drive for change in language pedagogy, in the form of the dilemma of continuity and change, is ever present, but particularly when introducing new methods for language teaching. Adapting the teaching of English to meet local needs and practices has been advocated by Kachru (2009) and supported by studies of English in contexts such as Pakistan and Saudi Arabia (Mahboob, 2009; Mahboob & Elyas, 2014).

Culture of learning

Culture of learning as a concept captures a number of factors relevant to English language learning and teaching. Cortazzi and Jin (1996, p. 74) developed it to account for Chinese students' experience of learning in Western/British academic settings:

> Different cultures of learning exist in Western and Chinese educational contexts which teachers need to be fully aware of and take into consideration while teaching English in China. These cultures of learning include academic and professional expectations, perceptions, attitudes, beliefs and values about what good learning is, what constitutes a good teacher and a good student; learning and teaching styles, approaches and methods; classroom organization, management, activities and behavior.

These factors play a significant role in language learning as they invalidate the "autonomous" assumptions and call for the "ideological" ones in language teaching (Coleman, 1996, p. 1). Language learners bring with them a baggage of learning experiences, what they want to become through learning a language, and what they ought to be (Dörnyei, 2009). At the level of culture of learning, Chinese students, for example, tend to believe that knowledge is from teachers and textbooks, education is accumulative, and teachers direct learning while students follow and work hard (Cortazzi & Jin, 1996; Hu, 2002).

Social and economic constraints

Asia is as huge as it is heterogeneous in several important ways. Geographically, it spans East Asia, Southeast Asia, Middle Asia, and West Asia. Culturally, the Confucian influence in East and Southeast Asia, Islamic influence in West and Middle Asia, and Buddhist influence in India and many other parts of Asia, complicated by political systems of socialism and capitalism, make the region culturally diverse. The stages of economic development are also different, with some nations being advanced and many others at varying stages of industrialisation. Within each country, in particular, developing countries, internal disparity such as between rural and urban locations, the economically powerful coastal regions, and the less developed inland areas, are recognised as factors relevant to education, in particular language pedagogy (Fang, 2012; Ho, 2002).

Taking China as an example, Hu (2005) identifies the influence on pedagogic practices of resource factors such as appropriate curricula, school facilities, and availability of properly trained teachers because of the imbalance of economic power in the affluent coastal areas and the poor inland provinces. This disparity entails a close examination of the match between proposed methodological affordances and constraints, and local social, cultural, and economic conditions.

The motivation for learning English, however, is high in China, for students at least. This is, in part, driven by the high-stakes examinations for admissions to middle school and university. For example, reading typically takes up 30% of the total score for an English test in the university entrance examination, excluding the need to read instructions for listening and writing tasks. However, the English examination is focused on verbal language, with visuals typically included as prompts for writing or glossing unfamiliar vocabulary. The national examination values print text rather than multimodal text, which is not untypical of centralised assessment regimes internationally and in Asia, for instance, Singapore (Tan, Bopry, & Guo, 2010).

Nevertheless, the curriculum environment is conducive to teaching multimodal reading in China's classrooms. The New English Curriculum and its framework calls for an all-round ability to use English and the task-based approach to language teaching. Multimodal reading draws on more explicit strategies for teaching: to relate sources of information and to evaluate messages central to the text. The explicit teaching of multimodal text features can be embedded within a task-based approach.

Ideology of text

Texts, no matter how they are defined, are the substance for reading. They are not neutral entities but permeated by ideology in the sense that text production, consumption, and transmission are part of sociocultural practices and ideologically driven (Fairclough, 1989). For example, English texts in Chinese school textbooks are constructed to embody mainstream Chinese socialist values such as priority of social harmony and communal well-being (Chen, 2010b). In other words, students are reading to learn to become communal members rather than individuals. When students have been socialised to read such texts, they may experience certain cultural dissonance when they are exposed to texts that promote individualistic values. This is subtle but important to reading, both for understanding the messages and practising skills for critical reading. As Kachru (2009, p. 455) points out, the messages in (varieties of English) should be "learned, acquired, absorbed, and appreciated within the cultural contexts" where they are produced. In the more participatory environment of the Internet, such texts, predominantly multimodal, provide opportunities for developing students' critical reading skills.

There is a tension between the text for teaching or promoting patriotism and the international outlook espoused by the New English Curriculum. In the former, the pursuit of the common good is embedded – the whole nation – while the latter is oriented to individual endeavor. This tension poses a challenge but can be a resource for critical reading. This may start from the viewing of images in the textbooks by deconstructing the interpersonal meaning around attitudes (Chen, 2010b).

Concluding remarks

The four levels of context discussed in the previous section represent challenges for teaching English in Asian contexts – the-one-size-fits-all mindset is unlikely to be effective or efficient in Asian English classrooms. When an approach is advocated or considered for adaptation, the local context, from the national culture of learning to the classroom situation, needs to be carefully addressed.

The potential for teaching reading in the online environment as a community activity in constructing and interpreting meanings in text (Tierney, 2013) is becoming a reality. As access to the Internet breaks down vertical hierarchies of power in cultures of learning, alternative spaces to crowded classrooms are being created for increased participation in collaborative knowledge production. The teacher is no longer the sole source of information and knowledge, since:

> cultural artifacts such as externally produced language textbooks and other teaching materials, English language media (including the internet) and the arts, all of which can be used to examine different images and perspectives of other cultures at both local and global levels.
>
> (Baker, 2012, p. 32)

With the proliferation of multimodal texts online, multiple entry points to complementary ways of meaning give students greater power to access meaning and engage with text. In this environment, as Gee and Hayes (2011, p. 120) argue, "we all need more experiences that allow us to be critical . . . asking whose interests are served and whose are not, and what the agendas were of the producers of those words, images, and texts". Teaching reading through multimodal texts opens up the space for an expanded repertoire of textual practices leading to critical competence.

Acknowledgements

The authors gratefully acknowledge the use of the following material in this publication:

1   Figure 4.2: Tourist map of Shanghai. Source: Shanghai Maps Free Download www.chinatouradvisors.com/travelguide/Shanghai/. Reproduced with permission from China Tour Advisors.
2   Figure 4.3: An example of a topological food web. Source: "Soil Food Web" by USDA – http://soils.usda.gov/sqi/concepts/soil_biology/soil_food_web.html via Wikimedia Commons. http://en.wikipedia.org/wiki/Soil_food_web. Licensed under Public Domain.
3   Figure 4.4: Haze is an annual problem in Northern Thailand. Source: www.straitstimes.com/asia/se-asia/haze-rises-to-unhealthy-levels-in-chiang-mai on the Asia News Network www.asianewsnet.net/. Reproduced with permission from The Nation Multimedia Group.

References

Ajayi, L. (2010). Pre-service teachers' knowledge, attitudes, and perception of their preparation to teach multiliteracies/multimodality. *The Teacher Educator*, 46(1), 6–31. doi:10.1080/08878730.2010.488279

Ajayi, L. (2012). How teachers deploy multimodal textbooks to enhance English language learning. *TESOL Journal*, 6, 16–35.

Archer, A. (2000). Communicative competence expanded: A 'multiliteracies' approach to English Additional Language teaching. *English Academy Review*, 17(1), 83–96. doi:10.1080/10131750085310101

Baker, W. (2012). Global cultures and identities: Refocusing the aims of ELT in Asia through intercultural awareness. In M. T. Muller, M. S. Herder, D. J. Adamson, & P. S. Brown (Eds.), *Innovating EFL teaching in Asia* (pp. 23–34). Basingstoke: Palgrave Macmillan.

Bezemer, J., & Kress, G. (2008). Writing in multimodal texts: A social semiotic account of designs for learning. *Written Communication*, 25(2), 166–195. doi:10.1177/0741088307313177

Bezemer, J., & Kress, G. (2010). Changing text: A social semiotic analysis of textbooks. *Design for Learning*, 3, 10–29.

Bull, G., & Anstey, M. (2010). *Evolving pedagogies: Reading and writing in a multimodal world*. Melbourne: Education Services Australia.
Chan, E., & Unsworth, L. (2011). Image-language interaction in online reading environments: Challenges for students' reading comprehension. *The Australian Educational Researcher*, 38, 181–202. doi:10.1007/s13384-13011-10023-y
Chen, Y. M. (2010a). Exploring dialogic engagement with readers in multimodal EFL textbooks in China. *Visual Communication*, 9, 485–506. doi:10.1177/1470357210382186
Chen, Y. M. (2010b). The semiotic construal of attitudinal curriculum goals: Evidence from EFL textbooks in China. *Linguistics and Education*, 21, 60–74.
Cheng, A. (2008). Analyzing genre exemplars in preparation for writing: The case of an L2 graduate student in the ESP genre-based instructional framework of academic literacy. *Applied Linguistics*, 29(1), 50–71.
Coleman, H. (1996). Introduction: Autonomy and ideology in the English language classroom. In H. Coleman (Ed.), *Society and the language classroom* (pp. 1–15). Cambridge: Cambridge University Press.
Cope, B., & Kalantzis, M. (2009). "Multiliteracies": New literacies, new learning. *Pedagogies: An International Journal*, 4, 164–195.
Cortazzi, M., & Jin, L. (1996). English teaching and learning in China. *Language Teaching*, 29, 61–80.
Dörnyei, Z. (2009). The L2 motivational self system. In Z. Dörnyei & E. Ushioda (Eds.), *Motivation, language identity and the L2 self* (pp. 9–42). Bristol: Multilingual Matters.
Fairclough, N. (1989). *Language and power*. London: Longman.
Fang, X. (2012). Teaching the new English curriculum: An ethnographic study in a Chinese high school. In M. T. Muller, M. S. Herder, D. J. Adamson, & P. S. Brown (Eds.), *Innovating EFL teaching in Asia* (pp. 9–22). Basingstoke: Palgrave Macmillan.
Farías, M., Obilinovic, K., & Orrego, R. (2007). Implications of multimodal learning models for foreign language teaching and learning. *Colombian Applied Linguistics Journal*, 9, 174–199.
Freebody, P. (2007). *Literacy education in school research: Perspectives from the past, for the future*. Camberwell, Victoria: ACER.
Freebody, P., & Luke, A. (1990). Literacies programs: Debates and demands in cultural context. *Prospect: Australian Journal of TESOL*, 5(7), 7–16.
Freebody, P., & Luke, A. (2003). Literacy as engaging with new forms of life: The 'four roles' model. In G. Bull & M. Anstey (Eds.), *The literacy lexicon* (pp. 51–65). Frenchs Forest, NSW: Pearson Prentice Hall Australia.
Gargesh, R. (2009). South Asian Englishes. In B. B. Kachru, Y. Kachru, & C. L. Nelson (Eds.), *The handbook of world Englishes* (pp. 90–113). Oxford: Wiley-Blackwell.
Gee, J. P. (2008). *Social linguistics and literacies: Ideology in discourses*. New York: Routledge.
Gee, J. P., & Hayes, E. (2011). *Language and learning in the digital age*. New York: Routledge.
Goodman, K. (1988). The reading process. In P. L. Carrell, J. Devine, & D. E. Eskey (Eds.), *Interactive approach to second language reading* (pp. 11–21). Cambridge: Cambridge University Press.
Graddol, D. (2006). *English next*. London: British Council.
Halliday, M. A. K. (2009). *The essential Halliday*. London: Continuum.

Haugen, E. (2006). The ecology of language. In A. Fill & P. Muhlhausler (Eds.), *Ecolinguistics reader: Language, ecology, and environment* (pp. 57–66). London: Continuum.

Hirvela, A. (2004). *Connecting reading and writing in second language writing instruction*. Ann Arbor, MI: University of Michigan Press.

Ho, W. K. (2002). English language teaching in East Asia today: An overview. *Asia Pacific Journal of Education, 22*(2), 1–22.

Hu, G. (2002). Potential cultural resistance to pedagogical imports: The case of communicative language teaching in China. *Language, Culture and Curriculum, 15*, 93–105. doi:10.1080/07908310208666636

Hu, G. (2005). Contextual influences on instructional practices: A Chinese case for an ecological approach to ELT. *TESOL Quarterly, 39*, 635–660.

Jewitt, C. (2005). Multimodality, "reading", and "writing" for the 21st century. *Discourse: Studies in the Cultural Politics of Education, 26*, 315–331. doi:10.1080/01596300500200011

Jewitt, C. (2008). Multimodality and literacy in school classrooms. *Review of Research in Education, 32*, 241–267.

Kachru, B. B. (2009). World Englishes and culture wars. In B. B. Kachru, Y. Kachru, & C. L. Nelson (Eds.), *The handbook of world Englishes* (pp. 446–471). Oxford: Wiley-Blackwell.

Kirkpatrick, A., & Sussex, R. (Eds.). (2012). *English as an international language in Asia: Implications for language education*. Dordrecht: Springer.

Kress, G. (2000). Multimodality: Challenges to thinking about language. *TESOL Quarterly, 34*, 337–340.

Kress, G. (2003). *Literacy in the new media age*. London: Routledge.

Kress, G. (2005). Gains and losses: New forms of texts, knowledge, and learning. *Computers and Composition, 22*, 5–22.

Kress, G. (2010). *Multimodality: A social semiotic approach to contemporary communication*. NewYork: Routledge.

Kress, G., & van Leeuwen, T. (2006). *Reading images: The grammar of visual design* (2nd edn.). London: Routledge.

Lemke, J. (2006). Towards critical multimedia literacy: Technology, research, and politics. In M. McKenna, D. Reinking, L. Labbo, & R. Kieffer (Eds.), *International handbook of literacy and technology V. 2.0* (pp. 3–14). Mahwah, NJ: Erlbaum.

Littlewood, W. (2007). Communicative and task-based language teaching in East Asian classrooms. *Language Teaching, 40*, 243–249. doi:10.1017/S0261444807004363

Lotherington, H., & Jenson, J. (2011). Teaching multimodal and digital literacy in L2 settings: New literacies, new basics, new pedagogies. *Annual Review of Applied Linguistics, 31*, 226–246. doi:10.1017/S0267190511000110

Mahboob, A. (2009). English as an Islamic language: A case study of Pakistani English. *World Englishes, 28*, 175–189.

Mahboob, A., & Elyas, T. (2014). English in the Kingdom of Saudi Arabia. *World Englishes, 33*(1), 128–142.

Muller, M. T., Herder, M. S., Adamson, D. J., & Brown, P. S. (Eds.). (2012). *Innovating EFL teaching in Asia*. Basingstoke: Palgrave Macmillan.

New London Group. (1996). A pedagogy of multiliteracies: Designing social futures. *Harvard Educational Review, 66*(1), 60–92.

New London Group. (2000). A pedagogy of multiliteracies: Designing social futures. In B. Cope & M. Kalantzis (Eds.), *Multiliteracies: Literacy learning and the design of social futures* (pp. 9–38). South Yarra, VIC: Palgrave Macmillan.

Royce, T. (2007). Multimodal communicative competence in second language contexts. In T. Royce & W. L. Bowcher (Eds.), *New directions in the analysis of multimodal discourse* (pp. 361–390). Mahwah, NJ: Lawrence Erlbaum.
Serafini, F. (2012). Expanding the four resources model: Reading visual and multimodal texts. *Pedagogies: An International Journal, 7,* 150–164. doi:10.1080/1554480X.2012.656347
Tan, H. Y. (2015, March 4). Haze rises to unhealthy levels in Chiang Mai. *The Straits Times Asia Report, Asia News Network.* Retrieved from www.asianewsnet.net/
Tan, L., Bopry, J., & Guo, L. (2010). Portraits of new literacies in two Singapore classrooms. *RELC Journal, 41*(1), 5–17. doi:10.1177/0033688210343864
Tan, L., & Guo, L. (2009). From print to critical multimedia literacy: One teacher's foray into new literacies practices. *Journal of Adolescent and Adult Literacy, 53,* 315–324. doi:10.1598/JAAL.53.4
Tierney, R. J. (2013). Multimedia digital engagements by readers and learners. In C. A. Chapelle (Ed.), *The encyclopedia of applied linguistics* (pp. 1–8). Oxford: Wiley-Blackwell.
Tomlinson, B. (2005). The future for ELT materials in Asia. *Electronic Journal of Foreign Language Teaching, 2*(2), 5–13.
Unsworth, L. (2001). *Teaching multiliteracies across the curriculum: Changing contexts of text and image in classroom practice.* Maidenhead: Open University Press.
Unsworth, L. (2014). Multimodal reading comprehension: Curriculum expectations and large-scale literacy testing practices. *Pedagogies: An International Journal, 9*(1), 26–44.
Yi, Y. (2014). Possibilities and challenges of multimodal literacy practices in teaching and learning English as an additional language. *Language and Linguistics Compass, 8,* 158–169. doi:10.1111/lnc3.12076
Zhang, B. B., & Freebody, P. (2010). Image, genre, voice and the making of the school-literate child: Lessons from multiliteracy teaching in China. In D. R. Cole & D. L. Pullen (Eds.), *Multiliteracies in motion: Current theories and practices* (pp. 42–58). New York: Routledge.

5 Supplementing extensive reading for Japanese EFL learners

Meredith Stephens

English as a Foreign Language (EFL) pedagogy in Japan continues to be characterized by the transmission style of education, in which the teacher transfers knowledge to the students, and the grammar-translation method (Nagatomo, 2012). Nevertheless, alternative or even complementary methodologies such as extensive reading are growing in importance. This is because educators recognize the many clear benefits Day and Bamford (1998) outlined, and they implement them in the hope that this will improve the English proficiency of Japanese students. The definition of extensive reading is taken from Day and Bamford's (1998, pp. 7–8) seminal work and is characterized as follows:

1 *Students read as much as possible*, perhaps in and definitely out of the classroom.
2 *Materials on a wide range of topics are available* so as to encourage reading for different reasons and in different ways.
3 *Students select what they want to read* and have the freedom to stop reading material that fails to interest them.
4 *Reading is usually related to pleasure, information, and general understanding*. These purposes are determined by the nature of the material and the interests of the student.
5 *Reading is its own reward*. There are few or no follow-up exercises after reading.
6 *Reading materials are well within the linguistic competence of the students* in terms of vocabulary and grammar. Dictionaries are rarely used while reading because the constant stopping to look up words makes fluent reading difficult.
7 *Reading is individual and silent*, at the student's own pace, and, outside class, done when and where the student chooses.
8 *Reading speed is usually faster rather than slower*, as students read books and other material they find easily understandable.
9 *Teachers orient students to the goals of the program, explain* the methodology, keep track of what each student reads, and guide students in getting the most out of the program.
10 *Teachers are role models for students* – active members of the classroom reading community, demonstrating what it means to be a reader and the rewards of being a reader.

Day and Bamford do not recommend follow-up activities such as comprehension questions that require students to retrieve irrelevant details (p. 141), but they do present numerous ways in which an extensive reading program can be effectively supplemented in the reading community: the current study is a further exploration of this issue. In particular, it will address how extensive reading can be supplemented with extensive listening and having students provide creative written responses.

Transferring reading skills to listening comprehension

Before the age of electronic communications in Japan, reading comprehension of second language (L2) English was a skill to be mastered in order to comprehend documents. Currently, this skill remains important, but because of modern technology, travel and migration, listening and speaking skills are also considered important. One of the assumptions educators may bring to extensive reading programs is that students will transfer the skills from reading to oral communication. However, students whose first contact with English has been in written form may have trouble transferring this skill to listening. Written words in English are separated by spaces, but the stream of spoken English is continuous. Crystal (2005) identifies an important feature of normal spoken language:

> Normal speech proves to be so rapidly and informally articulated that in fact over half the words cannot be recognized in isolation – and yet we have little trouble following it, and can repeat whole sentences accurately.
>
> (p. 48)

Unlike speech, written words *can* be recognized in isolation and are therefore more accessible for the L2 learner. Accordingly, skill in reading will not automatically equip the L2 learner to comprehend normal speech. This strengthens the case for practising simultaneous reading and listening.

Supplementing extensive reading with extensive listening

Traditionally, linguists have asserted the primacy of speech over writing because writing is a representation of speech and because children learn speech before writing (Allen, 1975). Furthermore, only 40% of human languages are represented in written form, and for speakers of these languages, language means speech (Crystal, 2005). However, in the case of L2 learners, Allen (1975) observes no advantage in preserving the order of first language (L1) acquisition. In contrast, he argues that adult learners may prefer to have oral language supported with written text and that this presents no barrier to them attaining oral fluency. If this view were applied to the practice of extensive reading and listening, students would not be disadvantaged from conducting these activities simultaneously.

Chang (2011) carried out a study of the effectiveness of the practice of simultaneous reading and listening; one group consisted of a 'reading-while-listening' group and the other a control group. The reading-while-listening group outperformed the control group in terms of both listening fluency and vocabulary gain. Chang and Millet (2014) conducted a further experiment on the development of listening fluency comparing three groups: reading only, reading-while-listening, and listening only. The reading-while-listening group achieved superior results to the reading only and listening only groups. Accordingly, Chang and Millet conclude that the most effective strategy is to have students first read and listen simultaneously and then listen only, and that this listening skill can continue to be activated for unfamiliar passages.

According to Masuhara (2007), L2 Japanese EFL learners lack the neural networks for an adequate aural/oral vocabulary, segmental and suprasegmental proficiency, and automatic understanding of English syntax (p. 24). Masuhara recommends that these L2 readers be taught to connect spoken language with its meaning. They need to become familiar with how prosodic features create meaning as a basis for learning to read (p. 29). According to this reasoning, it would appear advantageous for Japanese learners of English to engage in simultaneous reading and listening.

Walter (2008) presents a compelling case for L2 learners forming a mental representation of spoken language. She explains the role of the phonological loop, in which the last two seconds of what has been read or heard is stored in the working memory in order to better comprehend larger stretches of text. These insights from Walter strengthen the case for extensive reading to be supplemented with extensive listening.

However, some may question the need to perceive a phonological representation of the text while reading. Crystal (2005) explains competing points of view regarding this question of "reading by ear or by eye" (p. 123). The former asserts that a phonological bridge is necessary and the latter that "a non-phonological route from print to meaning must exist" (p. 125). Crystal concludes that both strategies are employed according to the stage of learning or reading material. If the latter approach is the one that applies in the Japanese context, it is possible that some students may make the grapheme to semantic connection without the phonological bridge, and in this case, extensive listening may be redundant for those who are simply aiming for reading comprehension.

Language as participation

Studies of first-language acquisition highlight the importance of feedback from the interlocutor. Wells (1981) explains how children confirm the effect of their utterances from the responses of their interlocutors: "Both listening and speaking, however, require that the child should have a conversational partner who is oriented to his needs as a language learner" (p. 109).

The importance of the interlocutor goes beyond the purely linguistic. Katherine's (1991) discussion of the role of the interlocutor in the development of an awareness of feelings: "We need a reaction, feedback, when we're feeling something. When the feedback is accurate, our feeling unfolds and becomes clearer. . .

An echo bounces your words back to you" (p. 19). Citing the work of Rogoff (1990, 1995), Sfard (1998). Donato (2000) and Pavlenko and Lantolf (2000), Block suggests that the acquisition metaphor of learning needs to be supplemented with a participation metaphor.

The discussion of the role of the interlocutor raises the broader concern of the participation of the learner not only with a single interlocutor but also with a range of interlocutors in the community. Mickan (2013) reminds us "we live in relationships and learn through relationships" (p. 32), describing the essential role of socialization in the learning of languages. Block (2003) highlights the interactional and interpersonal dimensions of Second Language Acquisition (SLA), reminding us that it is more than information exchange (p. 64): "Transactionally-oriented aspects of talk will be embedded in and intertwined with relational/interpersonal aspects" (p. 73). This suggests that learners in an extensive reading and listening program may benefit from opportunities for discussion and to provide written responses to the text.

Should extensive reading be supplemented with comprehension questions?

Comprehension questions sometimes feature in graded readers, but do not reflect the ideals of modern pedagogy. Bloom (Davidson & Decker, 2006) discriminated between lower and higher order thinking skills, with the lower ones consisting of knowledge, comprehension, and application, and the higher ones of analysis, synthesis, and evaluation. Comprehension questions belong to the category of lower order thinking skills. Nagatomo (2012, p. 163) observes a lesson in a university English class, which features comprehension questions, and makes the criticisms that it neither helps the student engage with the text nor make progress in English.

The case for supplementing extensive reading with creative written responses

Extensive reading and listening are intrinsically worthwhile activities, but providing a creative written response can harness this input to promote higher order thinking skills. Reading and listening are sources of unilateral input. Tokuhama-Espinosa (2008) describes sources for language learning such as television and computers as "passive tools" (p. 176). In contrast, "true learning comes with use, and use related to language implies practice with others" (ibid). Accordingly, learners in an extensive reading and listening program would benefit from the opportunity to reflect on what they have read or listened to. Tokuhama-Espinosa (2011) highlights the nature of learning in a social context. She describes this learning process as $1 + 1 = 3$, meaning "each person has his or her own ideas, but once shared, what is produced by the combined effort is greater than the sum of its parts" (p. 215). She urges teachers to provide opportunities for collaborative learning. Ideally, an extensive reading and listening program would need to provide such opportunities. Furthermore, Tokuhama-Espinosa advises teachers to provide instruction in different channels such as "discussion, readings, videos, debates, projects" (p. 164) in order for students to retain the information because it has been processed through different, albeit overlapping, neural pathways. Similarly, Puchta (2013, pp. 49–50) urges,

> Thinking actively – when we do things such as writing down our thoughts about something, talking aloud to ourselves, engaging in a discussion with someone, taking our time to silently reflect on something that engages us, or playing around in our mind with knowledge we have just acquired – can help us integrate recently acquired knowledge with prior knowledge, discover new aspects about something we already know, or develop a deeper understanding of a concept.

The act of writing helps clarify the student's response to a text. As Crystal argues, "Full meaning does not always exist prior to writing; often the process operates in reverse. A typical comment is Edward Albee's: 'I write to find out what I'm thinking about.'" (2005, p. 128).

Vygotsky (1962, cited in Wolf, 2008, p. 73) describes how the process of writing helps individuals refine and expand their thoughts. Writing fosters an inner dialogue within individuals as they hone their expressive skills by the sheer effort of finding the most fitting language. Accordingly, there are two kinds of dialogue that are characteristic of learning: the dialogue of collaboration, and inner dialogue that occurs when writing. Also citing Vygotsky (1981), Arnold and Murphey (2013) highlight "the importance of the *other* in learning is essential" (p. 7). They similarly explain Vygotsky's insight that learning is first intermental – that is, between individuals – and second intramental – that is, internal.

Teaching practices for L1 English-speaking middle school children affirm the importance of the inner voice when reading:

> Reading comprehension is an ongoing process of evolving thinking. When readers read and construct meaning, they carry on an inner conversation with the text. They hear a voice in their head speaking to them as they read a voice that questions, connects, laughs, cries. This inner conversation helps learners monitor their comprehension and keeps them engaged in the story, concept, information and ideas, allowing them to build their understanding as they go.
>
> (Harvey & Goudvis, 2007, p. 78)

Harvey and Goudvis continue to explain that "reading is a social act" (p. 82) because of the common practice of sharing what has been read from either a novel or the newspaper with others. They exploit this in the L1 classroom with an activity called "Read, write and talk." They urge children to jot down notes as thoughts occur to them as they read and respond to it with an activity called STR: stopping, thinking, and reacting. They insist that engagement and interaction with the story is necessary for constructing meaning and therefore comprehension: "Active reading is a dynamic process that puts the reader at the helm" (p. 84). Neurologist and teacher Judy Willis advises that memory and retention can be enhanced with strategies such as "individualized opportunities to verbalize, write or create something using a new language arts skill or new information students read in hopes of building more connecting dendrites" (2008, p. 36).

These studies and practices may offer insights into L2 pedagogy. Students should be encouraged to write about what they have read and listened to in order to develop their inner dialogue in the L2. Indeed, de Guerrero (1994) provides evidence that many adult learners do in fact experience inner speech in their L2, so this phenomenon is not confined to L1 learners. Hence the process of reading in the L2 should provide learners with the opportunity to practise inner speech in their L2 during the act of writing.

The interlocutor may require someone to reflect their ideas in order to help them define their English language selves. This is in fact evidenced in a study of Japanese high school learners of English. Watanabe (2013) describes the justification of one of the students in his study for not being willing to communicate in English: "Even if students are motivated to acquire practical English, they cannot build confidence in using English or be willing to communicate in the language without many chances to use it (p. 161)." Thus willingness to communicate seems to require the presence of an interlocutor who is a speaker of the L2. This raises the question of whether the task of responding to extensive reading and listening and the ensuing dialogue with the teacher who reads their response could fulfill that need.

The current study

Two classes of second-year university students in classes of Communicative English were assigned homework consisting of extensive reading of and listening to books of their choice for 14 weeks over a semester. This was a compulsory class for non-English majors. One class consisted of 22 students from the Regional Studies Department, and the other consisted of 20 students, mainly from the Civil Engineering Department. Permission was obtained from 13 members of the Regional Studies class and 13 members of the Civil Engineering class for their work to be cited for educational research.

The students were asked to read and listen to the story twice, and listen only one additional time. They were instructed to choose a book from the collection of graded readers in the library at whatever level they desired. Weekly homework consisted of a single-page essay about the graded reader, and the students were given a different essay question every week. The final homework was to write a reflection of how and why the listening and the reading had improved their English over the semester. The second question concerned gains in confidence in vocabulary, grammar, cultural knowledge, and listening. Responses have been selected from these essays, which relate to the questions of improvements in listening and providing creative written responses to the texts.

Student responses

Benefits of supplementing extensive reading with listening

Many students indicated the benefits of supplementing extensive reading with listening. However, a common theme was the difficulty of listening comprehension. This may be due to the small phonemic scale of Japanese. Tokuhama-Espinosa (2008, p. 40) posits that this small phonemic scale increases the likelihood of a Japanese speaker having an accent in a language with a larger phonemic scale. She attributes accents to difficulties in aural perception of the L2. This may account for the listening difficulties expressed by the students. Furthermore, as Crystal (2005) has explained, the individual words in normal speech are not comprehensible in isolation and yet become comprehensible in the stream of speech. This poses an additional problem for the L2 learners who have based their learning on the printed word. However, many students explained that repeated listening practice helped them improve their listening comprehension. It was possible for many of these students, already in their second year of university, to work at decoding the meaning of connected speech:

> "Listening is difficult. At first, I couldn't keep up with the CD. But I listen several times I could understand little by little. Beginning by getting used to English is important."
> "Listening and reading this semester improved my English."
> "I enjoy listening."
> "My English ability was improved in this class, especially listening. We listen to a CD every week so I think it approved the ability."
> "I think we are able to learn with our ears by doing homework while listening to the CD."
> "I feel more confident in listening a little, because I feel like it has become easy for me to understand spoken English. I think that the reason is that I listened to the CD repeatedly and got used to listening to English."
> "Three times listening was great training for me."
> "My listening skill improved greatly."

A major barrier to successful reading and listening comprehension is arguably a limited vocabulary. The Japanese language does contain many loanwords from English, which may be a source of positive transfer. However, the possibility of positive transfer of vocabulary is not on the same scale as that for learners from language backgrounds of similar typologies to English, such as French and German. Vocabulary acquisition is onerous for speakers of non-cognate languages. The following comment expresses the frustration experience by an inadequate vocabulary: "I don't feel confident in vocabulary so much. I think my vocabulary increased but they are not enough because I frequently couldn't understand words in the class and I couldn't compose English sentences without using a dictionary."

Traditionally, students have memorized vocabulary through looking at lists of vocabulary and their translations in special vocabulary books, with a special red transparent cover provided to hide the translations temporarily in order to aid memorization. Comments from students suggest that the alternative method used in the current study, reading and listening to new vocabulary in context, can also be effective:

> "I gained 'listening' and 'vocabulary' through this class."
> "Previously I learned English word for word in the English word book. Now through this class I have learnt that it is easy to remember to learn English words in a phrase."

One student was able to transfer skills gained from listening to the CDs to comprehending the teacher's English. As Crystal (2005) has explained, a majority of words in the stream of speech would become impossible to comprehend if uttered in the same way in isolation. However, the following student's comment suggests that the barrier of understanding the stream of speech has started to erode. Comprehension of the stream of speech rather than of single words may have been enhanced by this practice: "After listening to the CDs my ears became better and better. I recognized it when I could hear your fast English."

However, one respondent experienced a barrier to listening comprehension after a certain threshold: "It was difficult to understand the CDs above Level Three." Reading and listening were conducted simultaneously and therefore the visual support provided by print was present. A possible explanation for the earlier comment is that the contrasting word orders of English and Japanese render rapid processing of the languages to be challenging for L2 learners of the respective languages. The traditional approach for comprehending advanced texts has been *yakudoku* (Takeda, 2002), or 'translation reading'. The purpose of this methodology is to render difficult English texts into well-formed Japanese, rather than simply comprehending English in its own terms. Because of the contrasting word orders of the languages, the most efficient way to parse the sentences is considered to be from right to left. Nevertheless, the act of listening to English necessitates that it be processed in its natural order. Accordingly, Japanese students may have had limited practice of parsing English in its natural order. This may render simultaneous reading and listening to be a novel and challenging experience. This study was confined to simple texts, and therefore simultaneous reading and listening of advanced texts is also a topic that merits further exploration.

Benefits of supplementing extensive reading with creative written responses

Student responses confirm the value of providing a written response to the text:

> "However I have felt that I can write about my feeling by reading books in English. It was surprising for me because I didn't like English. Someday,

I got used to write English, and like reading English books. These books I chose were easy, so I, who did not like English, can read them easily."

This student derives an unexpected pleasure from reading because he is able to choose easy books and expresses satisfaction about being able to understand them and write how he feels about them. This confirms Day and Bamford's (1998) recommendation that students benefit from choice of book and level (p. 8). Furthermore, it confirms the value of being able to provide a personal response (arguably in contrast to responding to comprehension questions), as Puchta (2013) and Harvey and Goudvis (2007) argue concerning the enriching nature of reflection and expression.

The student's comment that he had not liked English is commonly heard. There is even a word in Japanese to express dislike of English: *eigogirai*. The reason for the dislike of English is arguably its role as a gatekeeper to higher levels of education. For students, English is inextricably associated with the arduous process of cramming for important exams and the concomitant threat of being unable to realize their ambitions. Many students would have had no experience of using English for communicative purposes. Hence the social purposes for language acquisition outlined by Block (2004) and Mickan (2013) earlier are arguably unfamiliar to these students. In providing a creative written response to the literature, the student has indicated that he was able to write about his feelings. This indicates that he has been able to create an interpersonal dimension to the study of English, which was likely to have been hitherto absent. This is the beginning of learning English, which conforms to Block's (2003) participation metaphor.

Another student indicated the value of dialogue with the teacher in terms of the written feedback received from the teacher. Again, this indicates that the role of English is one of participation: "I feel more confident in grammar because the English sentences I composed really weren't wrong. So I was looking forward to having my submitted homework returned every week."

Despite the challenge of writing a response in English, these students indicated that the effort was worthwhile. The following comments indicate enjoyment of reading and responding to texts. Responses concerning the enjoyment of reading were unsolicited and therefore can be considered to be particularly important.

"It was hard for me to do homework every week, but I enjoyed reading books and writing my idea on paper."

"It was very hard for me to write the essays every week, but I could understand the importance of reading English books. I am very glad to have improved my English skills. I want to improve them more and more."

"When this class started I had a hard time finishing reading a book, but I was getting used to reading a book by reading different books every week. At the very least, reading an English book and writing my opinion were getting easy. Also, I came to like and enjoy English."

"I've improved writing and vocabulary skills, because I can write long English sentences and I can enjoy to write English."

> "At the very least, reading an English book and writing my opinion were getting easy."

These comments highlight the pleasure some students derived from extensive reading and listening. Students' personal responses ranged from faint praise: "I came not to dislike English," to effusive: "I fell in love with English here for the first time."

Recently, the importance of positive emotion for learning (Willis, 2008) and for successful language acquisition (see Schumann, 1997; Tokuhama-Espinosa, 2008) has been explored. Accordingly, further research could identify whether the long-term practices of extensive reading, listening, and responding continued to provide students with the enjoyment of learning a language and the concomitant improved proficiency. Nevertheless, there was some negative feedback about providing written feedback to the story:

> "The homework was very hard [. . .] because I must read a difficult book."
> "Sometimes I read a strange story and it was difficult to write a remark."

This may be due to cultural barriers in the genres of English language fiction. However, this comment is not in itself a reason to abandon stories, which are unfamiliar in the learners' milieu. This comment reflects the effort identified by Crystal (2005) that writing imposes in order to clarify thought. It is precisely this kind of effort that teachers hope will assist students to refine their thinking skills. It is unlike the kind of effort previously expended by Japanese students necessitated by English examinations, which test reading comprehension. This kind of struggle implies development of higher order thinking skills employed in reflecting on rather than simply comprehending the text.

Unexpected findings

An unexpected finding of this study, because it was unsolicited, was that some students indicated that they had not read a book in English before. In fairness, this must also be true of many native English-speaking learners' experience of reading books in Japanese.

> "Before I attend this class, I read English book hardly anything at all."
> "It was the first experience to finish reading one book written in English."

The novelty of extensive reading and listening suggested by comments such as this suggest that this methodology is a departure from those that students had previously experienced. This conforms to the findings of Nagatomo's (2012) recent study. Many educators lament the progress of English language learners in Japan (see Nagatomo, 2012, p. 15; Seargeant, 2009, p. 47). One reason may be that extensive reading is not as widely practised as traditional pedagogies of grammar, translation, and comprehension questions. Further research could investigate whether extensive reading and listening could serve to bridge this gap.

Conclusions

The major gain from this project were the feelings of success that the students expressed at sensing that they had improved their listening skills. It suggests that these students had begun to experience the skill highlighted by Masuhara (2007) and Walter (2008) of connecting spoken English with its meaning and, importantly, that many of them were able to gain a sense of pleasure from their reading. With practice, it is anticipated that students can extend the skill of listening comprehension to texts of increasing complexity. One student indicated a barrier to listening comprehension to texts above Level Three of the graded reader series. This highlights the need to facilitate listening comprehension of texts of greater lexico-grammatical complexity.

As for the value that they ascribed to providing a written response, some students perceived this positively, whereas a few students considered it to be a burden. Those who perceived this positively derived the benefits identified by Puchta (2013) of self-expression, and gains in confidence. Generally, this study supports the notion that students perceive benefits from an integrated approach to extensive reading. Certainly, the reading is the core of the approach, but providing students with opportunities to reflect on their reading, respond to it, and receive feedback can only consolidate and extend their gains. It demonstrates a move from the passive goal of the comprehension of English, to the use of English as a form of participation, as outlined by Block (2003).

Teachers are obliged to assess, and those with large classes of 40, 50, or even more students may have no option but to assess extensive reading and listening with comprehension questions, which can be administered online. However, for those with the luxury of smaller classes, extensive reading and listening can be usefully supplemented with activities designed to elicit personal responses to the literature.

References

Allen, J. (1975). Some basic concepts in linguistics. In J. Allen & S. Pit Corder (Eds.), *Volume Two: Papers in applied linguistics* (pp. 16–44). London: Oxford University Press.
Arnold, J., & Murphey, T. (Eds.). (2013). *Meaningful action: Earl Stevick's influence on language teaching*. Cambridge: Cambridge University Press.
Block, D. (2003). *The social turn in second language acquisition*. Washington, DC: Georgetown University Press.
Davidson, K., & Decker, T. (2006). *Blooms and beyond: Higher level questions and activities for the creative classroom*. Marion, IL: Pieces of Learning.
Donato, Richard.(2000). Sociocultural contributions to understanding the foreign and second language classroom. In James Lantolf (Ed.), *Sociocultural theory and second language learning* (pp. 27–50). Oxford: Oxford University Press.
Chang, A. C-S. (2011). The effect of reading while listening to audiobooks: Listening fluency and vocabulary gain. *Asian Journal of English Language Teaching, 21*, 43–64.
Chang, A. C-S., & Millett, S. (2014). The effect of extensive listening on developing L2 listening fluency: Some hard evidence. *ELT Journal, 68*(1), 31–40.
Crystal, D. (2005). *How language works: How babies babble, words change meaning, and languages live or die*. New York: Penguin.

Day, R., & Bamford, J. (1998). *Extensive reading in the second language classroom.* Cambridge: Cambridge University Press.

de Guerrero, M. C. M. (1994). Form and functions of inner speech in adult second language acquisition. In J. Lantolf & G. Appel (Eds.), *Vygotskian approaches to second language research* (pp. 83–115). Westport, CT: Ablex Publishing.

Harvey, S., & Goudvis, A. (2007). *Strategies that work: Teaching comprehension for understanding and engagement.* Portland, ME: Stenhouse Publishers.

Katherine, A. (1991). *Boundaries: Where you end and I begin: How to recognize and set healthy boundaries.* Center City, MN: Hazelden.

Masuhara, H. (2007). The role of proto-reading activities in the acquisition and development of effective reading skills. In B. Tomlinson (Ed.), *Language acquisition and development: Studies of learners of first and other languages* (pp. 15–31). London: Continuum.

Mickan, P. (2013). *Language curriculum, design and socialization.* Bristol: Multilingual Matters.

Nagatomo, D. (2012). *Exploring Japanese university English teachers' professional identity.* Bristol: Multilingual Matters.

Pavlenko, A., & Lantolf, J. (2000). Second language learning as participation and the (re) construction of selves. In J. Lantolf, (Ed.), *Socio-cultural theory and second language learning* (pp. 155–177). Oxford: Oxford University Press.

Puchta, H. (2013). Engaging adult learners: What ELT can learn from neuroscience and educational theory. In J. Arnold & T. Murphey (Eds.), *Meaningful action: Earl Stevick's influence on language teaching* (pp. 45–61). Cambridge: Cambridge University Press.

Rogoff, B. (1990). *Apprenticeship in thinking: Cognitive development in social context.* Oxford: Oxford University Press.

Schumann, J. H. (1997). *The neurobiology of affect in language.* Malden, MA: Blackwell.

Seargeant, P. (2009). *The idea of English in Japan: Ideology and the evolution of a global language.* Bristol: Multilingual Matters.

Sfard, A. (1998). On two metaphors for learning and the dangers of choosing just one. *Educational Researcher, 27,* 4–13.

Takeda, C. (2002). Phonics: The key to solving a fundamental problem in English L2 Education in Japan. *Ehime University Journal of English Education Research, 1,* 87–103.

Tokuhama-Espinosa, T. (2008). *Living languages: Multilingualism across the lifespan.* Westport, CT: Praeger.

Tokuhama-Espinosa, T. (2011). *Mind, brain, and education science: A comprehensive guide to the new brain-based teaching.* New York: W.W. Norton and Company.

Vygotsky, L. (1981). The development of higher forms of attention in childhood. In J. V. Wertsch (Ed.), *The concept of activity in Soviet psychology* (pp. 144–188). Armonk, NY: M. E. Sharp.

Walter, C. (2008). Phonology in second language reading: Not an optional extra. *TESOL Quarterly, 42,* 455–468.

Watanabe, M. (2013). Willingness to communicate and Japanese high school English learners. *JALT Journal, 35,* 153–172.

Wells, G. (1981). *Learning through interaction.* Cambridge: Cambridge University Press.

Willis, J. (2008). *Teaching the brain to read: Strategies for improving fluency, vocabulary, and comprehension.* Alexandria, VA: Association for Supervision and Curriculum Development.

Wolf, M. (2008). *Proust and the squid: The story and science of the reading brain.* Thriplow, Cambridge: Icon Books.

6 Teaching writing to multilingual learners using the genre-based approach

Justina Ong

The current writing pedagogies include the process-based, genre-based, content-based (including theme-based), task-based, problem-based, and project-based approaches (Hinkel, 2006). The process- and genre-based approaches have become the most influential writing instruction for learners. These approaches have been used to teach first language (L1), second language (L1), and multilingual learners (Gentil, 2011; Leki, 2011). The process approach emphasizes the cognitive processes (e.g., planning, transcribing, and revising) (Flower & Hayes, 1981; Scardamalia & Berieter, 1987) and the effective management of these processes in a writing task (Manchon, Roca de Larios, & Murphy, 2009; Ong, 2014). Previously, the genre-based approach was regarded as a product-based approach because of its emphasis on linguistic features of texts. Consequently, there is a perception that the genre-based pedagogy and process-based pedagogy are competing against each other (Racelis & Matsuda, 2013). However, the genre-based approach to the teaching of writing entails both product and process approaches, which Tardy (2009) highlighted in her four dimensions of genre knowledge: formal, process, rhetorical, and subject-matter knowledge. According to her, formal knowledge includes the lexico-grammatical conventions of the genre, the structural moves that are common to the genre, and the modes and media through which the genre may be communicated. Process knowledge refers to the procedural practices through which a genre is carried out; this includes the composing processes for the written genres. Rhetorical knowledge refers to the genre's purposes and learners' awareness of the dynamics of persuasion within a socio-rhetorical context. Finally, the subject-matter knowledge is the specialized content knowledge required in a writing task.

The underlying assumption of the genre-based theory is that writing is both a solitary and a social activity. Writing is a solitary activity because writing involves planning, transcribing, and revising, and the effective management of these processes (Ong, 2014). This is typically shown when learners independently construct texts at the later stages of the genre-based pedagogy. Writing is a social activity because the final piece of writing is often the result of social and cultural constructs (Prior, 2006). This is shown by the role played by the teacher, particularly during the earlier stages of the genre-based instruction when they model and deconstruct a text. The socio-cultural elements (e.g., scaffolding, guided practice, and co-participation) appear in their instructional discourse. Teachers rely on their instructional discourse (e.g., modelling, prompting, instructing, explaining, thinking-aloud, and scaffolding) and use instructional tools (e.g., graphic organizers, text structures, mnemonics, spellchecks) to teach writing skills. Social practices and cultural conventions are made accessible to learners through their instructional discourse (Englert, Mariage, & Dunsmore, 2006). In this sense, the writing activity is not only a solitary one.

Drawing upon Halliday's (1994) systemic functional linguistics (SFL), this chapter offers a genre-based approach to analyzing two advertising texts and focuses on the deconstruction of the texts using Feez's (1998) teaching-learning cycle. Classroom teachers could apply such an approach to a variety of selected texts for different age groups and proficiency levels of students (see Widodo, 2006). The main aims of this chapter are to raise second or foreign language learners' awareness of the functional use of language in achieving a social and communicative purpose of persuasion for authentic advertising texts and to offer language teachers a few practical suggestions for modelling and deconstruction of comparable texts through thinking-aloud.

Since 1981, genre has become an important concept in second-language writing studies (Tardy, 2011). Genres are ways in which people achieve their objectives through their use of language in particular contexts (Paltridge et al., 2006). Genre in SFL emphasizes "a purposeful and sequential character of different genres and the systematic links between language and context" (Martin, 1992, as cited by Hyland, 2007, p. 153). The use of language is, nevertheless, conformed to some socially recognized ways of using it. These socially recognized ways of using language permit a variety of texts to be roughly organized under a particular genre category – for example, informational genre, descriptive genre, and persuasive genre – although in real-life contexts, a more hybrid type of genre typically exists – for example, advertising brochures, notification letters, news reports, emails, blogs, and chat rooms. Schools have been strongly encouraged to use authentic texts to teach students writing skills because such texts are what learners are truly exposed to in their everyday lives. Examples of authentic texts are the two advertising brochures in which I have selected for demonstrating the genre-based approach to teaching writing.

Genre is typically defined as 'staged' and 'goal oriented social processes' (Christie, 1998; Derewianka, 1996; Martin, 1989; Painter, 2001). According to several SFL genre analysts, language has three meta-functions: the ideational, textual, and interpersonal functions (Christie, 1998; Derewianka, 1996; Halliday, 1994; Hyland, 2003, 2007; Martin, 1989; Painter, 2001; Schleppegrell, 2004). These meta-functions are used to achieve a particular social goal. The ideational function has to do with content or field representation. It centrally addresses what a text is about. The interpersonal function focuses on the relationship of the participants involved in using the language. The textual function deals with how language features 'hang together' in a cohesive manner. The genre-based approach to teaching of writing highlights the meta-functions of sample texts to learners.

Hyland (2007) identified the main elements in genre-based pedagogy and illustrated how this pedagogy plans learning, sequences learning, supports learning, and assesses learning of writing. Drawing upon Feez's (1998) prominent teaching-learning cycle, he showed how this pedagogy could be used to support learners' learning of writing. The teaching-learning cycle involves five major stages: (1) building the context: teachers teach the purposes of the genre and the contexts in which the genre is commonly used; (2) modelling and deconstructing the text: teachers, through their instructional discourse, analyze the key linguistic features and stages of representative samples of the genre; (3) joint construction of the text: teachers guide learners to compose in the genre; (4) independent construction of the text: teachers allow learners to independently construct the text; and (5) linking related texts: teachers relate to other genres and contexts. Accordingly, such a cycle is intended to be used flexibly. Based on learners' existing genre knowledge, learners can enter any one stage, teachers can return to an earlier stage of the cycle, and the stages can be repeated (Hyland, 2007).

Christie and Martin (1997) advocated that genre pedagogy pulls language, content, and contexts together and offers language teachers a systematic and explicit manner of teaching writing. They addressed how writing works to communicate its underlying goals. Expanding on the advantages of genre pedagogy, Hyland (2004) suggested that this approach to teaching of writing is "explicit, systematic, based on students' needs, supportive, empowering, critical, and consciousness-raising" (Hyland, 2004, pp. 10–16).

More recently, researchers attempted to apply genre-based analysis to learners' writing so as to track their language development (see Christie, 2012a, 2012b, 2012c; Christie & Derewianka, 2008). For instance, Christie (2012a, 2012b, 2012c) used genre-based analysis to track the writing development of L1 learners. In her study, she has extracted authentic texts from school textbooks and obtained learners' writing for analysis. She found that early childhood learners, who are in the age ranges of five to eight years old, learn to translate speech to writing, use simple words, construct simple sentences, expand their writing through relating to place and time of events, use frequently used conjunctions to connect sentences, and foreground the self using personal pronouns. Late childhood learners, who are in the age range of 9 to 12 years old, learn to deal with un-commonsense knowledge, learn to progress from speech-like writing to writing mode, learn to use lexically denser words, expand noun groups, use a larger prepositional phrase, display their emotions and attitudes through writing, and use a greater variety of conjunctions and thematic structures. Christie (2012c) further observed that, as learners reach adolescence, they learn to master abstraction in English, history, and science subject domains. In the case of English language, learners learn to evaluate the texts that they read. They learn how complex themes and rhemes are built up; how nominalizations and abstractions are used; how values, attitudes, and emotions of the writers are embedded through the use of language in a text; how distance is created with less reliance on personal pronouns; and how to manage clause complexity. Tracking learners' language development using genre-based analysis has proven useful in informing

86 *Justina Ong*

educators about learners' language needs. Additionally, the benefits of genre-based approach to teaching and learning writing can be reaped on a prior condition that language teachers could effectively 'talk about texts' in the classroom. Deconstruction of texts serves to heighten learners' awareness of how language can be used to achieve its purpose, and it is an important stage of the genre-based pedagogy.

Analysis: text deconstruction

In this analysis, I focus on the deconstruction of two short advertising brochures, which typically occur at stage two of genre-based pedagogy. In doing so, I adopt a think-aloud approach. The selection of two advertising texts allows me to demonstrate the functional use of language in both texts. Text 1 is labeled Kaikoura (Figure 6.1). Text 2 is labeled Blue Mountain (Figure 6.2).

Ideational meaning: lexis

How is the field of both texts constructed? I consider the choice of lexical phrases, the process, circumstances, and the participation types of the texts. Painter (2001) proposed that the lexical choices and the process, circumstance, and participation types construct the ideational function of a text. In a similar

---

Text 1: Kaikoura

(C1) Today, you will have the morning free (C2) to explore the sights and sounds of Kaikoura. (C3) If you are a nature lover, (C4) why not sign up for an optional dolphin excursion, (C5) where you may have the opportunity (C6) to swim with friendly and intelligent creatures? (C7) If you prefer (C8) to stay dry (C9) and yet have a close encounter with the ocean wildlife, (C10) you can go whale watching. (C11) Take a cruise out to the waters in the open sea, (C12) where you may be lucky enough (C13) to catch a sight of migrating whales breaking the surface. (C14) For a unique way to view the whales close up (C15) without disturbing them, (C16) you may take a flight to whale watch instead.

(C17) In the afternoon, we depart for Ashburton. (C18) Experience the hospitality of the locals with a STAY WITH A NEW ZEALAND FAMILY. (C19) The group will be split into smaller numbers (C20) to enjoy a maximum comfort. (C21) Receive a warm welcome from your new found friends (C22) as you get a glimpse of their laid back lifestyle (C23) and hear them share snippets of information about life in their country. (C24) They will be interested (C25) to hear about your country too, (C26) so why not bring a gift from home (C27) to introduce them to your homeland?

Figure 6.1 A brochure from the Chan Brothers Tour

> **Text 2: Blue mountain**
>
> (**C1**) The blue mountains are set within the wild wilderness of a national park. (**C2**) It's an area full of spectacular scenery from towering escarpments to hidden rainforests. (**C3**) Because of its ruggedness, (**C4**) many areas of the blue mountains are inaccessible to the majority of visitors.
> 	(**C5**) This wilderness experience traveling by four wheel drive will help you (**C6**) enjoy a sense of excitement and adventure in the great outdoors. (**C7**) Your guide will not only show you some breathtaking sights over one of the mountains most rugged valley systems (**C8**) but also explain the incredible diversity of flora and fauna (**C9**) as you enjoy a guided walk to the edge of the escarpment. (**C10**) To top it off, (**C11**) you will enjoy a cup of traditional Aussie Bush Tea.

Figure 6.2 A brochure from the Aussie Tour

vein, both Halliday (1994) and Christie and Derewianka (2008) pointed out that the nouns, verbs, prepositional phrases, adverbial adjuncts, and other resources for time, place, and manner reveal the ideational function of a text. Christie and Derewianka (2008) further distinguish the lexico-grammatical features at the clause level and the lexico-grammatical features beyond the clause level. At the clause level, Christie and Derewianka discussed the participants involved in the types of processes and circumstances. Beyond the clause level, they discussed the logical relationships between the events. In my analysis of the ideational function of the two advertising texts, I look at the choice of lexical phrases used by the writers, followed by the process, circumstances, and participation types.

First, what lexical phrases are used and why are they used? The writer of Text 1, *Kaikoura*, used ordinary phrases such as *the sights and sounds* (C2), *a close encounter with* (C9), *to catch a sight of* and *migrating whales breaking the surface* (C13), *to view the whales* (C14), *receive a warm welcome* (C21) and *get a glimpse* (C22). These phrases were used to arouse the senses of the audience or readers. Many activities such as *dolphin excursion* (C4), *take a cruise* (C11), *to catch a sight of* (C13), and *take a flight to whale watch* (C16) were foregrounded to promote the activities offered in Kaikoura. With lexes such as *nature lover* (C3), *swim with creatures* (C6), *encounter with ocean wildlife* (C9), and *laid back lifestyle* (22), the image of Kaikoura is portrayed as a carefree and relaxed place; one that could bring tourists close to nature. Contrary to Text 1, the writer of the *Blue Mountain* text used predominantly adjectives to describe the place. For examples, *wild wilderness* (C1), *spectacular scenery, towering escarpments*, and *hidden rainforest* (C2), *wilderness experience* (C5), *great outdoors* (C6), *breathtaking sights* (C7), *rugged valley systems* (C7), *incredible diversity* (C8), *guided walk* (C9), and *traditional Aussie Bush Tea* (C11). The lexes such as *escarpment, rainforest*, and *valley systems* entail technicality; hence, they created a more specialized effect.

88 *Justina Ong*

The image of Blue Mountain is projected to be wild, mysterious, magnificent, and adventurous.

Despite a similarity in the persuasive purpose of both texts, there is a disparity in the choice of lexis used. Evidently, the ideational function of Text 1 focused on the activities one could do at different times of the day, whereas the ideational function of Text 2 focused on the distinctive features of the place. Comparatively, the field of Text 1 is less technical and more commonsensical than Text 2.

Ideational meaning: processes

What processes, circumstances, and participation types are used and why? Apart from the lexical items, the ideational function of texts is realized through the transitivity patterns known as the process types (Halliday, 1994; Painter, 2001). The process types specify the actions, events, or relationships between the implicated participants. The processes are typically situated circumstantially, for time, place, or cause (Halliday, 1994; Painter, 2001). By examining the transitivity patterns, which involves the identification of the process, participants, and circumstances in a clause, one can explain how the field of the texts is constructed – e.g., we can describe what is being talked about (Eggins, 1994). There are six main types of processes: material, mental, relational, behavioral, verbal, and existential (Halliday, 1994). A comparative analysis of the types of processes reveals that Text 1, *Kaikoura*, has predominant use of material and mental processes, but Text 2, *Blue Mountain*, has predominant use of relational and mental ones. Text 1 used material processes of 'doing' to construct actions through presenting the activities one can do there. Text 2 used relational processes to relate or connect participants to each other without any actions (see Figure 6.3).

Even though both texts used mental processes, a closer investigation of the subcategories of the mental processes further reveals that Text 1 has a mixture of perception, affection, and cognition, but Text 2 has predominant use of affection processes. For example, in Text 1, the perception processes are *to catch a sight of* (C13) and *experience* (C18); the affection processes are *enjoy* (C20) and *receive a*

Text 1: Material process

In C1–C2, "*Today, you will have the morning free* **to explore** *the sights and sounds of Kaikoura*".

Text 2: Relational process

In C1, "*The blue mountains* **are set** *within the wild wilderness of a national park*".

Figure 6.3 An example of material process in Text 1 and relational process in Text 2.

warm welcome (C21), and, finally, the cognitive process is *prefer* (C7). In Text 2, the affection process is *enjoy* (C6, C9, and C11). Thus Text 1 is richer ideationally compared to Text 2, as it appeals to the senses, affect, and cognition of readers, whilst Text 2 appeals to readers' affect only.

Ideational meaning: participants

The participants referred to in Text 1 are *you* (C1, C3, C5, C7, etc.), *we* (C17), *the group* (C19), and *they* (C24). As Text 1 is centrally concerned with actions, there is a foregrounding of human participants 'doing' the actions. Whether it is the actor in the material processes or the sensor in the mental processes, the writer predominantly used 'you'. Contrary to Text 1, Text 2 has mostly nouns as carriers in the relational processes – e.g., *The Blue Mountain* (C1), *It* (C2), *Many areas* (C4), and *This experience* (C5). These nouns carry attributes. From C7 in Text 2 onwards, there is a shift of participants from nouns to personal pronouns. This is likely because of a shift in the field; the text producer moved from a description of the place to what the tourist would be expected to experience. In brief, the prevalent use of personal pronouns as participants, rather than the use of nouns in Text 1, makes the field of the text more commonsensical and of the 'everyday' domain.

Ideational meaning: circumstances

Another key difference in the ideational function of Text 1 and 2 lies in the selection of the type of circumstances (Figure 6.4). The most significant distinction is in the time and place circumstances, not in manner, extent, role, nor cause circumstances. Text 1 used time circumstantially – e.g., *today* and *morning* (C1), and *afternoon* (C17) – to sequence activities one could do in chronological order and also place circumstantial – e.g., *open sea* (C11), *Ash burton* (C17), *country* (C23), *home'* 26), and *homeland* (C27). However, Text 2 used only

---

Text 1: Time and place circumstances

In C17, "***In the afternoon***, we depart for ***Ashburton***".

Text 2: Place circumstance

In C1, "***The blue mountains*** are set within the wild wilderness of ***a national park***".

Figure 6.4 An example of time and place circumstances in Text 1 and place circumstance in Text 2

place circumstantially – e.g., *national park* (C1), *rainforest* (C2), and *many areas* (C4) – to describe the place.

Interpersonal meaning: speech function

How is the tenor of both texts constructed? To discuss how interpersonal meanings of Text 1 and 2 are constructed, I look at the writers' choice of mood, modality, and attitudinal adjuncts. The interpersonal function of a text is constructed by the use of mood (i.e., statements, questions, and commands), modality (i.e., modal verbs and adverbs), and other linguistic resources, which show evaluative and attitudinal meanings (Christie & Derewianka, 2008; Halliday, 1994; Painter, 2001). Martin and White (2005) have proposed an appraisal framework that focuses on the evaluative and attitudinal meanings of the texts. The framework emphasizes the linguistic resources that reveal writers' attitudes, graduation, and engagement. Writers' attitudes can be expressed using emotional reaction (i.e., affect), evaluation of the worth or quality of things or processes (i.e., appreciation), and judgment of behavior of others (i.e., judgment). Graduation denotes the strength of emotions, viewpoints, and judgments that are displayed by writers. Engagement reflects writers' involvement in the issue or topic of discussion. The choice of mood in Text 1, *Kaikoura*, is more varied than Text 2, *Blue Mountain*. Text 1 consisted of statements, commands, and offers; however, Text 2 consisted of only statements.

First, Text 1 used commands in the form of imperatives – e.g., *Take a cruise* (C11), *Experience the hospitality*, (C18) and *Receive a warm welcome* (C21). When these imperatives are used, they typically signal an unequal relationship between the writers and readers, with the writers having greater power and possessing greater expertise compared to the readers (Halliday, 1994). However, contrary to the typical function of imperatives, these imperatives were used to capture the readers' attention and not to command or instruct them. Second, Text 1 used modulated interrogatives (Eggins, 1994), which employ the speech function of an offer (Figure 6.5).

Modulation is a way for 'speakers' to express their judgments or attitudes about actions and events (Eggins, 1994). The writer of Text 1 employed modulated interrogatives in the form of suggestions. The choice of commodity is a type of service – e.g., *dolphin excursion* (C4) – and a product – e.g., *a gift* (C26). The

---

Text 1: Modulated interrogatives

In C3–C4, "*If you are a nature lover,* **why not sign up** *for an optional dolphin excursion...*"

In C23–25, "*They will be interested to hear about your country too, so* **why not bring** *a gift from home,...*"

Figure 6.5 Examples of modulated interrogatives

use of *why not* as a proposition, in negative polarity, was not to make it mandatory for tourists to sign up for a dolphin excursion or to bring a gift, but rather to suggest that they might do so if they prefer to. The reason the writer of Text 1 used modulated interrogatives is because all the activities in Kaikoura would cost the tourists money; therefore, the writer had to make the activities optional or suggestive.

Interpersonal meaning: modality

The difference between Text 1 and Text 2 lies in the intensity of modality used, not in terms of the frequency of use. The intensity of modality in Text 1 is low and medium, but the intensity of modality in Text 2 is medium. Text 1 used low intensity of modality – e.g., '*may*' (C5, C12, and C16) and '*can*' (C10) – in order to be less assertive and less authoritative when persuading readers to join the activities. For example, 'may' indicates an option. The medium intensity of modality in Text 2 – e.g. '*will*' (C5, C7, and C11) – makes it more certain. The writer of Text 1 sold the activities; the tourists would have to pay for them, thus, the choice of intensity of modality was low. However, the writer of Text 2 advertised the place as a whole tour package, thus, his choice of medium intensity modality is appropriate. In addition, the writer of Text 2 used intensifying adverbs to quantify the extent of the beauty of the place. High intensifying adverbs such as '*full of*' (C2), '*many*' (C4), and '*majority*' and '*most*' (C4) were used to express the writer's affect towards the place; this was completely absent in Text 1. In this sense, the interpersonal meaning in both texts is constructed differently.

Another significant aspect of interpersonal meaning is the attitudinal affect encoded in the texts. More attitudinal affect appears in Text 1 than Text 2. The writer of Text 1 used attitudinal affect to create an intimate relationship with the readers. He described the dolphins as having human characteristics such as '*friendly and intelligent*' (C6). He used '*a close encounter with the ocean wildlife*' (C9) to create an impression that the tourist 'is meeting with' the whales, but it is simply about watching the whales. In addition, the adjective '*migrating*' (C13) is commonly used to describe movement of people, but it is used in this text to illustrate movement of whales. The dolphins and whales are personified as humans to appeal to the potential tourists. The writer also suggested to readers that they could '*view the whales close up without disturbing them*' (C14–C15). A less positively attitudinal laden word 'disturbing' was used to appeal to the new-age travelers who would probably not like to be disturbed and also the animal lovers who respected and cared for the freedom of animals. The noun '*the opportunity*' (C5) reflects the writer's attitudinal affect towards the activity of swimming with dolphins – i.e., it is a rare chance. He also used '*lucky enough*' (C12) to express his affect towards catching the sight of '*migrating whales breaking the surface*' (C13) to imply that tourists who see whales are indeed fortunate. In Text 2, the writer used many positive adjectives such as '*spectacular*' (C2), '*breathtaking*' (C6) and '*great*' (C7), etc. to show his positive affect towards the place and '*incredible*' (C8), '*guided*' (C9), and '*traditional*' (C11), etc., to show his positive affect towards what would be offered at Blue Mountain. The scenery was described as '*spectacular*' (C2) and the sights over one of the mountains were described as '*breathtaking*' (C6).

In summary, the writer of Text 1 sequenced a list of activities tourists can do in the morning and afternoon. However, the writer of Text 2 described Blue Mountain and the tour experience. The macro-structure of advertising texts appears to be less structured because they are hybrid genres. Although the purpose of both texts was that of persuasion, the ideational and interpersonal meanings were constructed differently. In terms of ideational function, Text 1 (Kaikoura) had generalized lexes that are of everyday domain, unlike Text 2 (Blue Mountain) which had more semi-technical lexes. As Text 1 foregrounded the activities one could do there, the processes were mainly material and mental ones. However, Text 2 foregrounded the features of the place; as such, the processes were predominantly relational ones. Text 1 had a more varied use of mental processes than Text 2 (e.g., Text 1 used perception, affection, and cognitive processes, but Text 2 used affection processes only). Whereas Text 1 used predominantly personal pronouns as participants, Text 2 used both nouns and pronouns. Whereas Text 1 situated the time and place circumstances, Text 2 had only the place circumstances. In terms of interpersonal function, the writer of Text 1, through the choice of language use, attempted to build a more intimate relationship with the readers compared to the writer of Text 2. Text 1 had a greater diversity of mood choice – e.g., modulated interrogatives and imperatives. Furthermore, the intensity of modality used in Text 1 was of low and medium ranges, whereas the intensity of modality used in Text 2 was of medium range. The ranges invited a more imaginary dialogic interaction between the writer of Text 1 and its readers. Finally, Text 1 was written not only for those who enjoyed guided and planned tour but also for those who regarded themselves as new-age travelers, nature lovers, and animal protectors. The tour agency sells not only the image of place but also the image of the consumer – that is, anyone who travels with Chan Brother is a modern traveler. Aussie Tours in Australia wrote Text 2 mainly for adventurous backpackers. The writer of Text 2 might have believed that the scenery of Blue Mountain would naturally attract anyone who would like to visit the place; thus, the writer focused on the attractiveness of the place.

Research studies in the genre-based approach in Asian contexts

In this section, I review a few recent research studies that looked into the genre-based approach to teaching Asian learners of English. Myskow and Gordon (2010) and Firkins, Forey, and Sengupta (2007) described the genre-based approach to teaching writing to English as a Foreign Language (EFL) learners. The instruction focused on the modelling and deconstruction of genres, which is similar to the focus of this chapter. Myskow and Gordon (2010), for example, described the genre-based approach to teaching university application letters to six Japanese EFL high school learners. Their instruction looked into the rhetorical patterns and language used in university application letters. In the contextual analysis stage, the social context of letter writing such as understanding the values and beliefs of readers of their application letters was emphasized. This aspect emphasized the importance of considering the perspectives of readers. In the textual analysis stage, learners analyzed the rhetorical and linguistic features and the organization structure of sample application letters. In another study, Firkins, Forey, and Sengupta (2007) incorporated an activity into the genre-based approach to teaching procedural and information report writing to 32 low-proficiency EFL Hong Kong secondary-school students. The instruction on modelling and deconstruction of stages again focused on the structure and lexico-grammatical features of texts. The researchers concluded that the genre-based approach benefits EFL learners in their organization of writing.

There are a few recent studies that examined the effects of the genre-based teaching approach on EFL learners' writing. Chen and Su (2012), for example, investigated the effects of genre-based writing instruction on 41 Taiwanese University EFL students' summary writing using a test and retest design over a period of seven weeks. The learners were explicitly taught the structure of a prototypical narrative genre and linguistics features for writing narratives based on the teaching-learning cycle of the genre-based approach. Chen and Su (2012) found that the learners improved in content and rhetorical organization rather than linguistics accuracy and lexical density of their writing after the intervention. Another study is that of Yasuda (2011) who examined how 70 college-level Japanese EFL learners had developed their genre awareness, linguistic knowledge, and writing competence for email-writing tasks in a writing course. In implementing the genre-based approach, Yasuda included the idea of phases of tasks from task-based language teaching and learning. Yasuda (2011) found that learners' genre awareness was heightened and that learners' emails improved in task fulfilment and appropriacy, cohesion and organization, grammar, writing fluency, and language sophistication, but not lexical diversity after the intervention.

Implications of the genre-based pedagogy for Asian learners

There is a large number of Asian learners of English. The number of learners of English from China alone approximates to 390 million (Wei & Su, 2012). Given this large number of Asian EFL learners, it seems clear that more research in L2 learning and teaching of writing on this population and others is needed. The explicit focus on textual and linguistic features and the systematic instructional stages of the genre-based pedagogy make this writing approach a useful one for L1 or EFL learners. However, a one-size-fits-all writing approach will not work well for Asian learners who are different from L1 learners. First, unlike L1 learners, L2 learners have their L1 genre knowledge to draw from when writing in L2 (Gentil, 2011). Some writers rely on L1 genre knowledge to compose in L2, particularly if they have low L2 proficiency. The use of L1 vocabulary as substitution of L2 vocabulary is most prevalent when learners learn to write in L2. Gentil

(2011) suggested that language teachers can identify prior knowledge that learners bring to a writing task so as to help them draw upon it as they develop the knowledge required for writing in L2. It appears intuitive to hypothesize that, if learners' L1 genre knowledge resembles L2, then transfer of this knowledge is likely to ease the process of writing and produce positive outcomes. However, if learners' L1 genre knowledge does not resemble L2, then learners have to relearn the appropriate L2 genre conventions.

Second, the cultural background of L1 or L2 learners differs markedly. There are differences in how L1 or L2 learners organize the structure of their texts, use vocabulary, perceive their audience, define the purpose of writing, etc. Leki, Cumming, and Silva (2008) attributed some of these differences to the cultural background of learners, lack of proper writing instruction, and lack of writing experience. Gentil (2011) hypothesized that if sociocultural expectations in realizing the L2 genre differ from the L1 genre, knowledge of the L1 genre is of limited use for learners writing in L2, even if learners have sufficient L2 proficiency and adequate L1 genre knowledge.

Third, there are clearly individual differences between L1 and L2 learners and also among L2 learners. Individual differences such as motivation, attitudes to learning an L2, learning strategies and styles, etc., play an important role in learners' acquisition of writing in an L2. Ong (2015), for example, found that China EFL learners' interest level in writing an essay, familiarity with and self-efficacy in writing various genres, and gender explained 25% of the learners' writing ability variance and that gender was highly significant, and interest level in writing an essay was marginally significant, but familiarity with and self-efficacy in writing various genres were not significant.

Fourth, and finally, in the design and implementation of the genre-based writing approach, teachers should consider learners' age, L2 proficiency, L2 writing ability, language needs, task variables, and motivation, and how the variables affect processes of writing and text quality. Here are some suggestions:

- More scaffolding and guided practice activities in building the context of texts and in modelling and deconstructing of texts can be provided for elementary or low L2 proficiency or low L2 writing ability learners. Teachers can reduce the amount of scaffolding and guided practice as learners develop their genre knowledge and writing skills. The ultimate goal is for learners to develop a sense of personal control over their learning-to-write processes.
- Based on learners' language needs, teachers can emphasize targeted lexicogrammatical features when they model and deconstruct texts.
- Teachers can select a wide range of in-class reading topics to meet the diverse interests of learners. Teachers can include authentic texts (e.g., advertising texts, newspaper, magazines, emails, blogs, and business reports) that learners read in their daily lives. These increase the value of writing.
- As task demand of writing different genres varies, teachers can teach learners easier genres such as recount, narrative, and procedural text before

proceeding to more difficult ones such as argumentative text, information report, and academic text. Recount and narrative texts coincide with the knowledge-telling writing strategy that automatically creates coherence in writing, but argumentative text requires learners to transform genre and topic knowledge (Bereiter & Scardamalia, 1987).
- In implementing writing tasks, teachers can consider how task variables influence processes of writing (Ong, 2014) and text quality (Ong & Zhang, 2010, 2013; 2013; Ong, 2013). When EFL learners were given ideas for writing an argumentative essay and a sample macro-structure of the essay, the frequency of metacognitive processes reported were lower in both the planning and writing stages compared to when they were not given any assistance. Specifically, the frequency of generation and organization of new ideas during the planning stage and the frequency of elaboration and organization of new ideas during the writing stage were lower (Ong, 2014). When EFL learners were given ideas for writing an argumentative essay and a sample macro-structure of the essay, they also produced overall better quality texts (Ong & Zhang, 2013), better quality of ideas (Ong, 2013), and higher lexical complexity but not fluency (Ong & Zhang, 2010). The implication drawn is that emphasizing the organizational structure of genres in the genre-based pedagogy benefits the processes and products of EFL writing (see also Chen & Su, 2012; Firkins, Forey, & Sengupta, 2007).
- Learners who prefer collaborative group work can be given more opportunities to jointly construct texts with their teachers and peers. Learners who prefer to write independently can be given more opportunities to independently construct texts. Over time, teachers can encourage learners who prefer to write independently to do more collaborative writing tasks and vice versa.

Conclusion

In this chapter, I adopted a think-aloud approach which mimics instructional discourse on modelling and deconstruction of texts. I highlighted the differences in the use of lexico-grammatical features of two sample advertising texts that learners can model and teachers can use in their practice. The demonstration of think-aloud offers learners and teachers an opportunity to view this important stage of the genre-based pedagogy (Firkins, Forey, & Sengupta, 2007; Hyland, 2007; Myskow & Gordon, 2010). I also reviewed recent research studies that looked into the genre-based approach to teaching EFL learners and offered some implications of the approach for Asian learners.

References

Bereiter, C., & Scardamalia, M. (1987). Knowledge telling and knowledge transforming in written composition. In S. Rosenberg (Ed.), *Advances in applied psycholinguistics* (pp. 142–175). Cambridge: Cambridge University Press.

The Blue Mountain brochure. Australia: The Aussie Tour.

Chen, Y., & Su, S. (2012). A genre-based approach to teaching EFL summary writing. *ELT Journal, 66*, 184–192.
Christie, F. (1998). Learning the literacies of primary and secondary schooling. In F. Christie & R. Misson (Eds.), *Literacy and schooling* (pp. 47–73). London: Routledge.
Christie, F. (2012a). Early childhood: The initial challenges of school learning. *Language Learning, 62*, 33–70.
Christie, F. (2012b). Late childhood to early adolescence: Some transitional years. *Language Learning, 62*, 71–104.
Christie, F. (2012c). The years of mid-adolescence: Dealing with abstract knowledge. *Language Learning, 62*, 105–148.
Christie, F., & Derewianka, B. (2008). A functional approach to writing development. In F. Christie & B. Derewianka (Eds.), *School discourse: Learning to write across the years of schooling* (pp. 1–29). New York: Continuum.
Christie, F., & Martin, J. R. (Eds.). (1997). *Genre in institutions: Social processes in the workplace and school*. New York: Continuum.
Derewianka, B. (1996). Language in later childhood. In C. Reynolds (Ed.), *Teaching about language: Learning about language* (pp. 62–85). Melbourne: AATE/NPDP.
Eggins, S. (1994). *An introduction to systemic functional linguistics*. London: Continuum.
Engler, C. S., Mariage, T. V., & Dunsmore, K. (2006). Tenets of sociocultural theory in writing instruction research. In C. A. MacArthur, S. Graham, & J. Fitzgerald (Eds.), *Handbook of writing research* (pp. 208–221). New York, London: The Guilford Press.
Feez, S. (1998). *Text-based syllabus design*. Sydney: McQuarie University/AMES.
Firkins, A., Forey, G., & Sengupta, S. (2007). Teaching writing to low proficiency EFL students. *ELT Journal, 61*, 341–352.
Flower, L. S., & Hayes, J. R. (1981). A cognitive process theory of writing. *College Composition and Communication, 32*, 365–387.
Gentil, G. (2011). A biliteracy agenda for genre research. *Journal of Second Language Writing, 20*, 6–23.
Halliday, M. A. K. (1994). *An introduction to functional grammar* (2nd edn.). London: Edward Arnold.
Hinkel, E. (2006). Current perspectives in teaching four skills. *TESOL Quarterly, 40*, 102–131.
Hyland, K. (2003). Genre-based pedagogies: A social response to process. *Journal of Second Language Writing, 12*, 17–29.
Hyland, K. (2004). *Genre and second language writing*. Ann Arbor, MI: University of Michigan Press.
Hyland, K. (2007). Genre pedagogy: Language, literacy and L2 writing instruction. *Journal of Second Language Writing, 16*, 148–164.
The Kaikoura brochure. Singapore: Chan Brothers.
Leki, I. (2011). Learning to write in a second language: Multilingual graduates and undergraduates expanding genre repertoires. In R. M. Manchon (Ed.), *Learning-to-write and writing-to-learn in an additional Language* (pp. 85–109). Amsterdam: John Benjamins.
Leki, I., Cumming, A., & Silva, T. (2008). *A synthesis of research on second language writing in English*. New York: Routledge.

Manchon, R. M., Roca de Larios, J., & Murphy, L. (2009). The temporal dimension and problem-solving nature of foreign language composing process: Implications for theory. In R. M. Manchon (Ed.), *Writing in foreign language contexts: Learning, teaching, and research* (pp. 102–129). New York: Multilingual Matters.

Martin, J. R. (1989). *Factual Writing: Exploring and challenging social reality.* Geelong, Victoria: Deakin University Press.

Martin, J. R., & White, P. R. R. (2005). *The language of evaluation: Appraisal in English.* London: Palgrave Macmillan.

Myskow, G., & Gordon, K. (2010). A focus on purpose: Using a genre approach in an EFL writing class. *ELT Journal, 64,* 283–292.

Ong, J. (2013). Discovery of ideas in second language writing. *System, 41,* 529–542.

Ong, J. (2014). How do formulation time and task conditions affect metacognitive processes of L2 writers? *Journal of Second Language Writing, 23,* 17–30.

Ong, J. (2015). Do individual differences matter to learners' writing ability? *Asian Journal of Applied Linguistics, 2,* 129–13.

Ong, J., & Zhang, J. (2010). Effects of task complexity on fluency and lexical complexity of EFL students' argumentative writing. *Journal of Second Language Writing, 19,* 218–233.

Ong, J., & Zhang, L. J. (2013). Effects of the manipulation of cognitive processes on English-as-a-Foreign-Language (EFL) writers' text quality. *TESOL Quarterly, 47,* 375–398.

Painter, C. (2001). Understanding genre and register: Implications and language teaching. In A. Burns & C. Coffin (Eds.), *Analysing English in a global context: A reader* (pp. 167–180). London, New York: Routledge.

Paltridge, B., Johns, A., Bawarshi, A., Coe, R., Hyland, K., Reiff, M., & Tardy, C. (2006). Crossing the boundaries of genre studies: Commentaries by experts. *Journal of Second Language Writing, 15,* 234–239.

Prior, P. (2006). A sociocultural theory of writing. In C. A., MacArthur, S. Graham, & J. Fitzgerald (Eds.), *Handbook of writing research* (pp. 54–66). New York: The Guilford Press.

Racelis, R. V., & Matsuda, P. K. (2013). Integrating process and genre into the second language writing classroom: Research into practice. *Language Teaching, 46,* 382–393.

Schleppegrell, M. J. (2004). Linguistic features of academic registers. In M. J. Schleppegrell (Ed.), *The language of schooling: A functional linguistics perspective* (pp. 43–76). Mahwah, NJ: Lawrence Erlbaum.

Tardy, C. M. (2009). *Building genre knowledge.* West Lafayette, IN: Parlor Press.

Tardy, C. M. (2011). The history and future of genre in second language writing. *Journal of Second Language Writing, 20,* 1–5.

Wei, R., & Su, J. (2012). The statistics of English in China. *English Today, 28,* 10–14.

Widodo, H. P. (2006). Designing a genre-based lesson plan for an academic writing course. *English Teaching: Practice and Critique, 5,* 173–199.

Yasuda, S. (2011). Genre-based tasks in foreign language writing: Developing writers' genre awareness, linguistic knowledge, and writing competence. *Journal of Second Language Writing, 20,* 111–133.

7 Teaching communicative vocabulary

Anna Siyanova-Chanturia and Paul Nation

Second language (L2) researchers, practitioners, and educators agree that mastering vocabulary is of great importance in becoming a mature language user. It is also one of the greatest challenges for a L2 learner. As Swan and Walter (1984, p. vii) put it, "Vocabulary acquisition is the largest and most important task facing the language learner." There is simply too much to learn in a limited period of time, with the opportunities to actually *use* the language, especially in communicative situations, being scarce. This chapter looks at the vocabulary and multi-word expressions (MWEs) needed to use the language communicatively and addresses a number of questions: How much vocabulary is needed for spoken language comprehension? What are MWEs and why are they important in communicative vocabulary teaching and learning? What is involved in teaching communicative vocabulary? What kind of communicative vocabulary activities can be used in and outside the classroom?

How much vocabulary is needed for spoken language comprehension?

> It has been proposed that an educated native speaker of English has a vocabulary of around 20,000 word families, or 32,000 vocabulary items (Goulden, Nation, & Read, 1990; Nation, 1990). However, these are relatively conservative estimates. According to some less modest ones, this number is around 50,000 vocabulary items.
>
> (Laufer, 2003)

A more important, and pedagogically interesting, question is not how much a native speaker, or a proficient non-native speaker may know – these are likely to be unrealistic goals for most L2 learners, especially in the English as a foreign language context (EFL) – but how much vocabulary is needed to engage in everyday activities in the target language, such as, for example, watching a movie or participating in a conversation. Nation (2006) found that, on average, 6,000–7,000 word families were needed to successfully deal with unscripted spoken language (which means gaining a coverage of 98%). Importantly, Nation (2006) also established that the greatest variation in vocabulary coverage occurs in the first 1,000-word families, which cover around 83% of spoken texts. The second 1,000-word families were found to account for 6% of spoken coverage, while the fourth and the fifth 1,000-word families were found to provide a mere 2% of spoken coverage.

The aforementioned figures highlight the value of high-frequency words in vocabulary learning. Evidently, the first 1,000-word families should be of primary focus in an English language-learning programme. Nation (2011) further points out that a considerable amount of spoken communication is possible even if a L2 learner knows far fewer than 6,000–7,000 English words. According to West (1960), the minimum vocabulary needed to converse over a range of topics in English is around 1,200 words (this figure, however, should be viewed as an initial goal).

Multi-word expressions: what are they and why are they important?

Thus far, we have talked about vocabulary in terms of *words*. However, our lexicon is not made up solely of single words (Siyanova, 2010; Siyanova-Chanturia, 2013; Siyanova-Chanturia & Martinez, 2014). MWEs, such as, collocations (*strong tea, do a favour, chicken wings*), multi-word verbs (*figure out, rely on, put up with*), idioms (*piece of cake, tie the knot, cost an arm and a leg*), binomials (*fish and chips, nice and easy, time and money*), speech formulas (*How's it going? What's up? No worries*), grammatical constructions (*the -er, the – er, this is X, these are Ys*), expletives (*Oh no! Damn it! What the hell!?*), and other multi-word items have been found to constitute around 28% of the spoken discourse analysed (Biber, Johansson, Leech, Conrad, & Finegan, 1999). On average, four such units are produced by a native speaker in every minute of spoken discourse (Pollio, Barlow, Fine, & Pollio, 1977). These figures suggest that MWEs (also known as formulaic sequences, prefabricated language, chunks, formulas, frequent phrases) are an important component of mature linguistic performance. Clearly, then, the focus in L2 communicative vocabulary teaching and learning should be not only on (single) words but also on a wide range of phrasal elements.

In addition to MWEs being an integral part of the mental lexicon, it is widely acknowledged that mastery of a word encompasses more than just knowing a word's form, meaning, and pronunciation (Nation, 1990; Richards, 1976). An important aspect of Richards's (1976) framework of word knowledge is that knowing a word also involves knowing the words that go with it – that is, its *collocates*. Richards (1976, p. 79) argues, "For many words we also 'know' the sorts of words most likely to be found associated with the word" – that is, knowledge of *collocation* assumes that on encountering the word *fruit* we can expect the words *ripe, green, sweet, bitter*, and for the word *meat* we might expect *tender, tough* (Richards, 1976).

Knowing which words collocate, or go together, with other words is important in order to sound idiomatic, or native-like (i.e., to achieve "nativelike selection" in the words of Pawley & Syder, 1983, p. 191). The appropriate use of a wide range of MWEs is considered to be a prerequisite for proficient language use (e.g., Wray, 2002). However, research has also shown that L2 learners often have problems with MWEs in their language (Nesselhauf, 2005; Siyanova & Schmitt, 2007, 2008). Researchers have suggested that L2 learners rely on creativity and make "overliberal assumptions about the collocational equivalence of semantically similar items" (Wray, 2002, pp. 201–202). That is, where words have a similar meaning, such as *heavy* and *strong*, learners are likely to assume their equally appropriate status, or mutual interchangeability, in collocations like *strong wind* and *heavy rain*. Although saying *heavy wind* or *strong rain* – rather than the more conventional *strong wind* and *heavy rain* – will not impede general comprehension and will not lead to a breakdown in conversation, these 'unidiomatic' instances will inevitably signal the nonnative-likeness of the speaker's vocabulary repertoire. Other instances of MWE misuse or avoidance may, indeed, lead to a breakdown in conversation (e.g., not knowing the conventional ways to greet or farewell, express feelings and emotions, show solidarity and sympathy, and other pragmatic aspects of MWE use; see the following text). Foster (2001) proposed that L2 learners, unlike native speakers, construct a large proportion of their language from rules rather than lexicalised or prefabricated routines, such as MWEs. That is, they learn words individually, out of context, without paying attention to their immediate environment, and, when trying to produce an MWE, such as a collocation, learners may combine words that do not normally go together (e.g., *heavy + wind* and *strong + rain*). These unexpected or infrequent word combinations can be perceived as atypical, making the learners less effective communicators and hindering their acceptance into the speech community.

We have so far argued that MWEs are important because (1) they constitute a large proportion of native-speaker discourse; (2) they are a necessary component of Richards's (1976) and Nation's (1990) frameworks of word knowledge; (3) their appropriate idiomatic use is a prerequisite for native-like performance. There are, however, other reasons why MWEs are an important aspect of communicative vocabulary knowledge and why such phrasal units should be taught.

Research suggests that using MWEs may be a quick way of developing fluency, particularly in the early stages of language learning (Wood, 2002). Wood (2002) argues that speech fluency lies in the control of a large number of MWEs and that many familiar concepts and speech acts can (and should) be expressed formulaically. That is, if a speaker can pull MWEs readily from memory as chunks, fluency can be enhanced. This process of 'chunking' is believed to reduce the amount of planning, processing, and encoding required, and "gives the speaker time to pay attention to the multitude of other tasks necessary while speaking, such as generating specific lexical items, planning the next unit of discourse, syntactic processing of novel pieces, and so on" (Wood, 2002, p. 7). Thus the key to speech fluency in a L2 may partially lie in the amassing and regular use of a rich repertoire of MWEs.

Finally, researchers have pointed out an important link between MWEs and pragmatic linguistic competence (and, correspondingly, performance). According to Coulmas (1979), MWEs provide the verbal means for a wide range of conventional actions. As Wood (2002) further notes, specific situations provide specific contexts for the use of formulas, and only "an understanding of the relevant dimensions of certain social situations and their relative value guarantees understanding of the meanings of the formulas that are highly likely to occur in them" (p. 8). Wood's observations are based on the studies that looked at the functions of the various types of MWEs in communication such as that of Bygate (1988) who researched formulaic use in adult learner interactions. Bygate (1988) reports on a wide range of L2 formulas used in a variety of conversational contexts and for an array of pragmatic purposes. It is believed that the use of MWEs can help the learner (1) cope with the complexity of numerous social situations, (2) structure their discourse in an orderly and unambiguous way, and (3) attain a sense of group identity (Wood, 2002). The latter is particularly important in the English as a Second Language (ESL) context.

In sum, based on the evidence discussed thus far, a strong case can be made for the inclusion of MWEs in communicative language pedagogies and practices, and making them a core component of a vocabulary-learning programme.

Multi-word expressions, frequency, and vocabulary learning

It has long been acknowledged that one of the ways of quickly becoming fluent in the language (or at least some aspects of it) is to memorise a range of useful MWEs (Nation, 2011; Palmer, 1925). The type and number of MWEs will depend on the learner's immediate needs (Nation, 2011). For example, for learners who want to learn some basic vocabulary in order to stay in an English-speaking country for a short period of time, Nation and Crabbe (1991) devised a 120-item list of words and phrases (which includes phrases such as *excuse me, how much does that cost? where is the toilet? thank you*, and so on). This survival vocabulary has been translated into several languages, available from Paul Nation's website (www.victoria.ac.nz/lals/staff/paul-nation/nation.aspx). This basic vocabulary can be learnt in a few hours over several days, and for a small investment of learning effort, it can give L2 learners a large return in communicative use (Nation, 2011). Whether or not L2 learners intend to spend a period of time in an L2 country, one of the ways in which teachers can help learners gain fluency in the early stages of L2 development is to encourage them to memorise commonly used MWEs, such as those in Nation and Crabbe (1991), as well as other frequent phrases. For example, Shin and Nation (2008) identified the most frequent MWEs in spoken English using the spoken section of the British National Corpus. Table 7.1 contains the 30 most frequent items from this study.

As can be seen from Table 7.1, the most frequent MWEs in spoken English comprise a variety of phrases: speech routines, discourse markers, verbs, collocations, lexical bundles, and so on. In addition, their length and (semi-)fixedness vary from two words (e.g., *thank you*) to longer constructions with slots to be filled (e.g., *(about) (No.) percent (of sth)*). What unites them is that they are very

Table 7.1 The most frequent MWEs in spoken English (Adapted from Shin & Nation, 2008)

1	you know	16	at the moment
2	I think (that)	17	a little bit
3	a bit	18	looking at (sth)
4	(always, never) used to {INF}	19	this morning
5	as well	20	(not) any more
6	a lot of {N}	21	come on
7	(No.) pounds	22	number {No.}
8	thank you	23	come in (swe, sth)
9	(No.) years	24	come back
10	in fact	25	have a look
11	very much	26	in terms of {sth}
12	(No.) pound	27	last year
13	talking about (sth)	28	so much
14	(about) (No.) percent (of sth), in sth, on (sth), for (sth)	29	{No.} years ago
15	I suppose (that)	30	{Det-the, this, a} county council

frequent in spoken English (e.g., the most frequent MWE *you know* was found to occur a staggering 27,348 times in 10 million running words). It is these and other frequent MWEs that teachers should focus on and should encourage their learners to learn and use.

It is noteworthy, however, that care should be taken when choosing items from the list (Shin & Nation, 2008). Specifically, teachers should bear in mind that the reference corpus used in the study represents both colloquial and formal British English produced by adult speakers. On the one hand, items such as *{No.} pounds, {No.} pound* and *{Det-the, this, a} county council* suggest the strongly British (and somewhat formal) nature of the corpus, or, at least, parts of it. The authors argue that such items can be ignored, where, for example, English is taught outside the United Kingdom. On the other hand, items such as *you know, a bit,* and *come on* (as well as many others that appear further down the list: *mind you, I bet, hang on*) are very colloquial and may, thus, be best approached through learners identifying and learning them in longer stretches of naturalistic speech (and in the context of a range of communicative tasks, such as dialogues, pair and group work), rather than teaching them explicitly (e.g., through memorisation). Interestingly, greetings such as *Good morning, Good afternoon, Good evening,* and *How are you?* were not found in the top-100 phrases. This suggests that while frequency is a very important (perhaps, a major) factor to consider when choosing vocabulary to focus on in or outside the classroom, it is certainly not the only factor. Clearly, teachers should also use their intuition and judgment when selecting the target items (see Siyanova-Chanturia & Spina, 2015, for an overview of the research into the accuracy of native and non-native-speaker intuition in the context of MWEs). As Shin and Nation (2008) conclude, although frequency in the language is an important criterion for selecting vocabulary items, it is only one of several criteria along with others such as learner needs, difficulty, teachability, suitability for the age, proficiency level, and background of the learners in question. Nevertheless, having a list of the most frequent MWEs in spoken English is a useful reference point for course designers, teachers, and learners alike, in particular, in the context of communicative vocabulary teaching and learning.

Teaching communicative vocabulary: the four strands

While the nature of MWEs, their importance in L2 learning, and the fact that L2 learners often have problems with MWEs are well documented, there is little research on what can be done to help learners achieve greater "nativelike selection" (Pawley & Syder, 1983, p. 191) and improve their fluency and communicative competence. In the remainder of the chapter, we focus on a range of approaches, activities, and principles aimed at increasing L2 learners' awareness of and exposure to communicative vocabulary, including both single words and MWEs.

According to Nation (2007), the activities in a language course can be classified into four distinct strands: *meaning-focused input*, *meaning-focused output*, *language-focused learning*, and *fluency development*. The rationale behind the use of the four strands is the assumption that for learning to occur, it is useful to adopt a *holistic* view of the opportunities for learning in any language-teaching situation. In a well-designed course, it is argued, there should be an even balance of the four strands with similar amounts of time dedicated to each strand (Nation, 2007). Next we discuss each of the strands, focusing on a range of activities that can be used in the context of communicative vocabulary teaching and learning.

Meaning-focused input

The strand of meaning-focused input assumes the learning of a L2 primarily through two activities: listening and reading. As Nation (2007, 2011) argues, these activities provide learners with the opportunity to learn vocabulary items *incidentally*, gradually increasing the breadth and depth of knowledge of single words and MWEs. Because listening comprehension is a key part in any spoken communicative activity, the meaning-focused input strand is especially important when preparing learners for spoken interaction. Classroom activities that can be used in the context of the meaning-focused input strand are listening to stories that are read aloud by the teacher or other L2 learners, participating in communicative activities (role plays, dialogues, presentations) as well as reading. However, there is a limit to how much time can be dedicated to vocabulary learning in the classroom. It may, therefore, be of considerable value to encourage L2 learners to engage in extracurricular out-of-classroom activities that promote the acquisition of new vocabulary. As Nation (2001) notes, opportunities for *indirect* vocabulary learning should occupy much more time in a language course than direct vocabulary learning activities. Such activities may, for example, include *extensive reading* and *extensive listening*.

Extensive reading can be used as a useful activity outside the classroom, both in the EFL and ESL contexts. Researchers have long acknowledged an important role of reading in vocabulary learning owing to repeated encounters with the same word over the course of reading (Day & Bamford, 2002; Pigada & Schmitt, 2006). Indeed, according to Nation's (2001) principles of vocabulary teaching, spaced repeated exposures are a necessary prerequisite for vocabulary learning. In addition, it also provides the learners with the opportunity to meet words in their *contexts of use*.

Researchers have proposed that for extensive reading to be effective, a number of conditions need to be met. For example, Day and Bamford (2002) put forward ten principles for an extensive reading approach: the reading material is easy; a variety of reading material on a wide range of topics must be available; learners choose what they want to read; learners read as much as possible; the purpose of reading is usually related to pleasure, information, and general understanding; reading is its own reward; reading speed is usually faster rather than slower; reading is individual and silent; teachers orient and guide students; and the teacher is a role model of a reader.

It, thus, appears that the key to extensive reading success is that the material contains mostly high-frequency familiar words, with only a very small proportion of new words or MWEs. In addition, learners should read for pleasure, and they should do so on a regular basis. Nation and Wang (1999) suggest that learners need to read one book per week in order to meet repetitions of a new word or MWE soon enough to reinforce the previous meeting. One of the most useful jobs that a teacher can do is to encourage the learners to engage in extensive reading. After all, as Nation (2001) points out, reading may be one of the few options for out-of-class vocabulary development for some learners (e.g., EFL learners).

Extensive listening, such as, watching *television*, is another extracurricular out-of-class activity that has been shown to lead to vocabulary learning (Koolstra & Beentjes, 1999; Lin, 2014; Meinhof, 1998). Nurweni and Read (1999) recommend promoting watching English-language television programmes outside the classroom. However, as Lin and Siyanova-Chanturia (2014) argue, access to North American, British, Australian, or New Zealand television programmes is not always easy. Satellite television can be expensive for an ordinary household, which means that the only practical way of accessing it may be the school library or self-access, language-learning centre. Evidently, this implies certain limitations in terms of where and when, as well as a limited choice of programmes. These authors point out, however, that *Internet television* can overcome most of these problems. They argue that EFL learners can take Internet television with them and watch it wherever they wish (while commuting, at home, at university). Internet television is accessible with a few clicks on an Internet-enabled smartphone (or another mobile devise), which means that learners can receive authentic input even if they only have a few minutes on a train (Lin & Siyanova-Chanturia, 2014).

According to Lin and Siyanova-Chanturia (2014), the following principles demonstrate the potential of Internet television, especially, in the context of communicative vocabulary learning: learners receive extensive exposure to English; learners have the opportunity to observe everyday English; watching television facilitates contextual vocabulary acquisition. Thus extensive listening via watching television is not unlike extensive reading. However, there are some differences that teachers should be aware of when encouraging their learners to engage in one or the other activity. One of the principles of extensive reading is that it should be easy (Day & Bamford, 2002). Because watching (traditional or Internet) television puts emphasis on authentic (unmodified) input, this principle is unlikely to apply to extensive listening. Thus while extensive reading is suitable for any level (graded readers should be chosen according to the learners' proficiency level: beginner, intermediate, advanced), television programmes may only be suitable for more advanced learners. Even then, however, learners may need help and advice on how to make watching television a valuable learning experience. The following strategies, adapted from Lin and Siyanova-Chanturia (2014), may help guide EFL learners:

1 *Repeated viewing*: Repeated viewing leads to repeated encounters with a vocabulary item.
2 *Training on contextual vocabulary learning skills*: This will help learners acquire skills implicitly from watching television.
3 *Programme selection*: Lin (2014) found that television programmes in the factual, drama, and comedy categories were more representative of everyday English than programmes in the music, learning, and religion categories. The programmes should, thus, be chosen accordingly.
4 *Narrow viewing*: Viewing programmes on the same or similar theme is likely to provide multiple repetitions of vocabulary items and help learners accumulate vocabulary on a particular topic.
5 *Subtitles*: Subtitles can be used in the same language as the programme (*intralingual* subtitles), or in another language, such as learners' first language (L1; *interlingual* subtitles).

Overall, researchers agree that extensive reading and extensive listening can be useful activities, promoting learner autonomy and enhancing indirect vocabulary learning.

The *key principles* of the meaning-focused input strand are as follows:

- vocabulary learning happens through reading and listening
- material is mostly familiar to the learners
- learners engage in reading and watching/listening for pleasure
- learning is aided by the use of context and cumulative background knowledge
- opportunities for large amounts of input (hence *extensive* reading and *extensive* listening) are available

Meaning-focused output

While the strand of meaning-focused input centres on the *receptive* skills of a learner – that is, language comprehension – the strand of meaning-focused output focuses on language *production*. It has been proposed that L2 learners may be unwilling to use vocabulary items they are unsure about, or those they may be able to comprehend but not necessarily produce correctly (this particularly applies to certain MWEs, such as phrasal verbs, collocations, and idioms that are more likely to be known receptively than productively). Therefore, meaning-focused output activities should build on meaning-focused input and previous deliberate learning (Nation, 2011). Meaning-focused output activities include speaking activities that draw on written input. For example, retelling activities, ranking activities, role-play activities, problem-solving activities, and activities that involve negotiation for meaning in pairs or small groups (Joe, Nation, & Newton, 1996). As Nation (2011) argues, if the task sheet contains some words and MWEs that are new to the learners but essential for the activity, a speaking activity can provide excellent opportunities for vocabulary learning. However, the new words and MWEs should be few, and the focus should be on high-frequency items (e.g., words from the first two 1,000-word families, see Nation, 2006 as well as MWEs from Shin & Nation, 2008 and other MWE frequency lists).

Nation (2011) recommends following the following guidelines when designing communicative activities within the strand of meaning-focused output:

1. *Amount of written input*: Learners should be provided with plenty of material on the handout or task sheet. It is recommended to include some new material (words or MWEs), although these should be few.
2. *Procedures*: It is important to include an element of repetition in the task. The target material should be repeated a number of times during the task.
3. *Creative use*: Learners should be encouraged to use the material in new contexts (i.e., they should not repeat the original contexts as they appeared on the handout/task sheet verbatim).
4. *Deliberate attention*: Learners' attention should be drawn to the new vocabulary items.

These guidelines can be applied to a range of communicative tasks, such as, ranking, problem solving, retelling, role-playing, and so on. For example, by following these guidelines, the commonly used task of *retelling* can be carried out as follows:

1. *Amount of written input*: The material can be newspaper and magazine articles and reports. There should be at least one article or report per learner. Ideally, the learners should be able to choose the text they want to retell (but different learners should choose different texts).
2. *Procedures*: The point is to retell the piece to a number of people. This will ensure repetition of the target material.

3   *Creative use*: The point now is to retell the same story from a different perspective, slightly modifying events, characters, and places (i.e., retelling the story not from the perceptive of the author of the text but, for example, from the perspective of one of the characters, witnesses).
4   *Deliberate attention*: A task can be added to make sure the listeners are not passive listeners but active participants in the task (e.g., they can ask questions, ask the speaker to repeat something, express their attitudes towards the story).

The *key principles* of the meaning-focused output strand are as follows:

- new vocabulary items are learned through speaking
- material is mostly familiar to the learners
- learners draw on a range of communicative strategies such as dictionary use or use of contextual cues
- opportunities for speaking are plentiful
- learners work in pairs or small groups

Language-focused learning

The strand of language-focused learning is meant to engage the students in the *deliberate* study of language features, such as pronunciation, vocabulary, grammar, and discourse. Some of the techniques for vocabulary learning are word cards, flashcard software, and vocabulary notebooks (Nation, 2001, 2008, 2013). *Word cards*, which are cards with a L2 word on one side and the L1 equivalent on the other, have been shown to be particularly useful in deliberate vocabulary learning. Nation (2001) defines 'learning from word cards' as the formation of associations between a foreign word *form* and its *meaning* (which could be a L1 translation, L2 definition, or picture). There is a long history of research on the use of word cards in vocabulary teaching and learning (Mondria & Mondria-de Vries, 1994; Nation, 1982, 2001, 2013). Research suggests that this technique (1) is efficient in terms of return for time and effort, (2) allows learners to focus on an aspect of word knowledge that is not easily gained from the use of contextual cues or dictionary use, and (3) allows L2 learners to control the amount of repetition (Nation, 2001). In addition, the knowledge gained through the use of word cards has been argued to be the kind of knowledge necessary for typical language use (Elgort, 2007).

Word cards have traditionally been used with words as the target vocabulary. However, they can also be useful in the learning of MWEs. Recent years have seen attempts to incorporate the use of word cards in classroom learning of chunks and phrases (e.g., Noonan, 2010). In addition, laboratory-based research has shown that some kinds of MWEs, such as idioms, can be successfully learnt using a paired-associate paradigm (e.g., Steinel, Hulstijn, & Steinel, 2007). The principle behind this paradigm is not unlike the principle behind the use of word cards – that is, the formation of association(s) between the form and meaning.

Another useful technique is recording new words and MWEs. Teachers may encourage their students to record new vocabulary items in a number of different ways – in boxes, word maps, and so on. It is particularly a good idea to keep a word or MWE *notebook* and add new items as the learners come across them in texts, during lessons, or when doing homework. Learners may find it helpful to categorise new items. For example, they can do so according to the type (e.g., part of speech), or based on the topic (hobbies, food and drink, school, home and family, sport, weather, and so on). It is important for the learners to revise and revisit the words and phrases in their notebooks on a regular basis as well as add new items as they encounter them in their input.

The *key principles* of the language-focused learning strand are as follows:

- focus is on deliberate learning of language features
- vocabulary learning is aided by the use of word cards, reading, writing, and translation
- focus is on form

Fluency development

The fourth and final strand is that of fluency development, which is particularly important in the context of communicative language learning. This strand does not involve the learning of new language features or vocabulary items. Instead, it focuses on becoming fluent in using what the learner already knows. For example, it is important to be able to process certain kinds of information fluently such as numbers (e.g., time, price), days of the week, months, other 'time' words, greetings and farewells, and so on. This fluency practice is best done in pairs or small groups with one learner leading the activity, although it can also be done in larger groups as a teacher-led activity (Nation, 2011).

One of the most effective activities for spoken L2 fluency development is the *4/3/2 technique* that involves repetitive reception and production of the same material (Nation, 2007, 2011). In the 4/3/2 technique, the learners work in pairs or triads with one learner speaking on a familiar topic for four minutes and the other learner(s) listening to the speaker. The pairs or triads change partners such that each speaker has a new partner(s) to whom they now deliver the same talk – this time, in three minutes. The pairs or triads change the partners again, and the same speaker now delivers the same talk in two minutes. The logic behind this activity is that the less time the speaker has to give a talk, the faster (more fluent) their speech will be. In other words, the talk delivered in two minutes should be more fluent and should contain fewer and shorter pauses than the same talk delivered in three or four minutes. The speakers within pairs or triads rotate until all the learners have delivered their talks three times: in four, three, and two minutes.

Research into the effectiveness of the 4/3/2 technique has showed a significant increase in speakers' rates as measured by words per minute as well as significant improvements in the quality of the speech such as fewer and shorter hesitations and pauses, and increases in grammatical accuracy and grammatical complexity (Arevart & Nation, 1991; Nation, 1989). The fact that both *quantitative* and *qualitative* improvements have been observed supports the use of the 4/3/2 technique in ESL and EFL classrooms as a useful activity for the development of L2 fluency (and, possibly, accuracy, as reported in Nation, 1989).

Particularly important, in the context of fluency development, are MWEs, which have been linked to a quick way of developing fluency (Wood, 2002). This is because operating with larger units (as opposed to single words) that are retrieved readily from memory as chunks may enhance the speaker's perceived fluency. The process of 'chunking' is believed to reduce the amount of planning, processing, and encoding needed for language comprehension and production (Wood, 2002). Thus one of the important features of fluent speech in an L2 (just as it is in a L1) is believed to be the knowledge and use of a variety of MWEs.

A useful task that can help raise awareness of MWEs in speech is *shadowing*. As Wood (2002) argues, shadowing is most valuable for dealing with spoken discourse. In this communicative task, L2 learners are encouraged to imitate the performance (fluency and intonation) of a native or highly proficient speaker. Students read aloud a piece of text with the help of a transcript provided by the teacher, while listening to a recording of the same excerpt. The excerpt normally contains a variety of MWEs. Given the abundance of MWEs in everyday language, it should not be difficult to find a suitable authentic text with instances of various MWEs. Students are encouraged to repeat the task until they are certain they have mastered the target phrases. Special attention is paid to the pronunciation and fluency of the MWEs, as well as the suprasegmental aspects, such as intonation contours and variations in speed. The students then perform their own reading aloud. Shadowing tasks, rich in high frequency and, hence, useful for communicative purposes MWEs, can help raise learners' awareness of the presence of larger chunks in language and improve their production in real-time speech (Wood, 2002).

The *key principles* of the fluency-development strand are thus:

- learners work with high-frequency, familiar material
- focus is on fluency (i.e., speed) rather than accuracy
- learner output is fast paced, free of hesitations and pauses
- focus is on listening and speaking
- opportunities for large amounts of input and output are available

Conclusion

This chapter has raised a number of issues with respect to vocabulary teaching and learning. Specifically, we have looked at the vocabulary needed to use the language communicatively. We have also introduced MWEs and presented the case for their key role in the development of fluency, pragmatic knowledge, and native-like selection. Critically, this chapter has argued that a language course should seek to employ and integrate the four strands of meaning-focused input, meaning-focused output, language-focused learning, and fluency development. The four strands are important in their distinct contributions to speaking and vocabulary development. One of the aims of the chapter was to show how teachers can design and use activities to aid vocabulary learning. The chapter has covered a range of activities that can be used as part of a four-strand approach to communicative vocabulary teaching and learning, both in and outside the classroom. We have maintained that vocabulary needs to be integrated into a variety of language use activities that draw on all four strands. All in all, the present chapter has provided a strong case for the inclusion of the communicative vocabulary component into institutional vocabulary-learning programmes.

References

Arevart, S., & Nation, I. S. P. (1991). Fluency improvement in a second language. *RELC Journal, 22,* 84–94.

Biber, D., Johansson, S., Leech, G., Conrad, S., & Finegan, E. (1999). *Longman grammar of spoken and written English.* Harlow: Longman.

British National Corpus – World edition, CD-ROM. (2000). Oxford: Humanities Computing Unit of Oxford University.

Bygate, M. (1988). Units of oral expression and language learning in small group interaction. *Applied Linguistics, 9*(1), 59–82.

Coulmas, F. (1979). On the sociolinguistic relevance of routine formulae. *Journal of Pragmatics, 3,* 239–266.

Day, R., & Bamford, J. (2002). Top ten principles for teaching extensive reading. *Reading in a Foreign Language, 14*(2), 136–141.

Elgort, I. (2007). The role of intentional decontextualised learning in second language vocabulary acquisition: Evidence from primed lexical decision tasks with advanced bilinguals (Unpublished PhD thesis). Victoria University of Wellington.

Foster, P. (2001). Rules and routines: A consideration of their role in the task-based language production of native and non-native speakers. In M. Bygate, P. Skehan, & M. Swain (Eds.), *Researching pedagogic tasks: Second language learning, teaching and testing* (pp. 75–93). Harlow: Longman.

Goulden R., Nation P., & Read, J. (1990). How large can a receptive vocabulary be? *Applied Linguistics, 11,* 341–363.

Joe, A., Nation, P., & Newton, J. (1996). Vocabulary learning and speaking activities. *English Teaching Forum, 34*(1), 2–7.

Koolstra, C., & Beentjes, W. (1999). Children's vocabulary acquisition in a foreign language through watching subtitled television at home. *Educational Technology, Research, and Development, 47,* 51–60.

Laufer, B. (2003). Vocabulary acquisition in a second language: Do learners really acquire most vocabulary by reading? *Canadian Modern Language Review, 59,* 565–585.

Lin, P. M. S. (2014). Investigating the validity of internet television as a resource for acquiring L2 formulaic sequences. *System, 42*(1), 164–176.

Lin, P. M. S., & Siyanova-Chanturia, A. (2014). Internet television for L2 learning. In D. Nunan & J. C. Richards (Eds.), *Language learning beyond the classroom* (pp. 149–158). London: Routledge.

Meinhof, U. H. (1998). *Language learning in the age of satellite television*. Oxford: Oxford University Press.
Mondria, J-A., & Mondria-de Vries, S. (1994). Efficiently memorizing words with the help of word cards and "hand computer": Theory and applications. *System, 22*(1), 47–57.
Nation, I. S. P. (1982). Beginning to learn foreign vocabulary: A review of the research. *RELC Journal, 13*, 14–36.
Nation, I. S. P. (1989). Improving speaking fluency. *System, 17*, 377–384.
Nation, I. S. P. (1990). *Teaching and learning vocabulary*. New York: Heinle and Heinle.
Nation, I. S. P. (2001). *Learning vocabulary in another language*. Cambridge: Cambridge University Press.
Nation, I. S. P. (2006). How large a vocabulary is needed for reading and listening. *The Canadian Modern Language Review, 63*(1), 59–82.
Nation, I. S. P. (2007). The four strands. *Innovation in Language Learning and Teaching, 1*(1), 1–12.
Nation, I. S. P. (2008). *Teaching vocabulary: Strategies and techniques*. Boston, MA: Heinle Cengage Learning.
Nation, I. S. P. (2011). Teaching communicative and interactive vocabulary for EFL learners. In H. P. Widodo & A. Cirocki (Eds.), *Innovation and creativity in ELT methodology* (pp. 135–144). New York: Nova Science Publishers.
Nation, I. S. P. (2013). *Learning vocabulary in another language* (2nd edn.). Cambridge: Cambridge University Press.
Nation, I. S. P., & Crabbe, D. (1991). A survival language learning syllabus for foreign travel. *System, 19*, 191–201.
Nation, I. S. P., & Wang, K. (1999). Graded readers and vocabulary. *Reading in a Foreign Language, 12*, 355–380.
Nesselhauf, N. (2005). *Collocations in a learner corpus*. Amsterdam: John Benjamins.
Noonan, A. (2010). Developing learners' lexicon through vocabulary cards. *MA TESOL Collection*. Paper 478.
Nurweni, A., & Read, J. (1999). The English vocabulary knowledge of Indonesian university students. *English for Specific Purposes, 18*, 161–175.
Palmer, H. E. (1999 [1925]). Conversation. In R. C. Smith (Ed.), *The writings of Harold E. Palmer: An overview* (pp. 185–191). Tokyo: Hon-no-Tomosha.
Pawley, A., & Syder, F. H. (1983). Two puzzles for linguistic theory: Nativelike selection and nativelike fluency. In J. C. Richards & R. W. Schmidt (Eds.), *Language and communication* (pp. 191–126). New York: Longman.
Pigada, M., & Schmitt, N. (2006). Vocabulary acquisition from extensive reading: A case study. *Reading in a Foreign Language, 18*(1), 1–28.
Pollio, H., Barlow, J., Fine, H., & Pollio, M. (1977). *Psychology and the poetics of growth: Figurative language in psychology, psychotherapy, and education*. Mahwah, NJ: Lawrence Erlbaum.
Richards, J. C. (1976). The role of vocabulary teaching. *TESOL Quarterly, 10*, 77–89.
Shin, D., & Nation, I. S. P. (2008). Beyond single words: The most frequent collocations in spoken English. *ELT Journal, 62*, 339–348.
Siyanova-Chanturia, A. (2010). On-line processing of multi-word sequences in a first and second language: Evidence from eye-tracking and ERP (Unpublished PhD thesis). The University of Nottingham.

Siyanova-Chanturia, A. (2013). Eye-tracking and ERPs in multi-word expression research: A state-of-the-art review of the method and findings. *The Mental Lexicon*, *8*, 245–268.
Siyanova-Chanturia, A., & Martinez, R. (2014). The idiom principle revisited. *Applied Linguistics*, *36*(5), 549–569. doi: 10.1093/applin/amt054
Siyanova-Chanturia, A., & Schmitt, N. (2007). Native and nonnative use of multi-word vs. one-word verbs. *International Review of Applied Linguistics*, *45*, 119–139.
Siyanova-Chanturia, A., & Schmitt, N. (2008). L2 learner production and processing of collocation: A multi-study perspective. *Canadian Modern Language Review*, *64*, 429–458.
Siyanova-Chanturia, A., & Spina, S. (2015). Investigation of native speaker and second language learner intuition of collocation frequency. *Language Learning*, *65*(3), 533–562.
Steinel, M. P., Hulstijn, J. H., & Steinel, W. (2007). Second language idiom learning in a paired-associate paradigm: Effects of direction of learning, direction of testing, idiom imageability, and idiom transparency. *Studies in Second Language Acquisition*, *29*, 449–484.
Swan, M., & Walter, C. (1984). *The Cambridge English course*, I, (Teacher's Book). Cambridge: Cambridge University Press.
West, M. (1953). *A general service list of English words*. London: Longman, Green & Co.
West, M. (1960). *Teaching English in Difficult Circumstances*. London: Longman.
Wood, D. (2002). Formulaic language in acquisition and production: Implications for teaching. *TESL Canada Journal*, *20*(1), 1–15.
Wray, A. (2002). *Formulaic language and the lexicon*. Cambridge: Cambridge University Press.

8 What EFL teachers should know about online grammar tasks

Reima Al-Jarf

English as a foreign or second language (EFL or ESL) teachers generally believe that the formal study of grammar is essential to the eventual mastery of a foreign or second language (L2) when language learning is limited to the classroom (Thu, 2009). However, teachers and students around the world feel that grammar constitutes a major difficulty in teaching and learning of a second/foreign language. For example in Oman, Al-Mekhlafi and Nagaratnam (2011) reported that teachers, as well as students, face difficulties regarding grammar instruction in EFL. In Greece, results of a needs analysis by Xenodohidis (2002) revealed that most of the students majoring in computer science mainly needed grammar, syntax, and speaking, as well as computing vocabulary, to be able to comprehend specific computing texts and to be better qualified for their careers. Half of the students rated grammar as a problem. In Iran, EFL college students have many grammatical problems when writing in English, the most prominent of which are the use of prepositions, concord, articles, distribution of verb groups, and tenses. To a lesser degree, they have problems in using relative clauses and plural morphemes (Golshan & Karbalaei, 2009). Other studies have shown specific problems that students have in learning L2 grammar such as the improper use of prepositions by EFL Jordanian Arab learners, even at advanced stages of learning (Tahaineh, 2010).

Difficulties in L2 grammar, as Xenodohidis (2002) found, may be attributed to the rare use of language in everyday life and at work, and to the lack of exposure to EFL, especially for older students. To overcome difficulties in learning L2 grammar, both teachers and students indicated that practice is of crucial importance to grammar learning (Thu, 2009). ESL learners also need explicit help to improve the grammatical accuracy of their writing (Hegelheimer, 2006).

With the latest developments in information and communication technology, more and more instructors around the world are seeking to enhance their language instruction through activities and experiences made available through technology. Many have integrated a variety of technologies in the teaching of grammar in foreign and L2 learning environments such as websites and CD-ROM virtual environments (Bowen, 1999); Cyber Tutor, which allows students to annotate sentences and provides them with instant feedback and help facilities (McEnery & Others, 1995); and Learning English Electronically computer software, which consisted of 43 lessons emphasizing grammar concepts and accurate sentence structure, and covering topics such as employment, food, health, school, and transportation (Schnackenberg, 1997).

In addition, explicit, implicit, and exploratory grammar teaching approaches that use word processing packages, electronic dictionaries and grammars, the World Wide Web, concordances, electronic mail, computer games/simulations, and authoring aids were combined to overcome the 'grammar deficit' seen in many British undergraduate students learning German (Hall, 1998). In addition, an interactive messaging system set up on the Internet enabled teachers of English in Hong Kong to discuss language-related issues as part of the TeleNex teacher-support network. Grammatical explanations based on the analysis of corpus data were routinely used to answer teachers' queries (Tyrwhitt-Drake, 1999). In another study, Hegelheimer (2006) used the *iWRITE* program, a prototype of a corpus-based, database-driven online grammar/writing resource for intermediate learners of English. This online resource was intended to improve advanced-level ESL learners' writing by increasing their grammatical awareness and their ability to correct grammatical errors in their own writing.

Moreover, several other prior studies have shown that the integration of technology proved to be effective in the teaching and learning of L2 grammar. For example, computer-assisted and web-based grammar teaching helped instructors devote class time to teaching communication skills and individualizing course work (Beaudoin, 2004). Journalism teachers and students found the web-based *Targeted Approach to Grammar System*, a kind of grammar checker, useful for teaching and learning basic grammar (Henderson, 2002). Language learners in an intensive English program benefited from web-based materials in learning ESL grammar (Quesada, 2000). *My Sentence Builder*, a computer-assisted treatment program for the remediation of expressive-grammar deficits in children with specific language impairment, was found to be effective in addressing expressive-grammar difficulties in children (Washington, Warr-Leeper, & Thomas-Stonell, 2011).

Furthermore, in Saudi Arabia, an online course was used in the teaching of English grammar to EFL freshman students from home. Pretest mean scores showed significant differences between the experimental and control groups in their grammatical knowledge. Following online instruction with Nicenet (an Online Course Management System), comparisons of the posttest mean scores showed significant differences in students' achievement as a result of using the online course in teaching and learning grammar. The online course helped motivate the students and enhance their learning and mastery of English grammar (Al-Jarf, 2005).

At Brigham Young University's English Language Center, a web-based oral grammar assessment tool that enabled teachers to assess students' mastery of the grammatical structures covered in grammar classes was created. The project consisted of an online database of speaking tasks designed to target specific grammatical structures. Students and teachers reported that the project was beneficial in providing practice and self-assessment opportunities. Most students like using the program and considered it helpful (Torrie, 2007).

Similarly, a multimedia instructional grammar program was used by Adult ESL learners at a Midwest community college to facilitate the transition of declarative knowledge of the English passive voice to procedural knowledge. Grammar instruction was introduced in the context of American history and geography. Students with low prior knowledge of passive voice grammar concepts, intermediate level of general vocabulary, and adequate basic knowledge of content (basic geography and history) benefited most from the program (Koehler, Thompson, & Phye, 2011).

Finally, students learning Japanese at a US university produced a Japanese grammar quiz on the World Wide Web in which they employed a Common Gateway Interface (CGI) script to produce a simple, well-designed website consisting of multiple-choice questions and CGI-generated answers with concise explanations. The process of web-page production was highly motivating for the students and served as an effective review of L2 grammar rules in a constructive mode. With appropriate content adjustment, the same process can be easily replicated in L2 courses for learners of all proficiency levels (Fukushima, 2006).

Need for the study

At the College of Languages and Translation (COLT), King Saudi University (KSU), Riyadh, Saudi Arabia, the author conducted an exploratory study in which a needs assessment questionnaire-survey, with open-ended questions, was administered to a sample of EFL students in the first four levels of the English-Arabic translation program, and another questionnaire-survey was administered to a sample of EFL instructors at COLT who have taught grammar and writing to students in the first four levels. Results of the needs assessment questionnaires showed that Saudi EFL students had several difficulties in learning and applying English grammar rules. Students had many weaknesses in using verb tenses, articles, prepositions, complex sentences, word order, singular and plural noun forms, subject-verb agreement, indirect speech, question formation. They could not produce grammatically correct sentences in free writing. The students had negative attitudes towards learning English grammar and felt that English grammar was difficult to master, and it was difficult to remember so many rules and specific details. They indicated that they did not know how to study English grammar. When they did an exercise, they did not know whether their answers were correct or incorrect. When they wrote a paragraph or essay, they did not know whether their sentences were grammatically correct or not.

In addition, both students and instructors indicated that time allocated to the teaching of grammar was insufficient for covering all of the grammatical structures that the students needed for translation. Instructors were unable to cover all of the grammatical structures. Allocated time was insufficient for practice in class and for following up with the students in and out of class, and checking their homework. The Interactions and Mosaic grammar textbooks assigned by the department did not have sufficient exercises for practice. The students needed extra practice, help, guidance, and individualized feedback.

Aims of the chapter

Based on the findings of prior studies reported earlier and results of the student and teacher questionnaire-surveys, this chapter proposes the integration of Internet grammar websites with different types of online tasks in EFL grammar instruction as a supplement to in-class grammar instruction. Specifically, the study gives examples of grammar websites that target specific grammatical structures and show the types of online grammar tasks that students can perform on their own out of class and the instructional stages that can be followed. It also gives guidelines for selecting online grammar websites and performing online tasks.

Use of supplementary online grammar tasks provides additional opportunities for practicing and mastering English grammar by translation students at COLT. Helping students at COLT master English grammar is important for their success in the English language courses (listening, speaking, reading, and writing) that they take in the first four semesters of the translation program and in the subsequent specialized content courses (semantics, stylistics, text linguistics, and linguistics) that they take in semesters 5–10 of the program. It is also important for comprehending oral and written discourse in the translation and interpreting courses, the translation project, and the production of target texts.

Context

The translation program at COLT, KSU, Riyadh, Saudi Arabia is 10 semesters or 5 years long. In the first four semesters, the students take English language courses: four listening, four speaking, four reading, four writing, two vocabulary building, and three grammar courses. Only two hours per week are allocated to each grammar course. Students in levels I, II, and III study the following textbooks that are assigned by the department:

- **Grammar I textbook:** Kirn, E., & Jack, D. (2007). *Interactions I: Grammar*. Silver Ed. New York: McGraw-Hill Higher Education.
- **Grammar II textbook:** Werner, P. K., Nelson, J. P., Hyzer, K., & Church, M. M. (2008). *Interactions II: Grammar*. Silver Ed. New York: McGraw-Hill Higher Education.
- **Grammar III textbook:** Werner, P. K., & Nelson, J. P. (2007). *Mosaic 2: Grammar*, Silver Ed. New York: McGraw-Hill Higher Education.

In semester I (Grammar I), the students cover the following grammatical structures: *parts of speech, prepositions, prepositional phrases, transitive and intransitive verbs, linking verbs, regular and irregular verbs, adverb placement, information, tag, negative and yes-no questions, negatives, regular and irregular plurals, use of definite* and indefinite articles, pronouns, subject-verb agreement, nine tenses, modals, pronunciation of -ed, -s, and -es at the end of verbs and nouns, spelling of -ing, -ed, -es.

In semester II (Grammar II), the students cover the following grammatical structures: *the past perfect, types of verbs (transitive, intransitive, linking), the passive voice (with simple present, modal auxiliaries), the direct and reported speech, non-finite verbs, gerunds and infinitives, types of phrases, dangling and misplaced modifiers, and first and second conditionals.*

In semester III (Grammar III), the students cover the following structures: *clause with that: reported speech; clauses with embedded questions; statements and requests of urgency; clauses as subjects of sentences; reduction of noun clauses to infinitive phrases; adjective clauses: restrictive versus nonrestrictive clauses; adjective clauses: replacement of subjects and objects; other adjective clause constructions; reduction of adjective clauses to phrases; clauses and related structures of time: future, present, past, and unspecified time; and clauses and related structures of result.*

Materials and tasks

Selecting online grammar websites and tasks

The course instructor can search for and make a list of useful English grammar websites related to the grammatical structures to be covered in the course. He/she may assign weekly grammar websites to be checked by the students. Grammar websites selected should focus on a single grammatical structure such as *information questions, tag questions, negative questions, a single verb tense, a modal, complex sentences (noun, adjective, or adverb clauses), imperatives, exclamatory sentences, correlative conjunctions, phrasal verbs, prefixes and suffixes or singular and plural forms,* and so on. Websites selected should provide definitions, explanations, examples, and supplementary exercises for extra practice and provide students with instant feedback. When posting a website, a brief description of the website should be given, and the website should be checked to see if it is appropriate for the grammatical structure under study, if it matches the proficiency level of the students, and if it contains enough material and items. Several websites that target a particular grammatical structure should be posted to accommodate different proficiency levels, different learning styles, and several tasks (definition and explanation, practice, assessment, and remediation). Clear, specific, and detailed instructions on how a particular task should be performed should be given.

The students may search for grammar websites on their own by enclosing the topic of interest such as "*English tag questions*", "*English complex sentences*", or "*English phrasal verbs*" in quotation marks in the Google search box and by connecting search terms with Boolean operators such as: "*and, or, not*".

The instructor can use an online course, an online discussion forum, a blog, or a wiki to post the grammar websites, post the tasks, provide practice, hold the discussion, and provide interaction and feedback.

Based on a review of the literature on the effective practices in L2 grammar teaching and learning, the following guidelines for selecting and using online grammar websites and tasks can be followed:

Teach grammar explicitly: Thu (2009) reported that ESL teachers at an English language school in San Diego, California, generally believe that EFL grammar is best taught explicitly, not implicitly. Explicit grammar instruction leads to gains in grammatical knowledge and writing proficiency in first-year students of French at a UK university. It was also found to be a powerful approach in bringing about improvement in the students' grammatical knowledge and production tasks (Macaro & Masterman, 2006).

To teach grammar explicitly, Paesani (2005) suggested using literary texts as comprehensible, meaning-bearing input. Literary texts serve as a basis of the inductive presentation of new grammatical forms and as a springboard for communicative practice of these forms after explicit instruction. They provide learners with meaning-bearing input to assist their acquisition of grammatical forms, to raise their consciousness about the target language, to encourage meaningful communication among learners, and to develop skills and strategies in the reading of literary texts.

Teach grammar inductively or deductively: Results of studies by Haight, Herron, and Cole (2007) and Vogel, Herron, Cole, and York (2011) supported using a guided inductive instructional approach to teaching grammar in the beginning-level foreign language classroom. Results also indicated that students who preferred explanations of the rules performed better with a guided inductive approach. However, use of the deductive or inductive approach depends on the level of language structure complexity. AbuSeileek (2009) found that more complicated grammatical structures, such as complex and compound complex sentences, need to be taught deductively and that computer-based learning was functional for more complex and elaborate structures.

Contextualize grammar instruction: Meyer, Youga, and Flint-Ferguson (1990) argued that grammar instruction can be more effective if put in a realistic context. Patterson and Pipkin (2001) recommended the listing of traditional grammar websites, including online handbooks and style guides, but warned that the isolated teaching of grammar has little impact on student writing. They recommended that websites show teachers how to contextualize grammar instruction. In another study by Baturay, Daloglu, and Yildirim (2010), elementary-level English language learners enjoyed using WEBGRAM, a system designed to provide supplementary web-based grammar revision material and audiovisual aids to enrich the contextual presentation of grammar and allow them to revise target grammatical structures using interactive exercises such as gap-filling, combo-box, and drag-and-drop exercises.

Teach grammar communicatively: Benander and Roach (1995) indicated that grammar must be taught as a way to convey meaning, not as an isolated skill. Teaching grammar communicatively helped students show improvement in production and recognition skills. Students should be provided with opportunities to actively use their grammar skills in listening, speaking, reading, and writing activities rather than passively responding to an unfamiliar text or isolated sentences.

Integrate grammar instruction with reading and writing activities: Haddox (1998) and Weaver (1996) recommended the integration of grammar and writing with all levels and found that the teaching of grammar in the context of writing to be an effective and successful strategy.

Hegelheimer, Volker, and Fisher (2006) addressed the need for explicit grammar instruction as part of preparing students to write by using a collection of learner texts and transforming that collection into an online grammar resource for intermediate non-native speakers of English. The use of learner texts, online interactivity, and advanced technology (e.g., XML) facilitated the implementation of iWRITE, an approach to embodying aspects of L2 acquisition theory while taking advantage of the web's potential for interactivity.

Freshman students at a Midwestern university participated in a study that investigated the impact of an Internet-based program, designed to improve basic writing skills, on grammar and punctuation scores on an English Competency Test. Results indicated that the group that used the program in conjunction with correcting rough drafts of assigned papers had higher scores than the groups that did not use the program or used the program on its own. The students reported that the program had improved their skills (Mills, 2010).

Smoot (2001) taught "little grammar" – i.e., sentence structure, parts of speech, and usage – and "big grammar", such as essay structure, points of an argument, and rhetorical devices, to his seventh grade students through reading meaningful texts drawn from their history class.

Increase students' grammatical awareness and promote noticing: Hegelheimer (2006) found that ESL learners need explicit help to improve the grammatical accuracy of their writing by increasing their grammatical awareness and ability to correct grammatical errors in their own writing. Similarly, Fotos (1993) found task performance, specifically teacher-fronted grammar lessons and interactive grammar problem-solving tasks, to be effective as formal instruction in promoting grammar consciousness raising.

Focus on metalanguage: Thu (2009) reported that ESL teachers at an English language school in San Diego recommended that metalanguage be used with learners of all proficiency levels. Similarly, Fortune (2005) found that advanced learners use metalanguage much more often than their intermediate counterparts, and he concluded that metalanguage can play a facilitative role in focusing attention and deciding which form to use. Likewise, a positive relationship was also found between metalinguistic knowledge and facility with metalanguage as a result of rule verbalizations by EFL young adult Chinese learners exposed to large doses of explicit grammar instruction (Hu, 2011).

Use a task-based learning framework: Huang (2010) recommended the use of Willis' task-based learning framework in grammar instruction for adults.

Accommodate different learning styles: Beaudoin (2004) stressed the need for structure and adaptability to different learning styles (such as visual, auditory, and kinesthetic) in L2 grammar instruction.

Integrate exchanges between learners: Beaudoin (1998) gave some factors that should be taken into consideration in creating a website for teaching French grammar at the University of Alberta, Canada. Those included the integration of exchanges between learners and exchanges between learners and the virtual Francophone community and English-speaking community in the case of English.

Provide guidance: Toth (2008) compared results for task-based L2 Spanish grammar instruction conducted as whole-class, teacher-led versus small group, learner led. Results on grammaticality judgments and guided production tasks indicated a stronger performance for the teacher-led group on both tasks. To facilitate L2 learning, teachers should direct students' attention to target structures and provide procedural assistance for processing output.

Provide answers with concise explanations: Fukushima (2006) conducted an experiment in which students learning Japanese at a US university produced a Japanese grammar quiz on the World Wide Web. The subjects employed a CGI script to produce a simple, well-designed website consisting of multiple-choice questions and CGI-generated answers with concise explanations. The process of web-page production was highly motivating for the students and served as an effective review of L2 grammar rules in a constructive mode.

Provide ongoing training and technical support: Quesada (2000) asserted that students need ongoing training and technical support in using web-based materials.

Types of online grammar tasks

The grammar websites to be selected and used as a basis for performing online tasks should include the following:

Online self-assessment: Websites should provide pre- and post-instruction self-assessment, include self-grading and interactive grammar quizzes, accommodate the different proficiency levels, and help the students diagnose their weaknesses, as well as enable them to assess their mastery of a specific structure. The following are examples:

- Test Your English Level: www.world-english.org/test.htm
- Interactive Grammar Quizzes by level: http://englishmedialab.com/beginnerquizzes.html
- Grammar Quizzes by level: http://a4esl.org/

- English Assessment Test: http://englishenglish.com/englishtest.htm
- More Assessment Tests: www.world-english.org/english_assessment_tests.htm
- Self-grading grammar quizzes (Interactive Grammar Quizzes):

    www.esltower.com/grammarquizzes.html
    http://englishmedialab.com/beginnervideos.html

- Mixed Grammar Gap-Fill Quiz: www.world-english.org/archery.htm
- Passive Test: www.world-english.org/passive.htm
- Parts of Speech: www.eslus.com/LESSONS/GRAMMAR/POS/pos.htm
- Prepositions quiz: http://a4esl.org/q/j/ck/mc-prepositions.html
- Definite & Indefinite Articles (Quiz): www.learn4good.com/languages/evrd_grammar/article_ex.htm

Websites that explain grammar rules or provide definitions

- www.uottawa.ca/academic/arts/writcent/hypergrammar/partsp.html

Single-structure grammar exercises and practice

- English Articles (A, An, The): www.world-english.org/articles.htm
- Articles: www.usingenglish.com/glossary/definite-article.html
- Articles (explanation & exercise): www.englisch-hilfen.de/en/grammar_list/artikel.htm
- Prepositions and Articles: www.world-english.org/degrees_online.htm
- Prepositions (On, It, By, etc.): www.world-english.org/prepositions.htm
- Prepositional Phrases: www.world-english.org/prepositionalphrases.htm
- Preposition + Noun: www.world-english.org/prepositions3.htm
- Preposition + Adjective: www.world-english.org/adjective-preposition.htm
- Preposition + Gerund: www.world-english.org/gerundprep.htm
- Comparatives/Superlatives: www.world-english.org/comparatives.htm
- Conditionals: www.world-english.org/conditionals.htm
- Quantifiers: www.world-english.org/quantifiers.htm
- Adjective Placement: www.world-english.org/adjectiveplacement.htm
- Modal Verbs: www.world-english.org/modals.htm
- Conjunctions: www.world-english.org/conjunctions.htm
- Question Tags: www.world-english.org/questiontags.htm
- Questions (comprehensive): http://english-zone.com/index.php?ID=1
- Questions English zone/Grammar: http://english-zone.com/index.php?ID=30
- Gerund Or Infinitive: www.world-english.org/gerunds.htm
- Reported Speech: www.world-english.org/reportedspeech.htm
- Pronouns: www.world-english.org/pronouns.htm
- Nouns From Verbs: www.world-english.org/nounsfromverbs.htm

- For Or Since: www.world-english.org/fororsince.htm
- The Passive Voice: www.ef.com/english-resources/english-grammar/punctuation/
- Future Forms In English: www.world-english.org/future_english.htm
- Simple Present Or Present Continuous: www.world-english.org/simplepresentpresentcontinuous.htm
- English Verb Tense Tutorial: www.englishpage.com/verbpage/verbtenseintro.html
www.dailygrammar.com/mobile/archive.html
- Rewriting Sentences: www.world-english.org/sentencerewriting.htm

A daily grammar lesson

- www.englishforeveryone.org/Topics/Sentence-Correction.htm
- www.worldenglishclub.com/grammar/daily-grammar-lessons/pronouns-5

Error correction tasks

- Correcting Sentences: www.world-english.org/correctingsentences.htm
- Correct The Mistake: www.world-english.org/correct_mistakes.htm
- Correct Word Order: www.world-english.org/correct_word_order.htm
- englishmedialab.com/grammar.html
- www.grammarly.com/newhp/index-check- landing.php?q=grammar&gclid=CP3rv56ltqsCFagntAod-mlbcQ

Production tasks: The students can perform teacher-generated tasks such as the following:

- *Read the following story and then write 10 negative questions.*
- *Read the following paragraph and then write information questions beginning with 'when, what, where, who, whom, why, how, how far, how much, how old' and so on.*
- *Write a few sentences about what you have accomplished so far since the beginning of the semester. Use the present perfect tense as much as possible.*
- *What are you going to do during Hajj break? Use the future tense as much as possible.*
- *What are you going to do during your next summer holiday? Use the future tense as much as possible.*
- *What are you currently doing during your Ramadan break? List some activities that you are currently doing over the break. Use the present progressive as much as possible.*
- *Write a story or summarize a movie using the historical present.*

The tasks can also be based on Internet websites as in

- www.training2you.com/information/443.php

Remedial tasks

- Diagnostic Grammar Test: www.world-english.org/diagnostic_grammar.htm
- Grammar Basics: www.englishchick.com/grammar/
- Common Grammar and Usage Mistakes: www.englishchick.com/grammar/

Awareness-raising tasks: The students double-check their own essays and paragraphs or those written by their classmates by reviewing grammatical structures they have studied one by one. For example, they go through their own essay, underline verbs and then make sure each verb agrees with its subject. Then they go through all of the verbs, checking the tense and making sure each is conjugated correctly. They underline all of the nouns and double-check the plural forms and so on.

Metalinguistic awareness tasks: Students are provided with two or three paragraphs (long stretch of discourse rather than single sentences), each using a particular verb tense. The students underline the tense markers in each or highlight the subject in each. They examine the context in which each tense is used and the tense markers associated with each. They note subject-verb agreement and give explanations of when each tense is used – i.e., they verbalize the rule and context in which each tense is used. They can be asked to underline noun, adjective, and/or adverbial clauses, reduced clauses, defining and/or non-defining clauses, or passive structures in a text and give explanations and verbalize rules.

They can also be given a paragraph (a long stretch of discourse rather than single sentences) with blanks and asked to fill the gaps with articles and prepositions, correct the verb tense, and so on. They can be asked to verify and justify when they have to use the definite article and cases in which they do not, why a particular tense is used in a particular case and another one is used in another, or for using certain punctuation marks and so on.

Leveling-up tasks: "*Leveling-up*" refers to practicing English grammatical structures in an online language learning community. This can be done on websites such as SharedTalk.com, which is a community of people from all over the world dedicated to language exchange and language learning. Students may practice a grammatical structure orally through voice chat and may practice it in writing through text chat. According to SharedTalk.com, groups of two or more people exchange their knowledge of particular grammatical structure and help each other to practice it. The students practice with a native speaker, learn slang and informal expressions, ask their partners for explanations about a grammatical structure, and receive encouragement and support. Other websites for language exchange are Paltalk, Polyglot club.com, Skype, and Facebook.

Differentiation tasks: According to Tomlinson (2001), "*differentiation*" refers to providing students with different opportunities for acquiring content, processing, constructing, or making sense of ideas. It also involves developing teaching materials and assessment procedures to help all students learn effectively, regardless of differences in proficiency level. The teacher creates an environment that is structured, positive, and supportive for each student. For example, to practice using the '*future* or *past tense*', each student can write a paragraph about his/her future aspirations or a past event of interest to him/her and with which he/she is familiar. When grading the students' paragraphs, the instructor can focus on strong points, such as correct verb forms, and areas of improvement in each student and commend those. Then the instructor can point out one or two weaknesses, such as faulty irregular verb conjugations or faulty verb forms following *will*, for each student to work on. The instructor starts with the simplest to the more complex ones, depending on the student's competency level.

General grammar reference websites

- Irregular verbs: www.englishpage.com/irregularverbs/irregularverbs.html
- Regular verbs: www.englishclub.com/vocabulary/regular-verbs-list.htm
- Irregular noun list: english-zone.com/spelling/plurals.html
- Prefixes and suffixes: www.advanced-english-grammar.com/prefixes-suffixes.html
- Idioms: www.goenglish.com/Idioms.asp www.learn-english-today.com/idioms/idiom-categories/alpha-list_A.html
- Phrasal verbs: www.learn-english-today.com/phrasal-verbs/phrasal-verb-list.htm
- Acronyms and abbreviations: www.acronymfinder.com/
- Collective noun list: www.ojohaven.com/collectives/

Self-improvement

- www.positivearticles.com/Category/Self-Help/54
- www.selfgrowth.com/successskills_articles.html

Overcoming test anxiety

- www.studygs.net/tstprp8.htm
- kidshealth.org/teen/school_jobs/school/test_anxiety.html

Examples of self-improvement and motivational topics written and posted by the students are "The Positive Side of Life", "14 Ways to Be Happy", "Alphabet of Happiness", "Forgive and Forget", "How I Studies Grade 12", "How to Study", "Inspirations", "Success", "The Don't Sweat Affirmations", "The Life of Helen Keller", "The Old Man and His Son", "These Things Are Great Things to Be Learned", "Lessons of Life", "Life", "Personal Skills".

Study skills

- www.studygs.net/

Instructional stages

Orientation

Instruction with online tasks can proceed in the following steps:

- Introduce the students to the online course, blog, or online discussion forum to be used for posting grammar websites and online grammar tasks.
- Give the students the URL and ask them to register and enroll themselves.
- Post a sample website or task and show the students what they are supposed to do and how and where to respond.
- Tell the students what is expected of them.
- Show the students how they can search Google for grammar websites targeting specific structures by selecting specific search terms, enclosing search terms in quotation marks, and using Boolean operators.

Pre-task phase

The teacher checks the websites, exercises, and quizzes to make sure that they match the grammatical structure under study, students' proficiency levels, different learning styles, and aim for which the students are using them – i.e., assessment, diagnosis, remediation, or practice. In the pre-task phase, the instructor sets goals for a particular task and introduces the website and the grammatical structure it targets, posts written instructions on how to perform the task, and tells the students what they need to do and focus on. The teacher presents what is expected of the students in the task phase. She can give pre-questions.

Task phase

The students perform the tasks on their own at home either before or after taking a class lecture. Online grammar tasks can be performed individually (each student answers on his/her own), in pairs (two students work on a task together), or in small groups (three or more students work on a single task together and produce one answer). They can be performed interactively (students react, respond, or comment on other students' answers) or collaboratively (each student performs part of the task or project and then parts are put together to make the whole project). They can be performed synchronously (all the students go online at the same time and work on the tasks at the same time), asynchronously (the students go online at different times – i.e. the students check the websites and perform the tasks, any time, at their own convenience). To help the students make the most of online tasks, they should do interactive exercises in which they take an active role. While doing the task, the students should be required to engage in, respond to, and actively participate in the task.

Post-task phase

The students can discuss answers to questions. The teacher can clarify or help with the problematic structures and items. The students may keep a log of the tasks and structures they have finished. They can also perform post-instruction assessment tasks and those who need extra help can do remedial tasks.

Role of the instructor

The instructor serves as a facilitator, observer, and counselor. The instructor's guidance is crucial in facilitating the use of online tasks to improve students' grammar knowledge. The instructor creates a positive and supportive online learning environment that is secure for making mistakes. She praises good performance and encourages the inadequate one. She encourages the students to respond to and comment on each other's performance. She encourages peer correction of errors. She responds to students' needs, answers queries, and provides technical support. To motivate students to do the online tasks, the instructor can give credit or include online website content on tests.

Reflections

The online grammar tasks described in the present chapter were used repeatedly with six groups of EFL freshman students at COLT over six semesters. Comparisons of the pre- and posttest scores for each group showed significant differences in student mastery of English grammar between students who received in-class instruction that depended on the textbook only (control group) and those who received a combination of in-class instruction and a variety of online grammar tasks (experimental group) in favor of the experimental group. This means that students who performed additional online grammar tasks such as self-assessment of their mastery of grammar, using websites that provide definitions and explain grammar rules, checking general grammar reference websites, practicing single-structure grammar exercises, taking the daily grammar lesson, and performing error correction, production of certain grammatical structure, awareness raising, metalinguistic skill acquisition, leveling-up, differentiation, self-improvement, and study skills tasks as a supplement to in-class grammar instruction made higher gains than students who were exposed to in-class instruction that depended on the grammar textbook only.

A qualitative analysis of the students' responses to the grammar posttest showed the following: fewer errors in using and producing grammatical structures with which they had difficulty before performing the online tasks such as tenses and verb conjugation; singular and plural forms; use of prepositions; complex sentences; question formation; use of the definite article; adding different suffixes to form nouns, adjectives, and verbs; and others. They could also construct sentences containing those structures correctly.

Effectiveness of the online grammar tasks with the experimental group is supported by the results of studies that used other types of technologies used by the researchers cited earlier. As in the Al-Jarf (2005), Fukushima (2006), Hall (1998), Hegelheimer (2006), Henderson (2002), Koehler, Thompson, and Phye's (2011), Quesada (2000), Tyrwhitt-Drake (1999), and Washington et al. (2011) studies, the online grammar tasks proposed herein helped students in the experimental group overcome grammar deficits by teaching and learning basic grammar. They addressed expressive-grammar difficulties and enhanced the students' learning and mastery of English grammar. The students benefited from the web-based materials, which served as an effective review of English grammar rules with appropriate content adjustment to the different proficiency levels. They also facilitated the transition of declarative to procedural knowledge of the English grammatical structures, increased their grammatical awareness and provided self-assessment opportunities, and developed their ability to correct their own errors.

Furthermore, analysis of students' responses to a questionnaire-survey revealed positive attitudes towards the online grammar tasks described earlier. Use of supplementary online grammar tasks was reported to have several advantages: the students could access the online grammar websites any time and perform the online grammar tasks at their own convenience. They could learn independently and at their own pace. They were in charge of their own learning. The material posted served as a reference. They could refer to it as many times as they wished and whenever they needed to. It could be re-used even after the end of the course. They could follow up on their own progress by using the online self-assessment tests as formative assessment tools and by keeping a log of their own progress. They acquired study and self-improvement skills that helped them overcome other grammar learning issues such as test anxiety.

The students added that the online grammar tasks met their needs by providing a variety of tasks and exercises that catered to the differences in ability and knowledge among the students by targeting their weaknesses in English grammatical structures, such as tenses and complex sentences; by filling up the gaps in their knowledge of prior grammatical structures that they studied in earlier stages; and by clarifying the structures that they have not mastered, or which they find confusing, such as English tenses, irregular singular and plural forms, complex sentences, negative structures, question formation, reported speech, and others.

Students who struggle with English grammar indicated that the online grammar tasks provided them with extra opportunities for practice with tasks and exercises they could manage. The online grammar tasks, they reported, helped them acquire cognitive and metacognitive skills and support skills.

Some of the responses that the students gave to the questionnaire are as follows:

Hanoof reported, "*It is a new way of learning which I find interesting and motivating, unlike the textbook and classroom. I could do far more exercises online than in the textbook without feeling that it is a chore*".

Maha commented, *"The exercises in the book were not enough for me. So the online grammar tasks provided me with extra practice"*.

Sara said, *"I did extra exercises that helped me overcome my weaknesses in distinguishing between present perfect and present progressive and present perfect progressive"*.

Alia wrote, *"I could take the online grammar tests every two weeks to find out how much I have improved"*.

Fatama indicated, *"The self-study guides helped me learn how to study, review, remember and apply English grammar rules, difficult and singular and plural forms and irregular verb conjugations which were confusing to me before"*.

Samia added, *"I found exercises that match my level and explanations that I could understand, unlike the textbook that all students had to use whether they understand it or not"*.

Conclusion

Use of technology in grammar instruction is becoming more and more popular. To help EFL college students master English grammatical structures, the author recommends use of online grammar tasks that the students can perform on their own out of class as a supplement to in-class grammar instruction, based on grammar websites that focus on single and specific grammatical structures under study in class. The students can check those websites and perform relevant tasks before or after the class lecture.

The author also recommends that a grammar website repository (eLibrary) be created by EFL/ESL grammar instructors and students in which grammar websites are classified and stored according to the specific grammatical structures they target. The grammar repository should have a comprehensive alphabetical index that facilitates the searching process and allows grammar instructors and students' quick and easy access to the grammar repository via the Internet. Students and instructors should be able to store, search, and retrieve grammar websites to be used as supplementary material. The online grammar repository should be interactive. Students should be able to post questions and receive answers and feedback to their queries. Grammar websites used should be constantly updated and reviewed, with new websites added and malfunctioning websites or those with broken links removed. These resources are believed to enhance teaching and learning of EFL grammar in language and translation schools.

References

AbuSeileek, A. (2009). The effect of using an online-based course on the learning of grammar inductively and deductively. *ReCALL, 21,* 319–336.

Al-Jarf, R. (2005). The effects of online grammar instruction on low proficiency EFL college students' achievement. *Asian EFL Journal, 7*(4). Retrieved from www.asian-efl-journal.com/December_05_rsaj.php

Al-Mekhlafi, A., & Nagaratnam, R. (2011). Difficulties in teaching and learning grammar in an EFL context. *International Journal of Instruction, 4,* 69–92.

Baturay, M., Daloglu, A., & Yildirim, S. (2010). Language practice with multimedia supported web-based grammar revision material. *ReCALL, 22,* 313–331.

Beaudoin, M. (1998). De l'enseignement de la grammaire par l'internet [grammar instruction using the internet]. *Canadian Modern Language Review, 55*(1), 61–75

Beaudoin, M. (2004). A principle-based approach to teaching grammar on the web. *ReCALL, 16,* 462–474

Benander, R., & Roach, T. (1995). *Teaching academic English grammar in its own context to non-native users.* ERIC Document No. ED414608

Bowen, C. (1999). Technology helps students learn grammar. *Communication: Journalism Education Today, 32,* 17–18.

Fortune, A. (2005). Learners' use of metalanguage in collaborative form-focused L2 output tasks. *Language Awareness, 14*(1), 21–38.

Fotos, S. (1993). Consciousness raising and noticing through focus on form: Grammar task performance versus formal instruction. *Applied Linguistics, 14,* 385–407.

Fukushima, T. (2006). A student-designed grammar quiz on the web: A constructive mode of grammar instruction. *Educational Media International, 43*(1), 75–85.

Golshan, M., & Karbalaei, A. (2009). Grammatical problems in the writings of EFL undergraduate learners. *South Asian Language Review, 19*(1 & 2), 1–10.

Haddox, G. (1998). Billy's story: Grammar in context (rainbow teachers/rainbow students). *English Journal, 87,* 90–93.

Haight, C., Herron, C., & Cole, S. (2007). The effects of deductive and guided inductive instructional approaches on the learning of grammar in the elementary foreign language college classroom. *Foreign Language Annals, 40,* 288–310.

Hall, C. (1998). Overcoming the grammar deficit: The role of information technology in teaching German grammar to undergraduates. *Canadian Modern Language Review, 55*(1), 41–60.

Hegelheimer, V. (2006). Helping ESL writers through a multimodal, corpus-based, online grammar resource. *CALICO Journal, 24*(1), 5–32.

Hegelheimer, V., & Fisher, D. (2006). Grammar, writing, and technology: A sample technology-supported approach to teaching grammar and improving writing for ESL learners. *CALICO Journal, 23,* 257–279.

Henderson, B. (2002). Improving student writing using a web-based targeted approach to grammar system (TAGS). *Journalism and Mass Communication Educator, 57,* 230–243.

Hu, G. (2011). Metalinguistic knowledge, metalanguage, and their relationship in L2 learners. *System, 39*(1), 63–77.

Huang, J. (2010). Grammar instruction for adult English language learners: A task-based learning framework. *Journal of Adult Education, 39*(1), 29–37.

Koehler, N., Thompson, A., & Phye, G. (2011). A design study of a multimedia instructional grammar program with embedded tracking. *Instructional Science: An International Journal of the Learning Sciences, 39,* 939–974.

Macaro, E., & Masterman, L. (2006). Does intensive explicit grammar instruction make all the difference? *Language Teaching Research, 10,* 297–327.

McEnery, T., Baker, J., & Wilson, A. (1995). A statistical analysis of corpus based computer vs. traditional human teaching methods of part of speech analysis. *Computer-Assisted Language Learning, 8,* 259–274.

Meyer, J., Youga, J., & Flint-Ferguson, J. (1990). Grammar in context: Why and how. *English Journal, 79*(1), 66–70.

Mills, R. (2010). Does using an internet based program for improving student performance in grammar and punctuation really work in a college composition course? *Education, 130,* 652–656.

Paesani, K. (2005). Literary texts and grammar instruction: Revisiting the inductive presentation. *Foreign Language Annals, 38*(1), 15–24.

Patterson, N., & Pipkin, G. (2001). Grammar in the labyrinth: Resources on the world-wide web. *Voices from the Middle, 8*(3), 63–67.

Quesada, A. (2000). Using the web to practice and learn grammar: ESL students' perspectives. *Mosaic, 7*(4), 3–6.

Schnackenberg, H. (1997). *Learning English electronically: Formative evaluation in ESL software.* ERIC Document No. ED403877

Smoot, W. (2001). An experiment in teaching grammar in context. *Voices from the Middle, 8*(3), 34–42.

Tahaineh, Y. (2010). Arab EFL university students' errors in the use of prepositions. *MJAL, 2*(1), 76–112.

Thu, T. (2009). *Teachers' perceptions about grammar teaching: Alliant International University.* ERIC Document No. ED507439

Tomlinson, C. (2001). *How to differentiate instruction in mixed-ability classrooms* (2nd ed.). Alexandria, VA: Association for Supervision and Curriculum Development.

Torrie, H. (2007). *A web-based tool for oral practice and assessment of grammatical structures.* ERIC Document No. ED508831

Toth, P. (2008). Teacher- and learner-led discourse in task-based grammar instruction: Providing procedural assistance for L2 morphosyntactic development. *Language Learning, 58,* 237–283.

Tyrwhitt-Drake, H. (1999). Responding to grammar questions on the internet. *ELT Journal, 53,* 281–288.

Vogel, S., Herron, C., Cole, S. P., & York, H. (2011). Effectiveness of a guided inductive versus a deductive approach on the learning of grammar in the intermediate-level college French classroom. *Foreign Language Annals, 44,* 353–380.

Washington, K. N., Warr-Leeper, G., & Thomas-Stonell, N. (2011). Exploring the outcomes of a novel computer-assisted treatment program targeting expressive-grammar deficits in preschoolers with SLI. *Journal of Communication Disorders, 44,* 315–330.

Weaver, C. (1996). *Teaching grammar in context.* ERIC Document No. ED393104

Xenodohidis, T. (2002). An ESP curriculum for Greek EFL students of computing: A new approach. *English for Specific Purposes, 1*(2). Retrieved from www.esp-world.info/articles_2/ESP%20Curriculum.html

9 Teaching pronunciation to adult learners of English

Karen Steffen Chung

This chapter is to a great extent based on the author's decades of experience teaching at the university level in Taiwan; however, most suggestions have wide application and can be easily tailored to individual situations and needs elsewhere. For example, first language (L1) influenced substitutions for certain vowels and consonants of English will differ according to the home country or region, but the principle of phoneme substitution remains the same. Teachers may find that this chapter challenges some of their personal notions about the role of pronunciation in language learning, or that it goes against the current of some recent schools of thought in pronunciation teaching. We can only respond that it is perhaps time to let some new voices be heard and to focus more on the exigencies of survival and success in a competitive world outside of sheltered and idealistic academia.

Teaching adult learners

Unlike children, adult students will in almost all cases have received previous instruction in English. This training will not only have helped shape the current state of their English but also will often determine *how* they go about learning a language. Rather than just 'teaching pronunciation,' you will benefit your students most by showing them *a new way to learn English*. This will be the hardest part of what you do, especially since it involves identifying and offering replacements for deeply ingrained *habits*, but it also has the potential for turning your students' English learning entirely around.

Children have certain advantages in learning their L1 – for example, virtually unlimited exposure to the target language as spoken (in most cases) by competent native speakers. They have the chance and are motivated to use what they learn immediately and usually get instant feedback. They benefit from lower expectations and a much higher tolerance for their errors on the part of their listeners. They have boundless curiosity and energy. Since the filters of a child's brain are at this point not yet fully formed, they will let just about anything in. Adults, on the other hand, often have many preconceived notions about how language should work and how it sounds; less exposure to the speech of native speakers; a tendency to experience fear; embarrassment, or even shame over making mistakes; and often a belief that they are just 'not good' at learning languages.

The ideal would be for the adult student to be exposed to as much native-like spoken input as possible, with persistent repetitions, ample opportunity for speaking practice, and patience on the part of their listeners. This is often not what happens, due to many factors. However, in a healthy human, the brain maintains its plasticity one's entire life (Doidge, 2007). In addition, adults bring many strengths to the table such as sharper analytical skills, greater knowledge and experience of the world, and high proficiency in at least one language already. The question becomes not whether adults can learn languages well, but how to harness the brain's robust plasticity, together with its other more developed skills, for the most efficient and effective results.

Thinking, fast and slow

The following is by far the most important point as regards our understanding of how we learn languages well and how we can do a better job of teaching them.

In his bestselling book, *Thinking, Fast and Slow*, author Daniel Kahneman describes the two main modes of thinking used by the human brain. The first, called *System One* by Kahneman, is our unconscious brain, which is responsible for *automated responses* and *habitual behavior*. Its reactions are almost instantaneous. *System Two* is what we use for *linear, analytic, conscious thinking*, and *problem solving*. It works much more slowly than *System One* (Kahneman, 2011).

Students in East Asia are typically trained to rely heavily on *System Two* in their English learning, when what is required for successful oral communication is management of the task by their intuitive, habit-executing *System One*. Lightning-fast mental processing is required in order to listen to and decode linguistic input and then come up with a reasonable response before the rhythm of the exchange breaks down and the other party becomes impatient – and *System Two* is simply *too slow* to handle this. So it is absolutely necessary that language learning be *automated* to the point where *System One* can do most of the legwork. This can be achieved by loading System One with commonly used stock phrases and related vocabulary items to which System Two will make quick, minor alterations to meet the needs of each specific situation when the learner is engaged in real-life conversation.

Lack of understanding of these two complementary modes of brain function and their respective roles in language learning lies at the heart of why English education in much of East Asia so often comes up wanting. Under current practices, it is common for students to be taught English mostly from a paper textbook. After a minimum of audio input from the teacher and recordings, students learn the spellings and meanings of individual vocabulary items, which they must memorize in order to pass tests. They mostly rely on murky impressions when deciding how to pronounce the words, and in many cases, the teacher's pronunciation is not very accurate, measured by any standard. They also learn rules of grammar, often in excruciating detail. To compose a sentence, they will attempt to analytically put together the two data sets they have on hand – i.e., isolated vocabulary words + mechanical rules of grammar. Aside from a number of shorter model sentences they may happen to get right – such as "Sorry!" and "How are you?" – these self-composed sentences tend to end up quite garbled or awkward.

Many learners take the "think directly in English" exhortation often given them very seriously *before* they have enough automated audio material in their head to think directly *with*. They will produce sentences such as *"Where are you come from?" for "Where are you from?" or *"I am very like traveling" for "I really like traveling." Here is a longer example from a recorded corpus: "I meet some students in the Beijing University or other college. I interact of them is very happy, but I think they are more interesting in politic issue than our student in Taiwan." Intended meaning: "I met some students from Beijing University and other colleges. Our interactions were very enjoyable, but I think they were more interested in political issues than most Taiwan students are." The English they produce in this way sounds like panicked stabs in the dark with whatever raw data they can grab onto as quickly as possible. In the heat of a conversational exchange, their slow System Two, which they are relying on heavily, has no time for further grammatical processing. What they end up with can only be called an ad hoc variety of Pidgin English. It is certainly not because of an inherent lack of aptitude for language learning; there is abundant anecdotal evidence of Japanese, for example, who have learned to a high level of proficiency any number of languages – *other than English*.

Not just pronunciation

At this point, it may seem that we have digressed from our topic and are talking about grammar and overall conversational ability rather than just pronunciation. But, in fact, problems with both of these core issues, along with poor listening skills, can be traced back to the same cause – *insufficient audio input and practice*. These problems can also be *fixed* by the same solution: *intensive listening and repetition practice*.

A little 'listen and repeat' now and then is *not* sufficient to create the kind of phonetic awareness and stored mental audio files needed for learners to really *hear* what is being modeled and to self-correct when they get it wrong. In the limited listen and repeat that is done, students often 'repeat' mechanically *even before the model has finished playing* – clear evidence that they are simply *reading* and hardly listening at all beyond cues to 'start' and 'stop.' Once stuck in habits such as these, students' ears will have effectively *shut down*.

If you give such a student (Taiwanese, in this case) a correct spoken model such as "the other one" (ði ˈʌðɚ wʌn), he or she will typically register and retain it as (li ˈʌlə ˈwʌn), and if asked to listen and repeat, that is likely what he or she will say. The original pronunciation is initially received correctly – this is evidenced by the student's ability to distinguish a native from a non-native speaker of English. However, in the process of matching incoming audio input with mentally stored forms, the input is re-processed into the *student's own version* of the words, and that is how it stays, in fossilized L2 form. The reason for this is the *default spoken model* that the student has more or less unconsciously adopted and *identifies with*. It is based not on a native-speaker model but on how the student is used to hearing his or her compatriots speak English and how the student has come to believe English *should sound when he or she speaks it*.

Students may assert that they are (x nationality), and so of course they speak with an (x L1) accent. They may point out a person speaking English with a French, German, or Danish accent is fairly easily accepted and accommodated (though they may at the same time complain how difficult Indian English is to understand). There does indeed seem to be a wide consensus that a 'light' accent is OK; in fact, a 'light' accent is often *attractive* or may add authoritativeness to a voice (van Hoek, n.d.). A casual look around the Internet will quickly reveal that in the popular mind, the accents most commonly considered 'attractive' are first various regional native English accents, with Standard Southern British English (BE) usually at the top of the list. Others, such as Australian, Irish, and Scottish, follow and then come a number of European non-native English accents, often led by French or Italian (Dahlgreen, 2014; The Telegraph, 2009). There is considerable disagreement from here on.

So a 'light accent' is one thing. However, pronunciation that is too different relative to the expected standard – e.g., with off-target vowels, wrong or missing consonants, misplaced stress, or odd intonation – is another. If you do a search on 'Asian accents' or 'Chinese accents,' you most often find these described in popular discussion forums as 'not very attractive' (Giant Bomb Forum, 2014). And if the *grammar* of someone speaking with an East Asian accent is incorrect as well, the two together deliver a double whammy that often discourages a listener from wanting to initiate or continue communication when not absolutely necessary. One online note to a woman who complained about negative reactions to her Chinese accent delicately suggests, "Lastly but by all means not least ensure that you use *the correct form of the third person singular of the verb* [emphasis added] so that you don't immediately identify yourself as a foreign speaker, e.g., *he walks, she walks, it walks* [not walk without the s]" (Yahoo Answers, 2008).

Beyond being judged as less attractive, a foreign accent can affect assessments of one's overall abilities. People who speak with a heavy foreign accent may be viewed as less intelligent, and their style of speaking as "comical," "cute," "incompetent," "not serious," or "childish" Beebe (1988). *Credibility* is also at stake. Experiments by researchers Shari Lev-Ari and Boaz Keysar found that speakers with a heavy foreign accent are *perceived as less credible* (Levi-Ari & Keysar, 2010). This makes pronunciation actually a pretty serious matter.

Assessments of foreign accents can be a politically sensitive issue and will often set off academic partisanship and debate, sometimes even international furor (*The Guardian*, 2015). However, some, such as entrepreneur Paul Graham, have had the candor to come out and say what they think on this point:

> The empirical evidence about very strong accents is striking. And I am talking about failure to communicate here. I don't mean strong accents in the

sense that it's clear that someone comes from another country. I'm talking about accents so strong that you have to interrupt the conversation to ask what they just said.

(Tiku, 2013)

We will make some brief comments here on the popular notion of *English for International Communication*, or *English as a Lingua Franca* (ELF), in which 'intelligibility' is emphasized over attainment of native-like pronunciation as measured against one of the standard dialects of English such as General American (GA) or BE (Jenkins, 2002). This approach stresses that some features of spoken English are more important to intelligibility than others and that these should be given the highest priority in English teaching and learning. There is really nothing here to disagree with so far. While it would certainly be better to try and cover everything we can to give our students the best preparation possible, we do need to set priorities when teaching time and other resources are limited. Jenkins proposes that certain features can be left as "optional," to be acquired and refined at the learner's own discretion; for example, L2-influenced substitutions such as /s/ and /d/ would be allowed for the "th" sounds /θ/ and /ð/ (Jenkins, 2002).

In addition, however, proponents of this approach suggest that it is not reasonable for the entire burden of successful communication in a foreign language to fall on the speaker; the *listener* should do what he or she can to facilitate the process and make it easier on the speaker (Jenkins, 2002). While this is undeniably an admirable ideal, we need to be aware that we have at this point strayed beyond the bounds of what we are here to do.

Let us take a minute to discuss the notion of 'intelligibility.' Intelligibility is *not* just about what the listener can with effort correctly decipher from what the speaker is saying. It is about *cognitive load* on the *listener*. With every little difference in pronunciation and grammar that diverges from the standard the listener is most accustomed to and expects, the listener must *make up for the deficit through his or her own mental processing*, just like our brain needs to supply the missing information when listening over a bad phone connection – think back on how long it took you to give up on a mobile phone conversation in such a situation. Depending on how degraded the signal is, the brain may be able to partially salvage and reconstitute it to what it was *supposed* to be. The problem is that this mental processing burns up a lot of brain energy on the part of the listener – energy they could use to do other important tasks – and causes what is called "listening fatigue" (NPR, 2009). Speakers who cause listening fatigue in others have a big strike against them when it comes to competing for social and other resources. Who wouldn't rather just deal with someone who doesn't run down his or her battery of finite available energy for the day so quickly?

As teachers, we must always remember *who* our paying customers are, who we have been hired to serve – namely, our *students*. It is our job to give our *students* the best preparation we can to help them compete as successfully as possible in an often harsh professional and social environment. If you wish to help the general public overcome their tendency to shy away from people with speech that tires them out, more power to you – just make sure you do it *on your own time* and *not* on the time your students have paid for. The students are in your class to learn, not to be indulged or falsely told they're wonderful just as they are when they aren't there yet. You don't see lowering of standards in this way in such subjects as math, history, science, or music. Why are we so ready to acquiesce to flabby standards for language? We are doing our students no favor if we wave them through with weak skills, thinking that it is enough. When students finally get accurate information on what points they should fix in their speech, a frequent reaction is *anger* – *not* at the correction, but rather that no previous instructor pointed these things out to them before so they could have fixed them much sooner. Students who have seldom been corrected will be in for some rude awakenings when they begin a new semester in a university program in an English-speaking country, when they try to socialize and joke around with classmates, or when they compete with hundreds of other applicants for a job requiring good English and are simply not up to the task, and don't even know how to improve. The problem in these cases is not so much deficiencies in the students, but in us *teachers*, in our ability and willingness to help and inspire our students to aim high and do better, and in not giving our students enough informed *feedback* in order to better guide them. This does not require that a teacher's own spoken English be perfect, but that he or she show students effective methods for learning English well, beginning with intensive *listening* practice.

The value of mistakes

We conclude this section with one final and crucial point: *there is no learning without errors*, or as Kathryn Schulz puts it, "wrongness is a vital part of how we learn and change. Thanks to error, we can revise our understanding of ourselves and amend our ideas about the world." (2010, p. 5). East Asians tend to have an especially strong aversion to making any kind of error in public – they would rather just keep quiet than risk being ridiculed for getting something wrong. In fact, questions and other class participation are *discouraged* in many East Asian classrooms. Teachers have the same abhorrence of being caught in a mistake and shamed since they believe it would threaten or diminish their authority. Many would rather rationalize an assertion that is later proved to be wrong, insist that *they are right*, or even reprimand the student. This never fools students, though they may be intimidated to where they no longer venture to ask questions or express a viewpoint and then end up passive and mechanical in their learning. What the students learn from this playacting and capitulation is that they also must always be right, or pretend to be right, regardless of how convincing evidence to the contrary might be, and that this is how they should teach their own future students and children. Mistakes = shame, which must be hidden, denied, and avoided at all costs in the future.

We need to revise our view of errors as a source of embarrassment and shame. Education is only meaningful in so far as it provides learners with what they actually *need*, and teachers can hardly know what their students need without observing their errors. Teach students that mistakes are *treasures* that can lead them to what they need most – that is, *when* the errors are identified and addressed. Of course, learners should try to avoid mistakes once they have been identified – but they have to first *make* the mistakes in order for them to be pinpointed. Always give kind, patient, *constructive* feedback in response to student errors. Ask your students to compile the corrections that both they and their classmates receive and to work actively on fixing them. Only by *embracing* error (Schulz, 2010) will they see progress. And be open and honest about your *own* mistakes, and correct them publicly so students can do as you do and not just what you say. Which brings us to the next section on practical suggestions for the teacher.

Practical guidance and suggestions for teachers

Your own preparation: learn phonetics

Teachers of English to Speakers of Other Languages (TESOL) programs typically do not include rigorous training in phonetics; however, a mastery of phonetics is the one best way, whether English is your L1 or an L2, to prepare yourself to help students with their pronunciation issues. It will give you valuable tools to analyze what you hear, identify what the issues are, and then propose ways for the student to improve. If you do not have a strong background in phonetics, do consider enrolling in or auditing a course at a local university or taking a course online.

The first and most important step is to learn the International Phonetic Alphabet (IPA). You do not necessarily have to teach it to your students or otherwise use it in your teaching, though students generally do just fine with it. Those teaching in North America tend to rely on spelling and phonics since that is what most grew up with and are comfortable with, but this really is no replacement for solid competence in IPA transliteration in which each sound is represented unambiguously by a single symbol rather than by a number of possible spellings. It is in fact not that difficult and is easily mastered with practice if you prioritize it in your learning. Dismissing it as 'too hard' for TESOL students to master reflects a patronizing and even insulting attitude toward the students' abilities. Usually it reflects insecurities in the teacher rather than any lack on the part of the students.

Language is constantly changing, but set a clear, stable target for your students to imitate

All languages are in a state of constant change – for example, /ɑ/ (as in *father*) and /ɔ/ (as in *law*) have merged into a single phoneme for many North Americans, and the 't' in 'often' is now being pronounced more frequently than previously. Standard Southern BE, previously called 'RP' (Received Pronunciation), is no longer spoken in its textbook form by many people. In addition to the United

Kingdom's numerous regional dialects, features of Estuary English, such as substituting /f/ for /θ/ (making *three* sound like *free*) and /v/ for /ð/ (making *other* sound like ['ʌvə]), originally Cockney features, are now commonly heard.

However, not sticking to some kind of a consistent standard when teaching *spoken* English will lead to all kinds of sloppiness and an attitude of 'anything goes.' Lack of consistency in speech is one way you increase the burden on your listener. By choosing one of the established standard varieties of English as the goal for your students to emulate, you will end up with at least something close to a variety most easily understood by the largest number of English speakers in the world. *Listening*, however, is another matter. English learners should be exposed to as many varieties of spoken English, both native and non-native, in their *listening* as possible so they can quickly adjust when speaking with someone who has an unfamiliar accent.

Be comfortable with – and honest about – your own English

For L1 English speakers: We *all* have an accent. If the variety of English you speak is close to one of the more standard varieties, then fine. If it has relatively strong regional features, go ahead and use it in class, though some teachers may choose to adopt more standard versions of certain features, and that's fine too. Whatever you do, be *comfortable* with how you speak and use English in class, and try to be *consistent*. Point out which features of your speech are more regional, and encourage students to notice and get used to them, just as they should learn to adapt to many varieties of spoken English in their *listening*. You may, however, choose for them to model their *speech* after recorded materials in a more standard target variety.

For L2 English speakers: Many teachers may have a vague or not-so-vague sense of their own strengths and shortcomings in speaking English. However, in order to teach your students effectively, you will need to have a clear idea of what you do well and what you still need to work on. You may want to get an experienced and kind-but-honest native speaker to help you assess yourself. Once you have greater self-awareness, you can capitalize on your strengths and work around your weaknesses. It is a big step to try to overcome a clinging to cultural notions and norms of Confucian patriarchy and authoritarianism, but your students will *respect you* for it. You are not only teaching them English but also modeling behaviors and attitudes for them to internalize and, above all, to embrace *honesty* about your inevitable human limitations. Your goal is not to fool students into thinking you speak perfect English – not even native speakers can claim this – and most certainly not that you are right all the time. If you try to fool them, you will miss an opportunity to break the dishonest, negative cycle of trying to make others think you are more than you are and covering up for your shortfalls.

Most East Asian teachers tend to be fairly good at grammar; they may be less proficient in listening, speaking, and, specifically, pronunciation. But this does not have to hold you back from being a good teacher and helping your students learn good listening and oral skills. Be up front about your limitations and provide lots of opportunities for your students to work with audio and video recordings, while constantly working to improve your own skills.

Learn a bit or a lot about the language(s) of your learners

The following is mainly directed toward L1 English speakers who are teaching in Asia or elsewhere abroad, but it can also apply to local teachers who are learning a new L2, or are working to further improve their English.

There are two highly compelling reasons why you should make a concerted effort to learn your students' L1 for classes in which most share the same L1. First is for your own convenience, independence, and self-respect in all your dealings in your host country. It will help enormously in enabling clear, ungarbled communications with your students, colleagues, and everyone else, and it will win you much additional respect and social and professional standing. We all learn more from *example* than from explicit teaching. Any effort you put into learning the local L1, however large or small, will bring you great benefits.

The second reason affects your effectiveness as a language teacher. It is easy to hear the flaws in our students' English and to jump in to correct them. However, it is hard to empathize with their struggle to learn a language very different from their own when we haven't been through or aren't currently going through a similar struggle ourselves. The importance of close and repeated listening, and in particular the power of the Echo Method (described next), for example, may not be brought home to you until you are floundering yourself and have trouble 'hearing' certain crucial distinctions in the target language.

In addition, when you know the students' L1, you will have a whole repertoire of handy references and comparisons to the target language. The benefits of having students relate sounds in the target language to similar ones in their native language far outweigh any possible drawbacks (Abercrombie, 1991). Many sounds will tend to be nearly identical in any two languages and thus present a zero-learning load (Strevens, 1991). When two sounds are not exactly the same, the small details that distinguish the two can be worked on once the student is close. Instead of struggling over something that seems exotic and insurmountable, the students will produce a form immediately and with *naturalness*.

If you succeed in learning the students' L1 well, you will probably also end up with higher standards for your students. No one will be able to accuse you of asking things of your students that you cannot do equivalents of yourself in their L1. You will know firsthand the satisfaction, pleasure, and positive feedback that go with getting a language right.

The classroom and beyond: methods that work

Choosing a personal internal model to emulate

A lot of what goes on when we are learning a language happens because of choices we have ourselves made early in the process, often without even being aware that we *had* choices and made them. One of the first such choices involves our own *internal model* that we strive to match when speaking a new language.

We receive constant feedback from our own ears and brain on how we sound to ourselves when we speak. If our internal checking system thinks what we said is OK, it is allowed to pass. If we make a slip, our checking system alerts us, and we either go back and correct it if we can, or we may just let it pass. People speaking a foreign language *get used to their own version of that language*, which is often based on the way many other L2 speakers in their environment sound, and they come to identify with it. In the process, they essentially *shut out* native-speaker models in which things are done differently. If they were at this point to consciously stop and *listen attentively* to the native-speaker model, they could probably imitate it quite well. However, upon producing a good imitation, they might laugh, because it is so different from what they believe is the 'correct' way for them personally to speak – i.e., what they are *used to*. Getting past this is one of the biggest hurdles in learning a more authentic and easily intelligible accent.

The cycle can be broken by making the learner aware of his or her self-selected internal model and guiding the learner to open his or her ears to a new model. If the student is motivated and makes the effort, he or she will begin to see a big difference in how he or she both listens and speaks in the L2. Here is the procedure:

1. The student needs to find his or her own personal native-speaker model, usually someone in the media, a celebrity, or a personal acquaintance.
2. The student needs to frequently listen attentively to this person speak. Eventually, the student's brain will be able to synthesize an auditory model from this input and call it up on demand.
3. The next step is for the student, before speaking, to mentally 'hear' what he or she is about to read or say *just as the student imagines his or her chosen internal L1 model would say it*. Typical L2 errors will sound out of place on the model.
4. The student will start to identify with a native-speaker model rather than his or her original L2 model, and the student will improve. However, additional tools are needed.

Fixing pronunciation and grammar at the same time: the echo method

The interminable search in East Asia for a nostrum to learn English well is much like the quest for a miracle diet – both more often than not lead to disappointment. In both cases, there is often an unwillingness to invest the needed effort, willpower, and persistence. But then again, a lot of effort applied with the *wrong* method will not succeed, and doing more of what brought poor results in the past is not likely to bring better results in the future. The listen-and-repeat model is a deeply ingrained default method in our approach to language learning that we do not even question because it does not occur to us to question it. However, conventional listen and repeat, together with 'free conversation,' will usually not produce good results; in fact, the many repetitions of defective forms may *further entrench* them and make them even harder to fix. Practice doesn't make perfect – it makes *permanent*.

There *is*, however, an alternative to listen and repeat, and it involves the use of *echoic memory*. Though echoic memory is usually not something we are consciously aware of, most of us have had the experience of not hearing clearly something that someone else has said, asking them to repeat it, but then suddenly figuring it out on our own before the speaker is even finished repeating it. What was said has just been 'played back' in your head, so you got the whole message on the second go yourself – through *echoic memory*. Some works call it the 'phonological loop.' Echoic memory lasts only for a few seconds and then vaporizes – certainly one reason why we do not notice it more. However, it is strange that it has not been exploited in language learning until very recently.

a **The Echo Method:** The *Echo Method* works first by disrupting mindless repetition or extemporizing with one's entrenched L1 patterns and by opening up the ears and brain to actual audio input. It lets the brain relax in quiet for a few seconds so it can play back and absorb the 'echo' of a spoken phrase, enabling the learner to attend to it closely and fully internalize it before imitating the phrase; for this reason, it is much more effective than shadowing. Here is how it works:

1 Choose a suitable, interesting audio file in the target language with a written transcription. Listen to the audio a few times and then look up all the unfamiliar words and expressions. Focus first on a small portion of the file, maybe about two minutes long.
2 Listen to the first four or five words of the audio file; intonational phrases are best if not too long; if they are, divide them up.
3 Press the PAUSE button, and listen attentively to the *internal echo* in your head.
4 Imitate the 'echo' you hear in your head; do not automatically use the pronunciation you are accustomed to.
5 Follow this routine of listen-internal echo-repeat with the same phrase over and over until it is thoroughly imprinted on your brain.
6 Move on to the next phrase and repeat the process in the same way. Continue for 10 to 20 minutes. Do this daily and keep a record of time spent on practice, noting milestones.
7 When possible, get feedback on how you are doing; at first, it may be uncomfortable, but it is what helps us improve and grow.

When learners repeat after their own internal echo, their pronunciation is generally much more accurate than with simple listen and repeat, since their brains have already fully and correctly *internalized* the utterance, much like a retinal afterimage. This method has radically improved the pronunciation of many students who started off with seemingly 'hopeless' problems. Successful learners often unconsciously use this method themselves without identifying it by a name, or realizing exactly what it is they are doing that works so well.

With the right preparation, students will catch on to the Echo Method in their very first repetition in the first class of the term, without 'jumping the gun' and repeating right after the model. From that point on, they are really *hearing*, not just *what* is said, but exactly *how* it is said, and faithfully reproducing it themselves. This will get them started on *mindful listening* without the automatic filtering and substitutions that usually take place. What you are really training, beyond just the correct pronunciation of English sounds, is a high overall sensitivity to sounds, which will eventually spread to all areas of the learner's life, in both concrete and abstract applications.

Watch that the students *do not move their lips when listening to the model*. This may seem counterintuitive, but anything you do yourself while listening will distract the brain with *proprioception* – receiving and interpreting events generated from the learner's own thoughts and actions. This will blur the sharp focus that is needed to hear the input clearly, with no distortions added in.

It is good to do as much echo practice in class as possible, but it will never be enough. Students need to move from a default of learning only when pushed for the sake of exams to wanting to learn better English for the sake of their own future plans and for its own sake. This mindset may be the most important thing your students take away from your teaching.

At the beginning of the semester, you can have the students record a written passage in English, then play it back, and write a page of feedback on what they hear. You can then have them replay this same recording at the end of the course, and write a new page of feedback describing what they now hear with their 'new ears.' This is useful in helping the students and you to see how much progress they have made over the course of the semester or school year.

Students can be required to keep daily listening logs in which they write down from what time to what time they did their 10 or 20 minutes of echo practice, and a description of the material they listened to. It's best at the beginning to offer very short, simple conversations – ones they will think are too easy for them, but which in fact they couldn't produce correctly or colloquially on their own without help. They need to listen-echo-repeat over and over and over until the conversation is finally engraved in their *unconscious brains*, at which point it will emerge from their mouths when needed *automatically*, managed by their speedy, reactive System One, and with perfect grammar and pronunciation. You can have the students perform the dialogues in pairs in class every week and correct them where their output strays from the recording. Having the students give feedback on their peers' performance can also help sharpen their ears and attentiveness to detail.

Ten or 20 minutes a day of echo practice is a big commitment, and not everybody will follow through. However, as a teacher, you can do your best to assign and check their listening logs and offer encouragement. As a convenience to the students, the teacher can use a recording program such as Audacity to produce pre-paused audio files for a., b., and c.-type practice and make them available to the students.

In their echo practice at home, the following steps can be added as the student is ready, for further reinforcement and to fully automate the audio content:

b   **Listen and repeat:** Once the learner has practiced the Echo Method on a chosen passage (say, a one-minute scene of an episode of a television series), having captured as much phonetic detail as possible, the next step is to practice with conventional listen and repeat. This should be done until the material is even more solidly mastered and can be produced without hesitation or a single mistake.

c   **Synchronous reading:** The next step is synchronous reading, or reading along with the model, at the same pace. By this point, the material should be so familiar that the learner can produce it without much conscious thought. Synchronous reading can help the learner get the *rhythm* right – if there is any deviation from the original, they will fall behind or (less often) surge ahead. The goal is not speed per se but to be able to produce the sentences with the same stress, intonation, and pauses as the L1 model.

Even with good listening, fine-tuning will be required. Phonetic categories and allophonic processes in particular are often carried over unconsciously from the native language, as are errors from previous learning. Therefore, a list and description of common learner errors for each L1 learner group can be highly useful to both teacher and student.

For more help in getting the rhythm right, the following method is useful:

d   **Arm circles:** Some students have a tendency to read each syllable with equal length. It is often not so much a problem of making stressed syllables long enough, but of making unstressed ones short enough (Chela-Flores, 2001). A whole-body aid in helping students get the stress-timed rhythm of English right is to have them stand up near their desks and make large circles with their dominant arm, making muscular effort to push the arm *down* on the stressed syllables. Since the stress timing of English is not perfectly regular, the circles sometimes have to be made more quickly or slowly depending on the length and prosodic structure of the phrase, but the continuous motion can help redistribute varying syllable lengths more in accord with native-speaker rhythmic patterns. This falls under what Acton (1991) describes as a "connection between certain non-verbal behaviours (such as speech-rhythm-related upper-body movement) and suprasegmentals," or *haptic* pronunciation practice (see h.).

e   **Cultivate sensitivity to feedback:** The importance of feedback cannot be overemphasized. McClelland et al. (2002; reported in Wyner, 2014) found that Japanese adults were able to distinguish /r/ and /l/ – notoriously difficult for Japanese L1 speakers – after one hour of practice with automatic *feedback*. Often speakers of an L2 are given explicit feedback outside of class on how they do; for example, the person they're speaking with may repeat the same phrase with the correct pronunciation and grammar. Sometimes, the feedback is more subtle – the listener may briefly knit his or her brow when a wrong pronunciation or form is used. Teachers can help students become sensitive to and avail themselves of both kinds of free training when they come by and not just forge ahead down their own panicked path with sensors shut down.

f **Shadowing:** Shadowing is mentioned here, not as part of the formal steps of the Echo Method, but as an alternate form of listening and oral practice, borrowed from oral interpretation training. In shadowing, the learner repeats what he or she hears in an audio recording almost the second that he or she hears it. This trains the student in listening, attention, quick reactions, rhythm, and pronunciation. One reason it is often recommended is because few teachers know about the Echo Method, and it is the best method they have encountered thus far. However, if you have a continuous audio stream coming in (as with a radio broadcast), you are constantly being exposed to new material without a chance to master the old. It also causes fatigue fairly quickly. The method is more viable if you have only a relatively short loop and you repeat it over and over.

g **Repeated choral readings:** Phonetician Olle Kjellin has developed a highly effective method of repeated synchronous reading with the volume progressively lowered on copies of the target practice form prepared with Audacity (see the resources at the end of this chapter).

h **Haptic pronunciation practice:** Arm circles are in fact only one example of using physical touch and body movements to learn and reinforce accurate pronunciation. This approach is sometimes called Haptic Pronunciation Practice (see the resources at the end of this chapter).

Conclusion: materials and tools

With the Internet and other kinds of digital media, it is now easier than ever for students to be independent and self-directed in their learning. Here are some resources you can encourage your students to use in their English improvement plans.

a **Online English dictionaries with sound files:** Pronunciation keys in American-published dictionaries are mostly ad hoc, differing from dictionary to dictionary, and they can be quite confusing. A better way to check or learn the pronunciation of a word is with an audio dictionary. The following audio dictionaries are available online for free, and all are excellent: Merriam-Webster Online (GA), Cambridge Advanced Learner's Dictionary (BE and GA), Oxford Learner's Dictionaries (BE and GA), the Macmillan Dictionary (BE), and the Free Dictionary (GA and some BE). A Google search will turn up more, but these are really more than adequate.

b **TV series:** In fact, *good* TV series are the very best way to practice English listening and pronunciation skills, and they are the best materials to use for Echo Method practice. Nearly *all* students with the best English in the author's experience, regardless of L1 and country of origin, learned it from *repeated* watching, with active listening and practice, of good TV series or movies. Encourage your students to choose a series, watch it first for entertainment and to become familiar with it and then use it for their daily Echo Method practice, starting with the pilot episode. It may take a semester or even a year to work through a single episode with the thoroughness required to automate what they learn. Some suggested series, new and old include *Gilmore Girls, Seinfeld, The Good Wife, Grey's Anatomy, ER, Mad Men, Six Feet Under, Modern Family, West Wing, The Office, Ugly Betty, Roseanne, Ally McBeal, MacGyver, The Wonder Years, M*A*S*H, Cheers.* You can add your favorites to the list. Try to choose shows with relevance to the students' lives – *Gilmore Girls* is especially good – and avoid shows (of which there are plenty) with too much emphasis on sex, drugs, crime, violence, and slapstick or silliness. Encourage your students to watch legally obtained versions; watching programs from pirate sites may cause harm to the user's computer.

c **Movies:** Movies can be good for learning and pronunciation practice, but are not usually as good as TV series since often more extreme things happen in movies, and you do not have the chance to get to know the same set of characters from episode to episode and season to season. However, they are another option. It's best to choose a movie that is as close to real everyday life as possible, avoiding adventure, science-fiction, horror, fantasy, cartoons, and overly sexy or violent films, as well as other genres less suitable for language learning.

d **YouTube:** Learners must be selective, but YouTube offers a virtually limitless selection of free videos that can be used for English learning.

e **Audacity:** This is a free recording program with many features. Students can use it to record themselves and self-assess, or for class assignments, or to record online audio streams for practice, among many other things. See Olle Kjellin's tutorial on how to use it for pronunciation practice on p. 148.

f **Language exchanges:** Students can set up language exchanges locally or online, for pronunciation, speaking, and writing practice. One good one is italki.com; a Google search with the keywords "language exchange sites" will turn up many others. There are also many English and pronunciation learning pages on Facebook and other social media to explore. Students should be reminded to exercise care and good judgment on any social media website to avoid scams and other dangers.

g **Websites, software programs, commercial apps:** There are simply too many of these to list; you can do an online search and see what you come up with, or check in mobile-device app stores. But be selective – quality varies greatly. Automatic feedback on pronunciation of recorded speech is not yet completely reliable, but it is getting better and can be a useful reference, opportunity for practice, and motivator. One good site is EnglishCentral.com; there are many others.

References

Abercrombie, D. (1991). Teaching pronunciation. In A. Brown (Ed.), *Teaching English pronunciation: A book of readings* (pp. 87–95). New York: Routledge.

Acton, W. (1991). Changing fossilized pronunciation. In A. Brown (Ed.), *Teaching English pronunciation: A book of readings* (pp. 120–135). New York: Routledge.

Associated Press, Buenos Aires. (2015, February 4). Argentina's president criticised for seemingly racist joke on key China trip. *The Guardian*. Retrieved from www.theguardian.com/world/2015/feb/04/argentinian-president-racist-joke-china-trip

Beebe, L. M. (Ed.). (1988). *Issues in second language acquisition: Multiple perspectives*. Boston, MA: Heinle & Heinle.

Brown, A. (Ed.). (1991). *Teaching English pronunciation: A book of readings*. New York: Routledge.

Chela-Flores, B. (2001). Pronunciation and language learning: An integrative approach. *IRAL*, *39*, 85–101.

Dahlgreen, W. (2014, January 18). It's true! Americans love British accents. *YouGov*. Retrieved from http://yougov.co.uk/news/2014/01/18/its-true-americans-love-british-accents/

Doidge, N. (2007). *The brain that changes itself*. New York: Viking (Penguin)

Giant Bomb Forum. (2014). *Are foreign accents attractive or unattractive?* Retrieved from www.giantbomb.com/forums/off-topic-31/are-foreign-accents-attractive-or-unattractive-1471529/

Jenkins, J. (2002). A sociologically based, empirically researched pronunciation syllabus for English as an international language. *Applied Linguistics*, *23*(1), 83–103.

Kahneman, D. (2011). *Thinking, fast and slow*. London: Penguin.

Lev-Ari, S., & Keysar, B. (2010). Why don't we believe non-native speakers? The influence of accent on credibility. *Journal of Experimental Social Psychology*, *46*, 1093–1096.

McClelland, J. L., Fiez, J. A., & McCandliss, B. D. (2002). Teaching the /r/ – /l/ discrimination to Japanese adults: Behavioral and neural aspects. *Physiology & Behavior*, *77*, 657–662.

NPR. (2009, December 31). *The loudness wars: Why music sounds worse* [Interview with Bob Ludwig, record mastering engineer, and Andrew Oxenham, Professor of Psychology, University of Minnesota]. Retrieved from www.npr.org/2009/12/31/122114058/the-loudness-wars-why-music-sounds-worse

Schulz, K. (2010). *Being wrong: Adventures in the margin of error*. New York: Harper Collins.

Strevens, P. (1991). A rationale for teaching pronunciation: The rival virtues of innocence and sophistication. In A. Brown (Ed.), *Teaching English pronunciation: A book of readings* (pp. 96–103). New York: Routledge.

The Telegraph. (2009, November 3). *Irish accent beats French as world's sexiest*. Retrieved from www.telegraph.co.uk/news/worldnews/europe/ireland/6490202/Irish-accent-beats-French-as-worlds-sexiest.html

Tiku, N. (2013, August 27). Major FWD.us Donor Says a "Strong Foreign Accent" Makes You a Bad CEO. *ValleyWag*. Retrieved from http://valleywag.gawker.com/major-fwd-us-donor-says-a-strong-foreign-accent-makes-1208418411

van Hoek, K. (n.d.). *When Is a foreign accent an asset?* Retrieved from www.chosen-voice.com/news/news_article/when-is-a-foreign-accent-an-asset

Wyner, G. (2014, June 12). How to teach old ears new tricks: Learn a new language more quickly by focusing on pronunciation first. *Scientific American.* Retrieved from www.scientificamerican.com/article/how-to-teach-old-ears-new-tricks/

Yahoo Answers. (2008). *Why Is Chinese accent ugly?* Retrieved from https://answers.yahoo.com/question/ index?qid=20081113000756AA9rYhN

Recommended pronunciation textbooks and references

For teachers wondering where to start, it's here:

Gilbert, J. (2012). *Clear speech* (4th edn.). Cambridge: Cambridge University Press.

The rest:

Baker, A., & Goldstein, S. (2008). *Pronunciation pairs: An introduction to the sounds of English* (2nd edn.). New York: Cambridge University Press.

Beisbier, B. (1994). *Sounds great: Low-intermediate pronunciation for speakers of English.* Boston, MA: Heinle and Heinle.

Brown, A. (2014). *Pronunciation and phonetics: A practical guide for English language teachers.* New York: Routledge.

Brown, J. D. (2012). *New ways in teaching connected speech* (New Ways in TESOL). Alexandria, VA: TESOL.

Celce-Murcia, M. (2010). *Teaching pronunciation: A course book and reference guide* (2nd edn.). Cambridge: Cambridge University Press.

Chan, M. (2009). *Phrase by phrase pronunciation and listening in American English* (2nd edn.). Sunnyvale: Sunburst Media.

Chung, K. S. (2012, January–February to 2014, November–December). *Professor's Corner. A series of 18 articles in Chinese explaining English pronunciation teaching points in detail; in the bimonthly teacher's magazine Hello! ET. Taipei: Cave's English Teaching (CET).* Retrieved from http://homepage.ntu.edu.tw/~karchung/Karen/Karen_Chung_publications.htm#CET

Dauer, R. (1993). *Accurate English: A complete course in pronunciation.* Englewood Cliffs, NJ: Regents Prentice Hall.

Gilbert, J. B. (2008). *Teaching pronunciation using the prosody pyramid.* Cambridge, New York: Cambridge University Press. Retrieved from www.cambridge.org/other_files/downloads/ esl/booklets/Gilbert-Teaching-Pronunciation.pdf

Gorsuch, G., Meyers, C. M., Pickering, L., & Griffee, D. T. (2010). *English communication for international teaching assistants.* Long Grove, IL: Waveland Press.

Graham, C. (1972). *Jazz chants: Rhythms of American English for students of English as a second language.* New York: Oxford University Press.

Grant, L. (2010). *Well said: Pronunciation for clear communication* (3rd edn.). Independence, KY: Heinle Cengage Learning.

Grant, L. (Ed.). (2014). *Pronunciation myths: Applying second language research to classroom teaching.* Ann Arbor, MI: University of Michigan Press.

Hahn, L. D., & Dickerson, W. B. (1999). *Speech craft: Discourse pronunciation for advanced learners.* Ann Arbor, MI: University of Michigan Press.

Hancock, M. (1996). *Pronunciation games* (Cambridge Copy Collection). Cambridge: Cambridge University Press.

Hancock, M. (2012). *English pronunciation in use* (Intermediate) (2nd edn.). Cambridge: Cambridge University Press.
Hewings, M., & Goldstein, S. (1998). *Pronunciation plus: Practice through interaction*. New York: Cambridge University Press.
Kreidler, C. W. (2004). *The pronunciation of English: A course book*. Oxford: Blackwell.
Levis, J., & Moyer, A. (2014). *Social dynamics in second language accent*. Berlin: DeGruyter Mouton.
Miller, S. (2005). *Targeting Pronunciation: Communicating clearly in English* (2nd edn.). Boston, MA: Cengage Learning.
Reed, M., & Michaud, C. (2005). *Sound concepts: An integrated pronunciation course*. New York: McGraw-Hill.
Shockey, L. (2003). *Sound patterns of spoken English*. Oxford: Blackwell.
Teschner, R. V., & Whitley, M. S. (2004). *Pronouncing English: A stress-based approach*. Washington, DC: Georgetown University Press.
Vaughan-Rees, M. (2010). *Rhymes and rhythm: A poem-based course for English pronunciation study*. Reading, England: Garnet Education.

Journal

Journal of Second Language Pronunciation edited by John M. Levis, John Benjamins. Retrieved from https://benjamins.com/#catalog/journals/jslp

Pronunciation conferences

1 **Phonetics Teaching and Learning Conference** http://10times.com/phonetics-teaching-conference
2 **Pronunciation in Second Language Learning and Teaching** http://jlevis.public.iastate.edu/pslltconference/

Online dictionaries with audio files

1 **Merriam-Webster Online Dictionary** (GA) www.merriam-webster.com/
2 **Cambridge Advanced Learner's Dictionary** (BE and GA) http://dictionary.cambridge.org/dictionary/british/
3 **Oxford Learner's Dictionaries** (BE and GA) www.oxfordlearnersdictionaries.com
4 **Macmillan Dictionary** (BE) www.macmillandictionary.com/
5 **The Free Dictionary (GA and BE)** www.thefreedictionary.com/

Easy online input of IPA symbols

1 **i2Spi:k Smart IPA Phonetics Keyboard** www.i2speak.com/
2 **Online IPA Character Input**: http://westonruter.github.io/ipa-chart/keyboard/

Recording and phonetics software and tutorial

1 **Audacity** http://audacity.sourceforge.net/
2 **Olle Kjellin.** *Quality practise pronunciation with audacity – the best method! a tutorial* https://dl.dropboxusercontent.com/u/51074116/Kjellin-Practise-Pronunciation-w-Audacity.pdf

3 **WASP** (Waveforms, Annotations, Spectrograms & Pitch) www.phon.ucl.ac.uk/resource/sfs/wasp.htm
4 **Praat: Doing Phonetics by Computer** www.praat.org/

Video resources

1 **Karen Steffen Chung: Online Introduction to Phonetics Course** Open Course Ware, National Taiwan University (taught in English and Mandarin) http://ocw.aca.ntu.edu.tw/ntu-ocw/index.php/ocw/cou/101S102
2 **English Central** Listening/speaking practice site with feedback www.englishcentral.com/videos#
3 **Gabriel Wyner: The Pronunciation Video Series**
  http://fluent-forever.com/chapter3/#.VBKHM1Ps02Y
4 **Adrian Underhill: Introduction to Teaching Pronunciation Workshop**
  https://www.youtube.com/watch?v=1kAPHyHd7Lo

Online language exchange sites

1 **italki.com** www.italki.com/

10 Fluency in language classrooms
Extensive listening and reading
Alistair Wood

The pairing of reading and listening together in one chapter might seem at first glance to be a somewhat strange combination since we have traditionally taught the four skills separately. Even when we teach integrated skills (e.g., Nunan, 1989), this is usually in terms of more authentic uses of the skills, which in practice are seldom separated. The justification, however, for discussing reading and listening in the same chapter is not in terms of the authenticity of their use together, but rather in the similarities that lie in the pedagogic approaches to both. Both these skills have been described as 'passive' skills, and although the active nature of reading is now widely recognized (e.g., Anderson, 2007–08), with listening later following in this recognition (Nation & Newton, 2009), there is a similarity between them in that both involve comprehension and decoding rather than production.

Both skills are also related in that they have both traditionally been taught by an emphasis on intensive study of relatively short sections of text, with a focus on understanding that text, often at the expense of other aspects. More recently, however, there has been a move away from the intensive study of short texts to appreciation that students must be able to handle longer texts. In addition, more broadly, there has been a recognition that students need to be exposed to much more language, whether written or spoken, than they traditionally meet with in the classroom (Day & Bamford, 1998).

Extensive versus intensive reading

Traditionally, language learning has been conceptualised as a long and arduous process, with the language to be learned broken down in the syllabus into easily learned chunks, whether these chunks are lexical, morphological, or syntactic. Even in later communicative and subsequent eclectic methodologies, which recognise more overtly the linkage between different parts of the system and thus the need for the learner to cope with these, there has still been an overall breaking down of the whole into its parts.

In reading, this can be seen in the division of reading into a plethora of specific skills: skimming, scanning, reading for gist, finding the topic sentence, and so on. This is quite reasonable as it recognises that the umbrella term 'reading' is in fact a superordinate that covers a wide variety of skills. These components, however we itemize them, would also include things such as being able to read quickly for the main ideas of a passage or being able to establish the point of view of the author. The focus on different types of reading skills and strategies has been clear since the 1980s to most English teachers via Christine Nuttall's influential book *Teaching Reading Skills in a Foreign Language* (1982), but there are numerous other studies that ground the teaching of reading skills and strategies on a solid research base (e.g., Anderson, 2005; Carrell, Pharis, & Liberto, 1989; Grabe, 2009). That teaching reading strategies can not only help students but also be taught to students by teachers is also fairly generally accepted (Block & Pressley, 2002, 2007; Hudson, 2007; Koda, 2005).

Nevertheless, although the use of comprehension strategies is certainly valuable to students, there is clearly a sense in which such overtly taught strategies are a help to reading rather than reading itself. If a fluent reader in his or her first language (L1) does not normally use such strategies, then it would seem to be the case that something more is necessary also in the reading classroom. That additional approach is often encapsulated in the contrast between 'intensive' and 'extensive' reading (Al-Homoud & Schmitt, 2009; Carrel & Carson, 1997; Day & Bamford, 1998; Mason & Krashen, 1997; Robb & Susser, 1989). Intensive reading is the norm, the unmarked member of the pair, which is what takes place in the typical reading classroom. Extensive reading, on the other hand, would seem to require somewhat more of an explanation and justification.

The main difference between extensive and intensive reading, as normally described, (e.g., Beglar, Hunt, & Kite, 2012; Day & Bamford, 1998, 2002; Hafiz & Tudor, 1989, Mason & Krashen, 1997) would seem to be, as the name suggests, that students read considerably more and at a lower level than they would in a typical intensive reading class. Thus Mason and Krashen's pioneering study took place over one semester, while Beglar et al. (2012) had their cohort of first-year Japanese university students read extensively over a period of one academic year. Judge's study (2011) was for an even longer period – two and a half years. Whatever the time frame, students are encouraged to read more materials than they would normally.

The basic approach of extensive reading then would be the provision of reading materials that students can cope with, often graded readers (e.g., Al-Homoud & Schmitt, 2009; Beglar et al., 2012; Day & Bamford, 1998; Beglar & Hunt, 2014), and for the reading to be of more materials than would normally be met with in an intensive reading course. For students to read more in a reading course would often be a goal in itself for many reading teachers, but there are other aims which are normally claimed for such extensive reading courses. One immediate aim is that students will find it pleasurable to read and enjoy an activity that they might not otherwise enjoy. Extensive reading does seem to have such positive benefits, and several studies have shown a correlation between extensive reading and positive attitudes to reading (Al-Homoud & Schmitt, 2009; Mason & Krashen, 1997; Robb & Susser, 1989; Taguchi, Takayasu-Maas, & Gorsuch, 2004).

The most basic aim, of course, in any reading programme would be that students become better readers, whether in terms of comprehension, reading rate, or vocabulary development. Typically, students in extensive reading programmes are measured against a control group who had a more traditional intensive reading programme. Thus in Tanaka and Stapleton's study (2007), it was found that the extensive reading group did significantly better than the control group in reading comprehension and reading rate. Similarly, Beglar et al. (2012) and Belgar and Hunt (2014) found that all of their extensive reading groups made greater gains in reading rate than the intensive group and that there was also a correlation within the extensive groups between the amount of reading and the corresponding increase in reading rate.

Extensive versus intensive listening

Extensive reading was a fairly straightforward response to some problems with traditional reading programmes, but the applicability of the concept to other skill areas is not obvious at first sight. Some people, whether students or anybody else, obviously read more, even a lot more, than others. Turning our attention to another skill, like listening, it would seem at first strange to apply the concept of intensive and extensive to listening. If we are not deaf, we spend a good part of our time listening to those around us, and while some may spend more time listening to the radio or music, for example, that does not mean they spend more time listening as such, in the way that someone who reads novels can be said to spend more time reading.

However, if we consider how we traditionally teach listening, it becomes apparent that the approach is very similar to that found when we teach intensive reading. Both are typically taught for comprehension, and comprehension questions are set after a listening passage just as they are after a reading passage. Similarly, too, there was a move in teaching listening towards teaching listening comprehension strategies paralleling the move with reading comprehension (O'Malley, Chamot, & Küpper, 1989; Rubin, 1994; Vandergrift, 1999). Thus learners are encouraged, for example, to be aware of the process of listening. However, to what extent this actually helps learners to understand more of what they are listening is debatable (Berne, 2004; Chen, 2005; Goh, 2002; Renandya & Farrell, 2010; Rubin, 1994; Siegel, 2013), as sometimes listening strategies are claimed to be effective (e.g., Siegel, 2011) and at other times less so (e.g., Blyth, 2012). On balance, nevertheless, it would seem to be the consensus that strategy instruction is useful.

However, it would seem to be more appropriate to adult and more advanced learners than younger and more intermediate students. If we examine the kinds of problems faced by learners when doing listening activities, they are likely to include things such as too rapid speech rate (Hasan, 2000). Especially in the initial stages of learning a language, it is often the case that we find it difficult to comprehend speech that often seems too fast. There is also often an inability to understand stretches of text despite the ability to understand specific individual words (Goh, 2000). Similarly, it is often the case that the sound of a word is rather different from the spoken form, and learners may find it difficult to understand words that they in fact know in the written form (Field, 2003; Goh, 2000; Wilson, 2003). None of these problems is particularly amenable to solving by means of cognitive or metacognitive strategies.

Many of the problems listed here are likely to be, if not solved, at least given the possibility of being ameliorated, if an approach similar to extensive reading is applied to listening. In recent years, the concept of extensive reading has been applied also to listening (Field, 1998; Renandya & Farrell, 2010; Waring, 2008). If we allow listeners to listen to materials for a longer time, including repeated listenings, then they are more likely to be able to understand the materials. As Field (1998) points out, in many listening lessons there is not that much listening going on. The tape is played for only a short time, and much of the lesson is made up of pre-listening activities and going over comprehension exercises. The actual listening may take up only a few minutes of the whole period, perhaps only about 5%. How are students then supposed to practice their listening when they in fact do very little of it?

It could perhaps be argued that students are spending a lot of their time in the classroom listening since they are interacting with other students and the teacher. This is indeed true, but in fact it proves the point about the necessity and appropriacy of extensive listening. Listening to other students is characterised by input which is at the level of the student, relatively slow, spoken in an accent they understand, and likely to be relatively short. This type of listening is not a problem – what is a problem is the rapid paced, often by a native speaker, focused on comprehension questions, type of listening that is prevalent in many schools. Even the English spoken by the teacher has the advantage of familiarity, being targeted at the learners and on topics that are often repeated and whose vocabulary is known.

In extensive listening, therefore, in a similar case to extensive reading, students have the opportunity to listen to materials which are at their own level and during which the listening takes place over a longer time than is normally the case with comprehension-focused materials. Renandya and Farrell (2010, p. 56) define extensive listening as follows: "Extensive listening is defined here to mean all types of listening activities that allow learners to receive a lot of comprehensible and enjoyable listening input." As well as being enjoyable, it is primarily the case that the material chosen should be at a level that is easily understandable by students and the topics appropriate. For Waring (2008), extensive listening "involves fluently listening to a lot of comprehensible language" (p. 7).

Both definitions, whether in terms of comprehensibility or fluency, emphasize the fact that learners should be able to understand the text they are listening to without having to stop the tape or ask the speaker to repeat what they are saying. Thus, as with reading materials, the speaking materials should be at a level that is easily coped with by the speaker, whether in terms of vocabulary or grammar. Since this is listening material, it should also be added that the pronunciation should not cause problems, so the speaker(s) should not have an accent or speak at a speed that makes the material difficult to follow.

Extensive reading and listening

Having looked at extensive reading and listening separately, we turn in this section to look at a relatively recent development in the use of extensive materials and that is combining together extensive reading and listening. Various authors (e.g., Chang & Millet, 2014; Chang, 2009, 2011, 2012; Gobel & Kano, 2014; Stephens, 2011; Woodall, 2010) have experimented in the last few years with using both reading and listening simultaneously. This is not just from a feeling that if extensive reading is a good idea and so is extensive listening, then the two together must be even better. Sushi may be good and ice cream may be good, but we do not normally eat them together!

It might be considered that if learners simultaneously listened to a text while at the same time reading the written version of the text, they are not likely to improve their listening skills since they may rely completely or mainly on the written text for comprehension. However, Chang (2009, 2011) found that learners improved their listening skills despite reading the text simultaneously. Although sometimes (Chang, 2009) the relative improvement in the combined mode versus the listening only mode was not particularly great, the students concerned greatly preferred the combined mode. Other studies showed greater gains (Chang, 2011) but also sometimes not so great (Chang, 2012). Notice here that the same researcher found varying gains with different groups, so it would seem to be the case that the type or the amount of listening does make a difference in how effective the combined mode is (Chang & Millet, 2014). Sufficient listening activity must take place or else students may simply rely on the reading channel for information (Chang & Millet, 2014). In this latter experimental study, of the three groups, the reading only group was outperformed by the listening only group, which in its turn was outperformed by the reading and listening combined group. It should be noted that the reading group was also given practice in listening via more traditional intensive listening practice. This would seem to indicate that extensive listening and, more particularly, combined reading and listening is effective in raising listening abilities.

In a completely different part of the world (Puerto Rico), Woodal (2010) also found that the reading and listening group came out ahead of the listening only group in comprehension. It should be noted, too, that this comprehension was in terms both of gist and detailed comprehension. As well as improving listening comprehension, this combined reading and listening was found to improve incidental vocabulary acquisition in a study by Brown, Waring, and Donkaewbua (2008).

It would seem, therefore, that combining reading and listening does improve listening comprehension. The most obvious reason for this is that reading while listening gives students the opportunity to check their understanding via one mode with understanding in the other mode. They thus have both (a) twice the input as via the unitary mode and (b) a cross check on their understanding. More exactly, reading a text while at the same time listening to it provides a solution to several of the problems identified earlier as being symptomatic of aural processing of input text. Thus a text that is spoken too fast for the learner, has words that are not recognized but actually known in the written form, or is spoken in a difficult to understand accent, can all be understood much more easily in the written mode while listening. That this is the case can be appreciated if we think how we react when seeing subtitles to a film in a language that we speak but do not speak too well, as we use the subtitles to help us with the incomprehensible dialogue.

The subtitles in a film example should show us that reading while listening is not such a totally alien concept outside the classroom. Granted that as adults we seldom listen to an audio text while at the same time reading it, this is not the case with our children. Parents not only read aloud to their young children when the child is totally unable to read but also when they are beginning to read, and our first reading experience is often while simultaneously being supplied with auditory input. If this is our experience in the L1, then it is reasonable to assume that it might also be useful in the second language (L2). Learners of English as a second or foreign language may have much greater reading skills than L1 listeners and are thus more likely to be able to make use of their reading skills, but they are also more cognitively advanced and thus able to more systematically compare the input in the two modes.

Nevertheless, the fear that learners may come to depend on the written mode is a reasonable one, and it is likely to be the case if learners do not get sufficient aural input to become confident in their listening skills, as Chang (2012) found. However, if the practice is really extensive, then students are liable to depend less and less on the reading mode and more on the aural input. It should be noted here that listening is a more natural mode than reading: everybody with normal hearing and mental abilities naturally listens to language and understands it. Thus as learners improve their listening, they will automatically begin to rely more on the auditory and less on the written input.

It does seem, though, that much of the work on simultaneous reading and listening has been done in societies where the level of English among learners is not particularly high and where often there is another script in use in the L1 (Chang in Taiwan, Gobel & Kano, and Stephens in Japan for example). It may be the case that for these learners the aural input and written input are mutually reinforcing since they would also find the written text relatively harder to process than those already used to the Western alphabet. Or it may be the case that the low level of English and a traditional reliance on grammar translation as a method in both China and Japan means that students have difficulty with activities that emphasize understanding of natural spoken language input. It is nevertheless of interest that much of the impetus towards combining extensive reading and listening is coming out of Asia and the focus of this volume on the teaching of English in Asia should make this approach of particular interest.

Extensive listening and reading and fluency

The definition quoted earlier from Waring (2008) was expressed in terms of fluency, and having looked at the ideas of extensive reading and listening, we need to turn now to the superficially familiar concept of fluency. Waring does not explain what he means by 'fluently listening,' and it is a concept not as easy to grasp as 'fluently speaking,' which we are all familiar with. In an everyday sense, we all talk about being fluent in a language, a term which is used by teacher and lay person alike to convey our idea about how much someone knows a language.

Clearly, as it has grown up over recent decades, the idea of fluency must be taken to mean something rather more than just an ability to speak well. Looked at a bit further, it is often contrasted with the idea of accuracy, as in titles such as *Communicative Methodology in Language Teaching: The Roles of Fluency and Accuracy* (Brumfit & Brumfit, 1984). In this communicative paradigm, the two are often seen as being somewhat in opposition so that one develops while the other does not. Consequently, there arises the idea that the one should not be at the expense of the other, as encapsulated in Hammerly's *Fluency and Accuracy: Towards Balance in Language Teaching and Learning* (1991).

Before we accept that there is necessarily a trade-off between fluency and accuracy, perhaps it might be a good idea to examine a little more closely what we mean by fluency. As indicated earlier, fluency can be said to have two separate meanings (Lennon, 1990, 2000): ability in the language and something more specific. What this something more specific is may be more difficult to pin down (Housen & Kuiken, 2009) but is frequently considered to relate to the automaticity of processing (Schmidt, 1992). This definition is more focused on fluency in speech, but the idea can be broadened out so that it covers the "rapid, smooth, accurate, lucid, and efficient translation of thought . . . into language under the temporal constraints of on-line processing" (Lennon, 2000, p. 26).

Two things are of interest here: first that the definition of fluency now encompasses more than speech and thus can be applied to other language skills such as reading or listening, and second, Lennon's definition also includes the concept of accuracy. This also relates to the other meaning of fluency, a high level of ability in a language, thus uniting the two meanings of fluency into one composite picture of smooth, fluid accurate use of the language. If we consider the link with online processing, too, this helps us to get away from a conception of fluency as just being an oral skill and broadens it out to cover all four skills, not only speaking but also, writing, reading, and listening.

If we transfer the concept of easy processing in real time, without having to rerun any language, from speaking, we can see its applicability to reading. Disfluent reading would involve having to go back and read something again for comprehension so that it was not understood as the reader read the text. Similarly, if the reader had to slow down from his or her normal reading speed in order to comprehend the text, this would not be said to be fluent reading. Applied to listening, this would mean that a student should be able to process the speech heard and understand it in real time as he or she listens to the speech without having to stop and re-process.

Taking into account the dual meaning of fluency, being able to process, but also having high ability, and thus including accuracy rather than being a counterpoint to that term, it should be clear that listening could not be said to be at all fluent if the listener processed the speech heard in real time but misunderstood what was said. As applied to reading, a student who increased his or her reading speed with extensive reading, but at the cost of comprehension, could not be said to be reading fluently. Thus Beglar et al. (2012) included a measure of comprehension among the students they evaluated to make sure that any increase in reading rate was not offset by diminished comprehension.

This would seem to go against the grain for extensive practice. In contrast to intensive reading, it is customary in extensive reading not to have much or indeed any comprehension activities since the aim is to increase reading speeds and foster greater pleasure in reading. This does not mean, however, that we can totally forget comprehension; rather, it suggests that the balance should swing away from too frequent or overt checking of comprehension, not that there should be no control of comprehension at all. It is possible to monitor reading progress without using comprehension questions (Renandya & Jacobs, 2002).

Given, therefore, that the conception of fluency does include accuracy, and that we have some checking of comprehension to ensure accuracy, we can see fluency as a necessary part of any foreign language programme. The two faces of fluency, online processing in real time and accurate understanding of the text, are therefore complimentary aspects of the same process. With extensive reading and listening, we are able to expose our students to greater amounts of written or oral text and thus give them greater opportunities to practice.

Extensive reading and listening in the classroom

Standard descriptions already exist of how to set up extensive reading programmes (e.g., Bell, 1998; Day & Bamford, 1998; Susser & Robb, 1990), so this section will focus more on extensive listening and extensive reading and listening. Compared to extensive reading, intensive listening has a rather shorter history, so how to run such programmes has not been worked out in practice to such an extent. In addition, it is not so obvious at first glance just how to go about setting up an extensive listening programme. Whereas graded readers have long been used and are widely available, and borrowing books from libraries is standard practice, it is not so easy to work out how to set up extensive listening.

The first problem is finding suitable materials. There are no exact equivalents of graded readers in listening materials. Having said that, most textbooks for beginning and intermediate learners include listening material, while it is also possible to listen to the radio, and even find listening material on the radio, which is spoken at a slower speed – e.g., the Voice of America broadcasts in Special English (Renandya & Farrell, 2010). Nowadays, however, there are literally hundreds of thousands of videos available on YouTube, most of which may be too difficult for beginners or intermediate learners, but that still leaves tens of thousands of videos which can be used. YouTube also has special channels where organisations or individuals can upload videos, and it is possible to subscribe to these channels.

This makes available much specialised material, which may not be suitable for all classes, but there is a lot of educational material around which can be used. Thus channels such as BBC Earth or Discovery have a lot of material which is broadly educational and can be used in the class, or similar websites can be used.

At higher levels, use can easily be made, for example, of Ted Talks, in which excellent speakers give short talks to an audience. These talks can be on all sorts of subjects and are not necessarily academic. Again, many will be too difficult for intermediate learners or beginners, but there are so many, and they are so well done, that it is easy to use them for listening practice. In the case of Ted Talks, there are also relatively few visual elements since it is just the speaker talking to the audience in most cases. This means that it is more truly just listening practice since there is little visual help to the learner.

Other documentary-type material online will likely have a larger visual element, but this can often be used as additional comprehension support and allow intermediate learners to cope with language that would otherwise be above their level. This is true obviously also of material on television, and film material should not necessarily be discarded just because there is a visual as well as an aural component. If the film is almost completely visual and can be understood just from viewing, then of course it should not be used, but the precise balance between visual and aural elements will depend on the learners' levels and interests, as well as the focus of the lesson.

It should not be forgotten that Internet radio now makes available listening material from all over the world and with much better sound quality than is traditionally available from, for example, the BBC World Service. Many such traditional international broadcasters are now available online, and they can be downloaded for use in extensive listening contexts. Aside from these, there are thousands of Internet radio stations available, ranging from outlets run by one individual to major international commercial organisations. However, the worldwide reach of Internet radio and the corresponding availability of specialist materials means that all kinds of materials at all levels can be found, from the recondite to the everyday.

Similar to this is the use of podcasts, which are also available on all kinds of topics and have the advantage over Internet radio of being more focused on the spoken word and less on music. Podcasts can be found on a huge array of subjects, from sport to science to various hobbies, so learners can follow a podcast that is in their area of interest. There are even podcasts available especially for learners of English so that the problem of difficulty level is eased. Since such sites are liable to change very quickly and sometimes have a commercial side, I do not provide any specific links here, but they can easily be found via an online search. One advantage of podcasts is that they can be listened to online on any personal computer or laptop, or downloaded for listening to later, even on a smartphone.

Another possibility that should not be ignored is television. A lot of material that might not be considered suitable for education can actually be used for listening. Although much of reality TV is of very low quality from the point of view of television, it does provide a lot of examples of people talking English to each other. *Keeping up with the Kardashians* might not be high-class television, but it is full of people talking to each other about everyday subjects and repeating the same ideas, and therefore vocabulary and structures, seemingly ad infinitum! Soaps are another example where the same topics are recycled and the same speakers appear, so learners can become used to vocabulary and individual ways of speaking.

If we turn from materials to how to use them, then there is a distinction here between use in and outside of the classroom, as there is with extensive reading. Some traditional teacher-centred techniques such as reading a story to a class or dictation can only be done in class, while many other sources, such as television, might more easily be done outside of class. However, a lot of sources, such as podcasts, could be listened to either inside or outside of the class, and with a little ingenuity they could be used in both situations; the determining factor would be how you wanted to use the materials, how the course was constructed, and how much work can be done inside or outside the classroom. Whether the listening is done mostly in class or outside may be something that is largely outside your control as a teacher in many cases, but it should not be a make-or-break decision most of the time.

The kinds of activities that can be done with the materials suggested largely parallel those for extensive reading. Students can listen to the material once or more than once, and there should be a fairly loose approach to monitoring. Extensive listening, like reading, does not require close comprehension questions. As with reading, as mentioned earlier, however, there should be some feedback from the students on their listening. There are various ways this can be done:

- A diary of their listening, what they listened to online, on TV, or on radio, with a commentary about what they liked, what they found difficult, what they found interesting
- A critique of a TV series they are following with comments on interesting characters
- A reaction report to a TV programme, podcast, online talk, or anything they have listened to
- A comparison between different TED talks, or similar listening events online
- A discussion of their favourite or most hated character in a reality TV programme or a soap – e.g., who they think should win a show like *Big Brother*.

The type of thing that is wanted should be clear. It is an overall impression to show that they have indeed listened to the material and for you as a teacher to gauge their response. This is a teaching programme not a testing programme, and although it would be possible to gauge whether extensive listening improved test scores (Gobel & Kano, 2014), this is not the focus of such activities. Over time, it will become clear in intensive listening classes whether students' listening comprehension is improving or remaining static.

If we turn to extensive listening and reading, then there is an obvious additional problem involved in that we need to find listening material for which there is also a written script available. In some cases, with commercially published listening materials, this is often the case. Where the listening material is available but not the written text, transcription by the teacher is possible, and where written material – e.g., a story – is available, the teacher may make an aural version by reading it, either live to the class or by making a recording. Clearly, it would be easier if we could find material, which is accessible both in aural and written form, to save the teacher's precious time if nothing else.

Either scripts or transcripts of television series are often available online. Since television series are now commonly sold as DVD sets, it is possible to get hold of both the script and the actual TV programme. With programmes currently running on TV, it is more difficult usually to get hold of the script. With students simultaneously reading the script as the programme is playing on TV, it is clearly impossible for them to both watch the television and read the script at the same time. It is possible either to make this a more purely listening exercise so that they just listen to the TV, or alternatively they first watch the programme and then read the script.

Another alternative and a way of getting round this dilemma is of course to watch television programmes or films which have subtitles. It is often possible to get subtitles for TV programmes, even if the TV programme is in the same language as the subtitles, for deaf viewers. Thus it is possible to get subtitles in English for English television programmes. Similarly, many movies have subtitles in English, even those films that are in English.

One unusual source for a listening text with written transcript that might not immediately spring to mind is the availability on YouTube of songs with their lyrics on the screen as they play. Although not something that could be used alone, these might be a useful additional source and likely to be highly motivating to learners if they can listen to their favourite groups or singers. Depending on the song, this can even be used with beginners or lower intermediate learners.

As regards how the 'extensive listening while reading' materials should be presented, it is possible to either have the listening and reading materials accessed simultaneously – i.e., the learner reads the text while listening to it – or alternatively the reading can come after the listening. Since the listening is the focus rather than the reading, it is preferable that the listening comes first rather than the reading if the materials are not presented simultaneously. But mostly such materials are presented simultaneously so that the learner is given support in comprehending the material at the time they most need it: as they listen.

Extensive reading and listening is still rather in its infancy compared to the other extensive approaches, but it is likely to grow in importance, and it is an interesting development. Since it is relatively new, ways of tackling it are still being developed, so there is still a lot of scope for development. Do not be afraid to experiment and try out different ways of doing it, to find what suits your students best. The best way is not what the book says but always what works best for your students.

References

Al-Homoud, F., & Schmitt, N. (2009). Extensive reading in a challenging environment: A comparison of extensive and intensive reading approaches in Saudi Arabia. *Language Teaching Research*, *13*, 383–401.

Anderson, N. (2005). L2 learning strategies. In E. Hinkel (Ed.), *Handbook of research in second language teaching and learning* (pp. 757–771). Mahwah, NJ: Lawrence Erlbaum.

Anderson, N. (2007–2008). *Active skills for reading* (2nd edn.). Boston, MA: Heinle & Heinle.

Beglar, D., & Hunt, A. (2014). Pleasure reading and reading rate gains. *Reading in a Foreign Language*, *26*(1), 29–48.

Beglar, D., Hunt, A., & Kite, Y. (2012). The effect of pleasure reading on Japanese university learners' reading rates. *Language Learning*, *62*, 665–703.

Bell, T. (1998). Extensive reading: Why? and how? *The Internet TESL Journal*, *4*(12). Retrieved from http://202.194.48.102/englishonline/jxyj/iteslj/Bell-Reading.html

Berne, J. E. (2004). Listening comprehension strategies: A review of the literature. *Foreign Language Annals*, *37*, 521–531.

Block, C., & Pressley, M. (Eds.). (2002). *Comprehension instruction: Research-based best practices*. New York: Guildford Press.

Block, C., & Pressley, M. (2007). Best practices in teaching comprehension. In L. Gambrell, L. Morrow, & M. Pressley (Eds.), *Best practices in literacy instruction* (3rd edn.) (pp. 220–242). New York: Guildford Press.

Blyth, A. (2012). Extensive listening versus listening strategies: Response to Siegel. *ELT Journal*, *66*, 236–239.

Brown, R., Waring, R., & Donkaewbua, S. (2008). Incidental vocabulary acquisition from reading, reading-while-listening, and listening to stories. *Reading in a Foreign Language*, *20*, 136–163.

Brumfit, C., & Brumfit, C. J. (1984). *Communicative methodology in language teaching: The roles of fluency and accuracy*. Cambridge: Cambridge University Press.

Carrell, P. L., & Carson, J. (1997). Extensive and intensive reading in an EAP setting. *English for Specific Purposes*, *16*, 47–60.

Carrell, P. L., Pharis, B. G., & Liberto, J. C. (1989). Metacognitive strategy reading for ESL reading. *TESOL Quarterly*, *23*, 647–678.

Chang, A. C-S. (2009). Gains to L2 listeners from reading while listening vs. listening only in comprehending short stories. *System*, *37*, 652–663.

Chang, A. C-S. (2011). The effects of reading while listening to audiobooks: Listening fluency and vocabulary gain. *Asian Journal of English Language Teaching*, *21*, 43–64.

Chang, A. C-S. (2012). Gains to L2 learners from extensive listening: Listening development, vocabulary acquisition and perceptions of the intervention. *Hong Kong Journal of Applied Linguistics*, *14*(1), 25–47.

Chang, A. C-S., & Millett, S. (2014). The effect of extensive listening on developing L2 listening fluency: Some hard evidence. *ELT Journal*, *68*(1), 31–40.

Chen, Y. (2005). Barriers to acquiring listening strategies for EFL learners and their pedagogical implications. *Teaching English as a Second or Foreign Language*, *8*(4). Retrieved from www.tesl-ej.org/wordpress/issues/volume8/ej32/ej32a2/

Day, R. D., & Bamford, J. (1998). *Extensive reading in the second language classroom*. Cambridge: Cambridge University Press.

Day, R., & Bamford, J. (2002). Top ten principles for teaching extensive reading. *Reading in a foreign language, 14*(2), 136–141.

Field, J. (1998). Skills and strategies: Towards a new methodology for listening. *ELT Journal, 52*, 110–118.

Field, J. (2003). Promoting perception: Lexical segmentation in L2 listening. *ELT Journal, 57*, 325–334.

Gobel, P., & Kano, M. (2014). Implementing a year-long reading while listening program for Japanese University EFL students. *Computer Assisted Language Learning, 27*, 279–293.

Goh, C. C. M. (2000). A cognitive perspective on language learners' listening comprehension problems. *System, 28*, 55–75.

Goh, C. C. M. (2002). Exploring listening comprehension tactics and their interaction patterns. *System, 30*, 185–206.

Grabe, W. (2009). *Reading in a second language: Moving from theory to practice.* Cambridge: Cambridge University Press.

Hafiz, F., & Tudor, I. (1989). Extensive reading and the development of language skills. *ELT Journal, 43*(1), 4–13.

Hammerly, H. (1991). *Fluency and accuracy: Towards balance in language teaching and learning.* Clevedon: Multilingual Matters.

Hasan, A. S. (2000). Learners' perceptions of listening comprehension problems. *Language, Culture and Curriculum, 13*, 137–153.

Housen, A., & Kuiken, F. (2009). Complexity, accuracy and fluency in second language acquisition. *Applied Linguistics, 30*, 461–473.

Hudson, T. (2007). *Teaching second language reading.* Oxford: Oxford University Press.

Judge, P. B. (2011). Driven to read: Enthusiastic readers in a Japanese high school's extensive reading program. *Reading in a Foreign Language, 23*, 161–186.

Koda, K. (2005). *Insights into second language reading: A cross-linguistic approach.* Cambridge: Cambridge University Press.

Lennon, P. (1990). Investigating fluency in EFL: A quantitative approach. *Language Learning, 40*, 387–417.

Lennon, P. (2000). The lexical element in spoken second language fluency. In H. Riggenbach (Ed.), *Perspectives on fluency* (pp. 25–42). Ann Arbor, MI: University of Michigan Press.

Mason, B., & Krashen, S. (1997). Extensive reading in English as a Foreign Language. *System, 24*, 91–102.

Nation, I. S. P., & Newton, J. (2009). *Teaching ESL/EFL listening and speaking.* Abingdon: Routledge.

Nunan, D. (1989). *Designing tasks for the communicative classroom.* Cambridge: Cambridge University Press.

Nuttall, C. (1982). *Teaching reading skills in a foreign language.* Portsmouth: Heinemann.

O'Malley, J. M., Chamot, A. U., & Küpper, L. (1989). Listening comprehension strategies in second language acquisition. *Applied Linguistics, 10*, 418–437.

Renandya, W. A., & Farrell, T. S. C. (2010). 'Teacher, the tape is too fast!': Extensive listening in ELT. *ELT Journal, 65*(1), 52–59.

Renandya, W. A., & Jacobs, G. M. (2002). Extensive reading: Why aren't we all doing it? In J. C. Richards (Ed.), *Methodology in language teaching: An anthology of current practice* (pp. 295–302). Cambridge: Cambridge University Press

Robb, T., & Susser, B. (1989). Extensive reading vs. skills building in an EFL context. *Reading in a Foreign Language, 5,* 239–251.
Rubin, J. (1994). A review of second language listening comprehension research. *The Modern Language Journal, 78,* 199–221.
Schmidt, R. (1992). Psychological mechanisms underlying second language fluency. *Studies in Second Language Acquisition, 14,* 357–385.
Siegel, J. (2011). Thoughts on L2 listening pedagogy. *ELT Journal, 65,* 318–321.
Siegel, J. (2013). Second language learners' perceptions of listening strategy instruction. *Innovation in Language Learning and Teaching, 7*(1), 1–18.
Stephens, M. (2011). The primacy of extensive listening. *ELT Journal, 65,* 311–313.
Susser, B., & Robb, T. (1990). EFL extensive reading instruction: Research and procedure. *JALT Journal, 12*(2), 161–185.
Taguchi, E., Takayasu-Maass, M., & Gorsuch, G. J. (2004). Developing reading fluency in EFL: How assisted repeated reading and extensive reading affect fluency development. *Reading in a Foreign Language, 16,* 70–96.
Tanaka, H., & Stapleton, P. (2007). Increasing reading input in Japanese high school EFL classrooms: An empirical study exploring the efficacy of extensive reading. *The Reading Matrix, 7*(1), 115–126.
Vandergrift, L. (1999). Facilitating second language listening comprehension: Acquiring successful strategies. *ELT Journal, 53,* 168–176.
Waring, R. (2008). Starting extensive listening. *Extensive Reading in Japan, 1*(1), 7–9. Retrieved from www.robwaring.org/el/articles/Starting_Extensive_Listening_ERJ_June_2008.pdf
Wilson, M. (2003). Discovery listening - improving perceptual processing. *ELT Journal 57*(4), 335–343.
Woodall, B. (2010). Simultaneous listening and reading in ESL: Helping second language learners read (and enjoy reading) more efficiently. *TESOL Quarterly, 1,* 186–205.

11 Literature in an age of distraction

Alan Maley

There can be no doubt that we live in an age of distraction. The impact of the Internet offering access to unlimited information and entertainment (Postman, 1985); the ubiquity of handheld devices, which induce a form of universal communicative addiction (however vacuous); the availability of games, videos and music; the advertising and peer-pressure to acquire goods in ever-increasing quantities, and to discard them ever more quickly; the near-extinction of the notion of silence as we are assailed by a barrage of music, sound and noise (van Leeuwen, 1999) – all of these factors raise formidable problems for the concentration and reflective modes of thought, which literature requires of its readers. There is even some evidence to suggest that the structure of our brains is being modified from exposure to the electronic envelope we are sealed in (Carr, 2010).

The survival of literature in the curriculum is also under threat from a control culture, which increasingly requires that everything be prescribed in detail and tested for immediate results. As Eisner succinctly puts it, "Such an image of education requires that schools be organised to prescribe, control, and predict the consequences of their actions, that those consequences be immediate and empirically manifest and that they be measurable" (Eisner, 1985, pp. 356–357). When education is reduced to the level of 'delivery' (one of the current prevailing metaphors), what chance does literature stand? And why should anyone bother with it? What use is it anyway? I shall return to these issues in the course of this chapter.

There are also a number of important differences in the current situation, which will affect the way we approach the use and teaching of literature. What are these new realities?

- As the demand for English as the language of opportunity continues to increase, there will be more students, many of whom will never have been exposed to literature before. This implies a democratic, inclusive, rather than an elitist, exclusive teaching approach. We can no longer expect students to come with a background in literary culture. And that may be no bad thing, for it gives us opportunities to re-think the way we present literature in the classroom.

- As English itself spreads, both geographically and functionally, it will continue to change rapidly and become more varied. New varieties are coming into being, and old ones are constantly evolving. This diversity has been recognised for a number of years now and needs to be taken into consideration. An exclusive focus on 'standard' English will no longer satisfy this reality. Yet one sees very little evidence of this recognition in practice. Non-canonical literature is one powerful way of acknowledging and celebrating this variety.
- As English becomes a necessary condition for personal or professional success, it will no longer be a sufficient condition to be able to use it averagely well (Graddol, 2006). Increasingly, the premium will be on those who can use it to a high degree of proficiency (Maley, 2009) and fuse it with 'life skills' (Clandfield et al., 2011; Rogers, 2008). Literature surely has a role to play, both as a counterweight to an excessively pragmatic view of language, but also as a necessary enrichment of language learning at the highest levels.
- As the opportunities for international exchanges become more frequent, there will be a corresponding need for social and cultural sensitivity. Social and emotional intelligence will become more important (Goleman, 1996, 2006; Spendlove, 2008). As we shall see in this chapter, one of the functions literature can usefully perform is to raise awareness of cross-cultural issues.
- As life in a consumerist world dominated by English becomes more demanding and more pressurized, the value of reflection and critical intelligence will be enhanced. (Fisher, 2001; Honore, 2004; Naish, 2008; Postman & Weingartner, 1976; Unrau, 2008). There is an increasing awareness that language learning is not simply a mechanical matter of acquiring the linguistic nuts and bolts, separated off from the world we live in. Increasingly, language learning is seen to include more broadly educational functions.
- As the demand for instant solutions and quick fixes in education becomes more insistent, the value of a more deliberate mode of thinking will become more urgent (Claxton, 1997). Literature is not usually about quick fixes, so once again it has a clear role to play in offering an alternative mode of perceiving the world.
- As English becomes more international, so will the movement to more local independence become more pronounced. The tensions between English as a medium for global communication and English as a badge of local cultural identity will be intensified. Local literatures in English have expanded in a spectacular fashion over the past 50 years or so. Literature in English is now well established in the Indian subcontinent, in parts of Africa, in Malaysia, in Singapore, in the Philippines, and in the Caribbean. That is hardly surprising given the colonial legacy of English in these territories. But we are now beginning to see original literature in English emerging from the so-called expanding circle (Kachru, 1992) – Nepal, Iran, Afghanistan, China, Vietnam, and so on. This provides a rich and varied resource for teaching, and an opportunity to develop new perspectives on other cultures.

Within the context of literature, I believe that such factors can to some extent be accommodated through the way we select the texts to which students will be exposed and by the manner in which we use these texts. The following sections should, therefore, be read against the earlier list of realities to assess the value of a new orientation toward the value of including literature in our programmes.

Why literature?

The justification for the place of literature in the language teaching curriculum is commonly made with reference to three main models: the linguistic model, the cultural model, and the personal-growth model (Carter & McRae, 1996; Duff & Maley, 2007, pp. 5–6; Maley, 2001, p. 182). Literary texts certainly offer a rich and varied linguistic resource and as such provide the kind of input for phonological, lexical, syntactical and discoursal acquisition regarded by many as essential for effective language learning, in contrast to the more restricted and narrow exposure offered by many pedagogically driven texts. Contrary to what is claimed by some critics, literary texts are not necessarily 'too difficult.' Literature is such a vast resource that we can find texts at all levels of linguistic (and cognitive) difficulty. They are also an ideal resource for the development of language awareness: of language variation (historical, geographical, professional, sociological), of social appropriacy and of ideological bias. Using texts like this can clearly sharpen students' critical thinking as well as their sensitivity to language.

In the international context of English use, where multicultural encounters are increasingly frequent and significant, and where misunderstandings so easily arise, the cultural potential offered by literature is also undeniable. This is not to claim that literature can be used to 'teach' culture except in the most limited sense, but it can illuminate the multi-faceted contexts, practices and beliefs our students may be expected to encounter in their professional and personal lives outside the classroom. This is particularly the case nowadays, when there is such a wealth of literature in English available from across many cultures. In the words of Kramsch (1993, pp. 233–259), it can create 'third places' from which students can critically examine both their own and other cultures. In the best of cases, this can lead to increased awareness of 'difference' and greater tolerance of 'the other.'

Literary texts have lost none of their power to promote personal growth, through better understanding of human motivation and action, both one's own and others'. Students exposed to such texts are opened to better critical understanding of themselves and of others in this rapidly changing and often confusing and paradoxical world. It is perhaps worth adding that literature has an enduring power to delight and to console. One of the criteria for evaluating a text (or any other art form, for that matter) is the extent to which we willingly return to it, relishing it anew each time, and always finding something fresh in it. Those who learn to appreciate and savour literature have the quality of their lives permanently enhanced. And in times of pain and suffering, literature has the power to console. It also offers an escape into an alternative world – which may be no bad thing sometimes!

Literature also has a unique potential to motivate and enthuse learners. The awareness that they are accessing 'real,' meaningful texts does wonders for their self-esteem. Literary texts are also highly salient and therefore memorable. Once learners are hooked, they are hooked for good. But, in an age of distraction, with so many competing attractions, just how can we hook them? The rest of this chapter will make some modest suggestions, fully conscious that there is no magic solution. All approaches are less than perfect, and no one approach will ever satisfy everyone, but that should not inhibit us from making some practical suggestions.

Approaches to teaching literature

Traditionally, there have been three major approaches to the use of literature in language teaching programmes.

Literature as study

From earliest times, it has been traditional to focus on canonical texts as objects of study: set books, line-by-line analysis and explication, dry as dust analysis. This approach centres on *teaching about* literature. Typically, this involves a good deal of transmission of received opinions about writers, their lives and times, their influences, critical views of their work and so on. The whole emphasis is on 'telling' rather than on 'discovery' and on memorizing content and facts rather than on critical reflection and inquiry.

The *Literature as Study* approach also tends to focus on canonical texts drawn from inner circle countries (Kachru, 1992). Such texts are often far removed from students' lived experience and are often culturally inaccessible. Even when more local texts are chosen, the transmission-dominated model of methodology usually remains unchanged, and this is inappropriate in the current context where there is a need for students to become active participants rather than passive recipients. It is certainly unlikely to hook many students in an age of distraction!

Literature as resource

An alternative approach is to treat literary texts as a resource to draw on for the teaching of language. The texts chosen tend to be drawn from a wider range and are used either as samples of language use or as springboards into other language learning activities. In a sense, the literature is secondary to the language learning aims and objectives: it is a kind of vehicle for engaging with the language. This might be characterised as *teaching with* literature.

The *Literature as Resource* approach may also prove unsatisfactory. It may become nothing more than another way of introducing and practicing language as part of a pre-determined syllabus. The specifically literary value of texts may be overshadowed by the linguistic content and the methodological gymnastics played with it. There is a danger that this approach may be reduced to a box of tricks, which students rapidly tire of.

Neither the *Literature as Study*, nor the *Literature as Resource* models therefore seem to offer the kind of access to literature needed in an age of distraction. There is, however, a third possible approach, which may be called *Literature as Appropriation*.

Literature as appropriation

In this approach, the aim is to encourage and enable students to make literature their own, to appropriate it for their own learning purposes in ways they find relevant to themselves and to the context in which they find themselves. Both of the other approaches are to a greater or lesser degree external to the students, what I have termed elsewhere *literature from the outside in* (Maley, 2010). In the approach advocated here, I am suggesting ways of enabling students to engage with the texts in such a way as to get inside the skin of the texts – to apprehend them from the inside rather than simply to comprehend them from the outside – what I have termed *literature from the inside out*. We may characterize this approach as *learning through* literature, and it seems particularly appropriate in current contexts where a personalised and critical appreciation of English is crucial to students' development as independent users of the language. How might this be done? A number of possibilities suggest themselves: independent work on Extensive Reading and Listening; Performance of texts; Creation of texts by students themselves, both spoken and written; and a number of pedagogical techniques, including Project Work, where responsibility is passed largely to the students. These types of work will be described in greater detail later in the chapter. But first, a word about text selection may be appropriate, since the kind of texts we offer our learners is a crucial factor in the likelihood that they will engage learners.

Issues of text selection

To have any chance of engaging learners deeply with literary texts, we shall need greatly to expand both the range of texts, which will form the basis of selection, and the mechanisms used for making the selection greatly. This will serve at least three purposes. It will better reflect the 'balance of power' between Englishes in the increasingly globalised world. It will offer a window into the numerous differing realities in that world. It can also make access to literary texts less difficult by offering students content with which they are relatively familiar. So how might this all be achieved?

Extending the geographical range of texts

As already noted earlier, there has been a spectacular growth of literature in English written by those for whom English is not a first language (Skinner,

1998). This abundance and sheer variety of new literatures, with their English tongue rooted in non-English soil, offers unparalleled opportunities to extend the boundaries of choice of texts for use in language teaching programmes with an EIL (English as an International Language) orientation. Such texts greatly expand the linguistic varieties learners are exposed to, the range of geographical and cultural contexts they can learn about and the issues of living in a globalising world they need to be aware of.

Extending the range of text types for inclusion

A second way of expanding the range of choice would be to include other genres, not usually regarded as literature (with a capital L) (McRae, 1991). There is an abundance of literature written primarily for children, for teenagers and for fans of crime, mystery, romance and science fiction. We should also consider the inclusion of certain kinds of graded readers. Many people would exclude graded readers as exemplars of literature, but a persuasive case has been made for the recognition of a new genre: *Language Learner Literature* (Day & Bamford, 1998). The argument is that, just as we can identify other genres that target particular types of readers (children's fiction, teen fiction, popular romance), the books written for a language learner audience also constitute a specific genre. This is particularly true of the latest generation of graded readers which, rather than simplifying existing texts, create original works within the linguistic limitations of their learner-readers. Some of these manage to create highly compelling fiction within a limited vocabulary. They also deal with significant subject matter, which can help develop world knowledge and critical thinking: civil war (Moses, 2004), immigration (Hancock, 2005), Alzheimer's disease (Maley, 2011), corruption (McAndrew, 2006) and so on. Even simplified fiction would qualify for inclusion if well done and oriented to non-inner circle worlds. The Oxford Bookworms titles anthologising Asian and African fiction are a good example of this (Bassett, 2008; West, 2010).

There is also a strong case to be made for including literature written by teachers and their students. The poems and stories produced by just one small group of such teacher writers in Asia, is a case in point (http://flexiblelearning.auckland.ac.nz/cw).

Opening up text selection to students

Typically, texts are chosen by syllabus authorities, by textbook writers and by directors of studies and teachers. However well intentioned such choices may be, it is rare for those who will use these texts to be consulted about them in advance. One way of engaging with literature is to empower students by giving them a say in decisions about text selection. Such choices would entail major shifts of power and practice. For example, offering students the simple choice between a class reader, which everyone would read at the same time, and a class library from which each students would select a book, would imply massive change.

Similarly, offering students small samples of books they might consider before requiring them to choose one title is another form of student enfranchisement. Asking groups of students to review different books or texts and then to make a case for using them (or not) is another. For many more examples of extending power of choice to students, see Bamford and Day (2004). In this way, students acquire a stake in the texts they use, which can massively affect their motivation and commitment.

Literature as appropriation

This approach to using literature in language programmes is informed by a number of key questions:

Why do we expect students to understand everything in a text?

The compulsion to understand every single word is destructive of enjoyment and not necessary for overall comprehension. Students need to be educated out of this debilitating habit. Perhaps teachers do too.

> *In deciding on poems, I wasn't put off by some of the difficulties teachers are often bothered by – unfamiliar words and difficult syntax, for example, and allusions to unfamiliar things... I wasn't put off, either, by passages in a poem that I knew would remain obscure to them. To reject every poem the children would not understand in all its detail would mean eliminating too many good things... What matters for the present is not that the children admire Blake and his achievement, but that each child be able to find a tiger of his own (p li).*
>
> (Rose, Where Did You Get That Red? Kenneth Koch)

Why do we need comprehension questions to prove they have understood a text?

There are many ways to demonstrate that a text has been understood, as we shall see later in this chapter. And the very nature of comprehension questions, which all too often focus on isolated particulars rather than on essentials, ensures that what looks like comprehension is no more than a mechanical ability to retrieve details. What is more important is to apprehend the sense and significance of the text.

Why do we need to tell rather than allow discovery?

By explaining everything, we pre-empt the students' natural ability and interest in finding things out for themselves. In line with Carl Rogers's educational philosophy, "true education involves a change in self-organization: learning is maximised when learners have the freedom to select their own direction, formulate their own problems, discover the solution for themselves, and are responsible for such choices" (Bao, 2014, p. 156).

Why do we kill texts by solemnising them?

We need constantly to remind ourselves that writers of literary texts did not write them with a view to having them studied in educational syllabuses and then examined with questions set by pedants, nor did they write them in the expectation that they would become monuments of high culture. They wrote because they had something interesting, amusing or compelling to say, or because they needed the money! To treat literary texts as cultural icons is to do them a serious disservice and to put them out of the reach of our learners (Maley, 1989).

How can we engage students affectively and cognitively with literary texts?

This is the nub of the issue. In the next section, I shall suggest five main ways in which literature could be more effectively incorporated into language programmes. These are Familiarisation, Extensive Reading (and Listening), Performance, Creative Writing and Techniques for getting inside the skin of texts. I shall now briefly examine each of these in turn.

Familiarisation

It is important to de-mystify literature with the learners. There are many ways of doing this, including the following:

1   Showing that literature is, in a sense, all around us. For example, giving examples of shop signs, advertising slogans, newspaper headlines, book titles, etc., all of which frequently use ambiguity, rhyme, rhythm, parallelism and other literary devices to attract attention to themselves. This can be done by routinely bringing in examples and briefly discussing them. Here are a few examples: *Lunatic Fringe* (hairdressing saloon), *You shop: We drop* (supermarket delivery service). This could also be made into a project, where students produce a visual display of the examples they have researched.
2   Setting up routines for making literature an everyday event. For example, the teacher can start every class by reading or telling a short, engaging text – a poem, a joke, a wisdom story, a mini-saga. This is done without any commentary and is followed by no questions or activities. Students are only required to listen (Tomlinson, 2014). Here is an example:

> *A rich lady was having dinner in a restaurant. As she began to eat her soup, she noticed a large fly in it. She called the waiter over and asked him, 'Waiter! What is this fly doing in my soup?' The waiter bent down and looked at her bowl of soup very carefully for a long time. Then he said, 'Madame, I think it is drowning.'*
>
> (This is not copyrighted material)

At the end of each class, the teacher makes available copies of the text for those who want to read it again.

3. By reading aloud a complete extended text to students over a whole semester. This might only take up 15 minutes per lesson. But by the end of the semester or year, the students will have listened to a whole novel, or a series of short stories. Obviously, the text has to be carefully selected so as to be of compelling interest and not too long or too complex, and it should lend itself to being dramatized and serialised.
4. By bringing in book covers of recent books, including the back cover blurbs to make a display. This can form part of a permanent book corner where books too can be regularly displayed.
5. By choosing a poem for each week. The *Poem of the Week* can be read by the teacher or by a student. The poems can be displayed on a special display board or on the class website. At the end of each month, students vote for their favourite poem of the month. When students are used to this idea, they can be asked to bring in poems they have found and want to read. Here is an example:

> **Time by Alan Maley**
>
> *The terrible cascade of time-*
> *The slow dripping of seconds,*
> *Gathering into the rivulets of minutes,*
> *Trickling into the streams of hours,*
> *Flowing into the torrents of days,*
> *Down into the rivers of weeks,*
> *The flood of months,*
> *And the great waterfall of wasted years.*

6. By regularly giving out a text, prose or poem and asking students to choose a sentence, a phrase or a word they particularly like. Here is an example:

> *Milmaq was a solitary person. He would spend hours in the forest, not hunting, simply sitting still, watching, waiting for something to happen. A spider would swing its thread across the canyon between two branches. A woodpecker would drum at the trunk of a chestnut tree, its neck a blur of speed. Above all, the trees themselves would speak to him. He would be aware of them creaking and swaying in the wind. He could sense the sap rising in them in the springtime; feel their sorrow at the approach of winter. If he put his ear to the trunk of a tree, he could hear it growing, very slowly; feel it moving towards its final, magnificent shape.*
>
> (*The Man Who Talked to Trees*, Alan Maley)

7   By making storytelling a regular feature of classes. There are few if any more compelling resources than storytelling. If our aim is to hook our students on literature, stories are an excellent way in. There are now some excellent resources to help teachers use stories. (Heathfield, 2014; Wright, 2008)

The idea of all these activities (and many more could be devised) is simply to make students comfortable with the idea of having literature around, as something non-threatening and pleasurable.

Extensive reading

There has been a growing interest in the potential of Extensive Reading (ER) to promote language acquisition, especially of vocabulary, and collocation (Day & Bamford, 1998; Goodman, 1996: Krashen, 2004; Maley, 2009; Smith, 2004; Waring, 2000).

It is also obvious that, given the limited hours of instruction in most programmes, students will never be exposed to enough vocabulary, enough times, to acquire the necessary quantum in classrooms alone (Waring, 2006). Out-of-class learning is the only way, and one of the most convenient and proven ways of doing so is through massive independent reading, entailing repeated encounters with vocabulary in context.

However, as mentioned earlier, much of the material available for ER is literary in nature, if we accept Day's definition of *Language Learner Literature*. It gives students a way of accessing novels and short stories in a non-threatening way. ER does not only involve literary texts, of course, but they are among the most motivating genres. Moreover, although we cannot hope to 'teach' the many varieties of English which our students will encounter in the outside world, we can give a certain limited exposure to them through the medium of literary texts drawn from a variety of geographical sources (Bassett, 2008; West, 2010).

In a similar way, exposure to extensive listening texts can reinforce and extend language acquisition. There is now a wide range of recorded fiction and poetry available in the form of talking books, CDs, DVDs and film. Most of the graded readers' series now come with an accompanying CD. One particularly rewarding and motivating type of listening is to hear and watch authors reading from their own work. This is especially valuable with poetry (see for example, Maley, 2008). In this way, they can begin to tune in to the many authentic voices and accents of living writers. In the absence of recordings, clear and sensitive reading aloud by the teacher can be equally inspiring (Maley, 2009).

Performance

One of the most effective ways of getting inside the skin of a text is to perform it. To do this well, the students have to have understood it and lived with it. There are also clear benefits in memorisation (without tears), cooperation, self-esteem and motivation. Performance can take a variety of forms. It may consist simply of students performing short texts they have chosen and brought to class. The more involvement they have in choosing what to perform, the more committed they will be.

A more demanding and intensive type of performance is to ask students in groups of about six to prepare an orchestrated performance of a text. In doing so, they will need to consider parameters of volume, pace, pitch and rhythm, as well as which lines will be spoken by one or more speakers (Maley,1999, 2000). This is related to work in 'Readers' Theatre' by Shirley Brice-Heath (1983) and Courtney Cazden (1993) in the USA. The effects on retention and on motivation and self-esteem are remarkable. Students voluntarily spend long periods of time working together, and alone, on texts so as to produce something they can be proud of.

An even more demanding example is when students engage with the production of a full-length play. Lutzker (2007) has investigated in depth the effects of such a production on his students in Germany, in terms of their linguistic and personal development, and reports strong evidence of growth in both areas. If the plays for performance are well chosen, they can also lead to a better understanding of social and personal issues in the real world. Lutzker chose *The Diary of Anne Frank*, which led to some really deep reflection on the part of his German students! Locally written texts may be chosen, but localised versions of classics, including Shakespeare, can also be connected to local realities (Kott, 1967). The teacher too should always be on hand to act as a performer, giving a good model of reading stories and poems aloud to the class (see "Familiarisation").

Creative writing

The act of writing creatively has a number of well-documented positive effects both on the learning of the language and on personal and social development (for an example, see the website of the Asian Teacher-Writers' Group: http://

flexiblelearning.auckland.ac.nz/cw; see also Maley, 2012). Taking the place of the writer – in fact, becoming a writer – helps students develop greater sensitivity to the ways the language functions, with particular benefits for vocabulary, collocation, rhythm and syntactic variety. The gamelike activity of writing creatively in the foreign language promotes willingness to take risks, to try out new things in a blame-free environment, and in the process, it helps develop awareness of the language, of the world and of oneself. At the same time, the constraints which literary form places on the writer also acts as an important kind of scaffolding support. Even more importantly, perhaps, the act of creating original texts and 'publishing' them (whether on a notice board, a website or as a leaflet), empowers the students and enhances their self-esteem (Spendlove, 2008). They have in a sense *appropriated* the language – made it their own.

Space does not allow for detailed examples here, but there are now many resources available to teachers wishing to try out creative writing with their students (Koch, 1990; Maley & Mukundan, 2012a, 2012b; Matthews, 1994; Spiro, 2004, 2006; Wright & Hill, 2009).

Techniques for getting inside the skin of the text

There are so many of these that it is not feasible to attempt a detailed catalogue. Two examples must suffice:

1   Choose a short accessible text about the length of this one:

    > The first time we met, he smiled at me. The second time we met, we laughed and joked together. The third time we met, we kissed and loved each other. The fourth time we met, we argued about something silly. It was not important. We did not meet again.

Students work in pairs. They take turns to read successive sentences in the following way: [S1] reads it very loud. [S2] whispers it. [S1] reads it very fast; S1 reads it very slowly. S1 reads in a happy voice. [S2] reads in a very sad voice, etc. Finally, each student reads the whole in a normal way. The fact of having 'made it strange' helps to familiarise them with it and to read it more effectively. It also involves them in multiple repetitions of the text without the boredom we normally associate with repetition.

2   Take a longish poem. This poem has 24 lines. In groups, students have to use lines from it to make an eight-line poem, which retains the essential meaning of the original. To do this, students have to have understood the poem, and they have to negotiate with group members until they can agree on their eight-line poem. By the time they finish, they are thoroughly familiar with the poem and will have processed a lot of language. Repetition without tears again.

The daffodils

I wandered lonely as a cloud
That floats on high o'er dales and hills,
When all at once I saw a crowd,
A host of golden daffodils.
Beside the lake, beneath the trees,
Fluttering and dancing in the breeze.

Continuous as the stars that shine
And twinkle in the Milky Way,
They stretch'd in never-ending line
Along the margin of the bay:
Ten thousand saw I at a glance,
Tossing their heads in sprightly dance.

The waves beside them danced, but they
Outdid the sparkling waves in glee:-
The poet could not but be gay
In such a jocund company!
I gazed, and gazed, but little thought
What wealth the show to me had brought.

For oft, when on my couch I lie,
In vacant or in pensive mood,
They flash upon that inward eye
Which is the bliss of solitude;
And then my heart with pleasure fills,
And dances with the daffodils.
William Wordsworth

The following titles are a good starting point: Lazar (1993), Maley (1993, 1995), Maley and Duff (1985), Maley and Moulding (1985), McRae and Vethamani (1999), and Tomlinson (1986). Essentially, the activities offered in these books encourage students to engage personally with texts in interesting and challenging ways in order to uncover and discover them afresh.

Conclusions

I began this chapter by setting out the challenge which literature faces concerning the many sources of distraction in the current context. I also listed the factors, which characterise the new contexts in which English is being taught and used, all of which impact on the way literature will need to be taught. I then argued that literature might be perceived as more relevant if the way texts are chosen were to be extended. I then discussed three possible approaches to the use of literature in language programmes: teaching *about*, *with* and *through* literature, expressing a preference for the last of the three – *literature as appropriation*. I then proposed five major types of activity: *Familiarisation, Extensive Reading (and Listening), Performance, Creative Writing and Techniques for Apprehending Texts from the Inside.*

Throughout, I have had in mind the kinds of challenges students now face with respect to English, learning and life. Among the most important of these are

- The need to survive the culture of speed and info-glut somehow, which threatens to overwhelm them. This implies the need to restore control over time and information, and to make available time for reflection, discrimination and criticism.
- The almost exclusive focus on the short-term utilitarian value of education, with scant attention given to the long-term values of aesthetic appreciation. This implies finding a place for texts and practices, which do help develop aesthetic and affective appreciation (Jakobson, 1960).
- The all-too-frequent priority given to English at the expense of local languages and cultures. This implies the need to use English instead as a way of validating the local rather than submerging it and restoring self-respect and self-esteem to local languages and cultures.
- The gap between the model of English offered in the classroom and the plurality of English uses outside it. This implies exposing students to many of the varieties they will encounter, even if these cannot be taught explicitly.

I contend that literature can achieve some success in meeting these four challenges. Is this the answer to the challenge of living in an age of distraction? Of course not. There are no easy options, and no ready-made solutions. Some people will always regard literature as irrelevant; there will be a corresponding need to make a case for it in contrast to the more fashionable, the more 'modern,' the more technological, the more utilitarian approaches on offer. This entails constantly reinventing the ways literature is deployed, so as to keep it fresh, interesting and, thus, relevant. This seems to me to be an effort worth making.

References

Astley, N., & Robertson-Pearce, P. (Ed.). (2008). *In person: 30 poets*. Highgreen, Northumberland: Bloodaxe Books (includes 2 DVDs).
Bamford, J., & Day, R. (Eds.). (2004). *Extensive reading activities for teaching language*. Cambridge: Cambridge University Press.
Bao, D. (2014). *Understanding silence and reticence*. London: Bloomsbury.
Bassett, J. (2008). *Cries from the heart: Stories from around the world series/Oxford Bookworms*. Oxford: Oxford University Press.
Carr, N. (2010). *The shallows: How the internet is changing the way we think, read and remember*. London: Atlantic Books.
Carter, R., & McRae, J. (1996). *Language, literature and the learner*. Harlow: Longman.
Cazden, C. (1993). Performing expository texts in the foreign language classroom. In C. Kramsch & S. McConnell-Ginet (Eds.), *Texts and context: Cross disciplinary perspectives on language study* (pp. 67–78). Washington, DC: Heath.

Clandfield, L., Pickering, K., Robb Benns, R., Jeffreies, A., Campbell, R., Watkins, F., Moore, J., & Coxall, J. (2011). *Global intermediate*. London: Macmillan.
Claxton, G. (1997). *Hare brain: Tortoise mind*. London: Fourth Estate.
Day, R., & Bamford, J. (1998). *Extensive reading in the second language classroom*. Cambridge: Cambridge University Press.
Duff, A., & Maley, A. (2007). *Literature*. Oxford: Oxford University Press.
Eisner, E. W. (1985). *The educational imagination*. New York: Macmillan.
Fisher, A. (2001). *Critical thinking: An introduction*. Cambridge: Cambridge University Press.
Goleman, D. (1996). *Emotional intelligence*. London: Bloomsbury.
Goleman, D. (2006). *Social intelligence: The new science of human relationships*. London: Hutchinson.
Goodman, K. S. (1996). *On reading*. London: Heinemann.
Graddol, D. (2006). *English next*. London: British Council.
Hancock, P. (2005). *Within high fences*. Cambridge: Cambridge University Press.
Heath, S. B. (1983). *Ways with words: Language, life and work in communities and classrooms*. Cambridge: Cambridge University Press.
Heathfield, D. (2014). *Storytelling with our students*. London: Delta.
Honore, C. (2004). *In praise of slow*. London: Orion Books.
Jakobson, R. (1960). Closing statement: Linguistics and poetics. In T. Sebeok (Ed.), *Style in language* (pp. 350–377). New York: Wiley-Blackwell.
Kachru, B. B. (Ed.). (1992). *The other tongue: English across cultures*. Urbana, IL: University of Illinois Press.
Koch, K. (1990). *Rose, where did you get that red?* New York: Vintage.
Kott, J. (1967). *Shakespeare our contemporary*. London: Methuen.
Kramsch, C. (1993). *Context and culture in language teaching*. Oxford: Oxford University Press.
Krashen, S. (2004). *The power of reading: Insights from the research* (2nd edn.). Portsmouth, NH: Heinemann.
Lazar, G. (1993). *Literature and language teaching*. Cambridge: Cambridge University Press.
Lutzker, P. (2007). *The art of foreign language teaching: Improvisation and drama in teacher development and language learning*. Tubingen, Basel: Francke Verlag.
Maley, A. (1989). Down from the pedestal: Literature as resource. In R. Carter, R. Walker, & C. Brumfit (Eds.), *Literature and the learner: Methodological approaches* [ELT Docs. 130] (pp. 10–23). London: Modern English Publications with the British Council.
Maley, A. (1993). *Short and Sweet I*. London: Penguin.
Maley, A. (1995). *Short and Sweet II*. London: Penguin.
Maley, A. (1999). Choral speaking. *English Teaching Professional*, 12, 9–11.
Maley, A. (2000). *The language teacher's voice*. Oxford: Heinemann.
Maley, A. (2001). Literature in the language classroom. In R. Carter & D. Nunan (Eds.), *The Cambridge guide to teaching English to speakers of other languages* (pp. 180–185). Cambridge: Cambridge University Press.
Maley, A. (2008). Extensive reading: Maid in waiting. In B. Tomlinson (Ed.), *English language learning materials: A critical review* (pp. 133–156). London, New York: Continuum.
Maley, A. (2009). *Advanced learners*. Oxford: Oxford University Press.
Maley, A. (2010, October). Literature from the outside in and from the inside out (Unpublished paper). Asia TEFL Conference, Hanoi.

Maley, A. (2011). *Forget to remember.* Cambridge: Cambridge University Press.
Maley, A. (2012). Creative writing for students and teachers. *Humanising Language Teaching, 14*(3). From www.hltmag.com
Maley, A., & Duff, A. (1985). *The inward ear: Poetry in the language classroom.* Cambridge: Cambridge University Press.
Maley, A., & Moulding, S. (1985). *Poem into poem.* Cambridge: Cambridge University Press.
Maley, A., & Mukundan, J. (Eds.). (2005–2008a). *Asian poems for young readers* [*Vols. 1, 3,* 5, 7, 9]. Petaling Jaya: Pearson Malaysia.
Maley, A., & Mukundan, J. (Eds.). (2005–2008b). *Asian short stories for young readers* [*Vols 2,4, 6, 8*]. Petaling Jaya: Pearson Malaysia.
Maley, A., & Mukundan, J. (2012a). *Creative writing activities: Poetry.* Petaling Jaya: Pearson Malaysia.
Maley,A., & Mukundan, J. (2012b). *Creative writing activities: Stories.* Petaling Jaya: Pearson Malaysia.
Matthews, P. (1994). *Sing me the creation.* Stroud: Hawthorne Press.
McAndrew, R. (2006). *Strong medicine.* Cambridge: Cambridge University Press.
McRae, J. (1991). *Literature with a small 'l'.* London: Macmillan.
McRae, J., & Vethamani. M. E. (1999). *Now read on.* London: Routledge.
Moses, A. (2004). *Jojo's story.* Cambridge: Cambridge University Press.
Naish, J. (2008). *Enough: Breaking free from the world of excess.* London: Hodder and Stoughton.
Postman, N. (1985). *Amusing ourselves to death.* London: Penguin.
Postman, N., & Weingartner, C. (1976). *Teaching as a subversive activity.* London: Penguin.
Rogers, M. Taylor-Knowles, J., Wusniewska, I., & Zemach, D. (2008). *Open mind.* London: Macmillan.
Skinner, J. (1998). *The stepmother tongue.* New York: St Martin's Press.
Smith, F. (2004). *Understanding reading* (4th edn.). Mahwah, NJ: Laurence Erlbaum.
Spendlove, D. (2008). *Emotional literacy.* London: Continuum.
Spiro, J. (2004). *Creative poetry writing.* Oxford: Oxford University Press.
Spiro, J. (2006). *Storybuilding.* Oxford: Oxford University Press.
Tomlinson, B. (1986). *Openings.* London: Penguin.
Tomlinson, B. (1998). Seeing what they mean: Helping L2 readers to visualize. In B. Tomlinson (Ed.), *Materials development in language teaching* (pp. 265–278). Cambridge: Cambridge University Press.
Tomlinson, B. (2014). Looking out for English. *Folio, 16*(1), 5–8.
Unrau, N. J. (2008). *Thoughtful teachers, thoughtful learners* (2nd edn.). Toronto: Pippin.
van Leeuwen, T. (1999). *Speech, music, sound.* London: Macmillan.
Waring, R. (2000). *The 'why' and 'how' of using graded readers.* Tokyo: Oxford University Press. Retrieved from http://extensivereading.net/docs/tebiki_GREng.pdf
Waring, R. (2006). Why extensive reading should be an indispensable part of all language programmes. *The Language Teacher, 30*(7), 44–47.
West, C. (2010). *Leaving no footprint: Stories from Asia.* Oxford: Oxford University Press.
Wright, A. (2008). *Storytelling with children.* Oxford: Oxford University Press.
Wright, A., & Hill, D. A. (2009). *Writing stories.* Innsbruck: Helbling.

12 Expressing study abroad experiences in second language haiku writing
Theoretical and practical implications for teaching haiku composition in Asian EFL classrooms

Atsushi Iida

Constructing voice and expressing self in written form can be a challenging task for second language (L2) learners, especially English as a foreign language (EFL) students. This is partly because of a grammar-centered curriculum at the secondary level, which provides very few chances to express their thoughts or feelings in the target language. The focus on error reduction and memorization of linguistic forms leaves L2 learners at a disadvantage when they have to use English in real-world situations. One of the principal issues in this context is that it restricts the L2 learners from "learning around communicative contexts where students learn to express their *voice* – the articulation of their personal needs, interests, and ideas – in a social context that presumes an *audience* – the teachers, classmates, and even the community at large" (Iida, 2010, p. 28). In order to learn to write and communicate in the target language, however, it is necessary for the instructors to teach L2 learners how to discover and express their own unique perspectives on the world.

Expressive writing has the potential to overcome this issue (Hanauer, 2010, 2011, 2012b; Iida, 2012), and poetry writing, especially, is viewed as a way for L2 learners to construct, develop, and express their voices (Bishop, 1997; Elbow, 2007; Iida, 2010; Romano, 2004). According to Hanauer (2004), poetry is defined as "a literary text that presents the experiences, thoughts and feelings of the writer through a self-referential use of language that creates for the reader and writer a new understanding of the experience, thought or feeling expressed in the text" (p. 10). In this sense, poetry is the articulation of the writers' voices reflecting on their life experience and writing poems on personal life events is a process of self-discovery (Hanauer, 2010). What has been known about the study of expressive writing is that poetry is used as a form of literacy practice in first language (L1) education (Bizzaro, 2004; Romano, 2000; Young, 2003); on the other hand, there is scant reporting on empirical study of poetry writing in L2 contexts (Hanauer, 2010; Paran, 2008). It is crucial, therefore, to investigate whether poetry writing can be used as a means to explore L2 writers' personal experiences. The question is of interest both in relation to expressive abilities of L2 writers and in relation to the personally significant events themselves.

The aim of this chapter is to discuss the way in which EFL students at a Japanese university use *haiku* – a Japanese poem containing 17 syllables in a three-line 5–7–5 syllable pattern with the use of a seasonal reference[1] and a cutting word[2] – in an L2 to express their personal histories. First, it reviews previous research on expressive writing in L2 education. Second, it describes a case study of haiku writing on study abroad experiences in the Japanese EFL classroom. The main objective of the current study is to identify how EFL students understand and express their study abroad experiences in haiku and clarify the role of expressive writing in Asian EFL contexts. In doing so, this chapter intends to argue for the use of poetry as literacy practice in the L2 composition classroom.

Personal history and expressive writing in the L2 classroom

Expressive writing is the key pedagogical approach for the writers to construct and develop their thoughts. Iida (2008) argues the necessity of expressive writing and summarizes the potential contribution to L2 learning from two aspects. One perspective is to foster self-directed writers. Expressive pedagogy places students at the heart of the learning process and develops the ability to take control over their writing. The other is to develop their voices. Expressive pedagogy promotes their intellectual and psychological development in the process of negotiating meaning and constructing their voices in texts. Learner-centeredness, process-orientation, and voice construction in the pedagogy allow for "a deeper understanding of the connections between thought, words, and life" (Bishop, 1997, p. 17).

While expressive writing is still an unusual task for L2 writers (Chamcharatsri, 2013), Hanauer (2012b) has proposed a theoretical underpinning of teaching L2 literacy – *meaningful literacy* – in English as a Second Language (ESL)/EFL contexts. The concept of this literacy instruction is to decontextualize the traditional ESL/EFL pedagogy, which emphasizes the memorization of linguistic features and translation into L1, and to humanize the classroom in the way students reflect on their personal experiences, recreate each event through writing, and express their emotions in texts. Meaningful literacy practice puts "the individual learner and her/his personal experience, history and social contextualization at the center of the learning experience" (Hanauer, 2012b, p. 4). The use of personal experiences enables L2 writers to negotiate and express their voices in the target language and makes their learning more meaningful.

In addition to the theoretical rationale of expressive writing in the L2 composition classroom, a crucial issue in the field of applied linguistics is to investigate the use of expressive forms of writing as research (Hanauer, 2010, 2012a). Various types of literary writing have been used as a research method in L2 contexts: autobiography (Fujieda, 2010; Pavlenko, 2001, 2007), autoethnography (Lapidus, Kaveh, & Hirano, 2013), poetry (Hanauer, 2010, 2012b), poetic-narrative autobiography (Park, 2013), and personal narratives (Chamcharatsri, 2013). Regardless of the difference in genres, the purpose of these studies is to investigate the writer's, teacher's, and/or researcher's personal life histories through L2 expressive writing. What has been known so far concerning the research on literary writing and L2 writers is that expressive writing allows for a better understanding of experiences, emotions, and identities of the individual during language and cultural learning.

Poetry writing, a form of meaningful literacy practice, has been viewed as a means to understand the writer's personal experience (Hanauer, 2010, 2011). Taking this theoretical position, Hanauer (2010) conducted two case studies on poetry writing and ESL writers. One study aimed to investigate poetic inquiry in an L2 with the analysis of a book of poetry created by a Japanese ESL student. The book entitled *Family*, consisting of ten poems, involved her parents' divorce when she was 17. The results of content analysis of each poem illustrated her different subject position, which is a history of change in which she moved from shock and confusion at her parents' divorce to a position of accepting the reality, a more mature understanding of gender roles, and the ability to live by herself. This study revealed that the collection of poems consisted not of her simple descriptions of each moment, but of "the history of developing subject positions designed to explore, understand and negotiate different ways of being in the world" (p. 73).

The other case study conducted by Hanauer (2010) reported on the exploration of ESL students' study abroad experiences through poetry writing. A major finding in this study was that 78 poems, which described a significant moment of studying abroad defined by each writer, were categorized into five different experiences: self-positioning and the emotional experience of language, emotional responses to academic classroom experiences, experiencing American students, negotiating American culture, and homesickness. It also revealed that each poem involved ESL writers' quite deep emotional situations in which their study abroad experiences tended to be more negative than positive. The two studies indicated methodological guidelines for using poetry as a way to investigate and understand the writers' personal histories including their own voices and emotions in life experiences.

Park (2013) also conducted poetic inquiry into her personal identity. She used *autobiographic-poetic waves* through which she blended autobiographic and poetic discourse as a research method to look at four significant stages of her life: the emergence of hyphenated identities, the legitimization of hyphenated identities, the epistemological and ontological revolution, and the perception of Mama PhDs. The results of qualitative analysis of her poems and autobiographies illustrated her complicated, multiple identities, which consisted of a Korean-American woman, L2 writer, English teacher, teacher-scholar, and Mama PhD. In this study, she pointed out the value of autobiographic-poetic inquiry as a way to represent "snapshots of her personal, academic and professional life history" (p. 15).

In this way, previous studies report on the use of poetry as autobiographical research and suggest the potential to extend our understandings of the relationship between L2 writers and their personal histories. Following this theoretical and methodological framework, the current study aims to use haiku as a research method and to identify the way in which EFL college students at a Japanese university focus and express their personal histories in haiku writing. Specifically, the following question will be addressed: In what ways do EFL students understand and express their study abroad experiences in haiku?

Method

In order to investigate the question, the task of haiku writing was incorporated into a regular English writing course during a six-week period. In the current study, each participant created a book of haiku as one of the course requirements. The methodology chosen was a qualitative research design in which the use of poetry was as an autobiographical research method.

Participants

Twenty English major students registered in a first-year college writing course at a four-year Japanese private university. They were assigned in this class as a result of taking the TOEIC (Test of English for International Communication) as a placement test. Their proficiency levels ranged from 400 to 495 points on the TOEIC, which is approximately equivalent to 435 to 470 points on the TOEFL (Test of English as a Foreign Language) paper-based test. All participants had experience reading and writing haiku in Japanese at the primary and/or secondary level in Japanese schools.

Data collection procedures

The investigator implemented the instruction of reading and writing English haiku in this context. The goal of this haiku project was for each participant to create a book of haiku. A six-week teaching plan was designed in order for the participants to achieve this goal. This project was consisted of three stages. The first stage was to review the concept of haiku. The participants read both traditional Japanese and English haiku to discuss and review the concept of this poetic genre. Writing haiku was the next stage in this project. In this stage, the class format consisted of workshops and a series of exercises to help the participants to express their voices. The workshops required them to reflect on their experiences, choose 15 unforgettable moments in their lives, free write each moment, write one haiku per moment, revise them based on feedback from the investigator and classmates, and complete 15 haikus. The last stage involved the creation of a book of haiku. In order to publish it, the participants chose 10 haiku out of 15 depending on their themes. The booklet consisted of a table of contents, an introduction, and 10 haikus. In this way, the data collected were 20 books of poetry including 200 haikus.

Data analysis

Data were analyzed by Hanauer's (2010) methodological framework to investigate each writer's subject position in poetry. Since the participants were free to choose any topic to write haikus, not all poems collected were related to study abroad experiences. Data analysis was needed to begin with the selection of the thematic haiku.

The analysis was to collect haikus that came under the heading of study abroad experiences. In order to choose the thematic poems, decisions were made to define study abroad experiences according to the title and a description of each poem in the book of haiku. As a result, four haikus written by four participants[3] were chosen in the current analysis.

The second stage of analysis involved literary, linguistic, and content analysis of each haiku while recreating the writer's subject position expressed in the actual descriptions of the poem (Hanauer, 2010). Each haiku was carefully observed from the aspect of his/her specific perspectives, emotional contents, and understanding of the experience.

Findings

A Japanese female student, Kyoko Matsuyama, wrote a haiku entitled "Study Abroad in America." She participated in a homestay program in Kansas when she was a high school freshman. In this haiku, she described her feelings as a reflection on her first visit to the United States.

Study abroad in America

Very cold winter day
I saw many Kansas's view:
Want to go there again

This haiku expresses her emotion in visiting Kansas. The haiku starts with the statement, "Very cold winter day" to describe the context of the memory (e.g., when she visited Kansas or what the weather was like there). The second line addresses her experience in Kansas. She might have looked at the view of Kansas City from the car window, or she might have walked around the town and saw a different scene there. The last line, "want to go back again," reflects her direct response to this particular experience. This inner voice seems to be constructed from her current subject position, but it is true that her experience in Kansas was satisfactory, and that is why she wished to go back there. The use of "want to" in the last line clearly represents her desire to be there again.

The second haiku entitled, "Studying Abroad" was written by another Japanese female student, Shiho Kondo. She wrote the poem to reflect on the days she spent in Vancouver when she was 14. It represents her emotion when she took part in a homestay program there.

Studying abroad

> Fantastic summer
> Made friends with Canadian:
> My heart filled with joy

This haiku starts with the statement, "fantastic summer," which explains the situation in which the poet visited Canada in summer. At the same time, it makes readers imagine that the writer had an extraordinarily good time there. The second line addresses what made her feel fantastic. She made new Canadian friends during her stay in Canada. Her emotions can be seen from the last line, "my heart filled with joy," which represents her excitement and satisfaction with the experience of having made Canadian friends in ESL. Communicating and making foreign friends in the target language seemed to be a challenging task for her, but her emotion might have developed from a successful moment of making friends. This haiku clearly reflects her positive emotion during the study abroad experience.

A Brazilian student wrote the next haiku. Carlos Suzuki moved to Japan when he was six years old. He commuted to the primary and secondary school in Japan. He wrote a haiku, "Football Game with a Brazilian Team" to express his inner voice concerning playing a soccer game with Japanese and Brazilian friends.

Football game with a Brazilian team

> Using two languages:
> Japanese to make game plan
> Portuguese, grumble

This poem describes the poet's language use, Portuguese as his first language and Japanese as his L2 in playing soccer. The first line, "using two languages," addresses his possibility to manage two languages and different use of his L1 and L2. The next two lines clearly explain his different purposes of using the two languages. He uses Japanese for game making, which reflects his feelings that he does not want the Brazilian team to understand his strategy in the game. On the other hand, he uses his first language, Portuguese, to complain about the play in the game. He might not want to use Japanese to grumble to keep good harmony with his Japanese teammates, or since Portuguese is his L1, he might subconsciously complain in the language. However, it turns out that his strategic use of the two languages, especially his intentional use of Japanese language, refers to the representation of his desire to win the game as a member of the Japanese team.

The next poem, "First Day of School in Japan," was written by Kyine Nanda, an 18-year-old Myanmarese male student.

First day of school in Japan

Nobody knows me
But, drawing their attention:
"Can I make friends here?"

He moved from Myanmar to Japan at the age of 15. This haiku clearly signifies a meaningful moment of his new school life in Japan. It captures the scene in which the writer stands in front of the classroom, and his homeroom teacher introduces him to the class on the first day in his junior high school. The phrase, "Nobody knows me," in the first line infers that he is not physically alone but feels lonely in class. His loneliness is also seen from the next line, "drawing their attention," and as a new student, he just looks around the classroom while his classmates stare at him. In this situation, the writer must wonder if he can "make friends." His feeling at that moment was the nervousness and anxiety rather than the expectation or hope for his new school life.

The four haikus express each of the writers' emotional responses to their own significant moment during their study abroad experiences. The writer's emotions were directly expressed in both Keiko and Shiho's haikus. The poems show their positive experiences or good memories in English-speaking countries. On the other hand, no emotional word was used in the poems written by Carlos and Kyine. Carlos focused on his language use in playing soccer and expressed his thought: strategic use of his L1 and L2 in the game. Kyine also captured a specific moment in the classroom on the first day of Japanese school to express his worry in trying to adjust himself to a new social and cultural environment. Thus, overall, each of the haikus represents each writer's states of mind in his or her personally significant life event.

Discussion

Following Hanauer's (2010) theoretical and methodological framework for the usage of poetry in the L2 classroom, the goal of the current study was to identify how EFL students express and understand their study abroad experiences in haiku.

As shown in the haiku, each of the participants expresses their experiences of studying abroad. Each haiku captures the writer's own significant moments of joining some activities (e.g., looking at the view of a city, making friends, playing football, greeting to new classmates) in a foreign country and represents his or her thoughts, feelings, and emotions as their reflections on those experiences. Linguistic choices including the use of emotional words, seasonal references, and punctuation marks such as colons, semicolons, or question marks allow for the articulation of the writer's emotional states. Every single word in the poetry has a special meaning to construct and express the poet's thought that is produced as a result of a reflective and linguistic negotiation of a specific moment, which is significant to the writer. In this way, the writer's emotional concerns were represented in the texts as the manifestation of the writer's voices reflecting internal and external world of the individual.

The pattern of expressing the writer's thought varies depending on the participants. The Japanese female, Kyoko, used a phrase "want to" to show her desire to be back to Kansas City someday. Another Japanese female student, Shiho, used some positive phrases such as "fantastic" and "filled with joy" to represent her satisfaction with the experience of making friends in Canada. The Brazilian student, Carlos, wrote haiku by describing his language use in the football game to express his emotion. Regardless of whether the participants use explicit words to describe emotions (e.g., *happy, love, scary, embarrassed*) in the texts, their emotional contents were successfully presented in haikus. This finding extends our understanding of haiku writing and L2 writers. What we have known so far is that there was statistical evidence of a high frequency use of emotional words such as "happy" or "hot" in English haiku and of the writer's voice appearing more directly in English haiku than Japanese traditional haiku (Iida, 2012a). However, the results of the qualitative analysis of the haikus in the current study show that while explicit words to describe emotions are used in poetry, the writer's voice is not necessarily presented directly in the texts. This means that a poem describes a particular scene in the writer's life story and leaves space for readers to interpret the content including the poet's emotional states. This feature can be seen in Japanese traditional haiku: Japanese haiku consists of the description of a particular moment and the writers must insert spontaneous feelings in the texts through which they must first focus on and capture the moment immediately observed by the poets so as to share it with their readers (Higginson, 1985; Iida, 2012a). Therefore, no emotional word appeared in the texts. In this sense, similar to the characteristics of Japanese haiku, English haiku is based on the writer's thoughts, which develop with surface-level scenery and deep-level psychological descriptions (Minagawa, 2007; Uesaka & Koushima, 2009).

Pedagogical implications: teaching haiku writing in Asian EFL contexts

The current study exemplifies the ability of EFL learners to express and understand personal events through L2 expressive writing. This finding provides implications for teaching poetry writing as a way to humanize the L2 composition classroom. As discussed earlier, one of the challenges of teaching English in EFL contexts is to make the English class dynamic, communicative, and alive by deconstructing the traditional language classroom. From theoretical and pedagogical perspectives, poetry writing, as a form of "meaningful literacy" (Hanauer, 2012b), can overcome this issue. As shown in each haiku, poetry writing can enable L2 learners to be at the center of the learning process, to explore significant memories in their lives, and to work closely with their emotional contents in the moments.

The current study has focused on the study abroad experiences as a theme for haiku writing, but EFL writing teachers can have students choose and write any of their personal life events, which are defined as significant by each writer. The fact is that 200 haikus initially collected for this study included EFL college students' memories of high school life (e.g., entrance ceremony, commencement, or club activities), family trips, and first-time experiences in their lives (e.g., first time to play the guitar; first time to study English). Each of the students may explore and choose different memories for haiku writing, but the usage of their personal experience can motivate them to use the English and be students more engaged in L2 literacy practice.

From practical viewpoints, it is meaningful for EFL writing teachers to teach the process of haiku composing in the classroom. In general, poetry writing is an unfamiliar task for EFL writers, and they may find difficulty in working on this literacy practice. In order to make this language activity successful, teaching a step-by-step procedure is more important than just having them start to compose haiku. Following Hanauer's (2010) practical approach to teaching L2 poetry writing, this composing haiku exercise starts with making a list of significant moments in life. EFL students write down significant and unforgettable life experiences in the notebook. The next activity is to explore and free write each moment. This is regarded as a pre-writing activity for composing haiku, and students are expected to capture the sensory and emotional details of each moment. For instance, EFL writing teachers can ask the following questions in order for the students to describe the memory: *Who are you with? What are you doing? What do you see? What do you hear? What do you smell? What do you taste? What do you feel about?* A series of these questions help EFL students to collect materials for their haiku.

Once completing the free writing of significant memories, EFL students choose one memory and start to compose haiku. EFL writing teachers may have students underline some key words in the description of the free writing and use them in their haiku. Of particular importance of teaching haiku composition at this stage is to have students focus on their own emotional responses to the event and consider what they really want to express in the poem. In composing haiku, one of the challenging tasks for students is to adjust the 5–7–5 syllable pattern (Iida, 2012b). EFL writing teachers can provide some tips for this issue. For example, students can make adjustments by adding or deleting the article (e.g., *a, an, the*), using synonyms (e.g., *thought, viewpoint, i-de-a*) for a content word, or changing verb forms to gerunds or infinitives.

EFL teachers can also incorporate a peer-review activity into the lesson. A peer response activity for reviewing L2 poetry is useful for students in terms of developing the sense of voice in L2 writing while putting an emphasis on writer-reader interaction. However, EFL writing teachers need to provide students with explicit instruction and guide them to engage actively in the peer review activity (Iida, 2014). So it is important to for the teachers to train students to provide their classmates with constructive feedback, which is characterized as useful comments for revising poems. Based on Iida's (2014) approach, EFL writing teachers can pose some questions from the aspect of structure and content of the poem, and assign students to prepare their own answers in the peer-review activity: *How many syllables are used in this haiku? If the haiku does not consist of the 5–7–5* syllable pattern, what advice would you give to the writer for the syllable adjustment? What is the theme of the haiku? What emotion does this poet try to express in the poem? What is the story behind the poem? In order to make this activity more meaningful, EFL writing teachers encourage a pair of students to discuss their poems together and have them understand how the reader interprets his or her voice. It is also necessary for the teachers to have them clarify what to do for the revision to express and communicate their voice more accurately.

In this way, the task of composing haiku makes L2 learning more personal and meaningful. It also allows EFL students to engage more in literacy practice in the target language by developing awareness of the relationship among the text, meaning, and contexts surrounding them. Poetry as expressive writing has the potential not only of building the foundation for constructing and developing the writers' voices (Iida, 2012) but also of enabling them to understand their personal histories in the process of language learning (Chamcharatsri, 2013; Hanauer, 2004, 2010; Park, 2013).

Conclusion

The aim of this chapter was to identify the way in which EFL students used haiku to focus on and express their personal histories. The results of the current study illustrated the abilities of EFL students to express personal events in L2 poetry writing. This study also revealed that haiku writing on lived experiences consisted of both the description of each moment and the depiction of the writer's emotional states, and that the voice is articulated as a result of his or her reflective and linguistic negotiations of personal experiences.

L2 poetry writing is still an unusual task in Asian EFL contexts, but it opens a new possibility for L2 pedagogy in Asian English language classrooms. As discussed in this chapter, poetry writing as a form of meaningful literacy practice can transform the language classrooms into sites not only for developing L2 linguistic knowledge but also for exploring and reflecting on EFL students' personally significant life experiences. In this context, the students will be able to understand themselves better during the process of poetry writing in the target language.

Notes

1 A seasonal reference is not always shown in English haiku.
2 A cutting word which can be seen either as an actual word or an exclamation mark, including a colon or semicolon, has a specific rhetorical function: it is to divide one haiku into two parts.
3 All the names shown in each haiku are pseudonyms.

References

Bishop, W. (1997). *Teaching lives*. Logan, UT: Utah State University Press.
Bizzaro, P. A. (2004). Research and reflection in English studies: The special case of creative writing. *College English, 66*, 294–309.

Chamcharatsri, P. B. (2013). Emotionality and second language writers: Expressing fear through narrative in Thai and in English. *L2 Journal*, 5(1), 59–75.

Elbow, P. (2007). Voice in writing again: Embracing contraries. *College English*, 70, 168–188.

Fujieda, Y. (2010). Complexities of academic writing in English: Difficulties, struggles, and clashes of identity. In M. Cox, J. Jordan, C. Ortmeier-Hooper, & G. G. Schwartz (Eds.), *Reinventing identities in second language writing* (pp. 163–168). Urbana, IL: NCTE.

Hanauer, D. I. (2004). *Poetry and the meaning of life*. Toronto: Pippin.

Hanauer, D. I. (2010). *Poetry as research: Exploring second language poetry writing*. Amsterdam: John Benjamins.

Hanauer, D. I. (2011). The scientific study of poetic writing. *The Scientific Study of Literature*, 1, 79–87.

Hanauer, D. I. (2012a). Growing up in the unseen shadow of the kindertransport: A poetic-narrative autoethnography. *Qualitative Inquiry*, 18, 845–851.

Hanauer, D. I. (2012b). Meaningful literacy: Writing poetry in the language classroom. *Language Teaching*, 45, 105–115.

Higginson, W. J. (1985). *The haiku handbook: How to write, share, and teach haiku*. Tokyo: Kodansha International.

Iida, A. (2008). Poetry writing as expressive pedagogy in EFL contexts: Identifying possible assessment tools for haiku poetry in EFL freshman college writing. *Assessing Writing*, 13, 171–179.

Iida, A. (2010). Developing voice by composing haiku: A social-expressivist framework for teaching haiku writing in EFL contexts. *English Teaching Forum*, 48, 28–34.

Iida, A. (2012a). The value of poetry writing: Cross-genre literacy development in a second language. *Scientific Study of Literature*, 2, 60–82.

Iida, A. (2012b). Writing haiku in a second language: Perceptions, attitude, and emotions of second language learners. *SINO-US English Teaching*, 9, 1472–1485.

Iida, A. (2014). Responding to second language poetry: Critical self-reflection on peer review activities in the Japanese EFL classroom. *The Journal of Literature in Language Teaching*, 3, 52–61.

Lapidus, A., Kaveh, Y., & Hirano, M. (2013). ESL teachers/ ESL students: Looking at autoethnography through the lens of personetics. *L2 Journal*, 5(1), 19–42.

Minagawa, N. (2007). The review for psychological properties for empathy and positive influence of composition and appreciation for linguistic arts, especially a Japanese haiku poem, on the development of an emphathy. *Research Bulletin of Educational Sciences Naruto University of Teacher Education*, 22, 10–23.

Paran, A. (2008). The role of literature in structured foreign language learning and teaching: An evidence-based survey. *Language Teaching*, 41, 465–496.

Park, G. (2013). My Autobiographical-poetic rendition: An inquiry into humanizing our teacher scholarship. *L2 Journal*, 5(1), 6–18.

Pavlenko, A. (2001). "In the world of the tradition, I was unimagined": Negotiation of identities in cross-cultural autobiographies. *The International Journal of Bilingualism*, 5, 317–344.

Pavlenko, A. (2007). Autobiographic narratives as data in applied linguistics. *Applied Linguistics*, 28, 163–188.

Romano, T. (2000). *Blending genre, altering style: Writing multigenre papers*. Portsmouth, NH: Boynton/Cook.

Romano, T. (2004). *Crafting authentic voice*. Portsmouth, NH: Heinemann.
Toyomasu, K. G. (2001). *Haiku for people*. Retrieved from www.toyomasu.com/haiku/
Uesaka, Y., & Koushima, A. (2009). Sousaku to Kansyou no ittaika wo toriireta haiku sidou: Kokugo ni okeru aratana tangenkousei no teian. *Proceedings of the 17th Regular Meeting for Literature and Cognitive/Computers II (LCC II) in the Japanese Cognitive Science Society, 17*, 1–20.
Young, A. (2003). Writing across and against the curriculum. *College Composition and Communication, 54*, 472–485.

13 Exploring ICT tools in English language learning
Language, technology, and the globalized classroom

Paolo Nino Valdez, Neslie Carol C. Tan, and Lindsey Ng-Tan

Since technology has revolutionized our ways of thinking and communicating with each other, computer-mediated communication (CMC) and information communication technologies (ICTs) have likewise changed the landscape of education, becoming an essential part of twenty-first century pedagogy and literacy practices (Reid, 2011). The United Nations (2003) recognizes the active participation of youth in the new developments in ICT: "Youth are at the forefront of the information revolution," and they are capable of using these in varied innovative ways. Thus new forms of socialization overtake and challenge traditional ones within the family or in the school context (pp. 328–329).

Prensky (2001) observes that students today have radically changed from the students in the past. In fact, he asserts, "Today's students are no longer the people our education system was designed to teach" (p. 1). He refers to these "new" students as 'Digital Natives' since they grew up immersed in new technology, and are thus " 'native speakers' of the digital language of computers, video games, and the Internet" (p. 1). Their patterns of thinking and processing of information are fundamentally different from their predecessors, the 'Digital Immigrants,' who were not born into the digital world, but have adopted new technology later on in their lives (p. 2). Digital Natives are used to immediacy and connectivity, and have low tolerance for 'slow' step-by-step lectures or 'tell-test' instruction/assessment methods. Prensky (2001) further describes them thusly:

> Digital Natives are used to receiving information really fast. They like to parallel process and multi-task. They prefer graphics before their text rather than the opposite. They prefer random access (like hypertext). They function best when networked. They thrive on instant gratification and frequent rewards. They prefer games to "serious" work.
>
> (p. 2)

In his book *Grown Up Digital*, Tapscott (2009) calls this group the 'net generation' and further explains the eight norms that characterize their experience: (1) freedom – they value flexibility and mobility in doing their work; (2)

customization – they tailor-fit technology to their personal needs and preferences; (3) scrutiny – they use digital technology to carefully distinguish fact from fiction given the amount of unreliable information (spam, scams, phishers, hoaxes, etc.) online nowadays; (4) integrity – they tend to follow through with concrete action what they have discovered through their scrutiny (e.g. not supporting companies that are found to mislead consumers with false advertising); (5) collaboration – they thrive in collective digital projects where their personal opinions matter and they create connections with wider communities; (6) entertainment – they value amusement in their work and in their digital tools since they tend to be bored easily; (7) speed – there is a sense of urgency in their performance of tasks, and they are used to instant responses; and (8) innovation – they are immersed in a "culture of invention" and thus expect continuous novel and original ideas and tools (p. 95).

With these new norms and expectations from the Digital Natives/Net Geners, Prensky (2001) strongly advocates digital immigrant educators to adjust to the changing learning needs and styles of their digital native students: "*We need to invent Digital Native methodologies for all subjects, at all levels, using our students to guide us*" (p. 6; emphasis in the original). He proposes a radical reconsideration of both methodology and content. The former requires speed/urgency, more in parallel, and with more random access means of teaching, while the latter involves tackling both 'legacy' (traditional curriculum) and 'future' (technological matters) content.

This chapter aims to examine the context of use of social networking in a writing class in the Philippines. The chapter is divided into three sections. The first section presents the current thinking on ICT in ELT. The second section explores the potential of social networking in the ELT classroom considering the communities of practice framework, and the third section presents a sample case study, which contextualizes these concepts

Current thinking on ICT in ELT

With several innovations in technology, ELT practitioners have explored different tools to be used in the classroom.

The blog is the current inclination of Computer Assisted Language Learning (CALL) in reading into writing (Bakar, 2009; de Izquierdo & Reyes, 2009; Hardwood, 2009; Pinkman, 2005). Feedback is promoted, reading and writing are represented in blogging; moreover, informal language reading is offered in blogging, which gives comfort to the student to use the language (Bakar, 2009; de Izquierdo & Reyes, 2009).

Honing of the students' grammar editing skills is supported in blogging (Harwood, 2010), and this kind of CALL can encourage learner independence (Pinkman, 2005). Other than blogging, social networking sites (SNS) can be used in language learning and teaching in the aspect of reading into writing. For instance, the study of Valdez (2010) shows a case study on the usage of SNS as a platform to showcase output in a reading and writing class in a form of e-portfolio.

CALL is also widely used in developing writing skills, specifically in the preponderance of corpora. First, the corpus-assisted creative writing is explored in the study of Kennedy and Miceli (2010). Second, Yoon (2008) discusses the effects of corpus technology in the development of students' competency as second language (L2) writers; this includes the modification in students' writing process with the usage of a corpus. Third, the study of Park and Kinginger (2010) elaborates the integration of digital video and networked linguistic corpora in students' writing and thinking process. On the other hand, synchronous online interaction is used in a Taiwanese undergraduate EFL writing class (Liang, 2010), while asynchronous text-stimulated forum discussion was explored as a writing assessment (Kol & Schcolnik, 2008).

E-learning is also one form of CALL. Effects of e-learning on overseas student awareness of culture and interactive learning environment to develop English academic writing are studied by Xing, Wang, and Spencer (2008). As regards to collaborative writing among L2 learners, an academic web-based project is investigated through the lens of honing a collaborative writing (Kessler, Bikowski, & Boggs, 2012). In addition, the use of social technologies, such as wikis and chats, for the development of students' writing skills is a different treatment in collaborative writing (Elola & Oskoz, 2010).

Honing listening skills is considered as the most difficult among the macroskills. Accordingly, technology plays a significant role in the use of authentic materials for listening skills (Leloup & Ponterio, 2007a). The following are studies that discuss the usage of technology in listening skills. First, the impact of task-based listening skills through CALL on Iranians' learners is discussed in the study of Nobar and Ahangari (2012). Second, video-based methodologies are effective not only in the development of listening skills (Grgurovic & Hegelheimer, 2007) but also in speaking skills (Shrosbee, 2008), while captioned videos are effective for foreign language listening activity, as compared with non-captioned videos (Winke, Gass, & Sydorenko, 2010. Videos are also used in listening comprehension (Verdugo & Belmonte, 2007) and in listening assessment (Wagner, 2007).

Not only in listening does computer technology also have a significant role in honing speaking skills (Godwin-Jones, 2009). For instance, computer-based pronunciation can not only assess the correctness of stress patterns of the language learners but also develop stress patterns in words, phrases, and sentences (Abu-Seileek, 2007). Furthermore, podcasts are another tool that could be used in developing pronunciation skills (Ducate & Lomicka, 2009). Tanner and Landon (2009) investigated a self-directed, computer-assisted technique in oral readings, which hones students' production of pausing, word stress, and intonation. Comparison was done among AudCMC (audio group), VidCMC (video group), and FTF group (face-to-face) to explore the task-based, synchronous oral CMC (Yanguas, 2010). Collaborative dialogue through learners' interaction in self-access computer activities is investigated in the study of (McDonough & Sunitham, 2009). Moreover, a DVD player and a satellite are used to study the effect of autonomous CALL in speaking abilities (Younsei, 2012). While usage of English

Pronunciation Perceptual Training Program software shows an effective result in training pronunciation (Liao, 2010).

Social networking and communities of practice

Dudeney, Hockly, and Pegrum (2013) have also mapped out the digital literacies that educators must help develop in their twenty-first century learners. They explain that digital literacies refer to the combined media literacy skills and digital competencies that allow us to effectively use technologies in meaningful social contexts. They further classified the literacies into four main subgroups: those focusing on language (print and texting literacies), on information (search and information literacies), on connections (personal, participatory, and intercultural literacies), and on (re)design (remix literacy). This complex mix of skills is recognized as fundamental skills that will prepare today's learners for life beyond the classroom.

In their pilot study of ICT projects of English student teachers, Allen and Richardson (2012) noticed that connection-based literacy, which involves social media, is still quite underexplored compared to other areas of digital literacy (i.e., language-based literacy, information-based literacy, and (re-) design-based literacy) proposed by Hockly (2012). They surmised that this lack is due to the general impression that social media sites are used more for recreational purposes – "as part of their leisure identities rather than their professional practice as language teachers" (p. 9). They thus recommend that teacher training ICT courses "strive to emphasize the connecting possibilities afforded by Facebook and Twitter while counteracting their potentially distractive influence in the classroom" (p. 9).

Noting that collaboration is a key norm among the Net Geners, Tapscott (2009) encourages educators to take heed: they must adjust their one-size-fits-all pedagogy, which isolates the student in his learning process, and transform it into a more collaborative and customized model that allows student-centered, multiway flow of information and learning.

Researchers (Blattner & Fiori, 2009; English & Duncan-Howell, 2008; Massi, Patrón, Verdú, & Scilipoti, 2012; Reid, 2011) cite that some of the benefits of incorporating Facebook within the English language classroom are stronger learner motivation, increased sense of belonging with a group, improved use of the language in authentic interaction, and developed sociopragmatic competence (in terms of language awareness, participation, and language use in context/specific situations).

Massi et al. (2012) in particular emphasizes how Facebook can empower learners by allowing them to assume more active roles in their learning process, thus making them open up and construct their own identities without the usual constraints present in traditional methods. Facebook is thereby considered a 'safe platform' for sharing both academic and non-academic ideas that facilitate learning and strengthen relationships among peers and even with their teachers (p. 67).

The speed by which feedback is relayed also helps learners in their learning progress as they receive instant and regular responses and guidance from both their teachers and their peers.

Massi et al. (2012) conclude that Facebook adds "another dimension to the traditional ELT experience by contributing to an interactive space that promotes the development of awareness-raising and peer group collaboration" (Reid, 2011, p. 68). Blattner and Fiori (2009) encourage educators to capitalize on the tools such as Facebook that are already part of their students' routines.

What is interesting in a globalized classroom that incorporates ICT in practice is there is an extension of the notion of communities of practice. As Lave and Wenger (1991, p. 98) emphasize, a community of practice is a "set of relations among persons, activity and world over time and in relation with other tangential and overlapping communities of practice." In this regard, since social networking provides a venue for different learners to be part of different communities of practice, the extent of their participation has consequences not only in terms of their language learning but also their socialization skills.

Sample case

This case study was carried out in a private tuition tertiary institution in the Philippines, which is one of the leading research universities in the Philippines. We involved students of English taking an Academic Reading and Writing class in the school year 2012–2013. The class consists of 21 first-year college students majoring in biology; however, only 19 students participated because the other two students failed to comply with the requirements of the course.

The class met twice a week for their class, which is a foundational course that equips first-year college students with the necessary academic writing skills needed to become multiliterate and autonomous learners. The course has two major learning outcome outputs: (1) extended-definition essay and (2) argumentative essay/problem-solution essay (either of the two). In the case of this specific class, their learning outputs are the extended definition of an argumentative essay. Aside from the two major learning outcomes, by the last two weeks of the course, the students made an e-portfolio through the usage of the Facebook (henceforth, FB) note feature.

The class made an FB group as part of the course requirement and started with the extended-definition essay. The class followed the academic writing process: pre-writing, researching for topics, outlining, writing the thesis statement, drafting, revising, final editing, and proofreading for six weeks. After the final revision, the students submitted their final extended-definition essay by posting it to the note feature of FB on their respective accounts. The students then tagged their essay to the main class account (which was created by the teacher) for the checking process. The students were encouraged to solicit comments (at least five comments consisting of positive and negative feedback) through FB's commentary feature from their FB friends regarding their extended-definition essay. This solicitation of comments aimed to procure authentic feedback not limited to the teacher's and students' comments. These comments were also used to assist the students in revising their essay. The teacher gave a deadline for the solicitation of the comments.

The same procedure was made with the argumentative essay for the next six weeks. Out of the various feedback/comments that the students received from authentic audience, the students were made to choose the best essay between the extended-definition essay and argumentative essay. The chosen essay was then tagged to the class account, which is the mother account of the entire course. Through the class account, students were able to share their essays with other students from other sections taking the course from different colleges. Consequently, they were able to share, comment, and collaborate with their respective essay.

Based on the data gathered, several initial impressions can be made. First, there is a prominent use of other languages as a medium of providing feedback for students. In the first episode, English and Filipino are used in commenting on an extended definition about snakes.

Episode 1

1   A: Try mo maglagay nag according to. . . para hindi naman puro (Author, date).
2   B: Grabe tong magthesis partner oh.
3   C: tama si mr. Erke para hindi mukhang copy paste. Definition essay to diba? Lagyan mo nag personal definition mo:)) (yung yung turo smen) para maemphasize nag pagka extended-definition niya:)
4   D: idol!
5   E: 4 1/2 inch or 10mm is the possible that a snake can grow "parang kulang"?
6   F: A very well refined and educated essay I must say! Not only have you informed the readers about the characteristics of snakes but you have delivered it in an interesting manner. Ups on a very good introduction as well! I never knew you were a fan of snakes.
7   Writing is you asset, keep it up!
8   E: what I mean is parang ang gulo kung ano yung sinasabing "smallest possible" you mean be yung length niya?

All posts except for line 6 use Filipino and a code-switching variety to provide suggestions for the work. In line 1, member A suggests that instead of doing a parenthetical citation, 'according to' constructions may be used to show variety in citation use. In line 3, C comments that there is a need for a personal definition of the term "snake" and not just definitions sourced from scholarly sources. On the other hand, line 5 seeks clarification as regards the possible length of a snake and uses a borrowed expression "parang kulang" (something seems to be missing). The same participant (E) on line 7 further claims that there seems to be some confusion as regards the possible size of the snake in terms of length.

As seen in these stretches of posts, Filipino is used as a resource to negotiate meaning similar to other forms of classroom discourse (Ferguson, 2003; Valdez, 2008). From a community of practice perspective, this may be interpreted as a shared repertoire among participants as they comment on their peers' work. Interestingly, this also illustrates the ranging 'voices' figuring in providing comments. For instance, participant B in line 2, who pokes fun at the earlier post (the thesis partner is so intense with his feedback!), shows the interaction, which may not be related to the task of commenting itself but which shows ranging levels of participation among students.

Moreover, the data show that the participants not only examined local aspects of the work but also commented on the global changes that are needed to make the essay of their peers better. In Episode 2, participants A, C, D, and E do not only focus on the organization of the essay, which focuses on cloning but also features the emotional states upon reading the work of their peer hinting at a sense of mutual engagement in dealing with the piece.

Episode 2

1. A: Your opening line was quite an eye-catcher, it drew my attention and helped set the mood for the essay. I understood the essay the first time I read it and I also noticed.
2. That your main idea was clearly pointed out throughout the essay. . .
3. B: Thank you.
4. C: I admit that when I first saw your essay I felt lazy for it was quite long, But as I start reading it, I found myself reading it up to the last line. The topic was discussed thoroughly and clearly I admire on how you constructed your essay for the flow of your ideas were consistent that each sentence were related to each other.
5. B: Thank you.
6. D: The first sentence, in my opinion is not engaging as how it is not engaging as how it is expected to be. It seems common for such an essay. The thesis statement on the other hand, is explicitly stated. The paragraph and sentences in general are related to each other.
7. B: Thank you.
8. E: The first sentence is catchy but set a negative mood on the reader. The main idea is clearly stated and thoroughly discussed. It served its purpose as the whole essay revolved around it. It served its purpose as the whole essay revolved around it. The ideas in the paragraph are generally related to one another and follow a flow within the essay.

As seen in lines 1, 3, 5, and 7, the participants not only focus on aspects of the work that are positive but also provide a reader's perspective, which the writer may want to consider in revising his piece. For instance, citing a negative, uninterested mood in the introduction reveals emotional attachments from the audience's perspective, which is important to holistically make the work better.

Another aspect, which is seen in the data is the use of other multimodal resources such as icons, pictures that help reinforce the message posted using text. It would seem, therefore, that the participants in the group not only rely on their knowledge of language to providing meaningful feedback but also deploy a range of resources to assure that the meaning they wish to convey is strengthened. This reveals that aside from language, other competencies (technological and transidiomatic practices) are also at work in the feedback process.

Given these points, several inferences can be made. Considering the community of practice perspective, the learners participate by contributing to the different aspects of the paper, leading to the notion of joint enterprise, as all seem to have the goal of helping their peers improve their work through comments at the local and global aspects of the work. As Massi et al. (2012) emphasize, since social networking serves as a platform for collaboration, FB in our case study provides a space for meaningful engagement for learners as they gain meaningful input from peers. Moreover, the dialogic nature of this joint enterprise provides greater opportunities for learners to interact with the actual discourse community that will 'consume' their work. As observed in Valdez (2010), the use of social networking creates a greater space for learners to reach a wider audience for them to gain meaningful input to improve their work. Moreover, the use of FB affords them the opportunity to minimize direct, face-to-face confrontations, which may be face threatening if their peers criticize their work. This therefore leads to the notion that while FB appears to afford students a certain level of distance from criticism, they can gather meaningful input without being offended. This leads to the 'cultural' aspect of using social networking: digital tools help maintain smooth interpersonal relations, which are essential in cultural interactions.

Since these students are considered 'beginning' academic writers in the university, the use of FB can be seen as a 'safe practice' that allows learners to not only solicit feedback but also provide opportunities to improve their writing style. Moreover, since there is a joint enterprise through the use of FB, there is a shared repertoire among learners. This is not only confined in terms of the use of languages (English and Filipino) and styles of interaction (from informal-formal) but also multimodal resources are deployed to enhance the effect of their feedback. Also, the shared repertoire observed in this case not only refers to the use of linguistic, discourse, or multimodal resources but also technological competencies in using social networking. Characteristic of the net generation (Tapscott, 2009), the learners use technological skills acquired from familiar experiences, which make their shared repertoire in this community of practice helpful in the improvement of their writing skills. Based on the initial findings from this case, it can be said that the use of social networking in the classroom is also an opportunity for students to exercise different languages in their repertoires, as the highlight of activities done in an online environment is the negotiation of meaning. This in a way creates greater learning opportunities for students to engage, reflect, and improve their skills not only in language but also through the use of technology. Moreover, since cultural norms are observed in online interactions, they become more sensitive to the feelings of their peers.

Conclusion

As observed in the aforementioned case, the use of social networking in the ELT classroom creates interesting points/issues for further investigation and discussion. The use of social networking provides a virtual space where the use of languages (and not just simply the target language, English in this case) appears to be the norm. This hints at the growing multilingual/multicultural character of our teaching and learning opportunities, which should be positively recognized by different stakeholders in the educational system (parents, administrators, and subject area teachers).

First, given that the case study reported here was done in an English for Academic Purpose tertiary level setting, it would be interesting to find similarities and differences when the strategy is tried out in different grade levels. Also new insights may be gained if classrooms with students from different cultures take part in online EFL/ESL communities of practice. Moreover, considering that other content areas use FB as a means to improve instruction, it may be meaningful to examine if the language/multimodal practices observed in this case study are different or similar.

Second, multimodal resources appear to be a growing feature in the writing classroom as it becomes an instrumental tool for learners to strengthen their message. Therefore, the globalized classroom may no longer be confined to writing in the strictest sense but may be considered a multimodal one. Moreover, since multimodal resources require knowledge in technology use, educators need to be aware of how these technologies are used to benefit writing. One caveat though is that the notion of multimodal resources may also affect the notion of what constitutes norms of academic writing, which may affect practices of assessment focusing on aspects of writing.

Overall, the use of social networking in the language classroom may not only be considered a trend but seems to be a growing prominent feature in globalized classroom. This marks the effect of globalization as it not only creates a borderless world but also transcends in creating a borderless classroom.

References

AbuSeileek, A. F. (2007). Computer – assisted pronunciation instruction as an effective means for teaching stress. *The JALT CALL Journal*, 3(1–2), 3–14.

Ahangari, S., & Nobar, A. G. (2012). The Impact of computer assisted language learning on Iranian EFL learners task – based listening skill and motivation. *Journal of Academic and Applied Studies*, 2(1), 39–61.

Allen, C., & Richardson, D. (2012, 22–25 August 2012). Exploring digital literacy in student-teacher ICT projects. In L. Bradley & S. Thouesny (Eds.), *CALL: Using, learning, knowing* (pp. 5–9). [The EUROCALL Conference Proceedings at Gothenburg, Sweden, Dublin].

Bakar, N. A. (2009). E-learning environment: Blogging as a platform for language learning. *European Journal of Social Sciences*, 9, 594–604.

Blattner, G., & Fiori, M. (2009). Facebook in the language classroom: Promises and possibilities. *International Journal of Instructional Technology and Distance Learning, 6*(1), 17–28.

de Izquierdo, B. L., & Reyes, L. E. (2009). Effectiveness of blogging to practice reading at a freshman EFL program. *The Reading Matrix, 9*, 100–117.

Ducate, L., & Lomicka, L. (2009). Podcasting: An effective tool for honing language students' pronunciation? *Language Learning & Technology, 13*, 66–86.

Dudeney, G., & Hockly, N. (2012). ICT in ELT: How did we get here and where are we going? *ELT Journal, 66*, 533–542.

Dudeney, G., Hockly, N., & Pegrum, M. (2013). *Digital literacies*. Harlow: Pearson.

Elola, I., & Oskoz, A. (2010). Collaborative writing: Fostering foreign language and writing conventions development. *Language Learning & Technology, 14*, 51–71.

English, R., & Duncan-Howell, J. (2008). Facebook© goes to college: Using social networking tools to support students undertaking teaching practicum. *Merlot Journal of Online Learning and Teaching, 4*, 596–601.

Ferguson, G. (2003). Classroom codeswitching in postcolonial contexts: Functions, attitudes, and policies. *AILA Review, 16*, 38–51.

Godwin-Jones, R. (2009). Emerging technologies speech tools and technologies. *Language Learning & Technology, 13*(3), 4–11.

Grgurovic, M., & Hegelheimer, V. (2007). Help options and multimedia listening: Students' use of subtitles and the transcripts. *Language Learning and Technology, 11*(1), 45–66.

Harwood, C. (2010). Using blogs to practice grammar editing skills. *ELT World Online, 2*, 1–13.

Hockly, N. (2012). Digital literacies. *ELT Journal, 66*(1), 108–112.

Kennedy, C., & Miceli, T. (2010). Corpus-assisted creative writing: Introducing intermediate Italian learners to a corpus as a reference resource. *Language Learning & Technology, 14*(1), 28–44.

Kessler, G., Bikowski, D., & Boggs, J. (2012). Collaborative writing among second language learners in academic web-based projects. *Language Learning & Technology, 16*, 91–109.

Kol, S., & Schcolnik, M. (2008). Asynchronous forum in EAP: Assessment issues. *Language Learning & Technology, 12*, 49–70.

Lave, J., & Wenger, E. (1991). *Situated learning: Legitimate peripheral participation*. Cambridge: Cambridge University Press.

LeLoup, J., & Ponterio, R. (2007a). Listening: You've got to be carefully taught. *Language Learning & Technology, 11*(1), 4–15.

LeLoup, J., & Ponterio, R. (2007b). Listening: On the Net LiTgloss. *Language Learning & Technology, 11*(3), 4–7.

Liang, M. (2010). Using synchronous online peer response groups in EFL writing: Revision-related discourse. *Language Learning & Technology, 14*(1), 45–64. Retrieved from http://llt.msu.edu/vol14num1/liang.pdf

Liao, F. H. (2010). A new perspective of CALL software for English perceptual training in pronunciation instruction. *The JALT CALL Journal, 6*(2), 85–102.

Massi, M. P., Patrón, Z. R., Verdú, M. A., & Scilipoti, P. (2012). Aging Facebook in the ELT picture: Developing student motivation with social networks. In L. Anglada & D. L. Banegas (Eds.), *View on motivation and autonomy in ELT* (pp. 64–69). Argentina: United States Embassy.

McDonough, K., & Sunitham, W. (2009). Collaborative dialogue between Thai EFL learners during self-access computer activities. *TESOL Quarterly*, *43*, 231–254.

Park, K., & Kinginger, C. (2010). Writing/thinking in real-time: Digital video and corpus query analysis. *Language Learning & Technology*, *14*(3), 31–50.

Pinkman, K. (2005). Using blogs in the foreign language classroom: Encouraging learner independence. *The JALT CALL Journal*, *1*(1), 12–24

Prensky, M. (2001). Digital natives, digital immigrants. *On the Horizon*, *9*(5), 1–6.

Reid, J. (2011). 'We don't Twitter, we Facebook': An alternative pedagogical space that enables critical practices in relation to writing. *English Teaching: Practice and Critique*, *10*(1), 58–80.

Shrosbree, M. (2008). Digital video in the language classroom. *The JALT CALL Journal*, *4*(1), 75–84.

Tanner, M. W., & Landon, M. M. (2009). The effects of computer-assisted pronunciation reading on ESL learners' use of pausing, stress, intonation, and overall comprehensibility. *Language Learning & Technology*, *13*(3), 51–65.

Tapscott, D. (2009). *Grown up digital: How the net generation is changing your world*. New York: McGraw-Hill.

United Nations (UN). (2003). Youth and information and communication technologies (*ICT*). *World Youth Report* (pp. 309–333). Retrieved from www.un.org/esa/socdev/unyin/documents/ch12.pdf

Valdez, P. N. (2008). The Filipino bilingual's cultural competence: A model based on Filipino-English Codeswitching (Unpublished Doctoral Dissertation). Philippine Normal University.

Valdez, P. N. (2010). Reflections on using the digital portfolio in academic writing in a Philippine university: Problems and possibilities. *Philippine ESL Journal*, *5*, 160–170.

Verdugo, D. R., & Belmonte, I. A. (2007). Using digital stories to improve listening comprehension with Spanish young learners of English. *Language Learning and Technology*, *11*(1), 87–101.

Wagner, E. (2007). Are they watching? Test-taker viewing behavior during an L2 video listening test. *Language Learning and Technology*, *11*(1), 67–86.

Winke, P., Gass, S., & Sydorenko, T. (2010). The effects of captioning videos used for foreign language listening activities. *Language Learning & Technology*, *14*(1), 65–86.

Xing, M., Wang, J., & Spencer, K. (2008). Raising students' awareness of cross-cultural contrastive rhetoric in English writing via e-learning course. *Language Learning & Technology*, *12*(2), 71–93.

Yanguas, I. (2010). Oral computer-mediated interaction between L2 Learners: It's about time! *Language Learning & Technology*, *14*(3), 72–93.

Yoon, H. (2008). More than a linguistic reference: The influence of corpus technology on L2 academic writing. *Language Learning and Technology*, *12*(2), 31–48.

Younsei, M. (2012). The effect of autonomous CALL based task on speaking skill. *The Iranian EFL Journal*, *8*, 201–221.

14 The use of photo story in the Indonesian English language classroom
Working with multimodal tasks

Nur Arifah Drajati, Sri Rejeki Murtiningsih, Winda Hapsari, and Hasti Rahmaningtyas

The integration of technology into English classrooms has gained in popularity over the last 20 years. Despite the controversy whether this integration can boost or impede learning, teachers are geared to try out this new teaching-learning approach in their classes. As *digital natives* (Prensky, 2011), most of the learners are often more familiar with technology than their teachers. This fact motivates teachers and curriculum developers to include technology in the lessons.

Using digital technologies to teach narrative texts in English classes is one way to enhance learning as well as to facilitate the interests of the digital natives. One specific type of implementation of digital technologies in the classroom is the use of digital photo story (also known as digital storytelling). This digital tool uses a multimodal approach that is more functional and compelling for both teachers and students.

An array of research on digital photo stories has been undertaken to examine various aspects of learning, such as linguistic aspects (Royce, 2002) and writing skills (Cope & Kalantzis, 2000; Gee, 2003; Hocks, 2003). However, very few studies have been conducted to investigate the use of digital photo story designed to teach narratives in English as an additional language (EAL) classrooms, particularly in secondary schools. Thus the present study attempted to fill this gap. Anchored in multimodal theory, this study attempted to examine the use of digital technology in the teaching of narrative texts as part of the Indonesian secondary-school curriculum.

Literature and theoretical framework

Digital photo story

Digital storytelling, digital photo story, is the practice of combining multiple modes of technology, such as photographs, text, music, audio narration, and video clips to produce a compelling, emotional, and in-depth story (Bull & Kajdar, 2005; Castaneda, 2013) and to engage learners in authentic tasks that allow for self-construction of meaning (Jonassen, Peck, & Wilson, 1999) because it involves critical cognitive experiences (Fulwiler & Middleton, 2012). This digital photo story serves as a tool to help students visually illustrate a completed script as well as to make meaning of the story. Although this method of multimodal literacies is powerful, user-friendly, and affordable (Fulwiler & Middleton, 2012; Lambert, 2006; Robin, 2008), digital photo story is still under-practiced in EAL classrooms.

Lambert (2006) offers a set of elements involved in digital photo story. The first element is that students engage actively in developing a central theme of the story (*the point of view element*) and in creating a story line that captures the audience's attention (*the dramatic question element*). Other elements include allowing students to narrate the story to communicate their meaning-making, and to help the audience make meaning (*the gift of voice element*), and providing background music (*the power of soundtrack element)* to evoke audience emotion (*emotional content element)*. These can encourage students to engage in digital photo story activities. Lastly, students are encouraged to work on the linguistic part of the activities to tell the story (*economy of language element)*. This element also encourages students to make sure that speech is at reasonable speed and clear enough for the audience to understand the story (*pace element)*. Taken together, these elements are expected to enable students to engage with meaningful activities that involve multiple modes yet still engage in language learning since students have to produce a coherent and clear storyline both in writing and in speech. Obviously, when engaged in digital photo story activities, students will learn how to deal with computers and other devices because they need to organize selected images, record their voices, and learn to use the software. Robin (2008) indicates that digital photo story promotes other skills, such as cultural literacy, information literacy, and media literacy that students need in the real world. With this in mind, digital photo story needs to be included in language learning.

Digital storytelling provides students with a number of benefits. First of all, students can learn how to critique their own work as well as the work of others (Brenner, 2014; Robin, 2008). Using digital storytelling, teachers allow students to work collaboratively with their peers, to look at their own work and apply the revising skills they have learned. Also, teachers encourage students to provide constructive feedback to their peers' work. This collaborative process also facilitates social learning that stimulates students' emotional intelligence as well as critical thinking (Fulwiler & Middleton, 2012). According to Castaneda (2013) and Yang and Wu (2012), digital storytelling improves students' learning self-efficacy because they are likely aware that their work would be viewed by others; thus, they are motivated to create their best work and be more cautious with possible errors in their work. In addition, digital story allows computer users to be creative while going through the production process because students have to work closely with computers to download and upload the various modes they need to complete the tasks (Robin, 2008).

Despite the benefits of digital photo story, this tool presents a number of challenges. Empirical research conducted by Sadik (2008) revealed that collaboration in working on the digital story project was not done in an equal manner. Some students were more dominant and involved in the process than the others. Only a few students participated actively in preparing the content, design, and presentation of stories. These students showed a lower level of awareness towards views and opinions of other group members. The study found that students even spent more time browsing ideas and materials, which in turn caused them to pay less attention to the quality of the linguistic aspects, such as language use, vocabulary, and mechanics. The study also showed that teachers' lack of technical proficiency in the use of technology hampered the process. The teachers needed to allocate more time to better prepare for the lesson.

Time constraints were one of the main challenges in employing Photo Story. This challenge was reported in Brenner's (2014) study. Brenner (2014) reported that creating digital stories could be time consuming, especially for teachers and students who had never used digital production software. When it came to technology-mediated instruction in language learning, this unfamiliarity resulted in teachers and students turning to a more traditional approach of language teaching and learning.

Educational research on digital photo story

The use of digital photo story in the educational domain has been well-documented. In their experimental study with 110 high school students in Taiwan, Yang and Wu (2012) found that students' academic achievements, along with their critical thinking skills and learning motivation, improved after the use of digital storytelling. Digital storytelling also enhanced students' language performance in their speaking, writing, and listening. In terms of critical thinking skills, digital storytelling shaped how students evaluated arguments. In Yang and Wu's (2012) study, the students also reaped benefits from working collaboratively in the process of creating, revising, and clarifying the digital story that was instrumental in fostering students' performance in terms of evaluation of arguments. In another study, Hur and Suh (2012) investigated students' English language proficiency and development through the use of technology, one of which was digital photo story. This study showed that the digital photo story project helped students improve their research skills with active engagement in learning. In terms of writing and speaking skills, the students performed repeated practices, such as revising texts and reading the scripts. The results demonstrate that the digital photo story was an effective scaffolding tool. The activities allowed the students to practice English in a safe environment (i.e., home) where they had access to books and online resources. In addition to learning support, it was reported that the students were excited because they received firsthand experience in creating a digital photo story.

Castaneda (2012) used a case study to examine the effectiveness of digital storytelling in communicating students' emotion and presenting information before an audience. Overall, the findings of the study revealed not only that students could create digital stories but also that they could exceed the expectations of the teacher and the researcher. The students were able, willing, and proud to share personal stories in a foreign language. Once students became engaged in the process, in general, they found the drafting and editing process satisfactory. An added benefit was observed during the digital storytelling process. As the teacher pointed out, during the recording step, the students became aware of their language use.

In addition, Sadik (2008) looked into the effectiveness of technology integration for teachers and students by using digital photo story in schools in Egypt. The study showed that the use of technology could only be effective if teachers themselves possessed expertise in using technology in a meaningful way. The study also found that ineffective and inappropriate training in using the technology and teacher's lack of vision of technology's potential for improving learning became the main concerns in implementing technology-mediated instruction.

Multimodal approach

A multimodal approach refers to using a variety of resources or modes, which may appear in different forms – visual and auditory – to enhance learning (Jewitt, 2006). Naturally, digital technologies offer visual and auditory sources, such as images, background music, speeches, language, and movement. The multimodal approach is used to combine these different modes to make meanings beyond the language. Thus applying multimodality to an EAL classroom deals with learning beyond the linguistic aspects of communication. This means that visuals, sound effects, and colors are also tools for communicating meanings to others.

In terms of EAL learning, Krashen (1978) argues that exposure to English will provide students with elaborative inputs in their language learning, which will help students to make sense of the inputs. In turn, students will be able to use these inputs to use, manipulate, and develop their outputs of the new language they are learning. Similarly in multimodality, the use of multiple modes, particularly in digitally based learning environments, will facilitate students' understanding and students' language mastery (Moreno, 2002; Rance-Roney, 2010). Students learn English in different ways. Some students are more visual than others, while other students have a higher level of linguistic skills than their peers. Thus exposing students to different modes can enable students to be aware of their learning style and to focus on their strengths, but, at the same time, they also improve other skill areas that are less developed. Similar to elaborative inputs in language learning, exposing students to different modes is likely to encourage students to navigate, manipulate, and understand how these modes relate to each other (Mayer, 2003).

Multimodality also concurs with the types of digital modes that students are able to access from their environment quite easily these days. With the easy access to visual modes, for example, multimodality helps students "extract what visuals are trying to say and relate these messages to the linguistic aspect of the meaning" (Royce, 2002, p. 198). These activities will encourage students to reflect on their personal experience, to learn new information, to make meaning out of what they have learned, and to communicate their ideas to others in a way that they feel comfortable.

These days, different modes used in the multimodal approach may be presented in the classroom. One of the most common designs to utilize the modes in the EAL classroom is digital storytelling. In digital storytelling, students tell stories using different modes, such as in speech or in writing, with the help of computers and software. Integrating digital storytelling into the teaching of writing has also been a common practice in the EAL classroom. Studies show that the visual and aural modalities can teach students new strategies and approaches, which can be productively applied to their efforts at composing more traditional written compositions (Cope & Kalantzis, 2000; Gee, 2003; Hocks, 2003; Kalantzis, Varnava-Skoura, & Cope, 2002; Lankshear & Knobel, 2003; Wysocki, Johnson-Eilola, Selfe, and & Sirc, 2004).

The study

Thirty-five students participated in this study. The participants were twelfth graders at a private secondary school in a city in Indonesia. The participants worked in groups, which resulted in eight groups of four and a group of three. This digital storytelling project spanned three weeks. The participating students volunteered for extra grades in English.

For virtual discussion, the first author, an English teacher in the school, set up a Facebook (FB) group account and added the participants to the group. The other three authors were added to the FB account to analyze the data. Most instructions were posted on FB as well as participants' comments, questions, and assignments. The participants were given a link to Photo Story 3 for Windows, which was posted on the FB account. They were told to download photos, provide a background voice for the photos, and write narrative stories based on the photos and sound effects. The students were assigned to write individual self-reflection on working collaboratively, to give peer reviews, and to write their personal experiences in relation to being involved in the project. The teacher provided samples of these three pieces of work for students. At the end of the project, the students were interviewed to obtain richer data on the issues. The in-depth interviews were audio recorded and transcribed. These journal entries were later used as the sources of data. All the participants' written assignments were manually coded; the most frequently occurring codes were grouped into major themes. Member checking, suggested by Merriam (1998), was used to deal with trustworthiness of the data because the data were open for all the participants and the teacher to comment on and revise. The present study only used the latest revision if any work was revised.

Findings and discussion

Drafting and negotiating strategies for the creation of multimodal narrative texts

Central to the idea of a digital photo story project was to help them become autonomous learners. This was achieved by using a social medium, in this case,

FB, as the platform to learn new things, upload their work, and download others' compositions on which they worked further to write their feedback. The students were given freedom to choose their team members, topics, and photos for their texts, as well as time to upload their work, although deadlines were given.

Another purpose of this study was to provide students with more opportunities to read and write by using a digital photo story. Narrative texts were created in several steps, which moved from simple to complex types of writing, from more familiar to less familiar topics, from short essays to longer ones, and from concrete to abstract ideas. As the students were already familiar with the fact that past tense was commonly used in narrative texts, Task 1 started with assignments in which the students were required to write about their personal experiences. Assigning students to write a narrative text using past tense was also considered as encouraging students to tell their experience in chronological order (Yi, 2013) before moving to the use of present and future forms to write their stories. Meanwhile, the students performed the reading mainly by reading the pieces of writing from their peers.

During the process of creating narrative texts, the students were divided into small groups. Grouping was aimed at minimizing mistakes in students' writings, as Dobao's study (2012) found that working in small groups improved students' writing in terms of the number of mistakes the students made. Also, grouping was considered a form of learning from others, suggested by Vygotsky (1978) in his social-constructivism theory. This peer learning allowed the students to learn from each other.

In addition, the students were given freedom to decide how to complete a task. For example, although the students were free to select photos prior to writing the narratives, most – if not all – groups chose to write the narrative as the first activity before they picked pictures and assigned one of the team members to read the narratives as the background voice. This sequence was evident from Budi's writing about the narrative project. He wrote, "We [*he and his group*] discussed what narrative that attracts people. This discussion is important because it will become the foundation of our narrative."

In Task 2, the the students were assigned to provide feedback on their peers' writings. To help the students organize their feedback, the teacher provided a guideline or a rubric, which included organization, word choices, fluency, and sound effects. One group was assigned to review or comment on another group's work. This feedback was the basis for revising the work. While all groups wrote the narrative texts in the form of essays, they wrote their feedback in this particular task only in a few sentences for each point suggested by the teacher. The following was feedback provided by one of the groups:

> Organization: *You have a well-organized story, but there are some random plots.*
> Word choice: *Your chosen words are easy to understand. That way, we enjoy reading your story.*
> Grammatical pattern: *Your story has a good grammar. This is great and makes your story easy to understand.*
>
> (Group A, November 30, 2013)

In this feedback task, the students wrote a sentence or two for the feedback without providing supporting details to the sentence. The feedback from Group A mentioned previously, for example, showed that the group identified some random plots from their peers' work; however, Group A did not provide supporting details to which random plots they were referring.

This particular finding was closely related to writing models provided by the teacher. Tracey and Morrow (2006) argue that one way of learning is to observe other people. In this project, while the teacher provided a rubric and text sample for the students to write the narrative texts, she only provided a rubric for the students to write the feedback. As a result, all groups wrote the feedback like the model provided. The students were supposed to provide feedback beyond what the teacher modeled. Particularly in a feedback task, the students should have received different ways to provide feedback on each other's work. Despite this drawback, the students co-created the narrative texts using different negotiated strategies.

Framing the use of language in composing

Using the English language for the project was a challenge for most students, both in written and in oral form when they had to tell the story accompanying the photos. The data show that out of 23 reflection assignments submitted online, 9 students mentioned that one of the challenges they found in participating in the project was using English appropriately. Using appropriate grammatical patterns was understandable to the audience. This was one of the concerns the participants reported. Dinda, for example, stated that using English appropriately was one of the challenges she faced. She remarked, "Grammar is another challenge for me because, I think, using incorrect grammar gives a bad impression." Dinda was concerned that the audience of the video would not understand what she and her classmates were trying to say in the video because of the inappropriate use of grammar.

In addition to grammar, using standardized English became one of the challenges faced by the students. One of the students recounted that she and her classmates were accustomed to using non-standard English on many occasions, including for academic purposes, when they were supposed to use standardized English. As a result, this student found it hard to identify if English they used was standard or formal. For the purpose of the project, she and her peers felt that they were pushed to use standardized English. The student did not provide any examples or definitions of what she considered non-standard English. However, there has been a phenomenon in which English words or sentences are adapted based on the Indonesian context and are usually used in a non-formal daily conversation. This phenomenon commonly takes place among young people.

The students were also challenged with other language features, such as pronunciation and intonation. In this project, they were required to upload a set of pictures with read-aloud scripts, which were written in English. Reading the scripts aloud encouraged the students to ensure they pronounced the words properly so that the audience understood the story they presented. Choice of words was also mentioned repeatedly in the data as one of the challenges in relation to the language use. As a matter of fact, framing the language use was the most challenging part of the project. One of the students remarked, "The challenge on script writing was we must choose easy-to-understand words so it made sense to people." In short, writing a script and reading it aloud so that it made sense to the audience was a major concern among the students.

On the other hand, the students noted that they learned to use the appropriate grammar and other language skills from participating in this project. Because they were to show their projects to their peers and the teacher, they made sure that the audience enjoyed their work. Atika reported,

> Because we use our voice and pictures to tell the story, [the Photo Story video] had to be interesting enough [for the audience] to hear and see. We tried to fix our grammar and pronunciation, as well as be more careful with our choice of words.

The fact that the project was conducted in the English class made the students fully aware of their language. This was likely because they were aware that the language features were important for their audience to understand the meaning of the photos they presented. Some students even remarked that they made major changes to their script because they found grammatical and pronunciation mistakes in their first script. This awareness indicated that the digital photo storytelling activities also encouraged the students to do metacognitive activities in their language learning.

Collaborating on text creation and improvement

Drawing on the 23 reflection journals submitted, several challenges in relation to working collaboratively with their peers were identified. First and foremost, the software provided by the teacher was specifically designed for PC computers; thus, it posed a certain challenge for those who used Mac computers. Although, eventually, all the students were able to obtain computers that worked with the Photo Story software, they spent relatively more time familiarizing themselves with the operating system. Two groups mentioned that they did not use PCs for their daily technological work, which required them to design a strategy to solve the problem.

However, not all of the groups found the Photo Story software challenging. Nine students were happy with the software and stated that the Photo Story software was "simple and easy to use," "simply amazing," and "simple software." The user-friendliness of the software did not give them as many challenges as they had expected. In turn, they enjoyed using the software and the learning in general.

To be involved in this project, students "must make a variety of decisions about images, sounds and texts, and constantly address the effects" (Fulwiler & Middleton, 2012, p. 48). Making a variety of decisions was part of the challenges faced by students. While they were negotiating their other commitments, such as final test preparation and other school projects, the students in this study had to make decisions on topics, pictures, stories, and background music to meet the teacher's expectations. Atika articulated this challenge in her reflective journal: "The challenge is how to find a topic which is approved by everybody in the group." Finding certain types of pictures that matched their storylines was also a challenge. One of the students addressed this issue by stating the pictures that they needed were the ones that were eye catching and had a good resolution, and there were not many pictures that met their expectations.

Although the students were unable to meet every day work on their projects because of other school commitments, the collaborative work that they did with their peers was quite effective. The interview revealed that some groups actually finished the assignment in one meeting. This is evidence that the students worked effectively and independently. Although they received little instruction from their teacher, the students were able to solve the problems that they encountered.

Positioning roles of teacher and students in the entire learning trajectory

The main role of the teacher in this project was monitoring the whole learning process. The monitoring activities were also conducted through the FB account set up when the project initiated. For example, the teacher constantly reminded the students to make sure they did not miss the deadlines. In doing her role, the teacher also provided praise and questions to direct students to the goals of the learning process. At the beginning of the project, the teacher monitored the learning circle quite closely to make the students aware of the level of responsibility ascribed to the project. As the learning progressed, the level of teacher control was lowered.

In addition, one of the most significant roles of the teacher in the entire learning process was to provide scaffolding for the students. Since the project focused on improving writing skills, the writing assignment progressed from one paragraph for the first assignment to a journal entry that provided the students with a large degree of freedom to express their opinions. The data showed that the students wrote a paragraph, three paragraphs, and more than five paragraphs on average for the first, second, and third writing assignments respectively. The topic also moved from simple to more complicated. For example, for the first entry, the topic given was related to students' personal experiences. As the learning progressed, the students were required to present their personal opinion on some topics, to reflect on their learning, and to provide constructive feedback on their peers' works.

The most important role of the teacher in the learning trajectory was to facilitate a safe environment for students. This included providing a forum for students to accept constructive feedback from their peers and their teacher, and for students to provide justifications if they decided not to take the feedback. On the other hand, the students were also encouraged to give constructive feedback to their peers. They were encouraged to share their opinions in a respectful and non-offensive manner; thus, they felt secure when giving and accepting the feedback. This learning process enabled students to learn meaningfully from their social circle. Vygotsky (1978) maintains that students learn best from the social environment. The social interaction that took place among the students motivated them to use their social skills to solve various problems they encountered during the process. In terms of language learning, the teacher provided a safe environment for students to make mistakes in their work. Although grammatical errors and pronunciation were not the main foci of the project, the students were aware that grammatical and pronunciation errors might lead to misunderstandings. As a facilitator, the teacher reduced the amount of control to encourage student independence. For example, the teacher did not immediately intervene when a student updated the status on the FB group chat and stated that she encountered problems, although she closely monitored the interaction. This was aimed at observing students' attempts to solve the problems on their own. Also, it was intended to see if other students would work collaboratively to help the student solve his or her problem.

Likewise, the students played important roles in the whole learning process. The main role that students played was taking full responsibility for their learning in class and outside the class. Being more and more in charge of their own learning was a sign of students' autonomy/independence. The data showed that most students participating in the project did most assignments outside the classroom. In fact, many students posted their assignment on the FB group chat late in the evenings. The students participating in the project also set up meetings with their peers without the teacher's instruction. Students' journal entries showed that they made several attempts to solve the problems they encountered. For example, when a group of students were not able to install the software, which only worked with a PC laptop, they solved the problem by borrowing a PC laptop from one of their relatives without telling the teacher that they encountered the problem, and they did not post their problem on FB. Instead, they worked together to solve their problem.

In terms of language learning, the students were to be critical of their own language learning. While they were encouraged to be critical of their peers' language learning, the students were required to look at their own language learning as well. They were encouraged to make sense of the whole process of their language learning such as writing the script and understanding it when they read it aloud. Without being able to make sense of the linguistic features they used, it would be almost impossible to understand the effect of other features, such as music and photos, accompanying the texts that were used to communicate their ideas (Kress, 2000). On the other side, the students were also encouraged to make sense of their peers' work and provide comments that their counterparts could use to improve their work. The data showed that nine students found the comments and feedback they received from their peers insightful, and they made some improvement in their Photo Story videos so that the videos made sense to their peers.

Conclusion

The digital photo story is a way to introduce students to different modes and use them to improve their English ability. In this project, the students were required to perform a series of activities, such as selecting images and background music, writing scripts about the images, and reading aloud the script. The students were also involved in activating their background knowledge and providing constructive feedback on the work of their peers.

These activities allowed students to use their technological skills to participate in the project. This study found that drafting and negotiating the multimodal activities as a challenge for the students. The students had little interest in participating in the project because of their various school commitments and their unfamiliarity with the activities required for the digital photo storytelling. Although the students encountered problems with the technological devices, they were able to solve these problems with very little help from their teacher. Writing down their experiences and providing written feedback of their friends' compositions were activities that were new experiences for the students.

The digital photo story also improved students' awareness of learning English, especially their writing and speaking skills. At the outset, the students were concerned about the non-standard English they had been using and worried that non-standard English would interfere with their effort to make meaning and communicate their meaning to others. This concern led students to review their work continuously for grammatical mistakes and pronunciation to ensure that their peers were able to make sense of their work. It was evident that the students had a higher level of awareness of self-correction, which is crucial when learning a new or additional language. Additionally, the students worked collaboratively to perform digital photo story tasks, which proved that digital photo story had improved students' learning autonomy. With a decreasing level of control from their teacher, the students performed tasks and uploaded their work at their own pace.

To be able to perform all the tasks with which students were unfamiliar, the digital photo story project created a safe learning environment. During the project, the students received full autonomy to provide and receive feedback to/from others in a respectful manner. Digital photo story also enhanced students' responsibility and critical thinking skills regarding their own learning. Being able to make sense of their own work and others' was one of the main outcomes in the learning trajectory.

References

Brenner, K. (2014). Digital stories: A 21st-century communication tool for the English language classroom. *English Teaching Forum, 1*, 22–29.

Bull, G., & Kajdar, S. (2005). Digital storytelling in the language arts classroom. *Learning and Leading with Technology, 42*, 46–49.

Castaneda, M. E. (2013). "I am proud that I did it and it's a piece of me": Digital storytelling in the foreign language classroom. *CALICO Journal, 30*(1), 44–62.

Cope, B., & Kalantzis, M. (2000). *Multi-literacies: Literacy learning and the design of social futures*. London: Routledge.

Dobao, A. F. (2012). Collaborative writing tasks in the L2 classroom: Comparing group, pair, and individual work. *Journal of Second Language Writing*, 21, 40–58.

Fulwiler, M., & Middleton, K. (2012). After digital storytelling: Video composing in the new media age. *Computers and Composition*, 29, 39–50.

Gee, J. P. (2003). *What video games have to teach us about learning and literacy*. New York: Palgrave Macmillan.

Hocks, M. (2003). Teaching and learning visual rhetoric. In P. Takayoshi & B. Huot (Eds.), *Teaching writing with computers: An introduction* (pp. 202–216). Boston: Houghton Mifflin.

Hur, J. W., & Suh, S. (2012). Making learning active with interactive whiteboards, podcasts, and digital storytelling in ELL classrooms. *Computers in the Schools*, 29, 320–338.

Jewitt, C. (2006). *Technology, literacy, and learning: A multimodal approach*. New York: Routledge.

Jonassen, D., Peck, K., & Wilson, B. (1999). *Learning with technology: A constructivist perspective*. Upper Saddle River, NJ: Prentice Hall.

Kalantzis, M., Varnava-Skoura, G., & Cope, B. (Eds.). (2002). *Learning for the future: New worlds, new literacies, new learning, new people*. Altona, Victoria: Common Ground Publishers.

Krashen, S. (1978). The monitor model for second-language acquisition. In R. C. Gingras (Ed.), *Second-language acquisition and foreign language teaching* (pp. 1–26). Washington, DC: Center of Applied Linguistics.

Kress, G. (2000). Multimodality: Challenges to thinking about language. *TESOL Quarterly*, 34, 337–340.

Lambert, J. (2006). *Digital storytelling: Capturing lives, creating community* (2nd edn.). Berkeley, CA: Digital Diner Press.

Lankshear, C., & Knobel, M. (2003). *New literacies: Changing knowledge and classroom learning*. Buckingham: Open University Press.

Mayer, R. E. (2003). Elements of a science of e-learning. *Journal of Educational Computing Research*, 29, 297–313.

Merriam, S. B. (1998). *Qualitative research and case study applications in education*. San Fransisco, CA: Jossey-Bass.

Moreno, R. (2002). Who learns best with multiple representations? Cognitive theory implications for individual differences in multimedia learning. Paper presented at *World Conference on Educational Multimedia, Hypermedia, Telecommunications*. Denver, CO.

Prensky, M. (2011). Digital natives, digital immigrants. In B. Mark (Ed.), *The digital divide* (pp. 3–11). New York: Penguin.

Rance-Roney, J. (2010). Jump-starting language and schema for English-language learners: Teacher-composed digital jumpstarts for academic reading. *Journal of Adolescent & Adult Literacy*, 53, 386–395.

Robin, B. R. (2008). Digital storytelling: A powerful technology tool for the 21st century classroom. *Theory Into Practice*, 47, 220–228.

Royce, T. (2002). Multimodality in the TESOL classroom: Exploring visual-verbal synergy. *TESOL Quarterly*, 36, 191–205.

Sadik, A. (2008). Digital storytelling: A meaningful technology-integrated approach for engaged student learning. *Educational Technology Research & Development*, 56, 487–506.

Tracey, D. H., & Morrow, L. M. (2006). *Lenses on reading: An introduction to theories and models.* New York: Guilford Press.
Vygotsky, L. S. (1978). *Mind in Society: The development of higher psychological processes.* Cambridge, MA: Harvard University Press.
Wysocki, A. F., Johnson-Eilola, J., Selfe, C. L., & Sirc, G. (Eds.). (2004). *Writing new media: Theory and applications for expanding the teaching of composition.* New York: Hampton Press.
Yang, Y. T. C., & Wu, W. C. I. (2012). Digital storytelling for enhancing student academic achievement, critical thinking, and learning motivation: A year-long experimental study. *Computers & Education, 59,* 339–352.
Yi, Y. (2013). Questions arising from the assessment of EFL narrative writing. *ELT Journal, 67*(1), 70–79.

15 Social psychology of the language classroom

Hamzeh Moradi and Deepti Gupta

Social and psychological factors of language learning have been and indeed remain the focus of a significant amount of research during the few past decades. Whether it is Chomsky questioning the behaviorist stance or Krashen hypothesizing on the Affective Filter or Schumman placing social and psychological distance centrestage, the importance of social psychology facets in the language learning process is one of the most pervasive themes of research in second language (L2) acquisition. In fact, L2 acquisition is not only an innate cognitive aptitude and phenomenon but also a socio-psychological one and thus of great significance and value in order to investigate and consider the social and psychological conditions in which L2 learning occurs. This chapter reviews the most significant models related to the socio-psychological facets of language learning and clearly describes some of the indispensable concepts in the field such as self-efficacy, attitude, motivation, effort, literacy learning strategies and self-awareness while examining them further in the light of the Asian classroom. The focus of the present chapter is on the socio-psychology of the classroom to help teachers and language educators obtain a better understanding of socio-psychological forces related to language learning in the classroom, be cognizant of the implicit psychological features of the interaction between teachers and learners and, finally, to manage the classroom and learning environment and optimize classroom management.

Introduction

The continuous and ongoing process of globalization has led to the distribution and spread of English throughout the world, which stands reflected in the demands of its acquisition, learning and use. This has been well documented by sociolinguists (Crystal, 2003). As Dornyei, Csizer, and Ne´meth(2006) mention, possibly there are linguistic implications regarding globalization as well as economic interconnectedness. A substantial number of studies have been carried out by scholars to investigate how individuals learn languages other than their native language (e.g., Crystal, 2003; Dornyei et al., 2006; Kirkpatrick, 2007; Mesthrie & Bhatt, 2008; Seidlhofer, 2004, 2008; Sharifan, 2009). The literature on second/foreign language acquisition considers the social and psychological aspect as an obvious link between the language learning process and its success.

Those interested in the significance and intricacies of language in social life look to psychology and especially social psychology for some insight. Most of an individual's behavior takes place in a social context and is manifested linguistically and mediated by cognitive processes (Gardner, 1985).

Schools as the central societal institutions follow the goal of "to teach" and "to educate" the students. The classroom is a mini-society (Babad, 2009). It has a formal purpose and a fixed and defined structure. But beyond the universal formal and defined structure, every classroom has an informal structure that develops through student-teacher interaction. Teachers have dual roles in the classroom: as instructors who teach younger generations, help them to develop their intellectual capacities and lead them to academic progress and as socializers who help the students to develop values and social selves, their social conduct and a specific cultural level (Babad, 2009). Therefore, teachers should, first, consider the social and psychological forces in the classroom and second, pay more attention to the implicit and hidden psychological facets of the teacher-student interaction in order to improve their classroom management. It is obvious that in school students can acquire the basic social perception and mode of social behavior. These kinds of experience affect the students' self-esteem and self-concept, motivation and accordingly the formation of their attitude and values.

A large number of researchers argue that motivation and effort investment are variables which should not be neglected in the study of social psychology of language learning. Endorsing this idea, Boekaerts and Cascallar (2006) hold that learners should initiate activities that can set the scene for language learning, assign values to learning activities, motivate themselves and be persistent. Marinak and Gambrell (2010) point out teachers that can teach the learners reading and writing strategies, but learners may never reach their full potential if they lack intrinsic motivation to read and write and do not invest enough effort. The Asian teacher belongs to a highly culture-specific society, and in such societies, the teacher is usually looked up to as role model and guide, making the task of socializer easier.

According to Elisha Babad (2009), motivation is the main and central field of psychological theory and research. There are a large number of articles and books dedicated to the discussion of motivational processes (e.g., Dweck, 1986; Perry, 1991, 2003; Perry, Hall, & Ruthig, 2007; Wentzel, 1999, 2006). Elisha Babad (2009) mentions,

> Motivation is the fuel of our mental system, the force and the energy which activates us and leads our behavior to attain particular goals. Motivation is usually caused by inner demands and by the requirement and indispensability to satisfy those demands and needs.

Schutz (1958) and Schmuck (1978) were among the first who theorized about social needs and introduced a variation of three central social motivations as indicated in the following list:

1   *The need for affection (the need for warmth, to be liked and loved by others)*
2   *The need for inclusion (the need to be a member of the group and to avoid social rejection)*
3   *The need for power (the need to have control, power and influence in one's social environment)*

Gardner (1985), in his research, asserts that the social psychology approach straddles two domains:

> "*First, language and society are viewed as interdependent not as dichotomies as reflected in much traditional sociolinguistics*". It is extremely difficult to differentiate between linguistic and social processes in many instances. Therefore, not only does the individuals' language behavior reflect the norms of circumstances as understood by them, but that language behavior itself can usually function creatively to define or redefine the nature of the situation for the participants engaged.
>
> "Second, *attention is drawn to the fact that language behavior is likely to be dependent upon how speakers cognitively represent their social and psychological characteristics and subjectively define the situation in terms of its norms and their goals as is any objective classification of that situation imposed from without (e.g. by investigators)*". In this sense, cognitive representations are considered to be very important mediators between social context and language.
>
> (Gardner, 1985)

The notion that psychological adjustment and mental health should be perceived by the magnitude of the incongruity between the "ideal self" and the "actual self" was mentioned by Carl Rogers (1951, 1959, & 1961). The contribution of this concept is that it is the subjective ideal end-state and its congruity and incongruity with the real or actual self really matters (Babad, 2009).

John Dewey (1916) asserts that in order to give opportunities to students to expand and optimize their capacity for growth, they need to live in a democratic society. He mentions that mass education can occur only in societies where there is mutuality and where there is a chance to alter the social habits of institutions on a massive scale with great interest.

According to Gardner (1985), language learning should be culturally and socially bound. Gardner (2001) introduced three major factors which were related to social psychology to explain motivation: integrativeness, attitudes toward the learning situation and motivation. "Integrativeness represents a socially relevant, yet was opposed to an educationally relevant construct" (Gardner, 2005, p. 8). Therefore, "It is a positive disposition toward the L2 group and desire to interact with and even become similar to valued members of that community." (Dörnyei,

1994, p. 78). It is very important since it is related to the L2 learners' future pragmatic fluency and proficiency. Thus Dörnyei (1994) added three related components to the integrative motivation subsystem that include (1) interest in foreign languages, culture and people; (2) desire to expand one's view and avoid provincialism; and (3) desire to experience new stimuli and challenges. Therefore, integrativeness demonstrates a person's interest in learning the L2 in order to be much closer to the target language community. Integrative motivation orientation includes interpersonal (affective) temperament towards the target language group; hence, the language learner is interested to interact with and even become similar to the target language community in order to be a valued member of that community (Dörnyei, 2003).

This process constitutes a positive attitude towards the target language community. Therefore, the attitudes towards the learning situation entail attitudes directly associated with the learning process to describe simply how much the language learners enjoy the teachers and the materials. Motivation is the third factor that demonstrates the driving force in the system. This factor consists of three elements to describe its function in the process. First, motivation depicts how much energy a learner expends to learn the language. It means that students need to put forth consistent effort to learn the material. The second element demonstrates how much a learner states the desire to be successful and attempts to achieve the final goals. The last element is how much a learner will enjoy the task of language learning. So, in the Gardner socio-psychological system, Integrativeness and Attitudes towards the Learning Situation play a significant role in support of Motivation, so Motivation is considered the key element to support a learner's crucial behaviors to learn the target language.

Research on language learning motivation based on the social psychological emphasis was initiated in Canada. Gardner and Lambert's (1959) research was in fact the first study to depict the significance of social psychology of language learning as well as one of the first pioneering studies to use methodology in order to research motivation. This research engendered the field of language learning from the social psychological perspective and concentrated on attitudes towards the learning situation and motivation. According to Dörnyei (2001a), a key principal of the Canadian social psychological approach was the attitudes associated with the target community which maintain a great impact on language learning. The Asian learner of English is deeply influenced by the social attitudes towards the language. Since in most Asian countries, using English proficiently is taken to be a sign of inclusiveness in the global community, most learners are highly motivated. Motivation supports the Social-Education Model in a primary role.

According to this model, motivation is the key concept in order to inspire a person to learn a target language. It is linked with the attitudes towards integrativeness and the learning situation. This particular model concentrates on language learner roles of various types while learning a target language. It brings together the individual's effort, favorable and positive attitudes towards learning a target language and desire to achieve language skills and goals. The Attitude/Motivation Test Battery (AMTB) (Gardner, 1985) usually measured these kinds of variables. The AMTB is considered as a multi-component motivation test which includes 11 subcategories that could be grouped into 5 categories. First, Integrativeness, which involved integrative orientation, interest in foreign languages and attitudes towards French Canadians. The second category was Attitudes towards the Learning Situation, such as the Evaluation of French course and Evaluation of French Teacher. The third category was Motivation, which included Motivational Intensity, Attitudes towards learning French and Desire to learn French. The fourth category was Instrumental Orientation. Fifth, was Language Anxiety. It has been used in many databased researches of L2 motivation (Dörnyei, 2001b). Nevertheless, L2 motivation research apparently is going through a new and remarkable restructuring through the advent of a totally new theoretical framework – namely, the "L2 motivational system" proposed by Dörnyei (2006, 2009). L2 motivational system has three major dimensions, which include the ideal L2 self, the ought-to L2 self and the L2 learning experience:

- *The ideal L2 self:* Dörnyei (2005) asserts that the ideal L2 self is "the L2-specific aspect of one's ideal self" (p. 106). It demonstrates an ideal image of an L2 user, which bilinguals yearn to be in their future. As maintained by Ryan (2009) and Taguchi, Magid, and Papi (2009), the ideal L2 self as one of the main dimensions of L2 motivational system considerably correlates with integrativeness.
- *The ought-to L2 self:* as Dörnyei (2005) demonstrates, this less internalized facet of L2 self in fact describes the characteristics and attributes that individuals think they ought to possess on account of recognized and perceived responsibilities, requirements and obligations. Csizer and Kormos (2009), in their study in Hungary, revealed that there is a relationship between parental encouragements and the ought-to L2.
- *The L2 learning experience*: considers the attitudes of students towards learning an L2 and can be influenced by context-specific motivational factors associated with the immediate learning conditions, practical knowledge and experience. According to Csizer and Kormos (2009), the L2 learning experience, as one of the dimensions of the L2 motivational self-system, demonstrated the strongest effect on motivated and encouraged behavior.

Therefore, learning an L2 is mediated by a variety of cognitive representations analytically beyond the particular conceptual briefs involving other language-related procedures. In addition, Gardner demonstrates that not only is acquisition dependent on and influenced by individuals' social psychological structure but also social psychology makeup is moulded in part by the language fluency and proficiency attained by them.

Another important factor in the investigation of the social psychology of language learning is attitude. Attitudes have been, and actually remain, the central concern of a significant amount of research throughout the social sciences. Specifically, attitudes have been a key informative and explanatory variable in the field of social psychology. Research on attitudes has been conducted by social psychologists since 1920. Attitude has been defined from different perspectives according to various theories, which has led to semantic disagreement on the term.

Bohner and Wanke (2002, p. 5) define attitude as "a summary evaluation of an object or thought". According to this definition, an attitude is considered a "hypothetical construct", which means it cannot directly be inferred from observable responses (Eagly & Chaiken, 1993, p. 2). A specific problem with the definition of attitude is that it may overlap with some other concepts in social psychology such as "opinion", "value", "belief", "habit", "trait", "motive" and "ideology". However, Shaw and Wright (1967), state that it is in fact possible to differentiate between attitude and other related terms. Schwartz (2007, pp. 170–171), demonstrates that as compared to attitudes, values are more abstract because they transcend particular actions and situations. For example, the value of "freedom" may involve a number of attitudes towards public smoking, censorship and political correctness (Perloff, 2003, p. 44).

There are a few other terms which can be distinguished from attitudes in the field of social psychology. Bohner and Wanke (2002, p. 13) think that *habits* are considered fundamentally behavioral routines, while attitudes essentially can be determinants of behavior. Ajzen (1988, p. 7) distinguishes attitudes from *personality traits*, mentioning that, though both terms refer to a latent construct, attitude responses are considered to be evaluative, while traits are tendencies to behave in a particular way and do not concentrate on any specific external target. Garrett et al (2003, p. 11) state that ideology refers to "a naturalistic set of assumptions and values connected with a specific social or cultural group", while attitude is a central term in the field of social psychology and is less important in that of sociology where ideology is significant, central and crucial.

Sociological and psychological approach

Since the present research study incorporates a socio-psychological orientation, the two related approaches can be examined and discussed. They include the sociological and psychological approach.

Sociological approach

Language and society are inseparable. Hence the notion of language is regarded to be an index of social class and also as a symbol of family, status, home, country, ethnicity, etc. This means that acquiring a language involves acquiring the cultural and social norms of the language. In the situation of second/foreign language learning, learners need to adjust or adapt to the cultural and social norms of the target language. So teachers of languages should keep in mind that teaching a language as a second/foreign language to the students requires alignment into the life patterns, social and cultural norms of the members of the targeted speech community. For instance, a study of the Indian classroom proved that learners who were not motivated enough towards learning English earlier became strongly motivated when the liberalization of the Indian economy in the 1990s led to widespread use of the language in everyday professional contexts (Gupta, 2006, p. 102)

In his Social-Education model, Gardner (1985) introduced a number of factors that take into account the function of social factors throughout L2 acquisition. This particular model places four aspects of L2 learning within a mutual relationship, which includes individual learner differences (associated with the motivation and aptitude), the social and cultural milieu (which establishes beliefs about language and culture), the context (formal/informal) and, finally, learning outcomes (linguistic/non-linguistic). Within this specific model, motivation is thought to consist of three elements that include effort, desire and affect.

Effort, as its name suggests, refers to the time that individuals spend studying a language. Desire demonstrates how much the individual wants to become proficient and fluent in the language and affect indicates the individual's emotional reactions regarding language study. As mentioned before, there is a direct relationship between the attitudes of learners and their motivation towards learning an L2. Beginning with attitudes (motivation will be discussed in the next section – i.e. in Psychological approach), attitude is defined as a set of reference points to a set of values and beliefs that individuals hold and retain regarding the community of the target language – for instance, whether they are considered honest, dishonest, interesting or boring, etc. – and as well about their own culture and community.

In line with Wenden (1991), attitudes consist of three components: cognitive, affective and behavioural. A cognitive component comprises beliefs, values, ideas or opinions towards the object of the attitude. The affective component identifies the feelings, the impression and the emotions that an individual has about an object, "likes" or "dislikes", "with" or "against". Finally, the behavioural one which refers to an individual's consistent actions or regularly followed activities or behavioural motives and intentions towards the object. Attitudes can also functionally be crucial because they can contribute to the organization of knowledge and the guidance and avoidance strategies (Perloff, 2003, p. 74). Attitudes, thus, can carry out the knowledge function since they permit and enable individuals to enforce order on the world, make it more predictable and believe that individuals function efficiently and properly (Erwin, 2001, p. 11).

Language and social facets are integral and essential parts developing together in the language acquisition process and the learner simultaneously develops internal inducements that help acquiring first language (L1). These inducements are generally observed via an individual's cognitive, behavioural and affective processes. Nevertheless, in L2 learning, it is the external inducements that often are the reasons for the low proficiency of L2 learners.

Besides the aforementioned types of attitude, Gardner and Lambert (1972) have also introduced a number of different types of attitude that they regard as relevant to L2 learning. Stern (1983, pp. 376–377) classifies these types of attitude into three categories:

1   Attitudes towards the members of the target language community
2   Attitudes towards the learning of the language concerned
3   Attitudes towards languages and language learning in general, viewpoint

Considering these types of attitude, therefore, the more ethnocentric an L2 learner is, the less achievement or linguistic attainment can be achieved in learning the target language and the less ethnocentric the learners are the more linguistic achievement they attain. A

Psychological approach

Motivation as a cornerstone component of the psychological approach to language learning plays a substantial role in the acquisition of an L2. A highly motivated language learner attains desirable achievement in learning the target language. Gardner (1988), for example, thinks that "motivated learners are more active in the learning process". Harter (1981) points out that "motivated students consider themselves to be more competent and skilled learners". According to Cook (2001), "highly motivated individuals can perceive pragmatic functions of language". Therefore, to sum up, motivation is a fundamental and essential factor in L2 learning. It is one of the key elements that determines and fosters the achievement of L2 learning. The more the learner is motivated and encouraged, the more s/he can develop her/his language skills. Motivation is an essential factor for the success of second/foreign language learning. Motivation plays an indispensable role in the learning process. From a psychological point of view, motivation can be defined as a force or push within the learner characterized by a highly effective stimulation and arousal which drives the learner towards the expected objective, such as the objectives of second/foreign language program (McDonald, 1965). According to Crookes and Schmidt (1991), motivation is the learners' orientation with regard to the objective of learning an L2.

Motivation and attitudes to L2 learning are essential and crucial integral components in the process of language learning. Lack of motivation and sufficient enthusiasm of students may result in a situation where individuals do not demonstrate interest and desire for learning the target language. This kind of circumstance will probably influence the learner's success and achievement in language learning. Motivation is a key and significant factor that affects the success and rate of second/foreign language learning.

Similarly, the learners' attitudes towards the target language or towards the native speakers of the target language as an important social psychological factor of language learning may be positive or negative, and this can also influence the learners' motivation in language learning. Verspoor (2005, p. 72) points out that learners, teachers and researchers will all agree that a positive attitude towards an L2 and its speakers and a high motivation affect and help second language learning. These two factors, thus, are very important in the process of language learning.

The relationship between motivation and attitudes has been regarded as the primary concern in language learning research; there is a direct relationship between learners' attitudes and their motivations towards learning an L2. The motivation to learn a second/foreign language is dependent on the attitudes towards the other group or community, as well as the orientation towards the learning activity itself. Attitudes are very essential for learning language yet they provide inadequate indirect conditions for linguistic achievement; only if combined with motivation can suitable attitudinal tendencies related to the actual levels of the individual engagement in language learning provide appropriate conditions for linguistic attainment. To put it briefly, a better understanding of students' attitudes and motivation may well assist English as a Foreign Language (EFL)/ English as a Second Language (ESL) curriculum designers to create and develop language teaching programs that produce the motivation and attitudes most favourable to the creation of more successful language learners. Furthermore, it can assist material writers as well as teachers to choose activities or tasks that enhance and inspire learners' motivation and attitudes.

Self-efficacy, motivation, effort and literacy learning strategies

Some particular learner variables such as motivation, self-efficacy and effort can play a significant role in L2 learning. Bandura (1997) defines self-efficacy as the learner's perceived capabilities for learning or performing actions at designated levels. So as Schunk and Zimmerman (2007) also hold, the learners' level of self-efficacy can affect their choice of activities, persistence, effort and achievement. Individuals with positive self-efficacy have a strong sense of control over their learning and feel that they have the power and the capability to succeed, while learners with less self-efficacy feel just the opposite. Hence it is very important for language teachers to evaluate learners' self-efficacy and provide meaningful, systematic and motivational activities that will help the students to improve and enhance confidence in their ability. Therefore, self-efficacy, motivation and effort investment are variables that can make the teaching-learning environment much more fruitful and can be very effective and helpful for efficient learning.

Apart from self-efficacy, motivation and effort investment are also variables that should not be neglected. Learners need to trigger and perform activities that establish a particular arena or scene for learning, designating values towards learning activities, motivating and encouraging themselves and persevere. Teachers can certainly teach students writing or reading strategies; however, students may never ever achieve their total potential if they do not have the intrinsic motivation to read and write and do not invest adequate effort in learning the skills. Reading and writing are two basic skills of literacy which are very important to individuals' survival in this modern society. Reading, apparently an effortless, automatic, simple and easy activity in real-life situation is in fact a process that involves lots of strategic behavior on the reader's part. Since usually the main objective of authentic reading is for comprehension, it is therefore referred to as reading comprehension. Block and Duffy (2008, p. 21) depict that "comprehension is a strategic process" – i.e. good readers actively seek out the meaning of unknown words by using their background knowledge and text clues to create predictions, to keep track of those predictions, to re-predict whenever required and, usually, to create representations of the author's meaning. Afflerbach, Pearson and Paris (2008, p. 368) assert that reading strategies are "deliberate, goal-directed attempts to control and modify the reader's efforts to decode text, understand words, and construct meanings of text".

Writing also is a process that involves different strategic activities. Writing, as a productive skill, involves more deliberate control and objective-directedness, since, as Harris, Graham, Brindle and Sandmel (2009, p. 132) mention, the writer should consider the rules and grammatical frame of writing while preserving a focus on factors including purposes and objectives of the writing, organization, features and form, audience needs and considerations, efficacy and evaluation of communicative intent.

To enhance learners' literacy improvement, it is essential and significant to boost their awareness regarding the strategic nature and dynamic of the reading and writing process and make them familiar and conversant with the efficient strategies that good readers and writers usually use. Furthermore, we should also consider the learners' variables such as gender, motivation, self-efficacy, effort and contextual facets such as home language and culture. These types of factors are also identified to be closely associated with the literacy learning and strategy use. Learners' involvement and exuberance in literacy learning, self-rated writing and reading capabilities and effort in literacy learning are directly related to their strategy use.

Therefore, language teachers need to strengthen and reinforce the mutual ties between motivation, self-efficacy and effort and as well the frequent use of the effective learning strategies. By escalating the L2 learners' intrinsic interest in reading and writing activities, encouraging them to develop and enhance their self-efficacy and effort, language educators can make learners much more productive and active in performing strategic behavior in their literacy learning.

Self-awareness

Self-awareness in language learning is another crucial component of the sociopsychological aspect of language learning/teaching that has received a significant amount of research in recent years. Ways of improving students' self-awareness and its influence on language learning should be regarded as a significant phenomenon in the language learning and teaching process that can augment motivation and successful learning.

The last decade has demonstrated significant changes in language learning environments. The main objective of the latest strategies for language learning and teaching is to augment and boost learners' control over the learning process. These teaching/learning strategies concentrate on the importance of learning to learn. Therefore, it is essential to teach students the strategies that help them handle new technology as well as changed learning environment.

It is important for teachers to make students aware of the particular procedures involved in language learning and also to assist them to discover learning environments that suit their socio-psychological and linguistic requirements best. Language learners should be helped to engage exuberantly in the principles of autonomy in a gradual progressive way, but there should be a reasonable balance between providing chances for the students to take control over their learning environments and supporting those students who are not yet prepared to accept this responsibility for themselves.

The importance of students' self-directiveness and autonomy has been emphasized by many researchers. The improvement of student autonomy and self-directiveness at least to some extent seems to be almost universally considered as a significant and general goal of education.

The most commonly accepted definition of autonomy was introduced by Holec (1981). He defines autonomy as the capability to take responsibility of one's own directed learning. The students, therefore, need to improve specific skills for identifying and figuring out their own objectives, needs, methods of learning and evaluation. This is not simply something intrinsic that individuals are born with; the students need to be taught ways to help themselves and manage and control their own learning.

Boosting the awareness of one's own learning and attaining the perception of the procedures involved is a central and essential key for the improvement of autonomous learning. Developing the students' self-directiveness and self-awareness in L2 learning is very important, because without an explicit awareness about the procedures involved in L2 learning, language learners will not be in the appropriate state to make conscious decisions about their own learning. Therefore, language teachers should help students develop their understanding of the learning process so that they can acquire the linguistic skills consciously and consequently, they will be able to take control of their learning process.

Second/foreign language teachers should choose proper approaches for enhancing learners' awareness. They should take into account that learning a second/foreign language is a process of learners' progress in three interrelated areas – viz,

- personal awareness: self-direction, self-esteem and self-concept
- task-awareness: knowledge and understanding of language and communication
- awareness of the language learning process: process management and control

As a result, effective improvement in the learners' linguistic competence demands systematic and organized advancement of all three factors and the learners should acquire both cognitive and metacognitive strategies.

As mentioned, the role of language teachers in developing learners' self-awareness is crucial. They can help students discover, determine and make use of their own individual learning process and thus increase self-awareness. The enhancement of self-awareness and self-directed L2 learning should be an integral part of the language learning/teaching paradigm. Teachers should increase learners' awareness of their responsibilities and capacities; they should encourage students' self-study and take into consideration the students' interest and requirements that lead to an enhancement of their motivation in L2 learning.

Differentiated instruction: teachers' roles

The classroom is a stage for constant and ongoing role conflict between teachers and learners. Teachers have a clear image of the methods they would like to apply in their own roles and possess a clear perception of how they expect the learners play their roles. But the learners have their own image, expectation and perception that sometimes are in conflict with those of teachers. Some learners may have problems with learning and struggle with it, some may succeed beyond the expected level and still some others may be in between. Within each of these groups of learners, individuals furthermore learn language in a variety of different ways and have various interests. To fulfil the needs of a diverse learner population, many teachers differentiate instruction.

Differentiation involves the attempts of teachers to interact with and respond to variance among students in their classroom. When a teacher encounters a student or a group of students and decides to vary and alter his/her teaching method in order to create the most effective learning experience feasible, that teacher is in fact differentiating instruction. Based on the learner's interest, learning profile and readiness, teachers can differentiate among the four components of the classroom: one, content; two, process; three, products; and four, learning.

Content can be defined as what learners need to learn and how they will get access to the needed information – for instance, (a) using reading materials and resources at different legibility levels, putting text resources on visual tapes; (b) making use of spelling and vocabulary lists at readiness levels of learners; (c) delivering ideas and concepts via both auditory and visual means; and (d) meeting with a small group of students struggling with learning in order to re-teach an idea or concept, as well as organize meetings with the advanced learners to extend their thinking and skills.

Process includes differentiating activities or process such as (a) employing activities by which all students use the similar significant perceptions and skills; however, they carry on together with various amount of support, challenge and intricacy; (b) fluctuate the length of time a learner may need to complete an activity to give additional support for a struggling student or to motivate an advanced student to continue a topic in greater depth; and (c) developing personal agenda containing activity lists written by the teacher and consisting of both in-common tasks for the whole class and tasks that addresses personal and individual needs of students.

Products that implement differentiation include (a) providing learners options of how to express and convey expected learning, (b) employing rubrics which match and expand learners' various skills degrees, (c) letting learners to work individually or in small groups on their own products and (d) motivating learners to produce their own product assignments.

The learning environment can ensure differentiating by (a) ensuring that there are sufficient places in the room to work silently and without disturbance as well as places for collaborative working, (b) providing learning materials which can reflect a number of various culture settings of the target language and as well as native culture and (c) providing clear and unambiguous guidelines for working independently that matches individual demands.

If teachers want to increase their learners' individual potential, they need to consider the differences. There is a plethora of research evidence that learners are more successful and productive if they are taught in a manner which is more responsive to their interest, readiness level and learning profile. If teachers want to be more professional, competent and creative, they should work at differentiating instruction.

Differentiation helps learners to be more motivated to achieve and feel more engaged in the learning process and classroom activities. It will encourage students to engage in the tasks and thus learn more effectively. Therefore, it is of great help if teachers balance their own needs with those of learners if they want to become more effective and productive at differentiation. Living in a world that shrinks every day, dexterity in differentiation is definitely an asset for any teacher of language.

Conclusion

On taking an overview of the models available in this field to date, it is clear that each model is more complex than its predecessor and takes more variables into its field. While this means greater accuracy, it also implies that the realities of social psychology in the language learning paradigm are more complex than researchers recognize. This gives research a more fertile and busy field to work with. In order to be more effective as pedagogy, social psychological studies of language learning will need to have a greater empirical base. Just as the native-user construct has been re-modelled, once empirical data is firmly established, the next stage would be the testing of the hypotheses formed by the researchers on the basis of that data. Once a clear proposal emerges, then it would be possible to link research and pedagogy, leading to positive synergy in the field.

However, with respect to the Asian English language (EL) classroom, it should be understood that besides considering the socio-psychological aspects of language learning, it is essential to pay much more than usual attention to their social norms which are a set of fixed and standard rules that usually control the social behavior of the group members in a specific social context. Social norms are the particular reflections of a people's belief, values, culture and goals. Norms are usually shaped and preserved through the group, but they control and moderate the individual's behavior. Therefore, considering the fact that social norms of Asian students can sometimes significantly vary from Western social norms and hold the power to affect learning outcomes, it is essential that language teachers be aware of even those social norms that usually are hidden and implicit in Asian students. Language and society are interdependent, and it is extremely difficult to separate language and social process as the individuals' linguistic behaviors reflect significant social norms. Therefore, in addition to the discussed socio-psychological facets of language acquisition, in the Asian EL classroom, it is very important to consider the linguistic, social and ethnic diversification of Asian language learners.

As Moradi (2014) writes, "language and culture on the surface may appear to be two different and distinct fields, but it is obvious that they have an intertwined relationship and affect each other mutually". Learning a second/foreign language is different from other curriculum subjects, since it in fact requires language learners to incorporate and integrate elements and factors from another society and culture; as a result, reaction towards another culture and its social norms is of significant consideration. Such types of considerations shed light on the importance and complexity of motivation and attitude or the socio-psychological aspects of language learning especially when it comes to the EFL/ESL EL classroom.

References

Afflerbach, P., Pearson, P. D., & Paris, S. G. (2008). Clarifying differences between reading skills and reading strategies. *The Reading Teacher*, *61*(5), 364–373.

Ajzen, I. (1988). *Attitudes, personality and behaviour*. Milton Keynes: Open University Press.

Babad, E. (2009). *The social psychology of the classroom*. New York: Routledge.

Bandura, A. (1997). *Self-efficacy: The exercise of control*. New York: Longman.

Block, C. C., & Duffy, G. G. (2008). Research on teaching comprehension: Where we've been and where we're going. In C. C. Block & S. R. Parris (Eds.), *Comprehension instruction: Research-based best practices* (2nd ed., pp. 19–37). New York: The Guilford Press.

Boekaerts, M., & Cascallar, E. (2006). How far have we moved toward the integration of theory and practice in self-regulation? *Educational Psychology Review*, *18*(3), 199–210.

Bohner, G., & M. Wanke. (2002). *Attitudes and attitude change*. Hove: Psychology Press.

Cook, V. (2001). *Second language learning and second language acquisition: A research paradigm. language teaching*. London: Edward Arnold.

Crookes, G., & Schmidt, R. W. (1991). Motivation: Reopening the research agenda. *Language Learning*, *41*(4), 469–512.

Crystal, D. (2003). *English as a global language*. Cambridge: Cambridge University Press.

Csizer, K., & Kormos, J. (2009). Learning experiences, selves and motivated learning behaviour: A comparative analysis of structural models for Hungarian secondary and university learners of English. In Z. Dörnyei & E. Ushioda (Eds.), *Motivation, language identity and the L2 self: Multilingual matters* (pp. 98–119). Clevedon: Multilingual Matters.

Dewey, J. (1916). *Democracy and education.* New York: Palgrave Macmillan.

Dörnyei, Z. (1994). Motivation and motivating in the foreign language classroom. *The Modern Language Journal, 78*(3), 273–284.

Dörnyei, Z. (2001a). *Motivational strategies in the language classroom.* Cambridge: Cambridge University Press.

Dörnyei, Z. (2001b). *Teaching and researching motivation.* Harlow: Pearson Education Limited.

Dörnyei, Z. (2003). Attitudes, orientations, and motivations in language learning: Advanced in theory, research, and applications. *Language Learning, 53*(1), 3–32.

Dörnyei, Z. (2005). *The psychology of the language learner: Individual differences in second language acquisition.* Mahwah, NJ: Lawrence Erlbaum Associates.

Dörnyei, Z. (2006). Individual differences in second language acquisition. *AILA review, 19*(1), 42–68.

Dörnyei, Z. (2009). The L2 motivational self system. In Z. Dörnyei & E. Ushioda (Eds.), *Motivation, Language Identity and the L2 Self* (pp. 9–42). Clevedon: Multilingual Matters.

Dörnyei, Z., Csizer, K., Ne´meth, N. (2006). *Motivation, language attitudes and globalisation: A Hungarian perspective.* Clevedon: Multilingual Matters.

Dweck, C. S. (1986). Motivational processes affecting learning. *American psychologist, 41*(10), 1040.

Eagly, A., & Chaiken, S. (1993). *The psychology of attitudes.* Orlando: Harcout Bruce.

Erwin, P. (2001). *Attitudes and persuasion.* Hove: Psychology Press.

Gardner, R. C. (1985). *Social psychology and second language learning: The role of attitudes and motivation.* London: Edward Arnold.

Gardner, R. C. (1988). The socio-educational model of second language: Assumptions, findings, and issues. *Language Learning, 38*(1), 101–126.

Gardner, R. C. (2001, February 17, 2001, February 24). *Integrative Motivation: Past, present, and future.* Tokyo: Temple University Japan, Distinguished Lecturer Series. Retrieved from http://publish.uwo.ca/~gardner/docs/GardnerPublicLecture1.pdf

Gardner, R. C. (2005, May 30). *Integrative Motivation and second language acquisition.* Ontario: Canadian Association of Applied Linguistics/Canadian Linguistics Association Joint Plenary Talk.

Gardner, R. C., & Lambert, W. E. (1959). Motivational variables in second language acquisition. *Canadian Journal of Psychology, 13*, 266–272.

Gardner, R. C., & Lambert, W. E. (1972). *Attitudes and motivation in second language learning.* Rowley, MA: Newbury House.

Garrett, P., Coupland, N., & Williams, A. (2003). *Investigating language attitudes.* Cardiff: University of Wales Press.

Gupta, D. (2006). *Communicative language teaching then and now* (p. 102). New Delhi: Books Plus.

Harris, K. R., Graham, S., Brindle, M., & Sandmel, K. (2009). Metacognition and children's writing. In D. J. Hacker, J. Dunlosky, & A. C. Graesser (Eds.), *Handbook of metacognition in education* (pp. 131–153). New York, London: Routledge.

Harter, S. (1981). A new self-report scale of intrinsic versus extrinsic orientation in the classroom: Motivational and informational components. *Developmental Psychology, 17*, 300–312.

Holec, H. (1981). *Autonomy and foreign language learning*. Oxford: Pergamon.
Kirkpatrick, A. (2007). *World Englishes*. Cambridge: Cambridge University Press.
Marinak, B. A., & Gambrell, L. B. (2010). Reading motivation: Exploring the elementary gender gap. *Literacy Research & Instruction, 49*(2), 129–141.
Mesthrie, R., & Bhatt, R. M. (2008). *World Englishes*. Cambridge: Cambridge University Press.
McDonald, F. J. (1965). *Educational psychology*. Belmont, CA: Wardsworth Co.
Moradi, H. (2014). A sociolinguistic study of the importance of culture in language learning and teaching. *Asian Journal of Research in Social Sciences and Humanities, 4*(1), 190–204.
Perloff, R. (2003). *The dynamics of persuasion*. London: Lawrence Erlbaum.
Perry, R. (1991). Perceived control in college students: Implications for instruction in higher education. In J. Smart (Ed.), *Higher education: Handbook of theory and research* (Vol. 7, pp. 1–56). New York: Agathon Press.
Perry, R. (2003). Perceived academic control and causal thinking in achievement settings. *Canadian Psychologist, 44*, 312–331.
Perry, R., Hall, N., & Ruthig, J. (2007). Perceived (academic) control and scholastic attainment in higher education. In R. Perry & J. Smart (Eds.), *The scholarship of teaching and learning in higher education: An evidence-based perspective* (pp. 477–551). Dordrecht, The Netherlands: Springer Publications.
Rogers, C. (1951). *Client-centered therapy: Its current practice, implications and theory*. London: Constable.
Rogers, C. (1959). A theory of therapy, personality and interpersonal relationships as developed in the client-centered framework. In S. Koch (Ed.), *Psychology: A study of science. Vol. 3: Formulations of the person and the social context*. New York: McGraw-Hill.
Rogers, C. (1961). *On becoming a person: A therapist's view of psychotherapy*. London: Constable.
Ryan, S. (2009). Self and identity in L2 motivation in Japan: The ideal L2 self and Japanese learners of English. In Z. Dörnyei & E. Ushioda (Eds.), *Motivation, language identity and the L2 self multilingual matters* (pp. 120–143). Clevedon: Multilingual Matters.
Schmuck, R. (1978). Helping teachers improve classroom group processes. *Journal of Applied Behavioral Science, 4*, 401–435.
Schunk, D. H., & Zimmerman, B. J. (2007). Influencing children's self-efficacy and self-regulation of reading and writing through modeling. *Reading & Writing Quarterly, 23*(1), 7–25.
Schutz, W. (1958). *FIRO: A three-dimensional theory of interpersonal behavior*. New York: Rinehart.
Schwartz, S. H. (2007). Value orientations: Measurement, antecedents and consequences across nations. In R. Jowell, C. Roberts, R. Fitzgerald, & G. Eva (Eds.), *Measuring attitudes cross-nationally* (pp. 169–204). London: Sage.
Seidlhofer, B. (2004). Research perspectives on teaching English as a lingua franca. *Annual Review of Applied Linguistics, 24*, 209–239.
Seidlhofer, B. (2008). Language variation and change: The case of English as a lingua franca core. In K. Dziubalska-Kolaczyk & J. Przedlacka (Eds.), *English pronunciation models: A changing scene* (2nd ed, pp. 59–76). Frankfurt: Peter Lang.

Sharifian, F. (2009). English as an international language: An overview. In F. Sharifian (Ed.), *English as an international language* (pp. 1–20). Bristol: Multilingual Matters.

Shaw, M. E., & Wright, J. M. (1967). *Scales for the measurement of attitudes.* New York: McGraw-Hill.

Stern, H. H. (1983). *Fundamental Concepts of Language Teaching.* Oxford: Oxford University Press.

Taguchi, T., Magid, M., & Papi, M. (2009). The L2 motivational self system amongst Chinese, Japanese, and Iranian learners of English: A comparative study. In Z. Dörnyei & E. Ushioda (Eds.), *Motivation, language identity and the L2 self* (pp. 66–97). Clevedon: Multilingual Matters.

Verspoor, M. & et al. (2005). *Second language acquisition: An advanced resource book.* London: Routledge.

Wenden, A. (1991). *Learner strategies for learner autonomy: Planning and implementing learner training for language learners.* New York: Prentice Hall.

Wentzel, K. R. (1999). Social-motivational processes and interpersonal relationships: Implications for understanding motivation at school. *Journal of Educational Psychology, 91*(1), 76.

Wentzel, K. R. (2006). A social motivation perspective for classroom management. In C. Everston & C. Weinstein (Eds.), *Handbook of classroom management: Research, practice and contemporary issues* (pp. 619–643). Mahwah, NJ: Lawrence Erlbaum Associates.

16 The role of pragmatics in teaching English as an additional language

Andrew D. Cohen

For many learners of English as a Foreign Language (EFL) in Asia, the pragmatics of the language poses a major challenge. The concern is with meaning as communicated by speakers (or writers) and interpreted by listeners (or readers), with a focus on intended meanings, assumptions, and actions performed when speaking (e.g., *making a request*) (based on Yule, 1996, pp. 3–4). I personally have studied 12 languages beyond my native English over the course of my lifetime, and this has included two Asian languages, Japanese, and Mandarin.[1] While I have achieved relative pragmatic control in, say, four of these languages (Hebrew and three Romance languages), I have the sense that even with these languages I am capable of pragmatic failure (see Cohen, 1997, 2001). In fact, it is more my pragmatic failures than my pragmatic successes that have made me acutely aware that pragmatic performance benefits from explicit instruction – that learners do not just acquire pragmatic niceties through osmosis.

My concern in this chapter is to shift continually from theory to practice in providing insights for Asian learners of English as to how to be pragmatically appropriate in a host of language performance situations, whether in their perception and production of speech acts or in other areas. *Speech acts* are often, but not always, the patterned, routinized language that natives and pragmatically competent nonnative speakers and writers in a given speech community (with its dialect variations) use to perform functions such as *thanking, complimenting, requesting, refusing, apologizing,* and *complaining* (see Olshtain & Cohen, 1983, pp. 19–21; Cohen, 1996, pp. 384–385). Speech acts are a challenging area of pragmatic behavior because of the possible misfit between what one does or does not say or write in a language in the given speech act and what is meant by it. Speech act theory, in fact, provides a reliable and valid basis for examining pragmatic patterns that are primarily focused on selected utterances from the discourse (Mey, 1993). Beyond speech acts, there are numerous other areas of pragmatic focus. Thus this coverage of second language (L2)[2] pragmatics issues for Asian learners will start by looking first at the notion of research altogether, then at politeness, and then at speech acts, the favorite focus of pragmatics research. In addition, I will look at other areas of pragmatics: conversational overlap, back channeling, phatic communication, humor, sarcasm, and the pragmatic function of discourse markers. I will end by considering the teaching of L2 pragmatics, and the learning and performing of pragmatics. The main purpose of this effort is to identify areas of research on pragmatics, which can help to inform Asian learners of English as to how to be more pragmatically appropriate in their own uses of the language.

Themes in the research literature

Study abroad

Study abroad is a popular context these days for conducting L2 pragmatics research. One of the more creative studies was that conducted to describe pragmatic development of students while in study abroad, focusing on service encounters recorded in situ between L2 learners of Spanish and local Spanish service providers in Toledo, Spain (Shively, 2011). The participants in the study were seven US students who studied abroad for one semester. What made the research design innovative was that the data consisted of naturalistic audio recordings that participants made of themselves while visiting local shops, banks, and other establishments. The study was longitudinal with recordings made at the beginning, middle, and end of the semester by each student, for a total of 113 recordings. Additional data included students' weekly journals and interviews with participants. The analysis focused on openings and requests, and examined the ways in which students' pragmatic choices shifted over time, considering the role of language socialization and explicit instruction in pragmatics in that development. Overall, the changes in openings and requests suggested that the students learned and adopted some of the pragmatic norms of service encounters in the Toledo speech community.

Describing variation in intercultural pragmatics

Whereas in the Toledo study the innovation was in the way the data were collected, another line of research still in need of actualization would be to get at true variation in intercultural pragmatics. While *cross-cultural pragmatics* compares the pragmatics of one culture or subculture with that of another, *intercultural pragmatics* (at least as I define it) looks at cultures in contact and the hybrid forms of pragmatics that result from this interaction. So if we were to conduct genuinely intercultural pragmatics research, it would be important to include in the sample subjects who are likely to have elements of hybrid pragmatics in their data.

A hypothetical study was proposed in Cohen (2012a), focusing on doctor-patient interactions in the US Southwest in which intercultural pragmatics would be involved. The paper identified and discussed research design issues, types of data employed, the measures used, and concerns about data analysis. The proposed study was intended to highlight the number of variables that can lead to pragmatic variation in the research outcomes. When doctors use Spanish as a nonnative language, the question is how their pragmatics is perceived by their

Spanish-speaking Mexican immigrant patients and with what impact. The proposed study suggested comparing the pragmatics of this context with that of native Spanish-speaking doctors interacting with these same patients, English-speaking doctors interacting with mainstream patients in English in the US Southwest, and doctors in Mexico interacting with their patients. The purpose is to problematize just what the study of intercultural pragmatics involves when looking at speech communities in flux and taking into account individual variation.

So, for example, when an Asian learner speaks English, whose pragmatics is being used? Is it English with a pragmatics overlay from the first language (L1) language and culture? Even if there is an effort to reflect English language pragmatics, which English-speaking country's pragmatics are being adhered to, and if the speakers do not include any native English speakers, does it really matter if the pragmatics reflect approaches used by native speakers? In other words, in these cases is the issue of pragmatic failure due to violation of native-speaker norms even an issue? More will be said about this topic under the section "Teaching English as a *Lingua Franca*."

Politeness

A pervasive concern addressed in the pragmatics literature is that of politeness. Here let us sample just a few of the recent studies involving politeness – first looking at cross-cultural variation in the perception of impoliteness and at ethnic variation in perceptions of politeness within a country, and then at jocular insults and swearwords.

Cross-cultural variation in the perception of impoliteness

An investigation of cross-cultural variation in the perception of impoliteness was conducted based on 500 impoliteness events reported by students in England, China, Finland, Germany, and Turkey (Culpeper, Marti, Mei, Nevala, & Schauer, 2010). The analytical framework looked at rapport management, covering various types of face as well as sociality rights. An analysis of differences between the geographically separated data sets revealed that the England-based data had a preponderance of impoliteness events in which quality face was violated, whereas the China-based data had a preponderance of instances where equity rights were violated – where group values were prized more highly than individualistic ones.

Politeness and impoliteness in ethnic varieties

Building on earlier research describing pragmatic features of New Zealand (NZ) English, and identifying ways in which politeness was expressed in NZ workplace talk, Holmes, Marra, and Vine (2012) extended the sociopragmatic analysis of New Zealand English (NZE) in several ways. Using the theoretical model that the researchers had developed to analyze workplace interaction, they focused on intercultural interactions between Māori and Pākehā (i.e., Kiwis of European descent), and data from both Māori and Pākehā workplaces to throw light on distinctive features of politeness in NZE workplace discourse. For example, they examined the value of egalitarianism in NZ society, and explored its pervasive influence on the ways in which politeness was interactionally achieved in different NZ communities of practice. They then discussed how this related to the dimension of formality, exemplifying some distinctively NZ ways in which formality and informality were indexed in workplace interaction. The analysis illustrated how these influences were manifest in small talk, humor, meeting protocols, and extension of the distinctive pragmatic particle *eh* to new domains. So the findings from the study suggested how Māori ways of doing things were subtly influencing Pākehā norms and thus contributing to the development of a distinctively NZ set of values and pragmatic norms.

Jocular insults

A research project on leadership discourse and gender in Hong Kong workplaces looked at jocular insults in data from a business meeting in a small factory outlet involving three male and three female staff (Ladegaard, 2012). The two female leaders used jocular insults and other forms of verbal abuse repeatedly in what was interpreted as instrumental rudeness on the part of the two leaders. These discursive strategies were seen as having the purpose of attacking their interlocutors' face and thereby enhancing the leaders' power. The researcher pointed out that whereas jocular insults may not only function as a means by which superiors maintain their position in the workplace but also as a socially acceptable strategy by which subordinates challenge their leaders, in the present context, these strategies were used predominantly by the two leaders. The researcher argued that a careful consideration of the sociopragmatic norms of the micro- and the macro-context may explain why the subordinates would accept these insults.

In this particular case, the power distance and hierarchical relationships would explain why these leaders' demeaning discourses were not directly challenged. The researcher pointed out that normatively masculine and feminine management styles may be culturally specific. Generally, it is considered legitimate for Chinese leaders to adopt a paternalistic autocratic management style, and employees are expected to be deferential and obedient. In a culture that places great emphasis on power distance and filial piety, there is little to protect employees from exploitation. Bearing in mind that this study reported data from just one meeting in one workplace in Hong Kong, the study nonetheless lent support to more recent accounts in sociolinguistics arguing that women are not intrinsically more polite or considerate than men.

Swearwords

Knowing how to perform in a pragmatically appropriate way does not just mean knowing how to be polite. It also means knowing when and how to be impolite, and sometimes knowing how to swear plays an important role. Unfortunately, language teachers are often reluctant to teach learners how to swear, especially when teaching Asian students whose sensibilities may be easily offended by such instruction. In a study in NZ, over 2,000 interactions were collected in English (mostly English as an L1) (Daly, Holmes, Newton, & Stubbe, 2004). An extensive analysis of the corpus showed that among what was necessary for fitting in and becoming an integrated member of the workplace was the ability to curse affectively, especially using the f-word with fellow employees and even with the boss, as a way to fit in and bond. Nonnatives apparently can find themselves ostracized for *not* cursing like the rest. On the comprehension side, the learner may hear these invectives and be put off or even shocked, and certainly not eager to learn when and how to use them

Another study published at the same time investigated the perception of the emotional force of swearwords and taboo words (S-T words) among 1,039 multilinguals (Dewaele, 2004). The study was based on data drawn from a large database collected through a web questionnaire on bilingualism and emotions. As to the findings, *t*-tests revealed that the perceived emotional force of S-T words was highest in the L1 and gradually lower in languages learned subsequently. Self-reported L1 attriters were found to judge S-T words in their L1 to be less powerful than for those who were still dominant in their L1. Participants who learned their language(s) in a naturalistic or partly naturalistic/context gave higher ratings on emotional force of S-T words in that language than instructed language learners.

Cross-cultural speech act research

Research on speech acts often uses the paradigm of comparing L1 performance across languages. As an early researcher in the field of L2 speech acts, it is a pleasure for me to see how robustly this field has developed in the last 40 years – especially with regard to English as a second language (ESL) and EFL studies. Back in the late 1970s, there was little empirical data available on how natives and nonnatives performed pragmatics. Now there is a sizeable quantity of such data. Clearly, native speakers of certain languages have gotten greater focus, such as Spanish, Japanese, Chinese, and Korean speakers of English, but work has also been done in collecting ESL/EFL data from speakers of other languages, such as Persian, Arabic, and German. And every day there are new studies looking at pragmatics in languages other than English.

One area of development is an increase in the study of certain speech acts, with a focus on speech acts that had not been studied at all or only on a limited basis, such as the speech act of giving condolences or that of criticizing someone (i.e., beyond academic or literary criticism, as encouraged by teachers). Another is to look at written speech acts, such as in email messages. The following are two such studies.

Complaints

One study selected complaining as an under-represented speech act in cross-cultural pragmatics. Unlike the well-defined speech acts such as apologizing, requesting, and complimenting, the researchers viewed complaining as comparatively more complex in that it has no pre-determined forms and the interpretations are often negotiable (Chen, Chen, & Chang, 2011). In this study, a total of 20 Americans in the United States and 20 Taiwanese university students were recruited and asked to respond to a discourse completion task (DCT) containing eight complaint-provoking scenarios: the waiter spilling a drink on a patron's new shirt, discontent with the late shift at work, background noise while on the phone, someone cutting in line at a theater, a hole found in a new T-shirt, the tutee not paying attention, the chairperson forgetting an appointment with a member of staff, and a mother opening her child's mail. The DCT was used in the study because it clearly elicited the complaints under study and allowed for cross-cultural comparisons. Six complaint strategies (opting out, interrogation, accusation, request for repair, and threat) were identified and analyzed in terms of their overall and combined use across the eight scenarios. The quantitative results indicated that the American and the Chinese participants shared similar distributions in both overall and combined strategy use across the complaint situations. The qualitative findings, however, showed differences in choice of linguistic forms and expression of semantic content. The study revealed that compared to American complaints, the Chinese complaints seemed to be more sensitive to social power.

Requests

Another speech act study examined 200 email requests written in English by Greek Cypriot university students (non-native speakers (NNS) of English) at a major, English-medium university in Cyprus over a period of several semesters (Economidou-Kogetsidis, 2011). The emails were sent to 11 faculty members, 2 natives of English and 9 nonnatives, but with residence in the United Kingdom or United States for more than 10 years. The study examined forms of address (salutations), the degree of directness employed, and the degree and type of supportive moves and lexical/phrasal modifiers used by students in order to soften or aggravate their e-requests. The faculty members' communication style with their students could be characterized as friendly but formal (e.g., they did not encourage first name use with students and had contact with students only during class and office hours). Two of these faculty members were native speakers of English but had lived in Cyprus for more than 15 years at the time of the study. The rest were of Greek or Greek Cypriot origin, had lived in the United Kingdom or the United States for more than ten years, and had native-like proficiency in English. Twenty-four lecturers from 12 universities in the United Kingdom evaluated 6 archetype responses drawn from the email data. They were all British English native speakers and were teaching various subjects in higher education (other than linguistics).

Findings from the study showed that the NNS students' emails were characterized by significant directness (particularly in relation to requests for information), an absence of lexical/phrasal downgraders, an omission of greetings and closings, and inappropriate or unacceptable forms of address. Consistent with previous email studies, the results revealed that the NNS students resorted largely to direct strategies ("please" + the imperative) rather than more appropriate conventional indirectness, both in the case of requests for action and for information. The researcher argued that such emails could be perceived as impolite and discourteous and therefore capable of causing pragmatic failure. This was primarily due to the fact that such messages appeared to give the faculty no choice as to whether to comply with the request and failed to acknowledge the imposition involved.

Conversational overlap

One area of real concern for Asian speakers of American English beyond speech acts is how to break into an ongoing conversation, especially given the preferred politeness patterns in their native languages and cultures. Typically, the nonnative misjudges which kind of pause means it is OK to break in, since native speakers of different languages may have different attitudes about someone cutting into the conversation during someone else's turn. For example, research comparing conversational strategies in French and Australian English found that French speakers not only tolerate, but indeed expect, a variety of incursions into a current speaker's turn, unlike speakers of Australian English, and that these incursions are generally treated as collaborative strategies (Beal, 2010). Apparently, a conversational overlap in French is considered a feature of involvement and liveliness, lending a sense of joint purpose to verbal exchanges. By contrast, members of Anglo-Saxon speech communities, like English native speakers, regarded it as aggressive and unacceptable (Kerbrat-Orecchioni, 2005).

Against this research backdrop, a study was conducted focusing on overlapping talk as a feature of conversational management in multi-participant talk in advanced L2 French, in relation to L1 French and English (Guillot, 2014). The data collected consisted of multi-participant simulated television discussions on the topic of anti-smoking campaigns. They represented the communicative behavior of two main groups of subjects: advanced learners of French (four groups, two of pre-year-abroad subjects, two of post-year-abroad subjects) and native speakers of French (two groups) (25 subjects in all, four to eight per group). All groups were recorded twice, first in their L2 and then in their L1: The L2 recordings thus encompassed L1 and L2 French, and L1 and L2 English. The findings confirmed the active propensity of French speakers to use overlapping talk as an interactional resource than Australian English speakers. The frequency of use of overlaps in the L2 French post-year-abroad data, closer to L1 French than to L1 English, suggested that the greater interactional and strategic value of this type of overlap in L1 French may have been recognized and built on.

Back channeling

Another area of concern in terms of conversational management is how listeners use back channeling to signal that they are following a conversation. A recent study focused on listenership (consisting of back channel feedback) and its effect on intercultural communication in 30 dyadic conversations in English between Japanese and American participants (Cutrone, 2014). The findings of this study demonstrated several differences in how members of each culture used back channels in terms of frequency, variability, placement, and function. This study also found evidence supporting the hypothesis that back channel conventions that are not shared between cultures contribute to negative perceptions across cultures. The results of this study showed that, when compared to the American group, the Japanese group sent back channels far more frequently overall, which most notably included a greater percentage of simultaneous speech back channels and minimal responses. The American group, predictably, spoke a great deal more, posed a far greater number of questions, and produced a greater percentage of extended responses.

In addition, this study demonstrated a tendency in the Japanese participants to produce unconventional back channels in situations when they did not understand what their interlocutor was saying. The interpretation for this behavior was that Japanese L2 English speakers may sometimes feign understanding and/or agreement in order to keep conversations pleasant. This belief was further strengthened by several of the JEFLs' admission in the playback interviews that they often had employed a continuer, a sign of understanding, agreement, and/or support and empathy as back channels in situations when they did not understand (71%) and/or when they disagreed with what their interlocutor was saying (100%). Thus the findings of this study supported the conclusion that listenership warrants more attention in EFL classrooms in Japan, and by extension, in EFL classrooms in other Asian countries as well.

Phatic communication

Phatic communication or small talk has an important role in pragmatics. This non-referential use of language is enlisted in order to share feelings or establish a mood of sociability rather than to communicate information or ideas. It can be used to create, maintain, and/or enhance friendly relationships. The problem for Asian learners of English, however, is that they may not know how to make small talk effectively, since it requires a metapragmatic awareness of a wide range of complex and subtle issues, such as when and with whom to engage in it, the underlying reasons to do so, the types of phatic tokens that may be exchanged, the topics that such tokens may address, and the potential effects achievable

(Padilla Cruz, 2013). Although many didactic materials implicitly deal with some elements related to phatic communication, they apparently tend not to include it as an independent topic, nor do they neatly define it, distinguish its different manifestations or, address its sociocultural peculiarities.

It is this gap in the didactics associated with L2 pragmatics, which prompted a methodological proposal for teaching the pragmatics of phatic communication and for raising learners' metapragmatic awareness (Padilla Cruz, 2013). Based on an approach to teaching the pragmatics of specific L2 aspects (Martínez Flor & Usó Juan, 2006), this proposal integrated relevant findings about phatic communication from pragmatics and other neighboring disciplines, combines different approaches to teaching intercultural pragmatic issues in class, and includes tasks.

Humor

Also of great challenge Asian learners is to understand English language humor. Humor may fail for many reasons and the ways in which this happens are just beginning to be explored. One such exploration was aimed at examining L2 understanding of humor systematically (Bell & Attardo, 2010). Six advanced non-native speakers (three Japanese, two Korean, and one Chinese graduate student) of English, all studying to get a degree in an MATESOL program, kept diaries in which they recorded their experiences with humor in English over an eight-week period. Group meetings were held every two weeks during this time to allow the participants to elaborate on, interpret, and discuss their experiences. All instances of failed humor were extracted, coded, and used to construct a typology, which identified seven ways in which a speaker may fail to engage in a humorous exchange successfully:

1   failure to process language at the illocutionary level,
2   failure to understand the meaning of words (including connotations),
3   failure to understand the pragmatic force of utterances (including irony),
4   failure to recognize the humorous frame,
5   false negative: missing the joke,
6   false positive: seeing a joke where none was intended,
7   failure to understand the incongruity of the joke.

A follow-up study by one of the same researchers focused on native English speakers' handling of humor, as if to accentuate just how problematic responses to attempted humor can be, even for native speakers (Bell, 2013). The researcher looked at native-speaker responses to a joke that hinged on a rather subtle pun ("how's" = "house"). The pun situation involved the mailman inquiring about a homeowner's dog that had attacked him in the past but was not outside the last few days. When the postman asks, "How's your dog?," the homeowner, hearing (or pretending to hear?) "House your dog," responds, "I did." The joke was impossible for most hearers to comprehend without an explanation.

A total of 278 L1-hearer responses were elicited by 22 undergraduates enrolled in a sociolinguistics course at a large, public university in the Western United States. The most common reactions included non-verbal responses, explicit expressions of non-understanding (e.g. "I don't get it"), laughter, silence, and repetition of the punch line. Significant differences were found when analyzing the responses by gender and social relationship, but not age. The joke was met with laughter 28% of the time, even though many hearers did not understand it and so they responded with uncomfortable or nervous laughter.

Sarcasm

Equally as daunting for L2 learners as perceiving humor is perceiving sarcasm. According to Kim (2014), successful understanding of sarcasm in L2 can be a substantial challenge for learners for at least two reasons: (1) the inherent incongruity of meaning that is frequently exhibited in instances of sarcasm, and (2) the highly context-dependent nature of sarcasm. Native speakers of English possess top-down knowledge (e.g., intuitions and experiences) through which they can (in many cases) successfully interpret their interlocutors' sarcastic intent, while Asian learners have to use a bottom-up approach. As an example of recent research on this topic, a study examined how Korean adult learners of English interpreted sarcasm in spoken English (Kim, 2014). Twenty-eight Korean adult employees of a trading company in Korea participated in the study. Participants were asked to identify instances of sarcasm in video clips taken from the US TV sitcom *Friends* and then to assess the possible speaker intent and communicative goals associated with these sarcastic utterances. During individual interviews, participants reported the cues that they attended to while processing sarcasm. Analysis revealed that learners drew upon certain features of L1 schema during the L2 comprehension process.

According to the researcher, there were various explanations for why Korean participants did not perceive the use of sarcasm in *Friends*, such as lack of knowledge about how sarcasm is generally used in the specific L2 context, lack of linguistic data about highly conventionalized sarcastic utterances, and lack of knowledge about the types of cues used to convey sarcasm (Kim, 2014). For example, the majority of native-speaker participants not only saw the use of "Yeah, right" in *Friends* as an example of a conventionalized sarcastic remark, but also as a way of disagreeing or making fun of the interlocutor. For those 60% of the Korean participants who did perceive it as sarcasm, they all misperceived the intent as being that of simply trying to be funny. Many Korean participants also apparently lacked knowledge about how to interpret speakers' facial expressions, especially the use of a "blank face," which is one of the cues that sarcasm users in the United States typically adopt.

The pragmatic function of discourse markers

Discourse markers are an important means for signaling pragmatic functions, both in speaking and in writing. The following are two studies that highlight the issue.

Frequency of use of discourse markers

One study investigated the use of pragmatic markers by college learners of English in China (Wei, 2011). It compared the use of pragmatic markers by 141 English majors from three Chinese universities. The data consisted of responses to interview questions such as "How might your life look ten years from now?" Responses included descriptions of their homes, recent activities, and an apology to a friend for having missed a dinner engagement. While intermediate and advanced students used similar discourse markers and in the same order of magnitude ("I think," "well," "yes/yeah," "you know," and "please"), quantitative and qualitative analyses indicated that advanced students tended to be more spontaneous in their speech and more effective in managing spoken interactions and performing social functions to cater to contextual needs than were the intermediate students. These discourse markers – which the researcher referred to as *pragmatic markers* – were found to play a dynamic role in accomplishing more contextually bound coherence and to perform the important function of maintaining smooth interactions.

The cross-cultural misuse of discourse markers

A second study investigated the effect of native language (Mandarin Chinese) on the use of English discourse markers by L1 Chinese speakers of English (Liu, 2013). Ten graduate students originally from mainland China and five American English native speakers at the University of Florida served as subjects. All students were interviewed for 15 minutes in English by native English speakers. Topics for the interviews included hobbies, weekends, sports, favorite teachers, favorite movies and TV programs, and happiest experience. The Chinese students were interviewed on the same topics in Chinese. Results showed that three Chinese discourse markers were found to influence their corresponding English expressions. The finding that the L1 Chinese speakers used the deliberative function of "I think" in medial or final position, while the native English speakers did not, would suggest that they transferred this use of "I think" from their L1 (*woˇ juéde*). Second, the L1 Chinese speakers used "yeah/yes" as a back channel after the interlocutor's reaction "uh huh" or "OK," while the native English speakers did not. This use was also interpreted as negative transfer from the corresponding Chinese expression *duì* because *duì* has this function in Chinese. Finally, Chinese L1 speakers used "ah" to perform a clause-medial function (followed by self-correction) in the same way that *a* would be used in Chinese, while the native English speakers did not use "ah" in this way.

Teaching L2 pragmatics

Now that we have looked at a variety of issues regarding the "what" of L2 pragmatics, let us consider how to teach some of these important aspects of language behavior. Over the last few decades, the theme of interlanguage pragmatics and in particular the link between language and culture has gained increasing appeal internationally and has enjoyed attention in the field of language education. It is probably fair to say that pragmatics has become a mainstream concern in L2 teaching and learning. Nonetheless, there is a noticeable gap between what research in pragmatics has found and how language is generally taught today – thus a rather weak link between theory and practice. The reason why this chapter has concentrated on pragmatics research in leading journals was precisely to underscore the importance of a research basis for choosing pragmatic materials to teach. For example, research findings have tended to favor a deductive approach rather than an inductive one. Generally, explicit teaching about how language functions in discourse has been found to be more beneficial than leaving learners to figure pragmatic behavior out for themselves (Cohen, 2012b).

That said, a study by Takimoto (2008) found that learners who had to discover the underlying rules for downgrading requests were better able to process information about the target features and store it in working memory than those who simply received explicit information about making requests, without having to link the sociopragmatic and pragmalinguistic features in the information to various meanings conveyed by means of downgrading requests.[3] So it is still an open question as to how best to instruct learners regarding pragmatics, probably in part because learners differ as to their learning style preferences (see, for example, Cohen, 2012a).

Teaching criticism in an L2

Looking at the explicit teaching of a less taught speech act, a study evaluated the relative effectiveness of two types of form-focused instruction on the acquisition of the speech act set of constructive criticism by 69 Vietnamese learners of English (Nguyen, Pham, & Pham, 2012). Three high intermediate EFL intact classes (N = 69) of pre-service EFL teachers were recruited. Over a 10-week course, the explicit group (N = 28) participated in consciousness-raising activities, and received explicit metapragmatic explanation and correction of errors of forms and meanings. The implicit group (N = 19), on the other hand, participated in pragmalinguistic input enhancement and recast activities. The two treatment groups were compared with a control group (N = 22) on pretest and posttest performance, consisting of a DCT, a role play, and an oral peer feedback task. There was also a delayed posttest comprising the same production tasks to measure long-term retention. The results revealed that both of the treatment groups significantly improved in the immediate posttest over the pretest, outperforming the control group. The treatment groups also maintained their improvement in the delayed posttest. Of note, the explicit instruction group performed significantly better than the implicit group on all measures.

Teaching refusals in an L3

Another approach to pragmatics research regarding speech acts has been to look at the learning of pragmatics among multilinguals. One study examined the benefits that teaching the speech act of refusal from a discourse perspective had on third language (L3) learners' pragmatic knowledge (Alcón Soler, 2012). Retrospective verbal reports were used to examine the impact of instruction on attention and awareness of refusals, and to explore whether receptive and productive bilingual learners resorted to pragmalinguistic, sociopragmatic, and linguistic information in different ways during the planning and execution of refusals. There were 92 university students learning English L3 pragmatics in the study, 40 who had acquired Catalan as their L1 and Spanish as their L2 (referred to in the study as *productive bilinguals*), and 52 students who had acquired Spanish as their L1 and Catalan as an L2 (termed *receptive bilinguals*). Pragmatic input was provided using excerpts from the *Friends* sitcom series with the focus was on refusals to invitations in a situation of power and social distance. Retrospective verbal reports were used to examine the impact of instruction on attention and awareness of refusals, and to explore whether receptive and productive Catalan and Spanish bilingual learners resorted to pragmalinguistic, sociopragmatic, and linguistic information in different ways during the planning and execution of refusals.

The findings showed that teaching refusals at the discourse level increased the learners' pragmalinguistic awareness of refusals in English L3, regardless of their degree of Catalan and Spanish bilingualism. In contrast, productive bilinguals outperformed receptive bilinguals in L3 metapragmatic awareness. The interpretation provided was that the productive bilinguals had greater communicative sensitivity, in large part because they were already making more contrasts between the Catalan and Spanish linguistic systems and thus had a better sense of intended meanings and social variables affecting language use.

Teaching English as a lingua franca

In an increasingly global world, more and more people are communicating in English that is not the native language of either of them, in a context where there are no native speakers of English around to evaluate their pragmatics. So, as already queried earlier in this chapter, whose pragmatics do they use? A recent study performed qualitative analysis on a sample of data produced by a multicultural group of MA students for whom English was the *lingua franca* (Maíz-Arévalo, 2014). More specifically, the researcher sought to answer the following research question: In a multicultural class where English is the medium of instruction and students' peer-to-peer communication, whose pragmatic "rules" are followed? In other words, do these speakers stick to their own cultural pragmatic rules or follow native-like ones? More specifically, she focused on the speech act of disagreement, given its face-threatening nature and its disruptive potential if carried out in what interlocutors might perceive as the "wrong" way. Disagreement was also chosen because of the relative paucity of studies on this speech act.

Ten students from very different cultural backgrounds, studying English Linguistics at the Universidad Complutense of Madrid were asked to carry out a group assignment. The negotiation and discussion process was computer-mediated via the use of forums within their university's Moodle program rather than face-to-face. This allowed the researcher to collect 15,598 words of naturally occurring, spontaneous written data. By participating in an online asynchronous discussion, the students did not have to fight for conversational turns, but rather were able to contribute to the discussion at their own pace. Disagreement expressions were classified according to two main categories: strong and mitigated disagreement. The findings revealed that students on the whole showed a tendency to avoid strong disagreement and instead to favor mitigated disagreement – such as the use of hedges, asking for clarification, and giving explanations. Moreover, students with high linguistic proficiency displayed a wider range of strategies, following a more native-like pattern, following the pragmatic rules of British English, since most of them had lived in the United Kingdom for a while before coming to Spain. Students whose linguistic proficiency was lower also showed a tendency to avoid strong disagreement, but were much more limited with regard to their mitigating strategies, favoring the nonnative overuse of expressions of regret and hedges.

Materials development for L2 pragmatics

While textbooks are often authorized and treated as unproblematic, especially in foreign language contexts (Ishihara, 2011; Pulverness, 2003), many of them still fall short in terms of appropriate language use in context. However, publications in L2 pragmatics have begun to provide samples of instructional materials and lesson plans (e.g., Bardovi-Harlig & Mahan-Taylor, 2003; Houck & Tatsuki, 2011; Ishihara & Cohen, 2010; Martínez-Flor & Usó-Juan, 2010; Tatsuki & Houck, 2010). More extensive curricular materials include Riddiford and Newton (2010) for teaching a range of business or workplace interactions in ESL contexts, Sykes and Cohen (2006) for teaching communicative acts in Spanish, and Ishihara and Maeda (2010) for teaching speech acts in Japanese.

In order to provide an updated treatment of this topic, Ishihara and I looked at (a) what we know, (b) what we think we know, and (c) what we need to find out with respect to materials development in L2 pragmatics (Cohen & Ishihara, 2012). We concluded that although pragmatics is often neglected or only marginally treated in existing L2 curricula, further development of L2 pragmatics materials would support teachers in preparing learners to understand and use language effectively in context and to express their own voice as they wish in the target community.

Construction of websites

An area that has come into its own in research on L2 learning is that of language learner strategies and the application of strategies to the learning and performance of L2 pragmatics (Cohen & Sykes, 2013). The underlying concern is with the potentially important role of strategies in heightening learners' ability to make informed choices with regard to how they handle intercultural situations. The focus is on assisting learners in developing a more robust repertoire of strategies for their handling of pragmatics within intercultural communication. The aim is to support learners in building a toolkit of common pragmatic options that can be used as they co-construct communication in a variety of intercultural interactions.

To begin addressing these issues, a strategic approach to L2 pragmatics was included in a general pragmatics website that was launched under my direction in 2001 at the Center for Advanced Research on Language Acquisition (CARLA), University of Minnesota (www.carla.umn.edu/speechacts/index.html). Then a Japanese pragmatics website was launched in 2003 (www.carla.umn.edu/speechacts/japanese/introtospeechacts/index.htm), and a Spanish pragmatics website in 2006 (www.carla.umn.edu/speechacts/sp_pragmatics/home.html) (see Cohen, 2016 for more on these websites). Both the Japanese and the Spanish websites benefited from research in cross-cultural pragmatics and from interventional studies investigating the effects of explicit pragmatics instruction on the development of pragmatic ability. Their goal was to employ web-based strategy instruction: to enhance learners' development and use of language learner strategies, to provide guidance in complex pragmatic language use that is difficult to 'pick up,' and to facilitate learning through web-based materials.

A taxonomy of strategies for learning and performing L2 pragmatics was applied to the construction of the Spanish pragmatics website, *Dancing with Words*, aimed at facilitating the learning of pragmatics appropriate for Spanish-speaking world, with strategy material integrated into the website. Research was conducted by means of two studies, involving both this Spanish pragmatics website and a synthetic immersive environment (SIE), *Croquelandia*, which was designed as a 3-D immersive space for the learning of pragmatic behaviors in Spanish (Cohen & Sykes, 2013). Results showed some reported differences in strategy use in the two different kinds of digital environments, with the finding of most relevance to the notion of intercultural education being that in the SIE learners reported an increased use of metapragmatic strategies for dealing with L2 pragmatics. This finding highlighted the role of strategies in making informed choices about pragmatics.

A more recent expansion to the work begun at CARLA has been to set up a wiki focused on the teaching of L2 pragmatics, the Second and Foreign Language Pragmatics Wiki – wlpragmatics.pbworks.com. The main strategy is to use *crowdsourcing*, namely, soliciting contributions from a large group of people, and especially from the online community. The work has just begun to solicit a wide range of practical teaching materials and advice from language teachers and researchers worldwide who have successfully taught pragmatics to their students in a number of languages (see Cohen, 2016).

Assessment of pragmatics

Classroom teachers may avoid the assessment of pragmatics, especially nonnative teachers who feel that they themselves are incapable of judging what constitutes correct behavior. Nonetheless, there are various reasons for assessing L2 pragmatics in the classroom (Cohen, 2014):

- It sends a message to the students that their ability to be pragmatically appropriate in the comprehension and production of language in different sociocultural situations is a positive thing.
- Having such items on a test motivates students to study about the performance of speech acts.
- It gives teachers an opportunity to see the relative control their students have in what may at times be a significant area for L2 performance.
- It gives teachers an opportunity to see whether learners have learned the pragmatics that was included in the instruction.

A number of possible tasks have been suggested for assessing the comprehension of pragmatic performance. One approach is to have learners indicate how well they **think** someone else has performed pragmatically. There are also various ways to collect students' pragmatic production, such as through oral role play, written discourse as if spoken, multiple-choice, or short-answer responses. It would appear that if speech act situations, for example, are made realistic and if guidelines are provided to teachers on how to rate key aspects of pragmatics, assessment of pragmatics would be more prevalent (Cohen, 2014).

Bardovi-Harlig and Shin (2014) argued that testing in pragmatics had for too long relied on the same six measures of pragmatics assessment introduced by Hudson, Detmer, and Brown (1992, 1995). They demonstrated that there was a wealth of potential test formats in the L2 pragmatics acquisition literature that were as yet untapped resources for pragmatics testing. They introduced tasks that were used in pragmatic research which they considered innovative in the context of assessment, and addressed the potential of each task to enhance task authenticity, their practicality for testing, and their potential for broadening our construct representation. By format, the tasks that they presented for consideration included oral production (oral for oral), written production (written for written), and audio and/or audio-visual conversational excerpts with written/read interpretations. By area of pragmatics, the tasks covered conventional expressions, pragmatic routines, conversational implicature, pragmaticality judgments, sociopragmatic judgments, interaction of grammar and pragmatics, and speech act identification tasks. The production tasks simulated turn taking by providing unanticipated turns through computer generation or audio presentation, requiring responses from the test takers. They started with the production tasks, and then moved on to consider interpretation, judgment, and prediction tasks.

Learning and performing pragmatics

While it is crucial to focus on teachers and their teaching of pragmatics in Asia, it is equally important to focus on learners and the strategies that they employ in an effort to ensure that the input that they process is pragmatically comprehensible to them. Likewise, attention needs to be given to the strategies that learners can make use of so that their output is comprehensible pragmatically to their interlocutors (Cohen, 2011). This entails taking a close look at specific examples of what comprehensibility of language at the level of intercultural pragmatics actually means. In looking at both the comprehension and production of pragmatic material, the strategies that might be called on in order to avoid pragmatic failure need to be considered (Cohen, 2005). So this means looking at what it might take strategically in order to effectively comprehend input pragmatically, whether the input is through language, through gestures, or through silence. A strategy for understanding cursing at the workplace, for example, would be to pull over a working associate and ask to be briefed on the various ways to curse appropriately in that context (e.g., when in anger, when in jest, considering issues of age, status, and gender, and so forth).

In addition, it would be advisable for learners to consider using strategies for avoiding pragmatic failure in the production of language. Hence, they would need to know which strategies to use in order to avoid negative transfer of norms from the L1 or another language, overgeneralization of perceived L2 pragmatic norms, and the effect of instruction or instructional materials. They would also need strategies for communicating appropriately even if they have only limited L2 grammar ability, and strategies for dealing with their own resistance to abiding by the perceived L2 norms. Just with regard to avoiding negative transfer in dealing with speech acts, for example, learners may benefit from checking with local peers as to the most appropriate ways to respond to a compliment, as well as how to make requests that are likely to be responded to favorably in various situations in the given speech community. The ultimate concern is to identify strategies that might assist learners in their efforts to have their conversational partners correctly interpret the intended pragmatics in their communications, all the while being mindful of the role that ESL/EFL teachers can play in facilitating this process.

Conclusion

This review of research literature on L2 pragmatics has sought insights for Asian learners of English by first looking at approaches to research methods and by suggesting avenues for innovation since new technologies have provided us a host of new ways to gather and analyze data. We then looked at the issue of politeness, making the point that control of pragmatics includes knowing how to perceive impoliteness and how to actually be impolite at times when called for (e.g., knowing how to curse). Next, examples of recent speech act research were presented, both to illustrate study of a less commonly researched speech act (criticism), as well as to consider an innovative approach to research on a popular speech act (requests). After that, the focus was on other areas of pragmatics of concern to ESL/EFL teachers: conversational overlap, back channeling, phatic communication, humor, sarcasm, and the pragmatic function of discourse markers.

In an effort to move from theory to practice, the chapter also focused on L2 pedagogy: teaching L2 learners a less-commonly taught speech act (criticism), teaching L3 learners a commonly taught speech act (refusals), teaching pragmatics to learners for whom English is a lingua franca, materials development for L2 pragmatics, construction of pragmatics websites, and assessment of pragmatics. Of these issues, perhaps the ELF issue is the most provocative. Whose pragmatics should speakers of Asian languages use if they are interacting with other Asians without intervention by any native speakers? This issue is just beginning to be explored.

Finally, we focused on the learner and on strategies for the learning and performing of pragmatics. Teachers can do lots of exciting things in the language class, but learners need to take responsibility for their own learning. It helps if the learners make an effort to be strategic about their learning, especially when it comes to the challenging area of pragmatics.

Notes

1 Aside from numerous trips to Japan and China, I have traveled repeatedly to other Asian countries like Thailand and South Korea where cultural aspects of pragmatics are at times in noticeable contrast to those in English-language cultures.
2 In this chapter, L2 is used generically to represent either the teaching and learning of a second language – that is, one that is spoken in the given context – or a foreign language, namely, one that is not spoken in that context
3 *Pragmalinguistic* refers to what constitutes appropriate linguistic forms for expressing the intent of the speech act, taking into account the norms of behavior that apply in the given situation. *Sociopragmatic* refers to the norms of behavior for realizing the given speech act in a given context, taking into account (i) the culture involved, (ii) the relative age and gender of the interlocutors, (iii) their social class and occupations, and (iv) their roles and status in the interaction (Thomas, 1983).

References

Alcón Soler, E. (2012). Teachability and bilingualism effects on third language learners' pragmatic knowledge. *Intercultural Pragmatics*, 9, 511–541.

Bardovi-Harlig, K., & Mahan-Taylor, R. (Eds.). (2003). *Teaching pragmatics*. Washington, DC: Office of English Programs, US Department of State. Retrieved from http://americanenglish.state.gov/files/ae/resource_files/intro.pdf. (Note: Some of the individual chapters are still available at the same website)

Bardovi-Harlig, K., & Shin, S. (2014). Expanding traditional testing measures with tasks from L2 pragmatics research. *Iranian Journal of Language Testing*, 4(1), 26–49.

Béal, C. (2010). *Les Interactions quotidiennes en français et en anglais*. Berne: Peter Lang.

Bell, N. D. (2013). Responses to incomprehensible humor. *Journal of Pragmatics*, 57, 176–189.
Bell, N. D., & Attardo, S. (2010). Failed humor: Issues in non-native speakers' appreciation and understanding of humor. *Intercultural Pragmatics*, 7, 423–447.
Chen, Y., Chen, C. D., & Chang, M-H. (2011). American and Chinese complaints: Strategy use from a cross-cultural perspective. *Intercultural Pragmatics*, 8, 253–275.
Cohen, A. D. (1996). Speech acts. In S. L. McKay & N. H. Hornberger (Eds.), *Sociolinguistics and language teaching* (pp. 383–420). Cambridge: Cambridge University Press.
Cohen, A. D. (1997). Developing pragmatic ability: Insights from the accelerated study of Japanese. In H. M. Cook, K. Hijirida, & M. Tahara (Eds.), *New trends and issues in teaching Japanese language and culture* (pp. 137–163). (Technical Report #15). Honolulu, HI: Second Language Teaching and Curriculum Center, University of Hawaii at Manoa.
Cohen, A. D. (2001). From L1 to L12: The confessions of a sometimes frustrated multiliterate. In D. Belcher & U. Connor (Eds.), *Reflections on multiliterate lives* (pp. 79–95). Clevedon: Multilingual Matters.
Cohen, A. D. (2005). Strategies for learning and performing L2 speech acts. *Intercultural Pragmatics*, 2, 275–301.
Cohen, A. D. (2011). Learner strategies for performing intercultural pragmatics. *MinneWITESOL Journal*, 28, 13–24.
Cohen, A. D. (2012a). Strategies: The interface of styles, strategies, and motivation on tasks. In S. Mercer, S. Ryan, & M. Williams (Eds.), *Psychology for language learning: Insights from research, theory and practice* (pp. 136–150). Basingstoke: Palgrave Macmillan.
Cohen, A. D. (2012b). Teaching pragmatics in the second language classroom. *The European Journal of Applied Linguistics and TEFL*, 1(1), 35–49.
Cohen, A. D. (2014). Towards increased classroom assessment of pragmatic ability. *Iranian Journal of Language Testing*, 4(1), 5–25.
Cohen, A. D. (2016). The design and construction of websites to promote L2 pragmatics. In K. Bardovi-Harlig & C. Félix-Brasdefer (Eds.), *Pragmatics and language learning* (Vol. 14, pp. 341–356). Honolulu, HI: Foreign Language Resource Center, University of Hawai'i, Manoa.
Cohen, A. D., & Ishihara, N. (2012). Pragmatics. In B. Tomlinson & H. Masuhara (Eds.), *Applied linguistics: Connecting practice to theory through materials development* (pp. 113–126). London: Continuum.
Cohen, A. D., & Sykes, J. M. (2013). Strategy-based learning of pragmatics for intercultural education. In F. Dervin & A. J. Liddicoat (Eds.), *Linguistics for intercultural education* (pp. 87–111). Amsterdam: John Benjamins.
Culpeper, J., Marti, L., Mei, M., Nevala, M., & Schauer, G. (2010). Cross-cultural variation in the perception of impoliteness: A study of impoliteness events reported by students in England, China, Finland, Germany, and Turkey. *Intercultural Pragmatics*, 7, 597–624.
Cutrone, P. (2014). A cross-cultural examination of the back channel behavior of Japanese and Americans: Considerations for Japanese EFL learners. *Intercultural Pragmatics*, 11(1), 83–120.

Daly, N., Holmes, J., Newton, J., & Stubbe, M. (2004). Expletives as solidarity signals in FTAs on the factory floor. *Journal of Pragmatics*, *36*, 945–964.

Dewaele, J.-M. (2004). The emotional force of swearwords and taboo words in the speech of multilinguals. *Journal of Multilingual and Multicultural Development*, *25* (2 & 3), 204–222.

Dörnyei, Z. (2006). Individual differences in second language acquisition. *AILA review*, *19*(1), 42–68.

Economidou-Kogetsidis, M. (2011). "Please answer me as soon as possible": Pragmatic failure in non-native speakers' e-mail requests to faculty. *Journal of Pragmatics*, *43*, 3193–3215.

Guillot, M-N. (2014). Conversational management and pragmatic discrimination in foreign talk: Overlap in advanced L2 French. *Intercultural Pragmatics*, *11*(1), 83–120.

Holmes, J., Marra, M., & Vine, B. (2012). Politeness and impoliteness in ethnic varieties of New Zealand English. *Journal of Pragmatics*, *44*, 1063–1076.

Houck, N., & Tatsuki, D. (Eds.). (2011). *Pragmatics: Teaching natural conversation*. Alexandria, VA: Teachers of English to Speakers of Other Languages.

Hudson, T., Detmer, E., & Brown, J. D. (1992). *A framework for testing cross-cultural pragmatics* (Technical Report 2). Honolulu, HI: University of Hawai'i, Second Language Teaching and Curriculum Center.

Hudson, T., Detmer, E., & Brown, J. D. (1995). *Developing prototypic measures of cross-cultural pragmatics* (Technical Report 7). Honolulu, HI: University of Hawai'i, Second Language Teaching and Curriculum Center.

Ishihara, N. (2011). Co-constructing pragmatic awareness: Instructional pragmatics in EFL teacher development in Japan. *TESOL-EJ*, *15*(2). Retrieved from www.tesl-ej.org/wordpress/Issues/volume15/ej58/ej58a2/

Ishihara, N., & Cohen, A. D. (2010). *Teaching and learning pragmatics: Where language and culture meet*. Harlow: Longman Applied Linguistics/Pearson Education.

Ishihara, N., & Maeda, M. (2010). *Advanced Japanese: Communication in context* [*Kotobato bunkano kousaten: Bunkade yomitoku nihongo*]. London: Routledge.

Kerbrat-Orecchioni, C. (2005). Politeness in France: How to buy bread politely. In L. Hickey & M. Stewart (Eds.), *Politeness in Europe* (pp. 29–44). Clevedon: Multilingual Matters.

Kim, J. (2014). How Korean EFL learners understand sarcasm in L2 English. *Journal of Pragmatics*, *60*, 193–206.

Ladegaard, H. J. (2012). Rudeness as a discursive strategy in leadership discourse: Culture, power and gender in a Hong Kong workplace. *Journal of Pragmatics*, *44*, 1661–1679.

Liu, B. (2013). Effect of first language on the use of English discourse markers by L1 Chinese speakers of English. *Journal of Pragmatics*, *45*, 149–172.

Maíz-Arévalo, C. (2014). Expressing disagreement in English as a lingua franca: Whose pragmatic rules? *Intercultural Pragmatics*, *11*, 199–224.

Martínez-Flor, A., & Usó-Juan, E. (2006). A comprehensive pedagogical framework to develop pragmatics in the foreign language classroom: The 6R approach. *Applied Language Learning*, *16*(2), 39–64.

Martínez-Flor, A., & Usó-Juan, E. (Eds.) (2010). *Speech act performance: Theoretical, empirical and methodological issues*. Amsterdam: John Benjamins.

Mey, J. (1993). *Pragmatics: An introduction*. Oxford: Wiley-Blackwell.

Nguyen, T. T. M., Pham, T. H., & Pham, M. T. (2012). The relative effects of explicit and implicit form-focused instruction on the development of L2 pragmatic competence. *Journal of Pragmatics, 44,* 416–434.

Olshtain, E., & Cohen, A. D. (1983). Apology: A speech act set. In N. Wolfson & E. Judd (Eds.), *Sociolinguistics and language acquisition* (pp. 18–35). Rowley, MA: Newbury House.

Padilla Cruz, M. (2013). An integrative proposal to teach the pragmatics of phatic communion in ESL classes. *Intercultural Pragmatics, 10*(1), 131–160.

Pulverness, A. (2003). Materials for cultural awareness. In B. Tomlinson (Ed.), *Developing materials for language teaching* (pp. 426–438). London: Continuum.

Riddiford, N., & Newton, J. (2010). *Workplace talk in action: An ESOL resource.* Wellington: School of Linguistics and Applied Language Studies, Victoria University of Wellington.

Rogers, C. (1951). *Client-centered therapy: Its current practice, implications and theory.* London: Constable.

Rogers, C. (1959). A theory of therapy, personality and interpersonal relationships as developed in the client-centered framework. In S. Koch (Ed.), *Psychology: A study of science. Vol. 3: Formulations of the person and the social context.* New York: McGraw-Hill.

Rogers, C. (1961). *On becoming a person: A therapist's view of psychotherapy.* London: Constable.

Shively, R. L. (2011). L2 pragmatic development in study abroad: A longitudinal study of Spanish service encounters. *Journal of Pragmatics, 43,* 1818–1835.

Stern., H. H. (1983). *Fundamental concepts of language teaching.* Oxford: Oxford University Press.

Sykes, J., & Cohen, A. D. (2006). *Dancing with words: Strategies for learning pragmatics in Spanish.* Retrieved from www.carla.umn.edu/speechacts/sp_pragmatics/home.html

Takimoto, M. (2008). The effects of deductive and inductive instruction on the development of language learners' pragmatic competence. *The Modern Language Journal, 92,* 369–386.

Tatsuki, D., & Houck, N. (Eds.). (2010). *Pragmatics: Teaching speech acts.* Alexandria, VA: Teachers of English to Speakers of Other Languages.

Thomas, J. (1983). Cross-cultural pragmatic failure. *Applied Linguistics, 4*(2), 91–112.

Verspoor, M. & et al. (2005). *Second language acquisition: An advanced resource book.* London: Routledge.

Wei, M. (2011). Investigating the oral proficiency of English learners in China: A comparative study of the use of pragmatic markers. *Journal of Pragmatics, 43,* 3455–3472.

Yule, G. (1996). *Pragmatics.* Oxford: Oxford University Press.

17 Language classroom management

Zekiye Müge Tavil and Arif Sariçoban

In the process of teaching and learning, classroom management is of great importance. Effective teaching is generally synonymous with effective classroom management. Management on its own cannot be said to be teaching itself, but it is one of the cornerstones of teaching because many studies in the field suggest that if a classroom is managed effectively, teaching and learning are accordingly effective. However, the opposite spoils the teachers' desire to teach, increases burn out, and blocks the productive setting – no matter how well a teacher has been prepared for the lesson. This situation is the same in a language classroom.

The aim of learning a foreign language is basically communication. To achieve this aim, the ultimate need of learners is to develop four language skills, which are reading, writing, speaking, and listening. Active participation of the students facilitates communication and creates opportunities to speak, read, listen, and write; however, this circumstance may easily cause too much noise and disorder in the classroom. Owing to this, disruptive behavior and discipline problems may occur in an English as a Foreign Language (EFL) classroom, for example. The problem is how to manage and provide discipline by minimizing the disruptive behavior in the classroom. So here, it is better to make discrimination between classroom management and discipline. Martin, Sugarman, and McNamara (2000) define classroom management as the activities that classroom teachers apply in order to have effective teaching and learning within a positive classroom climate. Classroom management refers to the activities of classroom teachers that create a warm atmosphere within which effective teaching and learning may occur (Martin et al., 2000). Successful classroom management does not draw a picture of a class in which all the students sit at their desks and just listen to the teacher while copying all the instructions down. Conversely, effective classroom management is to provide student involvement and motivation, which facilitate a fruitful learning environment. Discipline focuses on misbehavior and punishment of an individual whereas classroom management underlines not only the positive behavior but also the teachers as decision makers. In other words, classroom management is teachers' strategies to enhance an effective learning environment whereas discipline is the teachers' attitude towards misbehavior.

Table 17.1 Strategies for handling disruptive behavior

Before the disruptive behavior	During the disruptive behavior	After the disruptive behavior
• Set rules and standards and be consistent in applying them. • Have a good knowledge of the field. • Plan and organize your lessons carefully before entering the classroom. • Make the aim of the lesson clear. • Make sure instructions are clear and brief. • Create a positive and stress-free atmosphere. • Keep in touch with what is going on.	• Anticipate problems and act quickly. • Deal with the problem quietly. • Keep cool; do not take things personally. • Do not threaten your students (unless you are prepared to implement them!).	• Explode yourself and display anger without losing your temper. • Give in. • Avoid oppositions. • Make them an offer they cannot refuse (postponement, arbitration, compromise). • Get help from administration if necessary.

Classroom management starts before the students enter the classroom. Simonsen, Fairbanks, Briesch, Myers, and Sugai (2008) state that teachers should organize the lay out of the classroom, determine student routines and expectations before the school year. Classroom management is a crucial area; thus, teachers should be trained about the strategies that they can use before, during and after the disruptive behavior. Some of the steps to be taken before, during, and after disruptive behavior that Wragg mentions include (cited in Sarıçoban & Barışkan, 2005) the strategies outlined in Table 17.1.

Although the importance of effective classroom management is often underlined, many novice teachers highlight the problems that they face because of lack of knowledge. Owing to the very important role language plays in education, the subject of the language instruction has been given a prominent place in the school curriculum in Asia (Chew, 2005). Therefore, this chapter is vital in pinpointing the key points not only for pre-service teachers but also for in-service ones who wish to combine theory with practice in EFL classroom management. A single model by itself may not provide adequate management strategy, so teachers should interweave all to coordinate the appropriate behavior in the classroom.

The intervening model

In the traditional theory of classroom management, the aim is to control the classroom, and this is teachers' responsibility. A traditional approach mainly focuses on behavioral principles in a teacher-dominant environment (Garret, 2005). "In a traditional EFL class, the teacher tends to achieve a control over the whole class by strict discipline so that s/he can convey her/his instructions and the students can copy them down" (Yi, 2008, p. 129). The teacher is the authority and the source of the target language, and tries to transmit the knowledge to the learners.

The basic principles of the interventionist model are stated as follows by Wolfgang and Glickman (1986).

- a teacher has primary responsibility for controlling the classroom
- the teacher sets the rules
- primary focus is on the behavior of the learners
- minor emphasis is on the individual differences of students
- a teacher should be quick to control behavior
- types of intervention are generally rewards and punishments

Management in traditional approaches is based on a behavioristic approach. Behaviorism focuses on learners' behavior and deals with them individually to encourage positive behavior in the classroom. The stages of the behavioral approach are as follows:

- establish clear expectations for positive behavior
- monitor positive behavior
- reinforce positive behavior

The aim of management in behavioral approaches is to replace inappropriate behavior with the appropriate one. Throughout the process, there are five basic behavior operations.

1. Positive Reinforcement: It is the effect that can be realized when a behavior continuously exists.
2. Negative Reinforcement: It is the removal of stimulus. In order to reach behavioral change in a positive way, the teacher removes the stimulus.

    a. Extinction: Extinction means ignoring in behavioral approaches.
    b. Response Cost Management: It is the removal of previous reinforcement owing to an inappropriate behavior.

3. Punishment: It is an application of stimulus when the students do not want to minimize the inappropriate behavior. Kauffman, Pullen, Mostert, and Trent (2011) underline the crucial aspects of punishment as follows:

    - punishment should be applied for serious misbehavior
    - instituted only in the occasion of ongoing behavior management
    - fair and consistent
    - reasonable intensity
    - should involve response cost
    - related to misbehavior to practice an appropriate behavior
    - discontinued if ineffective
    - written guidelines for specific punishment behaviors.

Table 17.2 Examples of setting rules

Elementary Level	Secondary Level
• Be polite and helpful. • Take care of friends. • Take care of yourself. • Hurt no living thing. • Take care of your school. • Do not hit or hurt others. • Keep the bathroom clean.	• Bring all needed materials to class. • Be in your seat and ready to work when the bell rings. • Get permission before speaking or leaving your seat. • Respect and be polite to all the other people. • Respect other people's rights.

In a behavioristic approach, setting rules is significant to conduct positive relationship and to prevent inappropriate behaviors. Brophy (1983) gives some examples of the rules in Table 17.2.

The interacting model

There are various key factors of the interacting model. The basic principles of the model are stated as follows by Wolfgang and Glickman (1986).

- Students and teacher should share the responsibility of control.
- A teacher sets the rules with the help of the student input.
- Initial focus is on behavior followed by the emotions of the learners.
- Emphasis is on individual differences of the students.
- The teacher allows some time for students to control behavior, but she or he decides at last.
- Types of intervention are consequences and class meetings.

Interactive models are basically based on logical and natural consequences, cooperative discipline, positive classroom discipline, and noncoercive discipline.

Logical and natural consequences

The result of an action a person does is called a consequence. In order to give responsibility to the learners, teachers should let the learners experience consequences. A natural consequence is directly related to the learners' actions whereas logical consequences include interference of teachers or parents.

Allen and Boelter (2008) categorized the use of logical and natural consequences as follows.

1 **Define reasons:** It is crucial for the teacher to understand why the learners misbehave. If the teacher understands the reason, then he/she can find out solutions to the problem easily. For example, the student may misbehave in order to get the teacher's attention, so it is better to ignore and pay no attention; otherwise, the misbehavior will go on.

2 **Try to understand whose problem it is:** As language teachers, we cannot solve or understand all the problems occurring in the classroom; however, some of the inappropriate behaviors may result from learner's personal problems. So if the results of the behaviors are not dangerous and cause much intervention during the lesson, teachers should give responsibility of the behavior to the learners.
3 **Offer choices:** The aim is to give responsibility to the learners and let them face with the consequences of their behaviors. If the learner insists on the misbehavior, the teacher may give alternatives to the learner such as "You should complete your homework; otherwise, it will be very difficult for you to play a role in the game because we need the information that you write in your homework in order to give you the appropriate role. You should make your own choice." By this way, the teacher tries to create a need for the learner to complete a task.
4 **Stand firm and calm:** At the end, if the student does not do his/her homework, the teacher should play the game with the students who have completed their homework. She/he should stand firm and not let the learner who does not carry out his/her responsibilities and take part in the game.
5 **Talk to your learners about choices in a positive way:** Giving a choice is better than threatening the learners. Offer them alternatives and let them take the responsibility of their own choices.
6 **Let your students know when they have done something good:** When the inappropriate behavior is replaced with the positive one, let your student know that and appreciate the appropriate behavior.
7 **If possible, let the learner help to decide on the consequence:** As the responsibility of the behavior is the learners', let the learner understand the results of the choices and talk about the positive results that may occur if the choices are different. This will help the learner make good choices.

Allen and Boelter (2008) underline the guidelines of using logical consequences and state the following:

1 Logical consequences acknowledge mutual rights and mutual respect.
2 Logical consequences are related to inappropriate behavior.
3 Logical consequences are not judgmental.
4 Logical consequences are directly related to current and future behavior.
5 Logical consequences are done in a firm but kind manner with a soft friendly voice.
6 Logical consequences give the learner an alternative.

Cooperative discipline

According to Albert (1992), the basic principles of cooperative discipline are capability, helping students connect and helping students contribute.

1 Capability

Albert (1992) defines a capability level as "I can" level, and it refers to the students' accomplishment capacity at school, and she suggests five tactics to increase students' performance.

- make mistakes normal
- build confidence
- focus on past achievement
- make progress tangible
- recognize success

Making mistakes is a natural part of language learning. When learners feel anxious, they stop trying. Albert (1992) suggests that teachers should talk about the natural sides of the mistakes with their learners in order to minimize the fear they may feel. Positive reinforcement and appraisal are very important in cooperative discipline as they help learners build confidence. Apart from that, teachers should focus on the success rather than mistakes in the classroom, and portfolios encourage the positive learning environment and make the progress tangible.

2 Helping students connect

According to Albert (1992), positive relationships with peers and teachers are really vital for management because when learners have good relations with their mates, they become more cooperative, and this not only increases acceptance but also supports achievement.

3 Helping students contribute

When a teacher is the authority and source of knowledge, students feel purposeless in the classroom. Thus, the teachers should make the contributions of the students to the learning and teaching process. Albert (1992) suggests some ways of doing that:

1 encourage student contributions in the class (asking for their opinions, having discussions in the classroom)
2 encourage student contributions to the school (dusting shelves, cleaning grounds)
3 encourage student contributions to the community (opening doors for people, preparing meals)
4 encourage students to work for protecting the environment
5 encourage students to help the other students

Positive classroom discipline

The aim of positive classroom discipline is mutual respect and relationship. By this way, effective communication and problem-solving skills develop in the classroom. The key points of positive classrooms are as follows:

1. Before starting the lesson, teachers should get the attention of each student. First, the teachers should settle down the class and then start lessons, so the students will understand that it is time to work. Novice teachers may try to speak loudly in order to catch all the students' attention, but it is better if the teacher speaks softly because the students will keep quiet in order to hear and understand the teacher.
2. The teacher should tell the aim of each activity and put time limit; thus, the students will be aware of what they are expected to do.
3. The teacher should walk around and observe the students while they are completing a task. By this way, the teacher may easily observe the problems and help the learners immediately. This can prevent the inappropriate behaviors to occur.
4. The teacher should provide examples to the learners. Teachers are the models in the classroom.
5. The teachers should use their body language properly. By their faces or mimes, teachers can control the classroom and express what they want to say.
6. The teachers can integrate personal items in their lesson plans, as the learners are curious about teachers' lives. This can increase their motivation and involvement.
7. The teachers should directly state how they want their students to behave, such as "I want you to stop that noise!" While listing the things the teachers should use positive sentences; for example, instead of "Don't fight," the teachers should say, "Work cooperatively."
8. Encourage, reinforce, and praise good behaviors.

Noncoercive discipline

Motivation is the key aspect of involving learners in the teaching and learning process. Students should make their own decision about their behaviors. Teachers have the power to guide students to the appropriate behaviors. Glasser (1986) states the nature of the behavior as follows.

- Virtually, all human behavior has intrinsic motivation and is chosen by the individual.
- All of our behavior is our best attempt to satisfy one or more of five basic needs built into our genetic structure.
- All human behavior is purposeful.
- We are responsible for our own behavior.
- Effective discipline is based on meeting students' needs for survival, belonging, freedom, fun, and power.
- All students can competently do some kind of work in school.

Noncoercive discipline gives equal rights to the students. It is no use to force a student to pay attention if he or she is not willing to participate, so the first rule is to catch the attention of the learners. As none of the behaviors are purposeless, there is a reason of inappropriate behavior in the classroom. The teachers should find the cause and then try to find solutions to misbehaviors in the classroom. The learners should have fun in the classroom; thus, the teachers should integrate enjoyable activities appealing to their learner's interest in order to involve the learners and increase motivation. The aim of the curriculum is to meet what the students need because of this; cooperative and collaborative activities should be placed into the lesson plans of the teachers. Generally, in language classrooms, students are given too much grammar, and they cannot use the language; therefore, the curriculum should be revised, and an adapted one should be implemented considering the needs of the learners.

Glasser (1998) argues that quality teaching can be accomplished by the following things.

- Provide a warm supportive classroom atmosphere.
- Use lead teaching rather than boss teaching.
- Ask students only to do work that is purposeful.
- Always ask students to do their best.
- Ask students to evaluate work they have done.
- Help students recognize that doing quality work makes them feel good.
- Help students see that quality work is never destructive to oneself, others, or the community.

The guiding model

In the guiding model, there is a shift from a teacher-centered classroom to a learner-centered classroom. With the help of this new perspective, during the last decades, management strategies have become constructive. A constructivist approach centers on the belief that learners should be involved in the process of learning and teaching actively rather than simply receiving knowledge from teachers; it reinforces critical thinking skills to become autonomous learners. There are several methods based on a constructivist approach, but most of them focus on learners' discoveries and elicitation instead of spoon-feeding. Teachers are just tutoring in a positive atmosphere; hence, creating a stress-free and warm atmosphere is one of the key points of management in the constructivist approach as learning takes place in a positive environment.

In a non-native language-learning environment, generally the learners' only chance to use and hear the target language is the classroom. The students are definitely in need of interaction as the primary aim of learning a foreign language is communication. When learners feel anxious, they are not taking part in the process and become passive. This reflects the importance of a positive classroom atmosphere in which the learners feel relaxed and are willing to get involved in classroom activities. As mentioned earlier, creating a positive atmosphere is crucial in a constructivist approach; however, the question is how to establish a positive setting in an EFL class.

The basic principles of the guiding (non-interventionist) model are stated as follows by Wolfgang and Glickman (1986).

- Students have primary responsibility for controlling their behavior.
- Students develop the rules with the teacher guidance.
- Primary focus is on emotions.
- Major emphasis is on individual differences of the students in the classroom.
- Teacher gives time to students to control behavior.

According to Fan Yi (n.d.), motivation, involvement, a relaxed atmosphere, and fluency are the major factors of creating a positive atmosphere.

1   *Motivation*

Motivation is a precious tool to prevent management problems because if students are interested in particular activities, they will not cause problems. In order to motivate the learners, the teacher should be aware of students' interests and prepare lesson plans considering the communicative needs of the students; thus, the students will produce language when they feel the need (Pitsoe, 2007; Simonsen et.al., 2008).

2   *Involvement*

Having students involved is a difficult task for teachers. Whilst preparing for particular activities, a teacher should prefer challenging ones because if the tasks are too easy, students may get bored and if they are too difficult, they may feel frustrated. Thus the teacher's job is to be aware of the learners' levels and prepare activities in accordance with the interests of the students. Apart from that, discovering a technique is very beneficial for the learners rather than copying from the board. Learning is learners' responsibility; they should formulate the rules from the context created in the classroom. By this way, the students will be busy with various tasks to complete, preventing the possible problems in the classroom.

3   *Relaxed atmosphere*

"Anxiety hinders learning" (Yi, 2008, p. 131). When the classroom is a place where learners feel nervous, they will feel reluctant to get involved in particular activities. Additionally, Brophy (1986, p. 6) mentions that "all research results show that in addition to dealing with the misbehaviors and problems effectively, to prevent them from occurring is an important aspect of efficient classroom management." Focusing on negative behaviors and criticizing the learners all the time because of their mistakes or errors may result in silent and passive learners. This is generally knowledge-based; learners learn grammar and memorize the formulas given by the teacher but cannot communicate in the target language because of lack of practice. However, the teachers' aim is to enhance communication in the classroom among students. Language teachers should keep in mind that mistakes are natural, and they are a sign of learning.

4   *Fluency prior to accuracy*

The teachers should be tolerant to the mistakes of their learners (Amarjit, 2009). When the learners' speech in the target language is understandable, the teacher should appreciate and motivate the learners to speak as the aim is to enrich communication. If the learners are always conscious of accuracy, then they will not become fluent (Oliver & Reschly, 2007).

Key factors in language classroom management

Effective teaching can be provided by effective management. In an effective classroom, students work together with their peers. Group work or pair work leads to cooperation and facilitates a positive environment. An educational environment, a social environment, a curriculum, teachers' and students' roles, setting rules, time management, lesson planning, reacting to inappropriate behaviors, and facilitating communication in the classroom are some of the key factors that the teachers should consider.

Educational environment

An educational environment cares everything related to a physical structure, such as size of the classroom, material appropriateness, or seating. The students should feel comfortable in the learning environment. To enhance communication and encourage learners to speak, seating arrangements are of great importance. In the traditional seating, teacher generally lectures, and there is not much space for teachers to move. In a language classroom, teachers need space to play or to complete information-gap activities whereas in a traditional seating, students generally sit still while listening to the teacher. This type is applicable, if the class is not crowded. It is easy to control students, and let them work cooperatively. This seating chart is called a horseshoe. It creates a space in the middle of the classroom. Everybody can see each other; students can easily cooperate. The teacher should choose the appropriate seating considering the needs of the learners.

Social environment

Social environment of a learner affects his or her behaviors in the classroom. There are two types of environments: close and distant. A close environment is directly related to the learners' lives like a classroom, school, and family. A distant environment is life styles, customs, cultural aspects, and beliefs. These surroundings affect a student's learning and teaching environment, and the teachers' one of the main aims is to minimize the negative influences of these factors.

Lesson planning

Good lesson planning is vital to improve communication in the classroom. Although teachers prepare the best plans, they may sometimes become worthless if the teachers cannot manage the classrooms. The lessons should be challenging and appealing to the needs and interests of the learners. The code of conduct in the classroom should be fair, responsible, and meaningful. While planning the lessons, the interactions should be considered. Student-student interaction increases the student talking time in the classroom. Individual difference should be considered, and the lesson plans should cover visual, auditory, and kinesthetic learners. The environment should be unthreatening to involve the students in the teaching and learning process. The instructions should be clear to help the learners to understand what they are expected to do. The first activity can be a motivating one to take the attentions of the learners. After the activities, the teacher should praise the learners to provide encouragement. The last but not the least important aspect that should be considered in the classroom is developing a positive teacher-student relationship.

Teachers' and students' roles

In the first lesson, the teacher should build a positive relationship in the classroom. He or she accepts student autonomy and involvement. In a constructive classroom, the teacher should use various materials to guide learners to classify, analyze, predict, and create things. Students are responsible learners. They formulate and test their opinions, make inferences, and draw conclusions. Students should work collaboratively and cooperatively. If the students are busy, they do not cause disruptive behaviors; the teacher should keep the learners busy with different and challenging tasks. The language that is used in the classroom should be in the target language. The teacher should reinforce the students to complete information-gap and opinion-gap activities together with their peers or in groups. The authentic and real materials facilitate communicative and grasp the students' attention.

Setting rules

Learners generally want to know the expectations of the teacher. The first lesson is ideal time for conducting classroom rules together with the learners by pointing out the expected behavior like "Look at how your friends at this table are listening." The rules should also be posted in the classroom in English with pictures to make the meaning clear. Making positive sentences is important while constructing rules (Table 17.3).

Table 17.3 Examples of constructing rules

Negative rule	Positive rule
Don't hit anyone	Have good relations with everyone
Don't push other students	Respect each other

Time management

Students should work more than teachers in the classroom. Time management is one of the crucial factors in the classroom management. Teachers should give enough time for certain activities. He or she should be aware of the learners' level of proficiency because time management of a lesson is related to the students' capacity. If the teacher gives too much time, the students who complete the task earlier may cause problem behaviors. If the time is not enough, the students may not complete the activity, and they may feel frustrated, which can bruise their self-confidence.

Reacting to inappropriate behavior

A positive reinforcement improves appropriate behavior. A classroom climate should also be positive. Students should feel relaxed. If the students are seated properly, this proper seating arrangement also lessens the inappropriate behavior. For example, Ata and Ege fight when they sit together, then it is better allow them to sit with other people in the classroom. Any appropriate behavior followed by a positive reinforcement becomes strong. Such behavior is more likely to occur again. A positive reinforcement becomes a reward here (Minden, 1982). Rather than punishment, teachers should focus on a reward and praise. Ignoring the negative behavior but reinforcing the positive behaviors is key points of enhancing appraisal behaviors in the classroom.

Communication

Students' lack of access to English-speaking users or native speakers is one of the drawbacks of learning a language in a non-native environment. Owing to this, having linguistic knowledge is no longer a goal of EFL learners, students need to be communicatively competent. Teachers should create needs for the learners to use the target language. This can be enhanced in a positive environment. Students should feel free to speak, and the teacher should praise their speech. Meaningful activities and authentic materials can take the learners' attention. The interaction should be student-student by the help of information-gap activities. Interaction may overcome the barriers and facilitates the communication in the classroom. Although studies reflect that the East Asian students as a group are reserved, so there are differences in the degree of their classroom involvement. For example, focusing on the researcher's observations in studies across several East Asian populations, East

Asians from Hong Kong have a tendency to be more interactional than students from Japan, Taiwan, or Korea.

Conclusion

Teachers play several roles in a language classroom, but surely the most dominant one is the role of a manager. Effective teaching and learning cannot take place in a poorly managed classroom. In a well-managed classroom, learning and teaching are fun, and the outcomes of learning will be fruitful. The responsibility of management should be shared by students. Students should be responsible for their own behaviors, and a teacher should be sensitive to the needs of the learners. By this way, a positive classroom climate will be enhanced, and well-established learning and teaching environment can be constructed, which also reinforces communication in an EFL classroom. It is known that anxiety blocks learning. When teachers manage their classrooms by threatening their students or through punishment, the communication breaks down. In order to reinforce students and to facilitate communication, positive behaviors should be encouraged.

Appendix

1. What is the significance of classroom management in a language classroom?
2. What is the difference between management and discipline?
3. What are the key factors of positive classroom atmosphere?
4. What are the basic differences of three management models (interventionist, interactionalist and non-interventionist)?
5. What are the key factors of a language classroom?
6. Mary was working as a teacher of English at a state school. There were 35 students in total in her class. It is really crowded. Two of the students were talking. Mary started the lesson, but they kept on talking. What would you do if you were Mary? Explain in accordance with each one of the models mentioned (intervening, interacting, and guiding).
7. What is the role of the teacher in a constructive classroom?
8. What is the difference between positive and negative reinforcement?
9. Which one is more efficient punishment or a reward?
10. What is the difference between a reward and punishment?
11. How should a teacher arrange the time of the activities?
12. When and how should a teacher set the rules?
13. How can you place your students if your classroom is crowded?
14. How can a teacher lessen inappropriate behaviors of the learners?
15. What can a teacher do to facilitate communication in the classroom?

References

Albert, L. (1992). *An administrator's guide to cooperative discipline: Strategies for schoolwide implementation.* Circle Pines, MN: American Guidance Service.

Allen, R., & Boelter, L. (2008). Using Natural and Logical Consequences. University of Minnesota-Extension. Retrieved from http://www.extension.umn.edu/family/partnering-for-school-success/structure/using-natural-and-logical-consequences/

Amarjit, S. (2009) *Classroom management: A reflective perspective*. St. John's: Memorial University of Newfoundland.

Brophy, J. (1983). Effective classroom management. *The School Administrator*, 40, 33–36.

Brophy, J. (1986). Classroom management techniques. *Education and Urban Society*, 18, 182–194.

Chew, P. G-L. (2005). Change and continuity: English language teaching in Singapore. *Asian EFL Journal*, 7(1), 4–24.

Garrett, T. (2005). Student and teacher-centered classroom management: A case study of three teachers' beliefs and practices (Unpublished Doctoral Dissertation). State University of New Jersey.

Glasser, W. (1986). *Control theory in the classroom*. New York: Harper Collins.

Glasser, W. (1998). *The quality school: Managing Students without Coercion*. New York: Harper Collins

Kauffman, J. M., Pullen, P. L., Mostert, M. P., & Trent, S. C. (2011). *Managing classroom behavior: A reflective case-based approach* (5th edn.). Boston, MA: Pearson.

Martin, J., Sugarman, J., & McNamara, J. (2000). *Models of classroom management: Principles, practices and critical Considerations* (3rd edn.). Calgary: Detselig Enterprises.

Minden, H. (1982). *Two hugs for survival*. Toronto: McClelland and Stewart.

Oliver, R. M., & Reschly, D. J. (2007). *Effective classroom management: Teacher preparation and professional development*. Washington, DC: National Comprehensive Center for Teacher Quality. Retrieved from www.tqsource.org/topics/effectiveClassroonManagement.pdf

Pitsoe, V. J. (2007). A conceptual analysis of constructivist classroom management (Unpublished PhD Thesis). University of Pretoria. Retrieved from http://upetd.up.ac.za/thesis/available/ etd-05202008–05171501/unrestricted/00front.pdf

Sarıçoban, A., & Barışkan, V. (2005). The effectiveness of pre-service teacher training in classroom management skills. *Journal of Language and Linguistic Studies*, 1(2), 124–135.

Simonsen, B., Fairbanks, S., Briesch, A., Myers, D., & Sugai, G. (2008). Evidence-based practices in classroom management: Considerations for research to practice. *Education and Treatment of Children*, 31, 351–380.

Wolfgang, C. H., &. Glickman, C. D. (1986). *Solving discipline problems: Strategies for classroom teachers* (2nd edn.). Boston, MA: Allyn and Bacon.

Yi, F. (2008). *Classroom management: A case study* (pp. 179–186). Retrieved from http://wlkc.nbu.edu.cn/jpkc_nbu/daxueyingyu/download/015.pdf

Yi, F. (2008). *EFL classroom management: Creating a positive climate for learning* (pp. 128–137). Retrieved from http://wlkc.nbu.edu.cn/jpkc_nbu/daxueyingyu/download/013.pdf

Index

accent 77, 134, 135, 138, 140, 146–8, 153, 154, 155, 174
Albert, L. 258, 259, 266
AMTB 219–20
Anderson, J. R. 15, 17, 24, 26–7
Anderson's model and top-down and bottom-up processes 6, 12, 24, 26–7; *see also* Anderson's model of language development
Anderson's model of language comprehension 15, 17
anxiety 14, 19, 22–3, 28, 124, 127, 186, 220, 262, 266
Asian contexts 1, 3–4, 63–4, 66, 92
assessment 54, 62–3, 65, 117, 125, 194
assessment of pragmatics 11, 248, 250
attitudes 64, 66, 85, 90, 94, 107, 115, 127, 138, 218–24, 239
Audacity 142, 144–5, 148
awareness-raising tasks 123

back channeling 11, 233, 240, 250
behavioral approaches 256
Biber, D. 99, 110
Blyth, A. 6, 12, 14–16, 18, 27, 152, 161
bottom-up process 6, 15, 17, 18, 22–3, 26, 27
Brophy J. 257, 262, 267
Brown, H. D. 21, 28, 147
Buck, G. 17, 19, 20, 23, 28
Bygate, M. 101, 110
Byram, M., 32–3, 45

CALL 193–4, 201
Cauldwell, R. 25, 28
Chamcharatsri, P. B. 181–2, 189–90
Chang, A. C-S. 23, 26, 28, 72, 81, 154, 155, 161
changing concepts of reading 51–4

changing nature of text 49–51
Chinese learners 36, 41, 44, 47, 119
choral readings 144
classroom discipline 257
classroom management 10–11, 63, 216–17, 232, 254–5, 262, 265–7
code-breaking activity 55–6
code-switching 197
coding competence 52–3
collaboration 63, 193, 195–6, 199, 204
collocations 8, 99–101, 106
community of practice 1, 10, 196, 198–9
comprehension questions 6, 16, 18, 26, 72, 74, 79, 80–1, 152–3, 157, 159, 170
connections 59, 181, 193, 195; *see also* collaboration
constructivist approach 261–2
cooperative discipline 257–59, 266
Corbett, N. 32, 35, 38, 45
creative thinking 6, 30, 35–6
creative writing 6, 9, 175, 189
creative written responses 7, 72, 74, 76, 78
critical competence 52–4, 67
critical thinking 30, 36, 45, 166, 169, 178, 204, 215
cross-cultural pragmatics 234, 238, 247, 252
cultural identity 165
Culture Corner 41
culture of learning 63–6
Cummins, D. D. 36, 46

Day and Bamford (1998) 71–2, 79, 104–5, 150–1, 157, 169, 173
deconstruction of text 7, 86, 95
deliberate learning 106, 108
differentiation tasks 123

Index   269

digital literacies 195, 201
digital photo story 203–8, 213
digital storytelling 203–5, 207, 213–15
discourse markers 11, 101, 233, 242–3, 250
Dörnyei, Z. 65, 68, 218–20, 230

ecology of English in Asia 63–4
Elbow, P. 180
embarrassment 39, 132, 136
English as a Foreign Language (EFL) 8, 14, 36, 50, 71, 92, 98, 180–1, 224, 233, 254
English as a Lingua Franca (ELF) 1, 135, 235, 245
English as an additional language (EAL) 10, 203, 233
English as a Second Language (ESL) 8, 101, 181, 224, 237
English for International Communication 14, 135
errors 114, 126–7, 131, 136–7, 140, 143, 204, 262
expressive writing 9, 180–2, 187, 189
extensive listening 7–9, 72–3, 103–5, 153–4, 156–7, 173
extensive reading 71–4, 76, 77–8, 80–1, 104–5, 151–4, 157, 159, 171, 173, 177
extensive reading and listening 7, 9, 72, 74, 80–1, 154–7, 160, 168

Facebook 123, 145, 195–6, 199–200, 207
feedback 128, 131, 136, 137, 139, 140, 141, 142, 143, 144, 145, 149, 159, 183, 188, 193, 196, 198, 208–9, 212
Field, J. 18, 26, 153, 162
formulaic sequences 99; *see also* multi-word expressions
functional use 7, 84, 86

Gardner, R. C. 217–23
genre-based pedagogy 83, 85–6, 93, 95
Glasse, W. 260–1, 267
globalized classroom 196, 200
Goh, C. 23, 24, 28, 152–3, 162
grammatical processing 133
guiding model 261

Haiku 9, 181, 183–9
Hanauer, D. I. 180–2, 184, 187–90
Holliday, A. 36, 46

ideational function 84, 86–9, 92
ideology of text 63, 66

Iida, A. 9, 180–1, 187–90
images 7, 23, 49–67, 88, 92, 165, 204, 206, 210, 213; *see also* images
innovating practice 7, 50, 63
Innovation and creativity 11–12
instructional discourse 84–5, 95
intelligibility 135
interacting model 257
intercultural communication 33–5, 38–9, 41–2, 44, 51, 240, 247
intercultural pragmatics 234–5, 249–52
interpersonal function 84, 90, 92
intonation 25, 27, 41, 109, 134, 141, 143, 194, 209

Jackson, J. 32, 34, 35, 36, 38, 46–47
Japanese learners 6, 14–15, 22, 25, 73, 231
Jenkins, J. 135, 146
jocular insults 11, 235–6
Jones, D. 19, 20, 23, 28

Kress, G., 49, 51, 212, 214

L2 motivational system 220
language comprehension 17, 106, 109
language-focused learning 103, 107, 110
Language Learner Literature 169, 173
language production 106
Laufer, B. 98, 110
learning environment 113, 194, 206
lexical coverage 21, 23
listen and repeat 133, 140, 141, 143
listening activities 16, 23–4, 26, 152–3
listening anxiety 23
listening comprehension 72, 77–8, 81
listening comprehension process 17
listening difficulties 14, 19, 20, 22, 23
listening strategies 23
literature as appropriation 9, 168, 170, 176
literature as resource 167–8, 178
literature as study 9, 167–8
local contexts 12, 50, 63

Maley, A. 9, 165–6, 168–9, 171, 173–6, 178
materials development 5, 11, 30, 179, 246, 250–1
meaning-focused input 103, 105–6, 109; *see also* vocabulary teaching
meaning-focused output 103, 106–7, 110; *see also* vocabulary teaching
meaningful literacy 10, 181, 187, 189, 190
meaning-making 51, 53–4, 56–8, 63, 204

metacognitive strategies 23–4, 26–7, 153, 226
meta-functions 84
metalinguistic awareness tasks 123
methodology in ELT 2–3, 5, 12
motivation 1, 10, 65, 94, 170, 174, 216, 217–24, 227, 229, 254–5, 260–2
multimedia resources 38
multimodality 206
multimodal reading 6, 52, 54, 62, 65
multimodal resources 50–1, 54, 199–200
multimodal texts 6, 50–4, 59–60, 62–3, 67
multi-word expressions 7, 98, 101

narrative texts 10, 95, 203, 208–9
Nation, I. S. P. 7, 21, 29, 98–101, 103–4, 106–7, 108–9, 111

online grammar tasks 8, 116, 120, 125–8
online tasks 8, 116, 120, 125–6

participation activities 6, 30, 41–2
personal histories 181–3, 189
phatic communication 11, 233, 240, 241, 250
phonological loop 25, 73, 141
photo story 10, 203; *see also* digital photo story
Piller, I., 35, 47
plasticity 132
poetry writing 9, 180, 182, 187–9
politeness and impoliteness 11, 235, 252
pragmatic competence 52–3, 60; *see also* sociopragmatic competence
pragmatic linguistic competence 100
prefabricated language 99; *see also* multi-word expressions
psychological approach 221, 223

reading competence 52
reading comprehension 72–3, 75, 80, 152, 225
reading-while-listening 72–3
reinforcement 143, 256, 259, 265–6
repeated listening 22, 77, 139
repertoires of reading 6, 50, 54
repetitions 104–5, 132, 141, 175
rhythm 22, 25, 27, 132, 143, 144, 148, 171, 174–5
Robin, B. R. 204, 214

sarcasm 11, 233, 242, 250
Schulz, K. 136, 137, 146

self-awareness 10, 138, 216, 225, 227
semantic competence 52–3
semiotic resources 49–50
setting rules 257, 263–4
shadowing 25, 109, 141, 144
simultaneous reading and listening 72–4, 78, 155
social media 10, 51, 145, 195; *see also* social networking
social networking 10, 193, 195–6, 199–200
sociological approach 221
sociopragmatic competence 195
speaking skills 26, 31–2, 34, 44–5, 72, 194, 205, 213
speech acts 100, 233, 237–9, 244, 246–9, 251
Spiro, J. 175, 179
spoken language comprehension 98
stock phrases 132
study abroad 9, 31, 35–7, 181–7, 234
swearwords 11, 235–6, 237
systemic functional linguistics 84

target cultures 32, 34
tasks 7, 10, 18, 39, 53, 93, 100, 117–18, 120, 122, 125–8, 204, 213, 224, 228, 241, 248, 262
Ted Talks 158–9
television 74, 104–5, 143, 158–9, 160
text-analyst 53
textbooks 6, 16, 32–4, 38–45, 50–1, 54, 64–6, 116, 157, 246
text selection 9, 54, 168
textual function 84
text-user 53, 58–9
think-aloud 86, 95
Tomlinson, B. 50, 70, 82, 123, 130, 171, 176, 178–9
top-down process approach 18, 27
traditional approach 78, 205, 255

Vandergrift, L. 17, 18, 23, 152, 163
visual texts 50, 52
vocabulary teaching 8, 98–9, 103–4, 107
voice 9, 50, 60, 62, 75, 134, 188–9, 210, 246
Vygotsky, L S. 75, 82, 208, 212, 215

Yoshida, K. 14, 15, 29
YouTube 145, 149, 157, 160

Zhu, H. 32, 35, 38